The Archaeology
of Harriet Tubman's
Life in Freedom

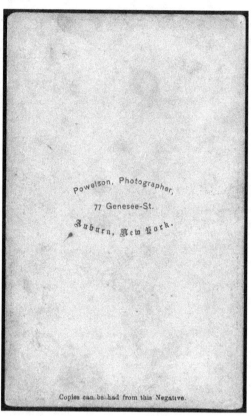

Harriet Tubman, Auburn, New York, c. 1868–69. From an album owned by Emily Howland (Sherwood, New York), a longtime friend. Photograph by Benjamin F. Powelson, 77 Genesee Street, Auburn (*back of photograph*). Photograph courtesy of the Smithsonian National Museum of African History and Culture, Object Number 2017.30.47, shared with the Library of Congress, Washington, DC.

THE ARCHAEOLOGY OF
Harriet Tubman's Life in Freedom

Douglas V. Armstrong

SYRACUSE UNIVERSITY PRESS

∞ The paper used in this publication meets the minimum requirements
of the American National Standard for Information Sciences—Permanence
of Paper for Printed Library Materials, ANSI Z39.48-1992.

For a listing of books published and distributed by Syracuse University Press,
visit https://press.syr.edu/.

ISBN: 978-0-8156-3736-3 (hardcover)
978-0-8156-3722-6 (paperback)
978-0-8156-5523-7 (e-book)

Library of Congress Cataloging-in-Publication Data

Names: Armstrong, Douglas V., author.
Title: The archaeology of Harriet Tubman's life in freedom / Douglas V. Armstrong.
Description: First edition. | Syracuse, New York : Syracuse University Press, [2022] |
Includes bibliographical references and index.
Identifiers: LCCN 2022000153 (print) | LCCN 2022000154 (ebook) |
ISBN 9780815637363 (hardcover) | ISBN 9780815637226 (paperback) |
ISBN 9780815655237 (ebook)
Subjects: LCSH: Tubman, Harriet, 1822–1913. | Tubman, Harriet, 1822–1913—
Homes and haunts. | Harriet Tubman National Historical Park (N.Y.) | African American
social reformers—New York (State)—Auburn—Biography. | Social archaeology—New York—
Cayuga County. | Auburn (N.Y.)—Antiquities. | Fleming (N.Y.)—Antiquities.
Classification: LCC E444.T82 A77 2022 (print) | LCC E444.T82 (ebook) |
DDC 973.7/115092—dc23/eng/20220118
LC record available at https://lccn.loc.gov/2022000153
LC ebook record available at https://lccn.loc.gov/2022000154

Manufactured in the United States of America

Publication supported by a grant from

The Community Foundation *for* **Greater New Haven**

as part of the Urban Haven Project.

To the memory of
HARRIET TUBMAN
and to all who have resisted tyranny and championed freedom, liberty,
and social justice through their actions, deeds, and words

For
WESLEY ALAN ARMSTRONG
and
WYATT JACOB ARMSTRONG

The midnight sky and the silent stars have been the witnesses of your devotion to freedom and of your heroism. Excepting John Brown—of sacred memory—I know of no one who has willingly encountered more perils and hardships to serve our enslaved people than you have. . . . Your friend, FREDERICK DOUGLASS

> —Frederick Douglass to Harriet Tubman,
> August 29, 1868 (in Bradford 1869, 7–8)

Contents

Illustrations

Tables

Preface

This study is the result of a cooperative effort between the Harriet Tubman Home, Inc., and archaeologists from Syracuse University. The study falls squarely within the definition of "interpretive archaeology." Interpretive archaeology has as its core objectives the exploration and communication of material and spatial data in ways that illuminate the past and engage the public in thoughtful consideration of past social contexts. In this case, the objective is to provide details on Harriet Tubman's life in freedom after the Civil War. I hope that the second half of Harriet Tubman's life is brought into sharp focus and that you gain a sense of the positive energy and unbounded faith that Harriet Tubman had in pursuit of her causes.

When I first started archaeological work at the Harriet Tubman Home for the Aged, I was surprised by stories of how some of Harriet Tubman's descendants did not know their kinship relationship or fully understand Tubman's contributions. Yet in the process of my studies of the Tubman Home, I inadvertently found a parallel gap in my knowledge of my own family history that connects with Tubman through John Brown. In 1908, when the Harriet Tubman Home for the Aged was formally opened, Tubman gave the remodeled brick structure that served as its primary dormitory the name "John Brown Hall" to honor him as a martyr in the fight for freedom for African Americans.

When I began archaeological studies of the ruins of John Brown Hall, I knew that my Quaker ancestors in Salem, Ohio, were abolitionists, but I had been told few details of their lives. In the early 1900s, my immediate ancestors moved west to a Society of Friends enclave in Whittier, California, and then blended into the California culture-scape and away from the Quaker church. The summer before I entered the eighth grade in 1967, my family went on a cross-country trek. One of my most memorable experiences from this trip was visiting the family's old stone house near Salem and learning about my Ohio and Quaker roots. I got excited about this history in part because issues of race associated with segregation and structured systems of inequality were being confronted in the late 1960s across America, including in my hometown, and my family, friends, and I were engaged in efforts for change.[1] That fall I returned to school and wrote a history paper about what I had seen and learned, only to have it graded down for its lack of verifiable detail and for relying too much on the anecdotal accounts of relatives. Upon reflection, the instructor was technically correct as issues related to lack of verification put limits on the veracity and accuracy of informal accounts associated with the inherent hidden history and mystery of the Underground Railroad. Still, in no small way, this "rejection" played a role in my interest in seeking tangible evidence related to issues of enslavement, the abolition movement, and emancipation. I am sure that many others have felt the frustration associated with not being able to know or substantiate one's history. For many African Americans, this "history gap" may be due to institutional structures that began with slavery and its recording of history. Fortunately, we now have new tools and sources of information to help us overcome gaps in the recording of history. One of these tools is the examination of the archaeological record preserved at the sites where people lived, worked, worshiped, and interacted. Archaeological sites and associated materials recovered from sites such as the Harriet Tubman Home provide a primary source of new, detailed, and important information about the past.

It was not until 2012, after most of the excavations and historical research upon which this study is based were complete, that I revisited the old stone house in Salem, Ohio, that had once been owned by my family. Although I arrived unannounced, the current owners graciously offered a tour of the house. My wife and I thought about also visiting the city's Society of Friends cemetery, but, not having time, we stopped at the nearby municipal cemetery.

1. My hometown, Pasadena, California, was at the time struggling with issues of segregation, and the trip made clear to me why in the 1950s my parents had stood up before the local school board to argue against redistricting that would have moved us and the children of Black families on our block out of our neighborhood school. This particular effort to redistrict and a pattern of segregation involving redistricting were later shown to be unconstitutional in *Spangler v. the Pasadena Board of Education* (US District Court, Civ. No. 68-1438-R, 311 F Supp. 501 [1970]; US Supreme Court, 427 US 424 [1976]). The case was decided on the basis of civil rights protections asserted in the Fourteenth Amendment and a precedent set by the landmark Supreme Court case *Brown v. Board of Education* (347 US 483 [1954]). The local case was initiated by the family of a friend in 1968, and I spent many hours in high school following it through the courts and sitting in on hearings. After the initial decision in 1970, the US District Court supervised the creation of the "Pasadena Plan" for desegregation, and my friends and I joined others at the American Friends Service Committee to staple together information packets designed to inform the public about the decision.

It was then that historical paths, academic interests, and personal history intersected.

As we drove through the Hope Cemetery in Salem, we were surprised to find a monument with the family name "Coppock" because we knew the Coppocks to have been Quakers, so we had not expected to find a member of that branch of the family in this municipal cemetery. As I got out of the car to look, my wife, whose car window was at eye level with the inscription on the substantial marker, said, "Doug, you really need to read this marker." It turns out that the commemorative marker had been placed in the municipal cemetery to honor a relative, an ancestral cousin, Edwin Coppock. Edwin was the youngest of John Brown's party at Harpers Ferry, Virginia, to have been hanged in 1859 for his revolutionary action in defiance of slavery. Originally buried in a wooden coffin in Virginia, Edwin's body was reburied in a metal coffin in Salem. As many as six thousand people viewed the body and participated in services. Later, at the end of the Civil War, the people of Salem paraded Edwin's original wooden casket through the streets, singing the words to what has become known as the "Battle Hymn of the Republic."[2]

Edwin and his brother Barclay Coppock had been among the band of twenty-five who had participated in the attack on the armory at Harpers Ferry on October 16, 1859, in an act that, even as it failed to directly spark a revolution aimed at freeing enslaved persons, is considered to have been a catalyst for the Civil War. When it was clear that the effort would not be successful, John Brown ordered his youngest son, Owen, and Barclay Coppock, the two youngest members of the raiding the party, to seek safety. Several were killed in the action, including three of Brown's sons, while John Brown and Edwin Coppock were among those captured. Edwin Coppock was tried, found guilty, and hanged on December 16, 1859, two weeks after John Brown. In captivity before and after the trial, Edwin refused to denounce his objection to end slavery and continued to write against slavery.[3] Half a century later, Eugene Debs was moved by this perseverance and included the full text of Edwin's final letter in a paper published in the journal *Appeal to Reason* (Debs [1914] 1916, 50–51). I, too, am moved by this letter, written by a man condemned and awaiting the gallows but remaining true to the hope for the future of freedom from slavery and oppression: "Hastening on that glorious

2. "Edwin Coppock" n.d.; see corollary of Tubman's singing this hymn in chapter 12.

3. In "The Coppock Brothers: Heroes of Harpers Ferry" ([1914] 1916), Debs recounted the role of the young Coppock brothers, who were among John Brown's band of white and Black revolutionary freedom fighters at Harpers Ferry.

day, when the slave will rejoice in his freedom and say, 'I, too, am a man, and am groaning no more under the yoke of oppression'" (December 13, 1859, quoted in Galbraith 1921, 429–31).

The remembrance of history can be odd and uneven, and although the abstract notion of family members engaged in the abolition movement had been instilled in me from birth and a statue of Lincoln was always displayed prominently on my grandparents' mantel, within this familial discourse the story of Edwin and Barclay had been omitted. Perhaps the omission was due to acts of violence being against Quaker religious doctrine, the measure of time and distance from the event, or even the fact that historical accounts tend to spell the brothers' surname "Coppoc" rather than "Coppock," as the family spells it. In 1908, nearly fifty years after the events of Harpers Ferry, Harriet Tubman chose to dedicate the dormitory of her long dreamed of and much cherished Home for the Aged in honor of John Brown for his role as a catalyst in pushing forward the cause of freedom through his actions at Harpers Ferry, an endeavor in which my relatives took part. I cannot help but contemplate the fact that this study began with an examination of John Brown Hall as a means of honoring the life and work of Harriet Tubman and with no knowledge of any connection to my own family. This serendipitous link drives home the fact that the quest for freedom affects everyone and that social justice has a wide footprint of importance to humankind.

Harriet Tubman was an inspiring freedom fighter; she repeatedly risked her life so that she and others could enjoy the basic liberties of freedom. However, for her, emancipation was just the beginning. Based at her home in Auburn and Fleming, New York, she continued to take action in support of social reforms related to women's rights, health care, and care for the elderly, particularly for African Americans. Now, more than a century after her death, many of the problems that Tubman confronted persist. Moreover, they have been compounded by the long-term impacts of continued social injustice experienced by African Americans, as demonstrated and accentuated recently by the senseless murders of African Americans, including George Floyd and Ahmaud Arbery. My hope is that this detailed study of Harriet Tubman's advocacy for and struggles on behalf of others during her life in freedom provide a model to continually inspire new generations to positive activism.

Acknowledgments

This archaeological and historical project has been carried out over nearly two decades. It has been both a research project generating new information and tangible material data as well as an engaged public interpretation project with the dual goal of expanding our knowledge and understanding of Harriet Tubman and enhancing the interpretive environment and knowledge base for those visiting the Harriet Tubman Home. The project could not have been carried out without the support of the Harriet Tubman Home Board of Directors, including Karen Hill, its executive director; Rev. Paul Carter, its resident manager; and Christine Carter, his wife. I am thankful to the board for allowing me to work on the property and to Karen Hill for her leadership in moving the mission of the Harriet Tubman Home forward, in tirelessly navigating the path toward the creation of the Harriet Tubman National Historical Park while retaining the ownership legacy of the African American Episcopal (AME) Zion Church, in proceeding with an ethos of historic preservation, and in targeting high-quality public interpretation of the site. I am particularly thankful for Karen's recognition of the important role that archaeology plays in the interpretation of the site and of the importance of developing a high-quality interpretive center so that this amazing site and, more importantly, the complex and important life and selfless life's work of Harriet Tubman can be properly presented to the public.

The initial archaeological work at John Brown Hall was a significant turning point for the Harriet Tubman Home in terms of historic preservation and site interpretation. Prior to that study, archaeology and its potential had not really been considered for the property. However, when I presented the findings from this site to the Harriet Tubman Home Board of Directors, I was rewarded by one of the most genuine outpourings of positive emotions I have ever witnessed. Members of the board responded positively and assertively to the revelations of the demonstrated value of the resources on the properties that they had spent so many years protecting—the tangible, intimate, and meaningful structural and material remains recovered from the ruins of

John Brown Hall, the primary dormitory and infirmary of the Harriet Tubman Home created through Tubman's efforts in concert with the AME Zion Church. The board members' faith in Tubman's legacy has been an inspiration to me and has made this archaeological project possible. Since 1903, the AME Zion Church has shepherded the properties through good times and bad and has strived to honor Tubman's legacy by holding the property intact and managing it in ways appropriate to her ideals. Without the legacy of the AME Zion Church's long-term support, Tubman may well have lost the property before her dream could be realized, and without the church's tenacious protection of the property through the years after her death the rich archaeological and historical contexts would likely not have survived intact.

This archaeological project was carried out over nearly twenty years and involved the assistance of hundreds of students and local volunteer participants, including Anna Hill, Kelton Sheridan, Heidy Murray, Charles Hartfelder, and Ben Jones, each of whom contributed multiple seasons and engaged in research and lab work associated with the project. I thank in particular Bonnie Ryan (Syracuse University librarian), who wrote her MA thesis based on studies of John Brown Hall and served as my field assistant for the first two seasons (Ryan 2000); Anna Hill, who became deeply involved not only in the archaeology but also in the pursuit of an engaged public interpretation of the site over a period of years; and Alan Armstrong, who spent several seasons as a field assistant, was always willing to head out to the Tubman Home to help me assess cultural-resource issues that arose during the restoration of Tubman's brick house and barn, and wrote his honor's thesis focusing on the brick kiln on the Tubman property and the social relations of brickmaking at the Harriet Tubman Home and in and around the South Street brickyards (A. Armstrong 2011). Over the past few years, the project has been greatly assisted by Jessica Bowes, a doctoral student who served as my teaching assistant and field supervisor. She has carried out a detailed examination of diet and dietary practice, including the study of animal bone remains and ethnobotanical remains recovered through flotation and fine-grain analysis of soil samples from all contexts at Harriet Tubman's house, barn, and yard.

The study has been greatly assisted by the assistance and support of Sheila Tucker, the Cayuga County and Town of Fleming historian, and of the staff of Syracuse University's Special Collections Research Center. Beth Crawford of Crawford & Stearns Architects and Preservation Planners in Syracuse provided guidance in relation to architectural features and historic-preservation issues. Beth has demonstrated an incredible dedication to the site and its restoration. Not only has she overseen the restoration of Tubman's barn and the efforts to restore Tubman's brick residence, but when I told her about archaeological evidence that indicated a fire had burned Tubman's house within a timeframe between 1880 and 1882, she quickly headed off to the archives and found a newspaper account of the fire that pinpointed the date of the fire as February 10, 1880. Judith Wellman, professor of women's history, emerita, at Oswego State University, demonstrated a generous willingness to share information from research she has carried out related to the location and historical significance of African American households in the Auburn area and general issues of women's rights and abolition in the Central New York region. Milton C. Sernett from Syracuse University's African American Studies Department came to visit the site while writing *Harriet Tubman: Myth, Memory, and History* (2007) and shared details of his historical findings. Both he and his book have served as a source of information on the details of Tubman's life and the way in which her activities have been perceived through the years. Kate Larson not only wrote the most definitive history of the life of Tubman from her birth forward, *Bound for the Promised Land: Harriet Tubman, Portrait of an American Hero* (2004), but has also been a generous contributor to this project and to the effort to move forward with the Tubman Home's historic preservation and public-interpretation mission. Not only is her book a wonderful resource that disentangles and makes sense out of Tubman's early life and her contributions during the Civil War, but it also provides a solid outline of Tubman's life in Auburn as well as her complex kinship and social networks and presents Tubman as a complex humane hero of her time.

Michael Long, the former director of capital projects and grants for the City of Auburn, New York, is responsible for the collection of a body of historical research involving primary sources and for many grants to the Harriet Tubman Home, including significant Save America's Treasures funds from the United States Millennial Fund (and a visit from then Senator Hillary Clinton) and funds from the New York State Environmental Quality Bond Act. The Preservation League of New York State also provided initial grants to document the Harriet Tubman connection to her brick home. The Thompson AME Zion Church and Tubman's grave site at Fort Hill Cemetery in Auburn formed the basis of National Historic Landmark designation, and the work of the US National Park Service and the Harriet Tubman Special Resources Study Act was supported by US senator Charles Schumer and congressman Amo Houghton. Subsequent congressional legislation to create Harriet Tubman National Historic Park in Auburn and Fleming, New York, was accomplished with bipartisan support in Congress led by Senators

Schumer and Kirsten Gillibrand and Representatives Daniel Maffei and John Katko, all of New York. Representative Katko was particularly helpful in the final push toward site designation. Michael Long took an active role in the Home's fund-raising and historic-preservation efforts, this time assisting the Home with its transition to a newly established National Park and bringing people together to focus squarely on the issues of funding necessary to establish a world-quality interpretive center at the site. Most recently, I had the pleasure of working with Michael and a range of specialists—including Larry Liberatore from the Beardsley Architects and Engineers firm; Karen Hill and the leadership of the Harriet Tubman Home; local community leaders, including the mayor of Auburn and representatives of both the City Council of Auburn and the town supervisor and town board for the Town of Fleming; representatives from the US National Park Service; and representatives from Syracuse University—to craft a proposal for the funding of this important interpretive center. The proposal was not funded, but the research and thought that went into it establish a new platform for quality historic interpretation of the Harriet Tubman Home property that will be invaluable as the site is developed.

From the inception of my engagement with the Harriet Tubman Home after a visit to the site in 1994, the archaeological project has focused on public involvement and interpretation aimed at both the process of data recovery and the use of this information to illuminate details of Harriet Tubman's life and the Harriet Tubman Home's role in her life. When the archaeological phase of this study began in 1998, very little was known about the complex array of structures, features, and ruins distributed across Tubman's thirty-two-acre property. Key structures associated with the Home, including the property's primary dormitory and infirmary at John Brown Hall, suffered first from years of neglect beginning in the late 1920s and then from demolition in the 1940s, and once these structures were eliminated from the visual-scape of buildings on the property, the location and significance of this important site and its residual ruins were lost from common memory. Archaeology provided a means of not only gathering details of life on the property and related to Harriet Tubman and her Home for the Aged but of re-registering the importance of these sites in the cultural landscape of Auburn and Fleming as well as of the region and country. In the process, new sites such as the brick kiln, the ruins of a burned house, a kitchen, and a cistern were uncovered that provide detail and context to the cultural landscape, and new information was recovered from the yards, foundations, and basements of standing structures, adding details related to activities on the property and changes in land use over time. From the inception of the project, the process of data recovery involved and was greatly assisted by volunteer participation of students from Syracuse University, who came back to the site year after year to reveal more layers of history and heritage on the property. Over the years, more than 350 Syracuse University students have contributed their time to the project as part of their formal field training during sixteen Syracuse summer field programs between 1998 and 2015 as well as in many quick-response field studies and site evaluations through 2022. In 2002, the Syracuse University student field team was joined by Professor Mark Hauser and students from Le Moyne College. In addition, I joined Agnus Maglioao and my graduate student Anna Hill to coteach a Syracuse University College of Visual and Performing Arts exhibit-design class to create models for museum presentation of archaeological and historical data for the site. I also assisted a Cornell University museum studies class in preparing field signage for the property. Early in the fieldwork, we held a series of very popular public-dig days involving hundreds of people from the Auburn community, but so many people wanted to get involved that we had to restructure such engagements and turned to more traditional site tours for groups visiting the site and to annual formal dig days involving an anthropology class from Nottingham High School, an urban public school in Syracuse. For two seasons, clearing and site preparation were assisted by men from the Butler Correctional Facility, who worked, sometimes in inclement weather, to clear the site for student and public digs.

Funding has come from several sources, but the bulk of the support for archaeological investigation came from the Summer Session and Continuing Education Programs as well as the Anthropology Department of the Maxwell School at Syracuse University. This was a project of engaged scholarship in which Syracuse University students contributed their time and energy to the project. While the Harriet Tubman Home, Inc., moved forward with its mission with funds from the Millennial Fund, funds from the New York State Environmental Quality Bond Act, and grants from the Lowes Foundation, Wachovia, and Bank of America, this study benefited indirectly from the preservation activities taking place but contributed all its services to date, including more than forty thousand hours of time, on a pro bono basis. In addition to support from Summer Sessions, this project was supported by grants from the Syracuse University Vision Fund, Syracuse University's Connective Corridor and Community Outreach Initiative, and the Maxwell School of Citizenship and Public Affairs. Alan Armstrong's contributions were supported by a Crown Scholarship and a National Science Foundation Mini-Grant (#802757) to run Neutron Activation Analysis samples at the

MURR Laboratory, University of Missouri. Michael Glascock and his laboratory assistants at MURR, Daniel J. Salberg and Jeffery R. Ferguson, ran the Neutron Activation Analysis of brick and clay samples from the Tubman site and carried out an interpretive analysis of findings (for an overview of Neutron Activation Analysis, see Glascock 2010).

When we needed to carry out remote sensing of the project quickly in order to test for possible and probable subsurface remains prior to planned development of key areas of the property, we received assistance from R. Christopher Goodwin & Associates and its staff, who conducted timely and significant remote sensing of the property that identified several key features, including magnetic anomalies defining features that we later excavated to rediscover a brick kiln on the property. Fieldwork was also assisted by Gordon DeAngelo and Barbara DeAngelo, who for this project and many others volunteered their time and expertise. Gordon came out on the first day of surveying in 1998 and generated the first formal survey map of the property and the grid system that we have used from that point forward. Gordon, who has since passed away, embodied the best of a generation of engaged amateur archaeologists who contributed significantly to the study of the region's prehistoric and historical archaeology. He always made himself and his survey equipment available, and his selfless service to archaeology and to sites such as the Harriet Tubman Home will long be remembered.

I extend my sincere gratitude and thanks to Rev. Paul Carter and Christine Carter, who not only manage but also serve as tour guides of the Harriet Tubman Home for the Aged. I met Paul on my first visit to the Tubman Home, and he not only allowed me to send my students out into the woods to find John Brown Hall but also understood the significance of the site and invited me to become involved with the Harriet Tubman Home. Over the years, it has been an honor to work with Paul and Christine. They have always welcomed my students and volunteers with a warm smile and words of encouragement. No doubt on many occasions our presence has increased their workload or caused them to alter their plans just so they could assist us in finding keys, moving artifacts, or providing resources to help us set up display cases of artifacts in the onsite museum. The two have been tireless workers for the cause of protecting Tubman's legacy. I am proud of the fact that Rev. Paul and Christine, Bonny Ryan, and I were honored with Syracuse University's Spirit of the Lantern award, and our group portrait now hangs in Hendricks Chapel on the Syracuse University campus. I have enjoyed working with them and look forward to their warm welcome each and every day that I arrive at the Tubman site.

I would also like to acknowledge and thank the extended family and descendants of Harriet Tubman. Over the years, I have come to know and appreciate the importance of Tubman's family to her during her life and to recognize their important place in the Tubman Home's legacy. Many descendants still live in the Auburn and Syracuse area, and several remain actively engaged in efforts to illuminate Tubman's life and the Home's mission (see, e.g., Jones and Galvin 2013). I am particularly thankful for the insights and encouraging support provided by Judith Bryant, Tubman's great-grandniece; for the stories and encouragement of Pauline Copes Johnson, Tubman's great-grandniece; and for the encouragement I received from other family members over the years. Judith Bryant opened her home and her files to me and most graciously allowed me to photograph family records related to Tubman's life. She and her mother are graduates of Syracuse University, and we are now in discussions regarding the donation of the Stewart Family Papers to the Special Collections Research Center at Syracuse University. These documents will add significantly to the already important body of records related to the Tubman Home at Syracuse University.

Finally, and most importantly, I thank my wife, Joan Armstrong, for her support and encouragement throughout the project. When our children were young, my efforts at the Tubman Home often meant more work at home on her part, particularly during the summer. However, our children, Alan and Amanda, fortunately always liked being on site and doing archaeology, so they were frequent site visitors and helpers. Joan has continued to support my efforts at the Tubman Home, hosting annual dig dinners for students and volunteers and showing understanding and support when I headed out to the site to address a problem or to Washington, DC, on short notice in the effort to get congressional support for the restoration of the Harriet Tubman Home.

The Archaeology
of Harriet Tubman's
Life in Freedom

PART ONE

Uncovering Inspiration

1

Underground No More

Uncovering Inspiration through Archaeology

If there is no struggle, there is no progress. Those who profess to favor
freedom and yet deprecate agitation are men who want crops without
plowing the ground. They want rain without thunder and lightning.
They want the ocean without the roar of its mighty waters. The struggle
may be a moral one or it may be a physical one, or it may both moral and
physical, but it must be a struggle.
—Frederick Douglass, "West Indian Emancipation
Speech," 1857

Introduction: Uncovering a Past and Exploring a Legend

Throughout her life, Harriet Tubman was actively engaged in the struggle for
freedom, liberty, and social justice (figure 1.1).[1] Her life projects the reality
and intensity of Frederick Douglass's words "If there is no struggle, there is
no progress" (Douglass 1857) as she repeatedly engaged in the moral and
physical demand for freedoms. Through resolve and tenacity, she helped to
liberate African Americans from slavery.[2] After the Civil War, Harriet continued the fight for freedoms, including advocacy of women's rights and care for

---

1. Details related to this struggle to live in freedom are elaborated in chapter 4, "The
Pursuit of Freedom and a Life of Liberty."

2. Tubman's early life conducting African Americans to freedom has been vividly portrayed in several books, such as Kate Larson's *Bound for the Promised Land* (2004), and in
many media over the years, including the movie *Harriet* (2019), in which Cynthia Erivo offers
an inspiring representation of Tubman's heroic efforts leading up to emancipation and for
which she received an Academy Award nomination. I had the good fortune to be invited to
join Tubman supporters, including many of her descendant relatives, as guests of the Harriet
Tubman Home and the producers at a preview of the film in Auburn, New York. The setting
was electric, and everyone was ready for the story of Tubman's continued efforts toward social
reform during the half century that she lived in freedom.

the elderly, for fifty years beyond the formal declaration of emancipation. This study remembers Tubman's commitment to social activism through the life that she lived at her personal home and farm and in relation to the Home for the Aged (the Home) that she created in Fleming and Auburn, New York. It is hoped that in learning the details of Harriet Tubman's steadfast efforts on behalf of others after the Civil War, the reader will be inspired to follow her path and work to assist those who are in need in today's world.

In the time since Tubman's death in 1913, the properties she once owned have continued to be held as a spiritual placeholder of her dreams and ideals. The properties constitute a landscape rich in artifacts, buildings, and meaning that derive from her life and her efforts on behalf of others. This study celebrates the process of healing and restoration associated with the reunification of Tubman's properties and their recognition in 2017 as a key element of the newly created Harriet Tubman National Historical Park (see US National Park Service n.d.). In the pursuit of understanding Tubman and the site, the study encountered many aspects of Tubman's life that had been lost. The process of rediscovery embraced the multivalent patina of freshly uncovered evidence of her life, including elements preserved in the site and in an array of newly examined documents. Together, these data inform us and provide depth and texture illuminating Harriet Tubman's life, the people with whom she engaged, and the cultural landscape of sites once warmed by Harriet Tubman's humanity.[3]

On the first day of our excavations outside Harriet Tubman's brick farmhouse in 2002, we uncovered a distinctive layer of gray and black ash just beneath the surface (figures 1.2–1.3).[4] This layer later informed us that Tubman's original wood-frame house had burned in a fire (*Auburn Herald*, Feb. 10, 1880).[5] The discovery was followed by the recovery of hundreds of burned

3. Shannon Dawdy's book *Patina: A Profane Archaeology* (2016) provides an excellent reminder of what archaeology can do in bringing forward the multilayered and at times imperfect patina of landscapes created in the past by others. In studying the landscape and Tubman's material world, we can bring forward the realities of that world and an awareness of her contributions.

4. The ash layers were found beginning at a depth of twenty to twenty-two centimeters (eight to nine inches) below the surface.

5. Tax and census records show a shift from wood-frame to brick construction, and the tax records indicate a doubling of property value associated with the new construction in the 1883 tax lists, confirming the completion of the new house by the beginning of 1883 (Cayuga County Tax Records, 1860–90, Cayuga County Clerk's Office, Auburn, NY; US census, 1890, Auburn and Fleming, Cayuga County Records Office, Auburn, NY).

artifacts among thousands of Tubman-era materials. Subsequent analysis of artifacts and historical research told us that the fire had occurred on February 10, 1880, and that the house had been reconstructed between 1882 and early 1883 using local brick made by local masons, including members of the Tubman household. Moreover, the ash and associated artifacts told us that Tubman-era deposits survived at the site and confirmed the importance of archaeology as a means of testing, evaluating, and learning new things about the events, places, and things of her life. Throughout this study, we uncovered evidence from a wide range of buildings and features across the thirty-two-acre Harriet Tubman Home property.

This study reconstructs the cultural landscape of the Harriet Tubman Home. Archaeological research was carried out as part of a restoration project that evolved into a successful effort to secure designation of the property as the Harriet Tubman National Historical Park. As a tangible aspect of uncovering inspiration, a group of metal "star" buttons recovered from deposits at her house (figure 1.4) are being included in the artwork of the Tubman $20 bill that has been approved by Congress and is currently being prepared for production by the US Bureau of Engraving (see chapters 7 and 13).

This study draws from a rich body of new information generated through archaeological and historical investigation of Tubman's house and farm (figures 1.5–1.6) as well as of the adjacent twenty-five-acre farm that she acquired in 1896 (figure 1.7). Tubman's seven-acre farm is located in the Town of Fleming on a parcel fronting the east side of South Street, just south of the City of Auburn line. Tubman owned this farm from 1859 until her death in 1913. In 1896, she acquired the adjacent property immediately north of her farm. The twenty-five-acre farm was made up of two farms, one located in the Town of Fleming and the other in the City of Auburn.[6] These farms came to be collectively known as the Harriet Tubman Home. In this setting, Tubman, her family, and those who came to rely on her created a place of engaged freedom.[7]

The archaeological record that Tubman left behind sheds light on her life and the ways in which she interacted with local and national communities.

6. Although this farm straddled the line demarcating Fleming and Auburn, formal records for it were generally kept by the City of Auburn, which accounted for the most acres. Unfortunately, over the years the positioning of the property line led to irregularities in mapping and in recording of buildings, taxes, and residential use.

7. In most cases, I refer to the Harriet Tubman Home for the Aged as "the Home." However, another home for elderly women in Auburn, the Home for the Friendless, was and is also called "the Home" (see chapter 8).

It also projects her strong, individually based spirituality and her relationship with the African American Episcopal (AME) Zion Church.[8] The AME Zion Church backed Tubman's struggle: first by working with her to open the Harriet Tubman Home for the Aged and then by keeping her dream and her legacy alive through the retention and preservation of her properties. However, within decades of the end of Tubman's life, the breadth and importance of her legacy were nearly forgotten by the broader American society. As the twentieth century progressed, the Home was closed, and the structures deteriorated, but the AME Zion Church managed to hold the properties together as a sacred trust. Fortunately, through perseverance and a reawakening to the importance of the many social movements with which Tubman was actively engaged, her properties were preserved, and the material record ensconced within these properties—including buildings, yards, ruins, and even a remnant apple orchard, all of which were important parts of Tubman's life—have been studied. In this setting, the past and present have become intertwined. Now, more than a century after her death, the property, which is still owned by the AME Zion Church through its not-for-profit unit Harriet Tubman Home, Inc., has taken on new symbolic meaning as a place of pilgrimage and national recognition, as a National Historic Landmark, and most recently as a National Historical Park.[9]

Archaeological studies began after I took my students to the property as part of a regional "freedom trail" and "social movements" fieldtrip for Syracuse University students in 1994.[10] As we walked across the property and into the small museum, my group and I were warmly greeted by the site manager, Rev. Paul Carter. Although feeling embraced by the welcome, I was instantly struck by the gap between my expectations for the site, given my understanding of the significance of Harriet Tubman's contribution to American and world history, and the less than expected scale and scope

8. The AME Zion Church is a historically African American denomination of the Methodist Church, a Protestant group, that was formed in New York City in 1821. The church integrates religious beliefs and a social ministry aimed at social change, outreach, and charity (see its website at http://www.amez.org/our-church).

9. A signing ceremony was held at the US Department of Interior on January 10, 2017, to commemorate the creation of the Harriet Tubman National Historical Park, the 414th National Park in the United States.

10. At the time, I was carrying out an archaeological study of the Wesleyan Methodist Church in Syracuse, New York, and wanted my students to get a broader perspective of the complex story of African Americans and the abolition and women's rights movements in Central New York (D. Armstrong and Wurst 2003; D. Armstrong, Wurst, and Kellar 2000).

of the property's presentation. I realize now that what I was experiencing was the product of changes in the landscape: missing buildings, misinformation on structures and their use by Tubman, and a general loss of interpretive connections to information on Tubman's life. Though the land had been retained by the AME Zion Church and the nonprofit Harriet Tubman Home, Inc., changes to the landscape during the decades intervening between Tubman's life and the present had resulted in significant losses in interpretive meaning. These changes were directional in that they were related to intervening social conditions and structures of social inequality, which, in spite of the AME Zion Church's good intentions, had resulted in limited resources and opportunities. Over time and through processes of physical decay, key elements of Tubman's legacy had been muted or muffled, and continuities inherent in the landscape obscured. Shannon Dawdy uses the biological concept of taphonomy, or change in the period between the actions of the past and the actions of the present, to frame consideration of the complexity of the "mix of accident and manipulation, the silences and erasures, the constraining structures, and the sudden ruptures that all go into the creation of history and into the formation of the 'ethnographic' present" (2006, 721). What I observed at the Tubman Home that day was in contrast to many other historic sites I have visited, such as Thomas Jefferson's Monticello and the nearby home of Tubman supporters William Henry and Frances Miller Seward, where every vista, room, and action from the past are amplified and illuminated.

As I toured the small museum, my eyes and thoughts focused on pictures of Harriet Tubman (figures 1.8–1.9). In these images, Tubman is sitting among a group of African Americans in front of a building identified as "John Brown Hall."[11] A third photograph taken at this time shows the group with an apple orchard and a small portion of the building in the background (figure 1.10). I had not seen the building in the modern landscape, so I asked Rev. Carter where the building was located. He responded that it had been torn down and was lost in the woods at the back of the property. My thoughts flashed back and forth between a feeling of loss and hope before focusing positively on hope. I asked him if we could go into the woods to look for it. He responded with a smile, saying, "By all means."

11. The photograph had a label identifying the structure as "John Brown Hall" along with the date 1911. Subsequent research indicates that the photograph was taken before 1909. It was probably taken at the opening of John Brown Hall and the Harriet Tubman Home for the Aged in the spring of 1908.

I gathered my students, and we all headed into the woods to look for the ruins. Partially in jest, I told the students that we couldn't have lunch until we had found John Brown Hall. Fifteen minutes later, they began eating their lunches at the site as Reverend Carter joined us on the newly rediscovered ruins.[12] We discussed the importance of the site, and I agreed, pending the support of the AME Zion Church, to excavate the ruins as soon as I finished another project. I remember thinking to myself as we returned home that day: "How could this site, a site associated with such an important woman, be so poorly understood? How could key elements of the story of her life be missing from the landscape and all but forgotten? And what other ruins lie hidden on the property?" I intended to make good on my promise to use archaeology to uncover the details of Tubman's life.

Four years later, we began our archaeological efforts at the Home with a survey and excavations focusing on the ruins of John Brown Hall. The success of this study demonstrated the value of archaeological reconnaissance and the potential of heritage-based interpretation for the site (Ryan and Armstrong 2000). The archaeological work at John Brown Hall began a two-decade-long quest to draw together the resources of archaeology, history, and the broader social-cultural landscape of the area to find new information on Tubman's life, to explain the social and spiritual contexts of her life, and to find tangible, material evidence of her daily life (D. Armstrong 2003b, 2003c, 2011, 2015; D. Armstrong and Hill 2009).

The actions of Harriet Tubman as an Underground Railroad conductor and leader within the abolition movement have secured her an honored place in American and world history as a champion of freedom.[13] Her name is globally invoked in the name of freedom and justice. She was a liberating conductor to more than seventy individuals on at least thirteen trips escorting refugees from slavery out of the southern states north and into Canada (Larson 2004). In the cause of liberation, she continued her activism as a Union soldier, a spy, and a nurse during the Civil War (Bradford 1869, 1886, 1901; Clinton 2004; Larson 2004; Sernett 2007). However, details of Harriet Tubman's life after

12. Though initially my challenge to students was tongue-and-cheek, the incentive of food to hungry college students was one of the best survey strategies I ever devised.

13. Another leader of the cause of freedom and social reforms was Sojourner Truth (c. 1797–1883). Truth was born into slavery before its abolishment in New York and did not wait for its dissolution to claim her own freedom in 1826 and to begin a long life dedicated to the abolition movement from her new home in Ohio (Painter 1997; Truth [1850] 2017).

the Civil War and her multifaceted legacy as an advocate for social
been obscured by time and changing social conditions since her
study combines a refined analysis of material goods recovered from exca-
tions with an array of seldom-explored documents, including accounts and
personal letters written by sponsors and supporters of her causes. The new
findings project details about Tubman's life, the problems she faced, and the
broader historical context of the era in which she lived.[15]

W. E. B. Du Bois (1903) described a "veil" that separates African Americans and often obscures their position in American society. Given this separation, it is not altogether surprising that the life of even such a respected
person as Harriet Tubman would be obscured by her position as an African
American woman. Unfortunately, the importance of Tubman's actions after
the Civil War was almost forgotten, covered up by social changes, including
growing racial separation and segregation in America in the decades following her life. By the early decades of the twentieth century, Central New York,
once a hotbed of social reform, was not immune to racism and segregation,
which resulted in difficulties in funding and operating a home for aged and
infirm African Americans. Interest in this woman of action dissipated. The
gaps in the memory of her actions forced us to reconstruct the record of her
life by weaving together the fragments of history and the cultural landscape of
her house and Home. Fortunately, the material record has been preserved in a
wide array of structures, foundations, and artifacts (ceramics, glass, brick, and
personal items such as beads, buttons, and tokens). Artifacts reflecting her life,
her family, and those whom she cared for are deposited in well-defined contexts at sites where she lived. Together the material and historical fragments
make the "veil" surrounding Harriet Tubman more transparent and provide
a means to gain an intimate understanding of her private life and its intersections with her public life.

14. Although details on Harriet Tubman's birth (born Araminta "Minty" Ross) are
incomplete, it is thought that she was born in February or March 1822 on the plantation
owned by Anthony Thompson in the Peters Neck District of Dorchester County, Maryland (Larson 2004, xvi, 301). Harriet was the fifth of nine children born to Harriet "Ritta"
("Ritte" or "Rit") Green and Benjamin Ross. At the time of their residence in Tubman's home
in Auburn, her parents were listed under the surname "Stewart."

15. This study also draws upon recent historical work completed while the archaeology
was under way, including books by Kate Larson (2004), Milton Sernett (2007), and Joyce
Stokes Jones and Michele Jones Galvin (2013).

A Landscape of the Past Inspiring the Future

In 1859, Harriet Tubman purchased a farm on South Street,[16] just beyond the Auburn city line in Fleming, New York.[17] This seven-acre farmstead was to become Tubman's home and a base of social interaction for the African American community through the last half of the nineteenth century and into the twentieth until her death in 1913 (figure 1.2).[18] Tubman's ownership of a house and farm provided her with the means to care for her family and others. It also projects her critical role as a female leader who was able and willing to negotiate complex actions for herself and on behalf of others. She had what Patricia Collins refers to in *Black Feminist Thought* (2009) as "the power of self-determination" (107–12; see also Battle-Baptiste 2011 and Gwaltney 1980). Tubman, the true social activist, used the property that she acquired on South Street to house and care for her extended family, including her parents, brothers, sisters, nieces, and nephews. As Cheryl LaRoche (2014a, 2014b) has reported for many emerging communities of migrating African Americans, people came together for mutual support. In reference to new free-Black settlements of the immediate post–Civil War era in Texas and the American South in general, Jannie Scott explores how mobility and community formation in new settings allowed the newly emancipated to "embrace their new identities as free people" (2018, 2). In Tubman's case, African Americans came to her and the Auburn/Fleming, New York, area because of her reputation. Many in her household and community had joined with her on her sojourns to freedom to New York and Canada. Ultimately, they congregated either near her or in her household to gain support and assistance, which she provided with almost limitless grace. Some stayed, but many others benefited from her kindness and then established their own homes in the Auburn area or moved on to new communities.

16. Prior to acquisition by Tubman, this farm was known as the "Barton Farm," named after a farmer who lived on the property in 1850.

17. Tubman and her family's movement from Maryland to St. Catherines, Ontario, Canada, and then back to Central New York was part of a much larger migration linked to self-emancipation and abolition (see Dodson and Diouf 2004; LaRoche 2014a, 2014b). Tubman's self-determination led those in her household in the defiant act of self-liberation, in the physical acts of relocation, and in the acquisition of property (see Collins 2009, 106–12; J. Scott 2018).

18. Harriet Tubman died on March 10, 1913, after a series of illnesses. At the time, she was a resident inmate of John Brown Hall at the Home for the Aged.

US senator William Seward and his wife, Frances, sold Tubman the seven-acre farm on favorable terms and held a note of mortgage.[19] The transfer of property to Tubman fit the Sewards' philosophy of securing a stable economic future for those who had made their way to freedom. The transfer is made more interesting and significant given that at the time Tubman was considered a free woman in New York State but still a slave under federal law, the Fugitive Slave Act of 1850. As such, she was subject to possible capture. Senator Seward and his wife took the liberty of not immediately recording the sale; rather, they simply held a personal note.[20] Prior to and during the Civil War, Harriet Tubman was occupied with activities away from her farm, first guiding people to freedom and then for the next few years serving as a soldier, nurse, and spy for the Union (Bradford [1886] 1993). When the war was over, Tubman returned to Central New York to pursue her life with her family on her farm.

By the mid-1880s, Harriet Tubman felt a calling to take in aging African Americans, and by 1895 she had chartered a Home for the Aged in her personal home. However, she needed more space, so in 1896 she attended an auction and purchased the adjacent twenty-five-acre farm with the intent of creating a home for the care of aging African Americans (figures 1.8–1.10). This farm had buildings that could serve as residential dormitories as well as barns, fields, and an apple orchard. Tubman hoped proceeds from farm crops and building rentals would facilitate a self-sufficient home for these aging African Americans. In the process, she took on significant debt in the form of a $1,250 mortgage on the new property.[21] Few outside the AME Zion Church took seriously her desire to create a home. The leadership and members of the AME Zion Church were behind Tubman spiritually and with what

19. The property had been inherited by Frances Miller Seward from her family and was her property under New York State law. She supported the sale and may have been more involved in it than William because he was in Europe at the time of the transaction.

20. The transaction was recorded in William Seward's financial records (archived in the William Seward Papers, Seward House and Cayuga Community College, Auburn, NY) but was not formally filed at the Cayuga County Records Office, perhaps to avoid a search of formal public records by bounty hunters looking for Tubman.

21. Tubman had enough pull within the Auburn community to be granted a mortgage by her friend Mr. William H. Meaker at the Cayuga County Savings Bank, a banker with whom she had done business for years. Meaker was a supporter of Tubman and was later among those proposed as a board member for the Harriet Tubman Home soon after the acquisition of the land by the AME Zion Church.

little funding they could raise, but they were by no means wealthy. However, some of her longtime friends and supporters were concerned about her personal economic welfare, her state of health, and her advancing age—she was, after all, around seventy-four when she purchased the additional acres. They saw the Home as a distraction and unnecessary burden. For example, Eliza Wright Osborne, a longtime supporter and noted women's rights activist, was generous in her direct contributions to Tubman,[22] but she was skeptical of Tubman's efforts to create a home for the elderly. Osborne's correspondence shows that Tubman was a continual focal point in her life but also that she thought Tubman's generosity was being exploited by ne'er-do-wells. At times, Osborne expressed frustration that resources targeted *for* Tubman were redistributed *by* Tubman to her charges.[23]

The cost of opening the Home for the Aged on the new farm was far greater than anticipated. Hence, Tubman's primary residence remained the de facto Home for another twelve years, until 1908. Finally, in 1903, faced with foreclosure and loss of the twenty-five-acre farm, she signed the deed to the property over to the AME Zion Church, which took over the property and the mortgage. It also began anew the process of fund-raising, but it was not until 1908 that the Home for the Aged was officially open. In 1908, following five years of planning and fund-raising and despite a bit of turmoil within the local church, a brick structure on the twenty-five-acre property was refurbished, named "John Brown Hall" by Tubman, and opened to elderly residents by the AME Zion Church (figure 1.8).

The AME Zion Church promised Tubman that it would take care of her in her old age, and it made good on that pledge. Following hospitalization for pneumonia in 1911, she was moved to the dormitory/infirmary at John Brown Hall and received care provided by the Home, organized by the AME Zion

22. Eliza Wright Osborne was the daughter of Martha Wright and the niece of Lucretia Mott. She was a lifelong supporter of Harriet Tubman and lived just up the street from her, on South Street, in Auburn. Eliza grew up among leading abolitionists and women's rights activists. Her husband, David Osborne, was also from an abolitionist family, and several of his brothers rode with John Brown in Kansas. David built a farm-equipment company that had a strong global presence. Their son, Thomas Osborne, sold the company to International Harvester in 1904. The Osborne Family Papers are housed in the Special Collections Research Center at Syracuse University, Syracuse, NY. The Osborne Center for Social Justice has summarized information on the family at http://osbornelibrary.com/yahoo_site_admin/assets/docs/osborne_family.362110612.pdf.

23. Eliza Wright Osborne to Helen Osborne Storrow, Dec. 16, 1906, Osborne Family Papers.

Church and overseen by the home's matron, Frances R. Smith.[24] A photograph of Tubman and the Home's "inmates" outside of John Brown Hall around 1912 was taken after Tubman had become a resident of the facility (figure 1.10).[25]

Harriet Tubman died on March 10, 1913, after a series of illnesses. Her death brought a short-lived flurry of funds donated in her honor that were used to make improvements to the wood-frame house (which I refer to as the "Legacy House") at the front of the property (figures 1.11–1.13). After Tubman's death, this house was no longer rented for income. By 1915, residents under the Home's care, referred to at the time as "inmates," were moved to this building, and John Brown Hall was rented. The Tubman Home continued to operate on the twenty-five-acre farm and to serve elderly African American women into the late 1920s. By 1928, though, the last of the elderly inmates died, and the Home was closed.

Through the very lean years of the Great Depression in the 1930s, the AME Zion Church retained the property. During the 1930s and 1940s, the physical structures rapidly decayed. Still, advocates who understood the importance of Tubman and her work obtained formal recognition of the property and sponsored the forging of a New York State Historic Site marker on South Street in front of the property. This marker has remained in place for nearly eighty years as a reminder of Tubman's works. Photographs from the late 1930s and early 1940s show John Brown Hall abandoned and the wood-frame house barely standing. Its wrap-around porch is missing, and nearly all its clapboard siding was stripped away for firewood (figure 1.13).[26]

24. Tubman was particularly appreciative of Frances R. Smith's efforts and included her among the three recipients of her estate, along with her niece Mary Gaston and her grand-niece Katy Stewart. Frances, the only nonfamily member among this group, was the wife of AME Zion minister and then Home superintendent Rev. Charles A. Smith. Earl Conrad interviewed Frances and found that the Smiths knew Tubman well and were at her side when she died (Conrad 1943; see also Larson 2004, 390).

25. The completion of a fund-raising effort to construct the porch shown in figure 1.11 is discussed in an article on the accomplishments of the Home published in the *Auburn Citizen* on June 11, 1910. The photo is labeled 1911, but it was taken before the construction of the porch. According to recent findings by Kate Larson, the last photo of Harriet Tubman was taken at the request of Anne Fitzhugh Miller for an article published in *American Magazine* (Miller 1912; Kate Larson, personal communication to the author, Aug. 5, 2017).

26. Alice Norris informed me that during the Depression members of their family would on occasion gather wood that had fallen from the white wood-frame house to burn in their furnace to heat the Norris house (formerly Harriet Tubman's brick house) (Alice Norris, personal communication to the author, May 22, 2002).

Yet the New York State Historic Site marker continued to serve as a sentry to remind passersby of the importance of Tubman's deeds and her place on the landscape.

Ultimately, the property was never reopened as a Home for the Aged, but beginning in the late 1940s the significance of Tubman's farms and the Home that she worked so hard to create began to be recognized. The period from the late 1940s through early 1960s was a difficult era for historic preservation in the United States. However, the AME Zion Church retained the property, and under the leadership of Bishop William J. Walls and with encouragement from Tubman descendants, funds were raised to rebuild the wood-frame house as a legacy to Tubman (US National Park Service 2001, 19).[27] Given the gap in active use of the property from the late 1920s to the early 1950s, confusion emerged regarding the context of the site and its structures. However, the AME Zion Church continued to maintain the property and to generate interest in Tubman and the Home.

In 1990, the church was able to acquire Tubman's seven-acre farm and reunite that farm and the twenty-five-acre property that she acquired to establish her Home for the Aged. The timing of this acquisition coincided with a revitalization of interest in Harriet Tubman and with social reform movements associated with abolition and women's rights.[28] By 1998, when I conducted my first survey and excavations of the property, efforts were under way to begin the process of gaining the funds necessary for a series of restorations. Those directly involved in the process clearly understood the importance of Tubman's brick farmhouse, barn, and the farm (A. Armstrong and D. Armstrong 2012; D. Armstrong 2003b, 2011, 2015; D. Armstrong and Hill 2009; D. Armstrong, Wurst, and Kellar 2000; Ryan 2000; Ryan and Armstrong 2000).

27. Judith Bryant and Fred Richardson have conveyed stories of how Tubman descendants were active supporters of restoration of the property, helping to spark interest in it beginning in the 1940s (Judith Bryant, personal communication to the author, Aug. 10, 2017; Larson, personal communication, Aug. 5, 2017).

28. This examination of the archaeology and history of Tubman's properties and the Harriet Tubman Home for the Aged is a direct outgrowth of this renewal of interest. During the 1990s, the Harriet Tubman Home, Inc., began the process of evaluating ways to best preserve the property and Tubman's legacy. Rev. Paul Carter was brought to the site as its resident manager, assisted by his wife, Christine. Michael Long, a City of Auburn community-development officer, worked closely with the Home to gain formal historic site designations and funding for restoration (US National Park Service 2001, 17), and the Harriet Tubman Home Board of Directors became active in finding ways to restore the site and put forward Tubman's legacy.

The Unknown Tubman: Reconstructing
a Historical Background and Social Context

The archaeological record provides important details pertaining to Tubman's life that are not otherwise available in the historical record. Growing up in slavery, Tubman did not have the opportunity for education. Hence, she did not write her own story, as did many of her peers, such as the African American activists Jermain Wesley Loguen ([1859] 2016) and Frederick Douglass ([1855] 1994).[29] Moreover, for an array of reasons, the details of her post–Civil War years had not been thoroughly compiled. She was an African American woman of marginal means, so her presence in the public eye ebbed with time and the passing of those with whom she had most prominently interacted in her roles as liberator, spy, warrior, and nurse before and during the Civil War. Although Harriet Tubman remained an engaged and public person throughout her life and until her death in 1913, her post–Civil War efforts were obscured by time and circumstance.

Today Harriet Tubman's role as an Underground Railroad conductor is known to just about every school child in America. In 2019, her early life and actions as a liberator and freedom fighter were the subject of the feature film *Harriet*, which earned actor Cynthia Erivo an Academy Award nomination. She is remembered for her role as a liberator and has once again become the symbol of a person willing to pursue acts of civil disobedience for just causes. However, her post–Civil War activism is less well known and unfortunately is often essentialized, and she is invoked only among lists of great contributors to the cause of freedom, without any specifics related to her later life and contributions. An example of how her name is mentioned to define the contributions of important women can be seen in Carole Davies's effort to describe the contributions of African American female activists. Davies simply adds Tubman's name to a list of African American "foremothers"—"Sojourner Truth, Harriet Tubman, Maria Stewart, and Ida B. Wells"—describing them as "women who were actively involved in a variety of movements against oppression" (2007, 13), but Davies provides no details of Tubman's contributions.[30]

---

29. Sojourner Truth dictated her life story (Truth [1850] 2017).

30. In *Left of Karl Marx* (2007), author Carole Davies shows how the social activist and feminist Claudia Jones struggled against prejudice and oppression. Davies often invokes references to Tubman on lists of forbearer activists, yet each time Tubman is cited (12, 19, 50), she is simply a name on a list with no substantive details pertaining to her contributions.

Tubman was a strong woman with deep spiritual beliefs and a willingness to open her home and extend her resources to others. Moreover, she was deeply respected not only by the African American community in Auburn and across the nation but also by a broader local and national community of persons engaged in social causes, activism, and civil liberties—without boundaries of color, race, gender, or ethnicity.[31] Although she did not write about her life, the activities she undertook as a conductor on the Underground Railroad and as an advocate for emancipation were the focus of an article by Franklin Sanborn published in the *Commonwealth* (Boston) in 1863. This account popularized Tubman's role as a liberator during the Civil War. Immediately after the war, Sarah Bradford wrote the first of her three Tubman biographies, which included Tubman's role as a conductor on the Underground Railroad and stories of her activities during the Civil War. Bradford's *Scenes in the Life of Harriet Tubman*, published in 1869, described Tubman as the "Black Moses" and popularized her iconographic and heroic roles.[32] Bradford expanded and republished this book in 1886 with the title *Harriet: The Moses of Her People*. This iconizing version was republished several times through the early 1900s as a means of raising funds to help sustain Tubman financially.[33]

Sarah Bradford (1818–1912) was an abolitionist who had taught Tubman's parents' Sunday school class in Auburn. The first version of Bradford's biography of Tubman was written to raise funds to help pay off part of Tubman's mortgage on her farm. It was written quickly in response to Tubman's immediate needs as Bradford prepared for an extended trip abroad. The publication was sponsored by a group of abolitionists, including Gerrit Smith

31. Elena Sesma provides an overview of how Black women in both slavery and freedom dealt with institutionalized oppression as they lived in settings at "the cross-roads of race, gender, class, and more" (2016, 41). Christopher Matthews (2019) discusses the importance of places of "refuge and support" for multiethnic and racial communities in North America, and Terrance Weik (2009) discusses settings of complex ethnic interactions at the Levi Colbert Prairie site in Mississippi.

32. Bradford published the first and second versions of her biography in 1869 and 1886, respectively, with different title, with a reprint of the second version done in 1897. The third version, published in 1901, retained the title of the second book, *Harriet Tubman, the Moses of Her People* (Bradford 1886), but added substantial revisions, including about fifteen pages of new materials based on new interviews and interactions between Bradford and Tubman. By the time this third version was published, both Tubman and Bradford were in their eighties.

33. Copies of the book and photographs of Tubman were sold to visitors to her home and at ceremonies associated with new printings of the books and at teas in the homes of women who supported her.

and Franklin Sanborn. In writing it, Bradford reached out to Black and white abolition leaders to ask them to provide letters to support the credibility of Tubman's deeds and character. Among those wrote letters were Gerrit Smith, Wendell Phillips, and Frederick Douglass (Bradford 1869, 4–8). Frederick Douglass's letter was written directly to Harriet:

ROCHESTER, August 29, 1868.

DEAR HARRIET: I am glad to know that the story of your eventful life has been written by a kind lady, and that the same is soon to be published. You ask for what you do not need when you call upon me for a word of commendation. I need such words from you far more than you can need them from me, especially where your superior labors and devotion to the cause of the lately enslaved of our land are known as I know them. The difference between us is very marked. Most that I have done and suffered in the service of our cause has been in public, and I have received much encouragement at every step of the way. You, on the other hand, have labored in a private way. I have wrought in the day—you in the night. I have had the applause of the crowd and the satisfaction that comes of being approved by the multitude, while the most that you have done has been witnessed by a few trembling, scarred, and foot-sore bondmen and women, whom you have led out of the house of bondage, and whose heartfelt "God bless you" has been your only reward. The midnight sky and the silent stars have been the witnesses of your devotion to freedom and of your heroism. Excepting John Brown—of sacred memory—I know of no one who has willingly encountered more perils and hardships to serve our enslaved people than you have. Much that you have done would seem improbable to those who do not know you as I know you. It is to me a great pleasure and a great privilege to bear testimony to your character and your works, and to say to those to whom you may come, that I regard you in every way truthful and trustworthy.

> Your friend,
> FREDERICK DOUGLASS
> (copied in Bradford 1869, 7)

In this letter, Douglass contrasts his work, carried out in public during the light of day to the acclaim of crowds, to Tubman's work and devotion to freedom, done away from the crowds and public eye and witnessed only by the

"the trembling, scared, and foot-sore bondsmen and women whom you have led out of the house of bondage and whose heartfelt 'God bless you' has been your only reward."

When the first edition of *Scenes in the Life of Harriet Tubman* was published, an announcement was placed in the January edition of the *Commonwealth*, the publication that had popularized Harriet Tubman's deeds in Sanborn's biography (Sanborn 1863). This announcement noted that Sarah Bradford "has made an interesting memoir of this devoted woman," "the proceeds of the sales of which go to her support" (Sanborn 1869). The announcement indicates a price of $1 for the book, which could be obtained at the Women's Club and the Freedman's Aid Society or by post. Sales of the book raised about $1,200 on Tubman's behalf and further popularized her efforts among women's groups and those who had supported the cause of abolition.[34]

The second version of Bradford's book was designed to raise money for "the building of a hospital for old and disabled colored people" (Bradford 1886, 78). By this time, Bradford had heard Tubman's stories often, and she expanded her base of Tubman sources to include material from new interviews in Franklin Sanborn's *Life and Letters of John Brown* (Bradford 1886, 96; Sanborn 1885; see also Drew 1856). Jean Humez suggests that the first, quickly written, and less-edited version of Bradford's biography "brings us closer to Tubman's own version of her experience" (1993, 165). The edits for the second version had the effect of making Tubman "less salty and more saintly" (165).

In evaluating Bradford's writing and its impact on our perceptions of Tubman, Humez wrestled with the problematic impact of Tubman's not writing her own autobiography. She notes that we are left to sift through "mediated" oral testimony and biographical information on Tubman's life as told by Sarah Bradford (1869, 1886), Franklin Sanborn (1863), and others, primarily white men and women of her era who, although sympathetic, did not fully comprehend Tubman's religious beliefs and spirituality (Humez 1993, 162). Humez points out that Bradford's writing projects a form of racism extant in the period she published the book and that the writer's literary interventions distort Tubman's original narrative, not just its spiritual inflections (163). Yet "this text is among the *fullest* repositories of Tubman's own speech to survive, if we are interested in the historical Tubman, we need to make it yield as much as we can" (163, emphasis in original).

---

34. The announcement of the book also mistakenly indicated that Tubman was very old and infirm, but at that time she was only forty-nine (assuming she was born in March 1822).

Milton Sernett illustrates the problem of Bradford's biographical intervention by comparing versions of the song "Hail, oh Hail, Ye Happy Spirits"
as presented in Bradford's *Scenes in the Life of Harriet Tubman* (1869) and
Harriet Tubman: Moses of Her People (1886) (Sernett 2007, 128–29).

1869	1886
Hail oh hail, ye happy spirits,	Hail oh hail, ye happy spirits,
Death no more shall make you fear,	Death no more shall make you fear,
No grief nor sorrow, pain nor anger (anguish)	Grief or sorrow, pain nor anguish,
Shall no more distress you there.	Shall no more distress you dere.
Around him are ten thousan' angels,	Around Him are ten thousand angels,
Always ready to 'bey comman';	Always ready to obey command;
Dey are always hobring round you,	Dey are always hovering round you,
Till you reach the hebbenly lan'.	Tell you reach the heavenly land.
(Bradford 1969, 26, and 1886, 37)	

In the first version, Bradford reports that the words were recorded exactly as
"Harriet sang them to me in a sweet and simple Methodist air" (1869, 26). In
the second, she admits the difficulty in recording the true and exact verse and
rewrites it, informing the reader that "the air sung to these words was so wild,
so full of plaintive minor strains, and unexpected quavers, that I would defy
any white person to learn it, and often as I heard it, it was to me a constant
surprise" (1886, 37). The side-by-side presentation of these versions, written
by the same person seventeen years apart, projects aspects of the subjective and
complicated nature of biographical recording as the shift in voice may reflect
not only subtle changes in Tubman's singing of the song but also a change in
the writer's understanding of the song's content and inflection.[35] Did Bradford know Tubman better the second time around, or did she wish to subtly
shift the message imbued in the selection of the verse attributed to Tubman?
With respect to intention, one must note that the objective of both editions of
the book was to raise money for Tubman, and all proceeds from these books
were given to Tubman, so whatever Bradford intended, it involved a degree

---

35. In telling Tubman's stories, Bradford makes reference to the fact that the songs sung
by Tubman during her flights to freedom often were specifically selected or varied in order to
convey messages to her charges as well as to those providing assistance.

of altruism. However, James McGowan and William G. Kashatus conclude in their biography of Tubman that the two versions, *Scenes* and *Moses*, project "a deliberate and conscious change of information" not just in the cited verse but in details found throughout the book (2011, 2). One of these changes is an increase of $500 in the size of the reward offered for Tubman's capture before emancipation. There are also substantive differences in the telling of the story of Tubman's first attempt at flight to freedom. In *Scenes*, Bradford describes how Harriet's brothers dragged her back to Maryland, where she had been enslaved, whereas in *Moses* she says that Harriet went back voluntarily. The unfortunate result is a degree of confusion regarding the details that require critical assessment (Humez 1993, 2003; McGowan and Kashatus 2011; Sernett 2007). Humez asserts that Bradford's biographies are valuable but that we must "begin by acknowledging that such a highly-mediated text creates daunting suspicion and resistance, especially for modern readers sensitive to racial power dynamics" (1993, 163). In critically examining the two versions, Humez notes that "while it is true that Bradford controlled the final form of the narrative as it was translated from talk to text, Tubman's own agency in the collaborative process of creating meaning can and should be stressed" (163). The story contains what Humez projects as "an essential spiritual transformation 'plot' that illuminates the inner sources of her social activist life" (163). Tubman had strong spiritual beliefs and felt a direct connection to God, who she says spoke to her personally and directly through dreams and inspired her to pursue her objectives, first freedom for herself and others and later women's rights and care for the elderly.

Bradford's books do much to frame the picture of Tubman's early life and chronicle Harriet as a "Moses" leading her people to freedom. Part oral reconstruction of conversations with Tubman and part acclamations of her deeds in the form of letters from abolition leaders such as Gerrit Smith, Wendell Phillips, and Frederick Douglass, the books document her contributions as a freedom conductor and a soldier. The first book, *Scenes*, takes aim not only at raising money for Tubman but at generating the documentary support for Tubman's request for a Civil War pension. This topic is addressed in letters from William Seward and Rufas B. Saxton (Bradford 1869, 1886). Ironically, the pension issue was not resolved until 1899, and the pension took years of work and an act of Congress to achieve.[36] As Bradford describes in her second

36. In October 2003, Senator Hillary Clinton won passage of an act providing $11,750 additional compensation for a widow's benefit withheld from Tubman between 1899 and her death in 1913. These funds were designated for "the descendants of Tubman" and were given

book, *Moses*, proceeds from the first book had been used to pay off or at least to make current the mortgage on Tubman's "little home," and the goal of the second was to assist her dream of a Home for the Aged: "The old parents, then nearly approaching their centennial year, were to be turned out to die in a poor-house, when the sudden determination was taken to send out a little sketch of her life to the benevolent public, in the hope of redeeming the little home. This object, through the kindness of friends, was accomplished. The old people died in Harriet's own home, breathing blessings upon her for her devotion to them" (Bradford 1886, 78). In the preface, Bradford wrote, "Her own sands are nearly run, but she hopes, 'ere she goes home, to see this work, a hospital well underway" (1886, 8).[37] Later, in describing the fund-raising purpose of the book, Bradford wrote of the intent to provide financial support for the "building of a hospital for old and disabled colored people":

> Now another necessity has arisen, and our sable friend, who never has been known to beg for herself, asks once more for help in accomplishing a favorite project for the good of her people. This, as she says, is "her last work, and she only prays de Lord to let her live till it is well started, and den she is ready to go." This work is the building of a hospital for old and disabled colored people; and in this she has already had the sympathy and aid of the good people of Auburn; the mayor and his noble wife having given her great assistance in the meetings she has held in aid of this object. It is partly to aid her in this work, on which she has so set her heart, that this story of her life and labors is being re-written. (1886, 78–79)

Newspaper accounts of sales of this book as well as the role of photographs of Tubman as fund-raising devices record fund-raising teas like one held at the home of Mrs. Telford on Grant Avenue in Auburn. Sales of books and photographs of Tubman are also discussed in Eliza Wright Osborne's correspondence.[38]

---

over to the Harriet Tubman Home, Inc., for use in the restoration of Tubman-related sites in Auburn.

37. A detailed discussion of Bradford's books on Tubman can be found in Humez 1993, 2003, and Sernett 2007, 105–30. There are many reprints of the 1886 edition, with page numbers that do not conform to the original version. For example, this quote is on page 7 of the 2004 Dover edition (Bradford [1886] 2004, 7); for purposes of clarity, I refer to the page numbering of the original 1886 edition.

38. Eliza Wright Osborne to Helen O. Storrow, June 15, 1906, Osborne Family Papers. Fund-raising events, including a tea at the home of the Mrs. W. Telford, also revolved around sales of the book.

Fortunately, despite Bradford's notion that Tubman was near an end in 1886, she lived for another quarter century. She did live to see the Home that she envisioned open and operating, though its materialization was slow in coming. For years, the Home operated within her personal residence, and finally in 1908 it formally opened as an institution dedicated to the care of elderly African Americans in a dormitory and infirmary located near the back of the Home for the Aged property in a building called John Brown Hall.

The opening of the Home was a tremendous achievement for both Tubman and the AME Zion Church, with which she worked closely for decades. The story of its opening reflects a spirit of collective generosity that began with Tubman and spread among those around her. It was no simple task opening a home for aging African Americans at the turn of the twentieth century, but she accomplished her goal, and for a few years the Home became a refuge for those in need. Unfortunately, the task of sustaining such a Home was difficult, particularly after Tubman's death. Auburn changed dramatically in the late 1910s; it was affected by World War I, a traumatic influenza epidemic, and a shift in its social and economic base. The local brickyards were closed, local corporations such as the Osborne Manufacturing Company were sold, and corporate management moved away. Both the small-scale brickyards and the large-scale manufacturing plants had been well known for hiring African Americans, including those in Tubman's household and neighborhood. Within two decades of Harriet Tubman's death, the social and political climate of Central New York and the nation changed dramatically.

Tubman's Presence and Absence in Published History

In *History of Cayuga County 1789–1879* (1879), the author Elliot Storke, a self-professed abolitionist, repeatedly discusses problems associated with slavery and positively proclaims the role of Cayuga County community leaders, including William Seward, in the abolition movement.[39] Yet he doesn't

---

39. Of particular note are abolitionist Rev. Henry Fowler and church organizations such as one connected to the Central Presbyterian Church (Storke 1879, 142). Other named abolitionists include the leaders of the Central Presbyterian Church, which broke away from an older congregation on the basis of strong antislavery views. Among the church elders and trustees were Lewis Seymour, Peter Burgess, Joseph Bailey, D. M. Osborne, Elliot G. Storke (the author of the 1879 history of Cayuga County), H. W. Dwight, Rugus Sargent, Charles P. Wood, D. T. Fowler, David P. Wallis, Rev. C. C. Hemenway, T. M. Davis, T. S. Gage, Zenas Howland, Charles M. Howlett, George Anderson, Wm. S. Shourds, Willis J. Beecher, Charles C.

mention Harriet Tubman, then a well-known resident in the county, which includes Auburn and Fleming, and only scantily discusses African Americans. The most specific details pertaining to African Americans are related to the AME Zion Church's history and leadership. Storke also reports a shift toward inclusion of African Americans in the education system of Auburn with the desegregation of schools in 1851, when the city was incorporated.[40]

Though missing from formal histories of the period, Tubman remained a well-known person and personality in the region during her life. This notoriety was based primarily on her role as an Underground Railroad conductor. Tubman was a colorful person who was known to evoke emotion, spirituality, and conviction, particularly with respect to causes centering on freedom and justice. During her life, she was also noted for her association with the early women's rights movement, African American women's organizations, and any number of groups supporting social reform, including those advocating education, temperance, and care for the elderly and indigent. Tubman's activities and her Home are well chronicled in sundry newspaper reports and feature articles of her day. But the African American community and to a lesser degree Tubman herself were cast to the periphery of society in Auburn, as in much of America.

Dwight, Theodore M. Pomeroy, William H. Seward, George H. TenEyck, William F. Wait, and Frank D. Wright (Storke 1879, 142). This list names only the male elders of the church, but in most cases the women were at least as active in the abolition movement as the men. Others involved in the abolition movement, as reported by Storke, included Joseph Letchworth (of Moravia and then Sherwood) and Edwin Goodwin (Storke 1879, 234, 66). Storke describes William Seward's brother-in-law W. T. Worton (resident of South Street) as "always an anti-slavery man, he insisted that all should be equal before the law and enjoy the same political rights" (234). The intensity of some individuals' position with regard to slavery is exemplified by John Stoyell, who at age sixty-one enlisted as a private in the Union army in 1861. Storke reports that Stoyell was adamant in his views toward temperance and abolition. It was his "anti-slavery proclivities which made him an abolitionist when the very name was a reproach, and led him at his own personal risk to feed, clothe and shelter, and often to forward in his own conveyance, the fugitive slave" (454). Stoyell died for the cause in the Civil War on July 5, 1863.

40. Prior to the incorporation of the City of Auburn, schools in the area were segregated (Storke 1879). Books on local history boast of the involvement of white leaders, such as the Seward and Osborne families, in the abolitionist movement. However, they entirely omit mention of Tubman and tell little regarding the local African American community. These accounts do mention that schools were integrated, provide some details on African American church congregations and clergy, and note the presence of a chapter of the Black Free Masons. Nelson Davis and several other boarders in Tubman's house and laborers in the local brick-yards are listed as members of an African American chapter of Free Masonry in the *Auburn City Directory* from 1870 to 1888 (Cayuga County Historian's Office, Auburn, NY).

Thus, just as her farms were positioned at the edge of city (Auburn) and town (Fleming), her life and life's works were not considered central to the region's formal history. To a certain degree, the history of the abolition movement and other social movements of the region was considered worthy of note, but the leading local protagonist was omitted from regional recollections of history and missing from the formal description of the social landscape. Even during her life, a combination of class-, race-, and gender-based social structures caused Tubman to be written out of the regional history and all but forgotten.

In 1908, the same year that Tubman and the AME Zion Church opened the new Home for the Aged in John Brown Hall, Benjamin Snow published a new *History of Cayuga County*, but once again this formal history omits mention of Tubman. The omission of Tubman from formal histories appears to be tied to complex social divisions within the region. Snow focuses on wealth and industry and those individuals who were perceived integral to their advancement and perhaps able to buy a copy of the book. The most significant mention of African Americans is in relation to their churches, with the AME Zion Church being well documented, but with little mention of African Americans living in the Auburn community. Certainly, in 1908 Tubman still retained a degree of respect and prominence, as indicated by the fact that she was seated at the podium of Auburn's Lincoln Centennial celebration and a participant in the parade associated with this event in 1909 ("All Honor Lincoln," *Auburn Citizen*, Feb. 12, 1909). In fact, based on the newspaper account, it might have been nearly impossible to have missed Tubman at these events because she had draped herself in small American flags and was fully engaged in the day's activities.[41]

In contrast to the formal histories of the region, newspapers did capture many details of the daily life of the community and regularly featured accounts of Tubman. More than three hundred accounts of Tubman and her Home were given in local and regional newspapers. One reason for Tubman's inclusion in this form of historical recording was that her friends in the Osborne family owned at least one local paper, the *Auburn Citizen*, and their reporters regularly wrote articles on Harriet Tubman, her Home for the Aged, and her

---

41. Harriet Tubman's longtime friend Emily Howland, an abolitionist and sponsor of educational institutions for African Americans as well as of free schools in New York, was unable to attend the festivities. Correspondence indicate that Tubman sent her one of these American flags (Emily Howland Papers, Howland Museum, Sherwood, NY, Cornell Univ., Ithaca, NY). I checked with the Howland Museum in Sherwood, New York, but it does not have the flag among its collections.

civic engagements. However, by 1913 Tubman was no longer alive, and by the late 1920s those civic connections no longer existed, and one finds only an occasional mention of the Tubman Home.

By the beginning of the 1930s, America had entered the Great Depression, and the buildings that had once served as the Home were abandoned and had started on a trajectory of rapid decay. By the early 1940s, when Earl Conrad attempted to publish a new biography of Tubman's life, there was so little interest in Tubman's deeds that he had a difficult time finding a publisher. Conrad's book was rejected by several prominent presses headed by white editors who had little interest in Tubman, saw poor possibilities for sales, and were critical of Conrad's activist writing style (Sernett 2007, 217). It took him three years to find a press for *Harriet Tubman: Negro Soldier and Abolitions* (1943) before he caught the interest of the Black publisher Carter G. Woodson at the Association for the Study of Negro Life and History and its publishing house, the Associated Publishers of Washington, DC (Sernett 2007, 196, 216).

Although Conrad's book has been repeatedly "rediscovered" and reprinted over the years, and although literally dozens of short children's books have been written based on Bradford's and Conrad's work, no significant historical biographies or studies using primary sources were undertaken to examine Tubman's life until the beginning of the twenty-first century with the works of Kate Larson (2004), Jean Humez (2003), Catherine Clinton (2004), and Milton Sernett (2007) as well as with publications associated with the current archaeological investigations detailed in this book (D. Armstrong 2003b, 2003c; D. Armstrong, Wurst, and Kellar 2000; Ryan 2000; Ryan and Armstrong 2000).

Recent scholarship has made great strides in compiling obscure sources that allow for detailed reconstruction of Tubman's early life and legacy. Larson's *Bound for the Promised Land* (2004) provides a compelling and engaging portrait of Tubman with an abundance of details on her pre–Civil War life. Books by Clinton (2004) and Humez (2003) provide additional details drawn from a collage of historical accounts, and Sernett's *Harriet Tubman: Myth, Memory, and History* (2007) challenges us to examine more closely the woman behind legend and the core values of humanitarian faith that she projected through her actions. Those interested in the life of Tubman as told by two of her descendants, Joyce Stokes Jones and Michele Jones Galvin, should read *Beyond the Underground: Aunt Harriet, Moses of Her People* (2013). This book weaves together family stories with recollections of Tubman's life and family relationships. Collectively, these histories focus their attention on the legacy of Tubman's role as an antebellum liberator and provide a baseline of information related to her early life as well as an outline related to her life in Auburn. These new histories are essential to the current work described here. However, they do not really focus specifically on the details of her life in Auburn, the complex social relations of Black and white communities, or the intimate details and refined contexts that can be derived from the material recovered from Tubman's personal residence or the Home for the Aged that she worked so hard to create.

The examination of Tubman's life in Auburn in this book draws from a rich array of archaeological and historical materials relating to Tubman's more than fifty years in Central New York and another century of remembrances of her life and humanitarian efforts. Hence, although the broad-overview histories of Tubman are important, so too is the suite of recent scholarship that looks closely and intimately at the setting and community in which Tubman lived and interacted. The interpretive meaning of the specific microhistory-scale recovery of material data from the Tubman sites was boosted significantly by the scholarship and scholarly exchange of ideas generated by Judith Wellman (2005), Beth Crawford ([2002] 2017), Sheila Tucker (1973), Rev. Paul Carter and Christine Carter of the Harriet Tubman Home, Inc., and waves of Syracuse University students who combed the local archives to find details that allow for a more complete understanding of Tubman in the Auburn community and of Tubman's legacy in Central New York. To this list, I add a series of cultural-resource reports that provide details of Tubman's life (A. Armstrong and D. Armstrong 2012; D. Armstrong 2003b, 2011; D. Armstrong and Hill 2009; Crawford & Stearns 2002; US National Park Service 2008). These recent histories were used as a baseline for getting to know the person (not just the legend) Harriet Tubman, her family, network of friends, and associates in Auburn. They were carried out in an era open to demanding a better understanding of her. In contrast, when Earl Conrad (1943) set out to research and publish a history of Tubman's life in the late 1930s, he received a less positive reception. Upon reflection, it is not surprising that this was the same period in which the Home for the Aged was closed and its structures rapidly slid into disrepair.

New Insights from Archaeology, Historical Research, and the Cultural Landscape

This study looks at the record of Harriet Tubman's life based on the buildings in which she lived, the fragmented ruins on the property, and the detailed material record of her life, along with that of her family and fellow residents.

Prior to site-based and landscape-focused study, many of the details of Tubman's life in Central New York remained unknown, untold, or misunderstood. The material record was recovered from well-stratified and well-defined archaeological contexts on the property. Our goal was, and still is, to identify and explain the archaeological resources present at ruins associated with her life to make that life relevant to new generations. Fortunately, the cultural landscape and artifacts recovered from Tubman's property can be integrated with formal records such as censuses, deeds, and tax records, enhanced by recurrent mention in the local press, and elaborated by personal accounts in letters and accounts of friends and visitors.[42] Throughout her life and particularly from 1896 on, Tubman and her care facility were a regular part of newspaper reportage, leaving us a continuous, albeit irregular, record of at least some of her activities and the activities of the Home for the Aged during this period.

Over the past decade, the Tubman site complex has undergone extensive archaeological, architectural, and historical investigations, and it is just beginning a process of renewal involving structural restoration, enriched historical interpretation, and renewed dedication to social activism—a mix that will position the legacy of Tubman's past with the people of the present to inspire social activists and social justice for the future. The Tubman properties in Fleming and Auburn are now listed as part of a National Historic Landmark and have been designated as a National Park, the first honoring an African American woman in the United States.[43] The new Harriet Tubman National Historical Park in Auburn and Fleming is being operated jointly by the Harriet Tubman Home, Inc., a not-for-profit established by the AME Zion Church, and the US National Park Service. The objective is not just to restore these historic sites but also to honor Tubman's legacy and to utilize these sites to engage, inspire, and assist.

Archaeological excavations demonstrate the value of the archaeological resources at the Home and will be of significance to public interpretation of the sites. For instance, an interesting aspect of the findings at both John

42. For example, letters in the Osborne Family Papers at Syracuse University and in the Emily Howland Papers at Cornell University.

43. Harriet Tubman National Historical Park was included in the National Defense Authorization Act of 2015, approved by the House of Representatives on December 4, 2014, and by the Senate on December 12, 2014, and signed into law by President Barack Obama on December 19, 2014. A second National Park honoring Tubman, the Harriet Tubman Underground Railroad National Historical Park, has been established in the vicinity of her birthplace in Maryland (US National Park Service 2017).

Brown Hall and Tubman's residence is the virtual absence of alcohol-related bottle glass, an item that is otherwise generally abundant at sites corresponding to the period. This attests to the importance of temperance within both the Tubman household and the philosophy of the AME Zion Church. Such findings allow us to triangulate beliefs, actions, and agency (Dobres and Robb 2000, 12–14) and to recover and interpret Tubman as a person and social activist as we examine her private and public life and their intersections, both in her personal farm and residence and in the more public Home for the Aged that she created. Elizabeth Brumfiel argues that agent-centered studies provide an argument for the "internal origins of social change" (2000, 251). This book purposefully highlights Harriet Tubman's agency, drawing upon the abundance of evidence uncovered from the ground or essentially forgotten in dispersed historical accounts: bits and pieces that individually may be anecdotal but that collectively allow us to frame a more complete picture of her life by compiling the details of her lived environment, the material record of her life, the landscape of her properties, and the social context of her house and the Home she created. The archaeological data and historical data are combined to form an "archaeography," much like a detailed "rich ethnography," to illuminate her life and contributions and to make her actions visible and relevant for today's and tomorrow's world. On many fronts—from abolition to her challenges to race and gender roles—she was an agent of social change. In this way, the reconstruction of Harriet Tubman's life brings her out from behind the veils of time and neglect by presenting the details of that life and her social relationships from a complex array of vantage points, including the cultural landscape where she lived; the artifacts, goods, and materials with which she lived; the hardships she encountered; as well as the ideals, problems, and idiosyncrasies associated with her daily life.

The words in the title of the book's last chapter, "the legacy of inspiration," relate to the important role that contemporary archaeology has in bringing Tubman's actions to life through interpretation of archaeological sites associated with her. We are fortunate that the land and sites associated with her life and continued legacy of social activism have survived, albeit in ruins and modified forms, and that we can now engage in the process of reconstructing and presenting her stories to the public (Brumfiel 2000, 252). The venue facilitates discussion of a wide range of social issues pertaining to American history, African Americans, networks of social interaction, women, the aged, and the combination of elements that constitute personal freedom.

Orientation to the Site: Spatial Layout,
Buildings, Ruins, and Archaeological Sites

Archaeological research at the Home involves the examination of a wide range of contexts through excavation, survey, and remote sensing, and it integrates information from historic maps.[44] Tubman's farms and those surrounding them were mixed agricultural farms on which fields were plowed, grains harvested, orchards tended, and stock such as hogs raised. Beneath the rich and agriculturally productive topsoil, at a depth of about one meter, the whole area is covered by a layer of fine glacial clay. A creek ran through the properties on the east side of the road and provided water for their various activities. Even before Tubman had acquired the properties, nearly all the farms on the east side of South Street bracketing the Auburn city line were engaged in brickmaking. Therefore, it is not surprising that many of the individuals in Tubman's household were involved with brickmaking (see chapter 11).

Archaeological surveys, remote sensing, and archaeological excavations resulted in the collection of more than fifty-five thousand artifacts, ranging from ceramics and glass and personal items such as broaches, buttons, and coins to dietary remains, architectural elements including locally made brick, and even a mason's pointed trowel. The latter item may have been used to construct her brick house and is very much like the trowels that we used to excavate the site. In the process of our studies, we defined and carried out excavations in eight areas, or loci, associated with well-defined buildings, ruins, and archaeological deposits spread out across the combined thirty-two-acre Tubman properties. Each distinctive cultural area within the overall site is considered a locus that consists of groupings of structures, ruins of outbuildings, and related cultural deposits (middens). Each locus and its associated archaeological deposits are discussed in detail as the study describes activities and interactions that took place on the property during Harriet Tubman's life or, as part of her legacy, after her death. To orient the reader and to emphasize the importance of understanding the context of the entire thirty-two-acre property to the story of Harriet Tubman's life after the Civil War, this study examines the cultural landscape of the array of structures and associated features at the site.

44. This information has been combined with archaeological survey and excavation data to compile an integrated geographic information system (GIS) map of Tubman's properties.

Locus 1

Harriet Tubman's brick residence and associated outbuildings and features (figures 1.2, 1.5–1.6). This grouping includes structures and features near Harriet Tubman's brick residence on the west end of a seven-acre parcel fronting South Street in the Town of Fleming. This locus includes the ruins of the wood-frame farmhouse purchased by Tubman in 1859 and the brick farmhouse built on the site by Tubman and her family after that earlier house burned on February 10, 1880. The locus also includes all the barns, outbuildings, features, and gardens associated with Tubman's initial seven-acre farm. The house, yard, barn, and outbuildings have been intensively investigated using a combination of pedestrian survey, remote sensing, shovel test pits, and excavation, including testing of features and refined testing of soils for dietary and environmental information.

Locus 2

A two-story wood-frame house that is currently painted white and has a wraparound porch. This house stands near the front of the twenty-five-acre farm purchased by Tubman in 1896 (figures 1.7, 1.11–1.13). Locus 2 includes the house, the archaeological ruins of a kitchen that was once attached to the house, as well as a series of outbuildings that once stood in the surrounding yard. This structure and associated ruins have a complicated history (see chapter 10). I refer to this house as the "Legacy House" in honor of its role in continuing the legacy of Tubman's goal of creating a home for the aged and in recognition of restoration and preservation efforts at the site. Because of its confused history, many still refer to it singularly as "the Harriet Tubman Home," and some continue to confuse it with Tubman's personal residence. In fact, it was an important part of a much more complicated history and did serve as the primary dormitory for the Harriet Tubman Home beginning in 1915, two years after her death, until the closure of the Home in 1928.[45]

45. In the early twentieth century, the *Auburn City Directory* usually referred to this house as 1 Danforth Street and John Brown Hall as 2 Danforth Street. However, on occasion it flipped the numerical designations. Also, the naming of the driveway as "Danforth Street" is also problematic because the name derives from a road that was planned for a property owned by Flavel Danforth north of the Tubman properties. The development plans were on a map from the 1880s, but the development and the road were never built. Those recording information for the city directories as well as census takers of the early 1900s simply mistook

Acquired along with several buildings that were present on the twenty-five-acre farm purchased by Tubman in 1896, this house was usually rented out by her to bring in some income until 1903 and then by the AME Zion Church, with the rent going to Tubman as a condition of the title transfer of the property to the AME Zion Church for the purpose of opening the Home. From 1903 to 1908, the goal was to turn this house into a school to train African American girls in the domestic services. However, the school was never opened. After Tubman's death, the house was refurbished with funds generated in honor of Tubman, and the color of the house was changed from red to a light cream with brown trim.[46] This house served as the dormitory for the Home from 1915 until the facility closed in 1928. Later, beginning in the late 1940s, after years of abandonment and neglect, it would be the focus of an effort to restore the Harriet Tubman Home by Bishop William J. Walls. The house was restored through the AME Zion Church's efforts, and it became a prominent centerpiece in an ongoing effort to restore the property and to use the site to interpret and project Tubman's legacy (see chapter 10).

Locus 3

John Brown Hall, the primary dormitory of the Harriet Tubman Home from the formal opening of the Home by the AME Zion Church in 1908 until 1915, two years after Tubman's death (figures 1.4, 1.8–1.10). Its ruins were rediscovered as part of this study, and it has undergone extensive archaeological investigation. The building was acquired as part of the twenty-five-acre farm that Tubman purchased for the Home, and it became the Home's primary dormitory. Like many buildings on the property, it has a complex history. It was constructed in the 1850s or early 1860s as a dormitory for a local brickyard. It was rented out for a few years while Tubman tried to organize funds for her Home. Between 1903 and 1908, it was refurbished by the AME Zion Church and was the site of the formal opening of Tubman's Home for the Aged in 1908. Tubman herself was cared for in this building from 1911 until her death in 1913. In 1915, though, the dormitory for the Home was moved to the Legacy House (Locus 2), and John Brown Hall was rented out

---

the unnamed driveway into the Tubman property for the designated but never constructed roadway that had been planned for the Danforth property.

46. The elderly women under the care of the Home were moved from John Brown Hall to this house in 1915, and the wood-frame home, Locus 2, thereafter became known as "the Harriet Tubman Home."

to the family of an African American Civil War veteran.[47] In the 1930s, the site was abandoned, and after a series of small fires it was declared derelict by the City of Auburn and torn down by the fire department in 1949 in spite of an effort by the AME Zion leadership to raise funds to restore it. We rediscovered the ruins in 1994 and carried out intensive archaeological surveys and excavations in 1998 and 1999. A few Tubman-era apple trees still survived in the surrounding yard.

Locus 4

Foundation ruins of a wood-frame structure that burned in a fire in 1903. These archaeological ruins are near South Street, south of the driveway that runs west to east through the property (figure 1.6). The possibility of ruins on the site was suggested by the presence of a building identified on a 1904 map of the City of Auburn (figure 1.14). The map shows a structure along South Street just south of the city line. The foundation of this structure was identified through a pedestrian survey, remote sensing, and test excavations in 2002. The excavations yielded data consistent with a terminus date tied to house fires in 1902 and 1903.[48]

Locus 5

A roadbed discovered during a winter snow and snow melt in 2002 (figure 1.6).[49] The roadbed runs from South Street at the north edge of Tubman's seven-acre farm and extends for more than five hundred meters east, crossing the creek over a culvert and ending near the ruins of John Brown Hall (which is on the north side). We excavated a cross section of this road to determine

47. Miss Winifred Johnson died while a resident at John Brown Hall on March 27, 1915.

48. The house shown on the 1904 map (archived at the Cayuga County Historian's Office in Auburn) had probably already burned prior to the publication of the map. It is also possible that the former tollhouse, previously located on the west side of South Street and about three hundred meters to the north, was moved to this site soon after the older house on the site burned. During the early 1900s, moving the tollhouse was discussed for its possible use as a dormitory for a proposed school for girls on the property. The school was never opened, and it is possible that the building was never moved to the site. Further archaeological exploration of the materials associated with this foundation might provide a clear use of this area in the early decades of the twentieth century.

49. A detailed discussion of this roadbed can be found in D. Armstrong 2003c. Small-scale excavation of a cross-section of the road was carried out in 2002.

details of the time of use and ways in which it was used. The bed forming this road was made up of layers of clam shell covered with a layer of approximately thirty to forty centimeters of fill. This fill was made up of waster brick (brick that was deformed in the firing process) from local brickyards, which indicates that the road's construction probably dates to the period of early use of the property for brick production. It was likely used to gain access to brick-producing areas at the back (east side) of the property and may have served as an access road for the brick building that was later reused for John Brown Hall. The materials in the roadbed indicate continual use through the Tubman era and into the first decade of the twentieth century. We noted the presence of Tubman-era trash deposits along the roadbed as well as of more recent trash and rubble accumulations on the north side of the roadbed.

Locus 6

A brick kiln and brick-production areas, including brick borrow pits (figure 1.6). The site of the brick kiln was first observed during surveys as a raised area in the grass to the northeast of the current museum building. In 2002, the area was projected as the site of possible construction, so testing was done to evaluate possible cultural resources. Remote-sensing techniques defined a very strong and distinct anomaly. Shovel testing identified the presence of a well-preserved base of a brick kiln, which was excavated in 2005 and 2006. In addition, a surface survey identified waster brick in the adjacent woods along with a very distinctive borrow pit where clay was mixed to make brick. The intensive survey and excavation of the brick kiln and surrounding area are the focus of archaeological studies presented in chapter 11. The study also includes a detailed examination of brickmaking and its role within the Tubman household and in the local African American community along South Street.

Locus 7

Possible ruins of William Henry Stewart Sr.'s house on a small half-acre property at the northwest corner of Tubman's twenty-five-acre farm. Half the property was a small parcel cut from Tubman's land, and the other half was at the southwest corner of what is now a property owned by the New York State Armory (figure 1.6). The presence of a structure is indicated in census records and on the 1904 map, but no surviving features or period artifacts have been observed. I have included it in this discussion because it was once owned by Harriet Tubman's brother William H. Stewart Sr. and represents a potentially important living area on a property adjacent to the Home. The area was surveyed in 2002, but no structure dating to the Tubman period was found. The survey was hindered by debris from a decomposed mobile home or trailer.

Locus 8

Possible structures in an area on which a wood-frame barn is indicated on the 1904 City of Auburn map (figures 1.6, 1.14). This area is very disturbed and covered with post-1950s municipal rubble and trash. Residual evidence in the vicinity includes evidence of an old roadbed (with asphalt) that was probably part of Danforth Street. The evidence of the possible feature includes a series of large stones and stone rubble. These stones suggest the presence of stone footings for the type of wood-frame structure indicated on the 1904 map. Unfortunately, earth movement and dumping of mid-twentieth-century trash have hindered investigation of this part of the site.

Inspiration to "Keep On Going"

The material and spatial record reveals Harriet Tubman's efforts to provide for those in need, her support of women's suffrage, and her efforts to create a special place where aging and homeless African Americans could find shelter and freedom from want. It is said that Tubman's motto was "keep on going." The record shows that she did just that—kept going on her own terms and in her own special ways. A common thread between her life and her social activism is her role as a lifelong advocate for the full expression of a life lived with dignity.

I am often asked to define the most exciting artifact that I have recovered through archaeology. This question used to stump me because I have been taught to value all the materials recovered and to respect each as an important element representing the story of someone else's past. In this book, I try to emphasize the importance of understanding the whole assemblage of artifacts to project the symphony of Tubman's life. In fact, many artifacts from the Tubman site have special meaning, and some I hope will take on new meaning to carry Tubman's legacy forward into the future. During the first season of excavations at the then recently rediscovered ruins of John Brown Hall, we uncovered a small heart-shaped metal pillbox (figure 1.15). It was not the only pillbox discovered at this care facility for elderly African Americans that Tubman had struggled so hard to create, but its heart shape makes it special. I do not know if it belonged to Harriet or to one of the others in residence. To me, it does not matter to whom it belonged because it projects a symbolic link among Tubman, those for whom she cared, and the legacy of her lifelong efforts as an activist for social reforms and justice on behalf of those in need.

This book is not simply a report of archaeological contexts pertaining to Harriet Tubman but a material demonstration of the qualities of the life she lived in service to others. The archaeological study is part of a growing body of what might be considered "activist archaeology" (Stottman 2010). Using archaeology at the Home, we have uncovered her past, exposed and assessed the material evidence of her life and deeds, and generated a material record with which to reflect upon her inspiration. The tangible artifacts recovered were used in daily life by Tubman, her friends, her family, and people who were reliant on her. They remind us that the message is not just to keep on going but, like Tubman, to keep moving forward with deliberate action and to fight for freedom and dignity on behalf of others. My hope is that in unearthing the archaeological record of her life, the new perspectives gained will serve to inspire new generations to action—to solve the social problems of today.

1.1. Harriet Tubman, late nineteenth century. From a women's rights album owned by Tubman's friends and women's rights advocates Elizabeth and Anne F. Miller of Geneva, New York. Album donated to the Library of Congress, Washington, DC (ID 3a10453w). This copy of the photograph is provided courtesy of Judith Bryant, Stewart Family Collection, Auburn, NY.

1.2. Harriet Tubman brick residence and farm, Fleming, New York, 2010. Photograph by D. Armstrong.

1.3. Excavations in 2003 showing ash deposits associated with the fire that destroyed Tubman's wood-frame house on February 10, 1880, and a builder's trench associated with construction of Tubman's brick house on the site of the burned wood-frame house in 1881–82. Photograph by D. Armstrong.

1.4. Pressed-metal buttons with six-pointed star pattern recovered from deposits associated with the fire that destroyed Tubman's wood-frame house on February 10, 1880. Images of these buttons have been incorporated on Tubman's clothing in the painting created for the engraving that will be used for the Harriet Tubman $20 bill. Photograph by D. Armstrong.

1.5. Harriet Tubman's farm in the winter after the completion of the restoration of Tubman's barn, 2015. Photograph by D. Armstrong.

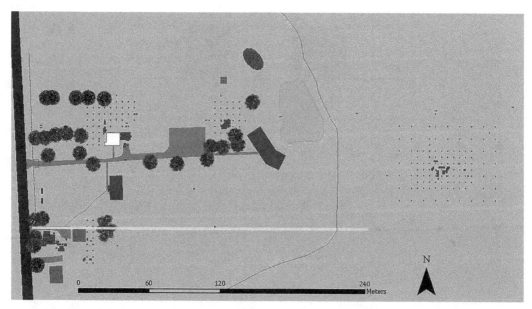

1.6. Map of the Harriet Tubman Home property, buildings, and archaeological sites (GIS map), 2016. Map compiled by J. Bowes and D. Armstrong.

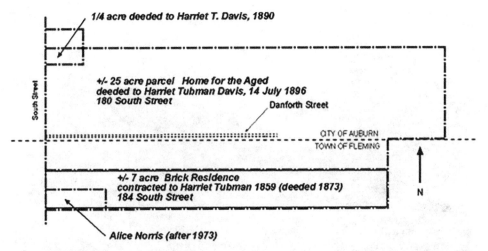

1.7. Map of Harriet Tubman Home showing boundaries of Tubman's farms. The seven-acre farm in Fleming, New York (south or lower part of image), was purchased from William and Frances Seward in 1859. In 1896, Tubman purchased the twenty-five-acre farm immediately north of her farm for the purpose of expanding the Home for the Aged that she had already established in her personal residence. Map by D. Armstrong.

1.8. Harriet Tubman, "inmates," and supporters in front of John Brown Hall, late spring of 1908. This building was constructed in the late 1850s or early 1860s and served as a dormitory for brick workers at local South Street brickyards. The ten-room structure was well suited for a dormitory and was refurbished by the AME Zion Church for the Harriet Tubman Home and opened in 1908 as the Home's primary dormitory. The photo captures an event celebrating the opening of the Home. Photograph courtesy of Harriet Tubman Home, Inc., Auburn, NY.

1.9. John Brown Hall, c. 1912. The porch on the north side of John Brown Hall was constructed with funds raised in 1909 and 1910. Photograph courtesy of Harriet Tubman Home, Inc., Auburn, NY.

1.10. Harriet Tubman and supporters in front of John Brown Hall, c. 1912, with apple orchard in the background. Photograph courtesy of Harriet Tubman Home, Inc., Auburn, NY.

1.11. The Legacy House (Locus 2) of the Harriet Tubman Home, 2012. When Harriet Tubman died in 1913, there was an outpouring of gifts from friends and supporters. Funds donated to the Home for the Aged were used to refurbish a wood-frame house that had previously been rented out to help support the Home. In 1915, when the fix-up was completed, the dormitory for the Home was moved to this wood-frame house. This house continued to be the primary dormitory for the Home through the late 1920s, when the Home was closed. The house fell into disrepair in the 1930s. In the late 1940s, a restoration effort was initiated by the AME Zion Church, and the house was restored in the early 1950s. Photograph by D. Armstrong.

1.12. The Legacy House (Locus 2) of the Harriet Tubman Home, c. 1915. This wood-frame building was painted red and rented by Tubman and then the Home until after her death. In 1914–15, the formerly red-colored house was refurbished and painted a cream color with brown trim. In the spring of 1915, the residential dormitory of the Harriet Tubman Home was moved to this building. Photograph courtesy of the Seward House Museum and Harriet Tubman Home, Inc., Auburn, NY.

1.13. The Legacy House (Locus 2) of the Harriet Tubman Home in a state of disrepair as it appeared in the late 1930s and 1940s. Even though the building had been
stripped of its porch and siding, a New York State Historic Marker continued to mark
the site as an important place in New York State history. Photograph courtesy of
Harriet Tubman Home, Inc., Auburn, NY.

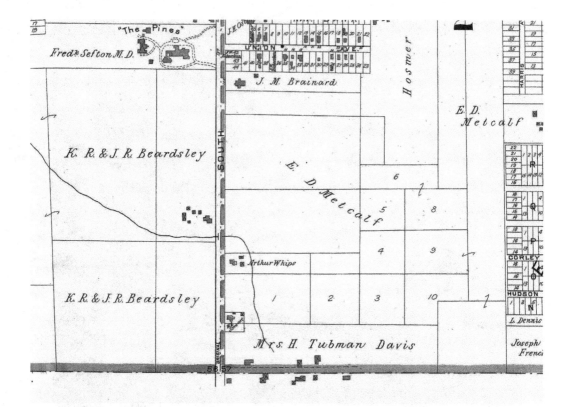

1.14. Section of a map of Auburn from 1904 showing the Harriet Tubman Home properties, which straddle the City of Auburn and the Town of Fleming. Buildings shown on the map include those that are part of the twenty-five-acre farmstead (a composite of two earlier farms) in the Town of Fleming. The map does not include buildings from Tubman's personal seven-acre farm (hence, her brick house and her barn are not shown). Map courtesy of the Special Collections Research Center, Syracuse University, Syracuse, NY.

1.15. Heart-shaped metal pillbox (lid and base) excavated at John Brown Hall (Locus 3). Photograph by D. Armstrong.

2

Interpreting the Evidence
of Harriet Tubman

This most wonderful woman—Harriet Tubman—is still alive. I saw her
but the other day at the beautiful home of Eliza Wright Osborne, the
daughter of Martha C. Wright, in company with Elizabeth Smith Miller,
the only daughter of Gerrit Smith, Miss Emily Howland, Rev. Anna H.
Shaw, and Mrs. Ella [Ellen] Wright Garrison, the daughter of Martha C.
Wright and the wife of William Lloyd Garrison, Jr. All of us were visiting
at the Osbornes, a real love feast of the few that are left and here came
Harriet Tubman.

—Susan B. Anthony, January 1, 1903[1]

A Past Worth Remembering

On New Year's Day in 1903, Susan B. Anthony, who had had a long association with Harriet Tubman based on their shared advocacy for the abolition
of slavery and women's rights, met Tubman for the last time in the parlor of
Eliza Wright Osborne's house at 99 South Street in Auburn, New York.[2] Earl
Conrad describes this meeting of women as "an intellectual salon, a gathering place of the last of the abolitionists, the oldest of the suffrage leaders, and
new generations of younger reformers" (1943, 216). Upon returning home,
Anthony wrote a note about the meeting in her copy of Sarah Bradford's biography *Harriet Tubman, the Moses of Her People* (1901).[3] Anthony's description

---

1. Susan B. Anthony, handwritten note, January 1, 1903, in her copy of Sarah Bradford's
biography *Harriet Tubman, the Moses of Her People* (1901), Susan B. Anthony Collection,
Rare Book and Special Collections Division, Library of Congress, Washington, DC.

2. This house was located a few blocks north of Tubman's house on South Street in
Auburn. It is currently the site of a Methodist church; however, the building that housed the
Osborne family library still stands on the property.

3. This gathering of women is reported by several sources, including accounts by Anna
Howard Shaw (1915, 240–41), Earl Conrad (1943, 215–17), and Milton Sernett (2007,
153–55).

of Harriet Tubman's entrance into this "love feast" of leading women's rights activists, nearly all with ties to earlier abolitionist activism, provides a momentary glimpse of Tubman's intersecting roles in diverse worlds and a new century.

I imagine the social setting in which "this most wonderful woman—Harriet Tubman" had quietly made the short but cold walk north from her farm and home on South Street to the warmth of the gathering in her wealthy neighbor's parlor.[4] Certainly, all the illustrious women meeting in the parlor knew and respected Harriet Tubman for her actions related to both abolition and women's rights, but how well did they know Tubman? What did they know of her household and daily life; and how did they perceive her dream to create a care facility for aging African Americans? Tubman was in fact "still alive" and actively pursuing her dreams for a home for the aged. Anthony describes Eliza Wright Osborne's beautiful home, but what was Tubman's house like, what was life like on her farm, and how were plans for her home for the aged progressing at the time of this sisterly "love feast"? In considering these questions, I draw upon the thoughts of the African American archaeologists Maria Franklin, Whitney Battle-Baptiste, and Anna Agbe-Davies in asking the same questions of contemporary scholarship. These scholars have identified flaws in the way archaeologists have tended to interpret the past (Agbe-Davies 2010, 2011; Battle-Baptiste 2011; Franklin 1997). Battle-Baptiste argues that archaeologists have fallen short in relation to engaging people of color, in particular Black women (2011, 70–71).[5] Agbe-Davies (2011, 2017) and Franklin (2001) have pointed out that African American women have not been fully considered for their important roles as agents of social change and social activism in the late nineteenth and early twentieth centuries. I take seriously these scholars' collective challenge to examine the significant role played by Black women as activists and advocates of social reform and justice. This focus on social justice is particularly relevant in examining the life of an activist such as Harriet Tubman.

Although we may never fully understand the intimate aspects of Tubman's relationship with Susan B. Anthony, Emily Howland, or Eliza Wright Osborne,

4. A unique mix of industrialist, abolitionist, and social reform–minded women's rights advocates lived on South Street in Auburn. The Osbornes lived in a mansion at 99 South Street, and Harriet Tubman at 128 South Street. Tubman's farms and the Osborne home were separated by a long block that included open land, much of which was owned by the Osborne family.

5. In relation to archaeology, see Battle-Baptiste 2011 and Sesma 2016. For a broader examination of Black feminist thought, see Collins 2009.

we can still examine the archaeological and historical record and understand it in terms of specific interactions recorded in historical accounts. The archaeological record provides materials used in daily life and allows us to focus on the material and social world of Harriet Tubman, her family, and those with whom she interacted. These material remains provide access to life as it was lived. Artifacts recovered include everything from intimate items such as buttons and other personal bits of clothing to nonpersonal items such as surprisingly informative bricks found in the walls, foundations, and walkways of structures. Not only are the bricks architectural items, but they also project more intimate contexts. On the Tubman properties, the bricks were made by the hands of family and associates from the local African American community in brickyards at these and adjacent properties (A. Armstrong and D. Armstrong 2012). The archaeological evidence also provides evidence of diet and dietary practice in dietary refuse such as animal bone, shell, and ethnobotanical remains as well as in the material remains of broken tableware and food-preparation bowls and utensils. These artifacts individually and collectively reflect the types and relative costs of goods utilized and the setting in which food was prepared and consumed. Items such as glass canning jars not only tell of the foods grown and put up on the farm but also provide a material trace of the foods regularly gifted by the community to Tubman and her household.

Tubman's residence and the Home for the Aged represent a nexus projecting the strength of an individual's actions in combination with complex networks of social interaction. Prior to this study, many of the details of Harriet Tubman's life in Central New York were unknown, untold, or misunderstood. This study looks at the direct record of her life based on the buildings in which she lived, the fragmented ruins on the property, and the detailed material record of her life and that of her fellow residents, recovered from well-stratified and well-defined contexts on the property. Once we began to examine the site, we found a robust material, spatial, and social footprint. The Tubman properties provide a temporal and spatial focal point by which an array of historical records can be examined to better understand Harriet Tubman and her interactions with family, friends, and the people for whom she cared.

Interpreting the Past Using Archaeology

Although Harriet Tubman was a strong woman, an African American, a head of household, and a person who has become an American icon, her life has been shrouded in the mists of Underground Railroad mythology (Sernett 2007). Archaeological investigation provides baseline data through which interpretation of the Tubman sites may be reconceptualized (Little 2002, 269, 2004). The material and spatial data that are recovered "combine to project compelling and interesting stories that engage the public" (Little 2004, 282). These data as well as a close examination of documents ranging from newspaper accounts to census records allow a more precise representation of life on Tubman's farmstead, within her home, and among her neighbors than had been previously available (D. Armstrong 2015; see also Aplin 2002, 39).

The term *farmstead* is particularly useful for the study of the Tubman properties because it refers not to her farmhouse or to a building in isolation but to the total landscape of her farm, its outbuildings and features, including fields, stone walls, fences, roadways, and brickyards (Pena 2000, 37). The spatial relationships between these structures and features are an important element of the farmstead concept. Hence, to understand the social setting in which Tubman lived her life on the farm, one must look at the totality of the encompassing cultural landscape and the surrounding communities with whom she interacted. Along these lines, Battle-Baptiste (2011) encourages us to focus on the ways in which households construct "personal landscapes" through differential use and perception of spaces within the domestic compound. The spatial and social context of the material remains recovered from the Tubman household provide "clues to the life histories" and a "archaeological biography" of Tubman and others who made up her household (Beaudry 2004, 255; Hendon 2006; Wilkie 2003). Much of Tubman's story emanates from her ability to use the farmstead to produce foods and resources to sustain those who lived there. For Tubman, the farm represented a means to provide the communal sustenance for her household. Beyond this, she hoped to utilize its resources to achieve her goal of providing for elderly African Americans in need.

As the nineteenth century ended, Tubman found herself called upon to take in and provide housing and care for relatives, aging African Americans, and other persons in need who came to her for support.[6] In fact, she had chartered a home for the aged in her own home before purchasing the adjacent farmstead. Tubman's idea was to create a self-sufficient cooperative farm

6. At the time that Tubman established her Home, there was another home in Auburn, the Home for the Friendless, located on Grant Avenue in Auburn, which was originally created to care for widows and orphans of the Civil War. It did not initially exclude Blacks. However, by the end of the nineteenth century admission required a significant donation. Chapter 8 discusses the Home for the Friendless and other charitable institutions in and around Auburn as a means of providing greater context for Tubman's Home.

on which the farm's goods and products could be used to sustain the home's inmates and generate funds for its management. When the neighboring farmstead came up at auction, she bid until she was the owner and then had to solicit support to cover the down payment and assume a personal mortgage on the balance.[7]

One of the problems in interpreting the sites connected to Tubman's life is the disassociation of the current landscape from the active setting of the nineteenth century. Evidence of this disassociation can be found in the fact that when referring to the Home, even the National Historic Landmark designation completed in 1999 refers to individual, isolated buildings and does not consider the fact that these residual structures were part of a far more complex farmstead landscape; everything else on the property is presented as ancillary (US National Park Service 2001). Likewise, when the place where Tubman lived is referred to, the most common reference point is her house, her residence—or, more specifically, the brick house. In each case, the specific building referred to represents an important but nonisolated element of two much more complex farmsteads, each of which has undergone transformative changes that significantly modified the form and material expression of the landscape. Today, much of the farmland on the collective thirty-two-acre Tubman property is covered by dense vegetation and trees. It is thus difficult for the visitor to imagine the property as an active farmstead with agricultural fields, animal pens, fruit-bearing orchards, brickyards, and kitchen gardens. Yet the combination of historical accounts and archaeology allows us to imagine the Tubman-era agricultural and industrial landscape. It also provides data by which the cultural landscape of the property in the Tubman era can be physically reconstructed so that visitors may more easily understand that the property is more than a series of isolated structures.

An equally compelling refining of history derives from the story of the white wood-frame house (Locus 2) at the front of the Home for the Aged property. This lone, standing Tubman-era building was until recently projected as the entire "Harriet Tubman Home." In fact, however, the Home included several structures in an active farm landscape that also had apple trees, grain crops, and domestic animal stock. The wood-frame house was certainly an important element of the Home, but so were Tubman's brick

---

7. Tubman received a lump-sum pension payment of about $500 in 1895. The pension, granted in 1899, resulted from her petition for Civil War widow's benefits, $8 per month, and a nurse's pension, $12 per month (see Sernett 2007, 99).

house (Locus 1) and John Brown Hall (Locus 3), as were other buildings on the two farms, produce from the fields, rents from several buildings, and both the economic activity associated with local brickyards (Locus 6) and the bricks themselves. The bricks not only were tied to African American labor but also were incorporated into several structures on the property, including the walls of Tubman's house, the foundation footings of her barn, and the kitchen of the wood-frame Legacy House.

This study draws upon the household perspective outlined by Mary Beaudry (2004) and frames it within a broader farmstead context. This approach derives in part from my studies of African Caribbean house and yard compounds (D. Armstrong 1991, 2003a). The approach to the cultural landscape highlights the interactive nature of household structures and their surrounding yards as well as the relationship of multiple households that operated within broader community structures. In the examination of Tubman's properties, a landscape-based perspective emphasizing the dynamic relationships expressed on these farmsteads assures an interpretation that combines people and place. It also allows us to see people as mobile, interactive players tied socially to the surrounding town and city (Brandon and Barile 2004, 6–7).

The parameters of inclusion within the Tubman household reflect the intimacy of an extended family and the trauma of separation caused by relocation. The Tubman household was at once a haven for refugees from the harsh institution of slavery and a reconstituted extended family of blood relatives, fictive kin, and persons in need who were attracted to the hospitality of a nurturing caregiver—Harriet Tubman. Thus, in conceptualizing this rather open household, one finds the pragmatic utility of Beaudry's suggestion that "archaeologists should take from the interdisciplinary literature on households what is most useful to them and to avoid adopting a single or monolithic definition of 'the household'; we encounter so many different sorts of domestic arrangements that there is simply not a one size fits all definition that can be of use to us" (2004, 255). In the case of the Tubman household, we find that it was in constant flux, even as it had Harriet Tubman as its continual anchor and head.

Agency and the Study of an Activist

The scope of this project is aimed at more than simply recovering data from sites associated with Harriet Tubman. Rather, it is aimed at understanding aspects of the daily life reflected in the material remains of sites owned and significantly impacted by Tubman's presence and at exploring how these data relate to broader issues of late nineteenth- and early twentieth-century life in America. These issues include the array of social movements and agency with which Tubman was associated: from resisting enslavement and living as a freeperson to owning property, advocating for women's rights, and being an activist who provided care to others. This study uses a pragmatic combination of contextual and interpretive approaches to the past that emphasize the impact of a well-known social activist, Harriet Tubman (Leone 2010). The notion of agency as applied to archaeology places the individual in the position of the actor but views the action through the material residue of the artifacts, objects, and structures that people devised and used within the site. The artifacts that were recovered reflect past actions but were not in themselves animate. Rather, our interpretation of the artifacts projects and implies the actions of those who used them.

Matthew Johnson defines agency as "the issue of how we think about intention, action and the resources needed to act" (2010, 237). The Tubman site is a model example for the role of "agency" in the archaeological record. Using agency as a model through which the material record is viewed allows us to see the artifacts and spatial array of structures and features on the landscape as the result of decisions made by, the belief systems of, and the values of a noted social activist. Virtually everything about the site correlates with the expression of social and political values related to living life on one's own terms. Although northern society accepted Tubman and honored her for her role as an activist in the cause of emancipation, her social activism continued to cross lines as she embraced women's rights and worked to create her Home for the Aged.

Tubman was an agent of change whose creativity and actions transformed social structures. The things she used in her daily life were modified at least in part to serve their own values and ideals rather than simply that of the dominant economic class or the world around it. The material record projects the lives and roles of individuals and of their community collectively. The record was deposited by people who were active in altering or redefining social structures in terms of agency. The study of Tubman's life projects an individual's active role in life and related material culture that is consistent with Pierre Bourdieu's (1977) approach, which sees individuals as engaged "social actors" for whom the active practice of their lives transforms the culture around them. Bourdieu emphasizes ways in which individuals bring on changes through their active practices (see also Johnson 2010, 108), and Tubman was certainly an active practitioner. Yet even as the site reflects a decidedly activist individual who was respected by many and who lived her life on her own terms, this does not imply a life without limits and constraints. In fact, even though Tubman was well known and honored across many social spheres, she lived with racial,

social, economic, and physical constraints: she was not wealthy or well edu-
cated, and, significantly for this era, she was an African American woman.
Moreover, even as she strived to assist elderly African Americans, as her life
went on, she, too, faced the increasing health problems associated with age.

The active role of individuals in their lives and culture is seen in many
forms in the archaeological record. For instance, archaeologists studying the
material remains recovered from female textile workers' quarters at Boott's
Mill in Lowell, Massachusetts, have uncovered acts of individual expression
(Mrozowski, Zeising, and Beaudry 1996). The material record at that site was
found to be in sharp disharmony with formal policies governing the behavior of workers. Ethnic, religious, and class-based alliance with Catholic Irish
identities was expressed in the material record through the active selection of
artifacts, including tobacco pipes embossed with the slogan "Home Rule"
(Mrozowski, Zeising, and Beaudry 1996, 71–74). In this case, workers of
Irish ancestry not only broke the formal rules regarding smoking but also did
so with pipes projecting their ethnic and religious identity as Irish Catholics.

Interpretation of the Tubman site recognizes the case-specific and icon-
ically Tubmanesque nature of the data. Rather than indicating resistance or
noncompliance, as in the textile workers' case, much of the material record of
the Tubman site projects the activist residents and their efforts to demonstrate
a set of values revolving around self-sufficient individualism, property ownership, and adherence to spiritual and social values consistent with those of the
AME Zion Church, with which Tubman became closely affiliated. The material record at the site reflects the broader matrix of material use and economic
structures of its era as well as the specifics of social relations revolving around
Tubman. Yet at the same time it is a setting defined by the parameters of life
for African Americans and the particularities of life in Auburn, New York,
as society shifted with the changing cultural landscape associated with the
transition into the twentieth century. Tubman was a national, if not global,
personality who traveled widely in the eastern United States as an advocate for
her Home and the cause of women's rights, yet she lived her life in her house
and for her Home.

The Importance of the Farm Setting
and the Archaeology of Farming

At first glance, the picture painted of Harriet Tubman's house and Home
focuses on the important person, Tubman, and the institution of care that she
created. One must look beyond the formal walls of each structure, though,

to find the broader farm and communal properties on which she lived and interacted, the complexity implied by the social and economic systems that she engaged in as a farmer, and her noted role as an activist. It takes an even deeper look to find the contributing contexts of social engagement implied by the connectivity between Tubman's farms and the local craft enterprises in which she and members of her household were engaged. The latter included production and sale of farm produce and jars of canned foods as well as a variety of activities about which the historical record is virtually mute, including involvement in a local small-scale brick- and tile-making industry as well as small-scale cottage craft industries such as the hand painting, or gilding, of bisque porcelain figurines, for which archaeology provides the only surviving record. It is important, when considering Tubman's life on the farm, to consider the total cultural and economic landscape and environmental setting of the farm on which she lived.

Archaeological studies of farms have been shown to be of use in providing a source of data that maximizes the interpretative potential of inadequately documented contexts (Little 2004). Effective site interpretation in historical archaeology relies upon reconstructing historical context. Historical context is used to address questions at different scales or levels of inquiry and refers to major trends that have had influence over the long-term historical development in different study regions (Groover 2008, 18). Farms hold a significant and relatively neglected place in the American landscape: even though many sites are known, "we don't know many of them thoroughly" (Rafferty 2000, 125). Most farms that have been excavated are in regions other than the northeast United States, and the majority of them have been only superficially excavated.[8] Their prevalence on the rural landscape allows us to drive by without considering them, unless perhaps in contemplation of the all-too-prevalent observation of an abandoned and collapsing barn or an abandoned farmhouse or the removal of these buildings in the process of widening a highway, constructing a shopping mall, or building a suburban housing development.[9] The Tubman farms, like several of its neighbors, was similarly fading into the landscape, many of its buildings lost, and Harriet Tubman's barn was in the late stages of collapse when, fortunately, a renewed interest in her legacy sparked a renewed effort toward restoration and interpretation.

8. Many studies involve small-scale investigations that are reported in archaeological contract reports.

9. The problem of identifying the significance of farms and farmsteads is discussed in Hart 2000.

The Tubman Farmsteads as Places of Social Engagement

The study of the Tubman farmsteads explores a household headed by a strong and famous African American woman, but the material record present at the site is the residue of actions and activities of a range of people over time,[10] including both Harriet Tubman and the many others, mostly African Americans, with whom she interacted. The men, women, and children there lived, worked, and interacted and in the process left a record of their daily lives and practices. The material record is thus polyvalent and projects "potentially contestable message, images, and actions" (Comaroff and Comaroff 1992, 10). The meanings reflected are subject to interpretation based on an evaluation of the context of use and discard. Hence, any interpretation is a story told about the past.

The material record represents the collective action of all present at the site. The data are a very intimate and personal record of common possessions and cherished items that eventually made their way into the ground and are the representative residue of more complete actions, events, and interactions.[11] This research can be viewed through several lenses, including the cultural landscape (Adams 1990; Armstrong 2003); the dynamics of the material culture associated with the household and housework (Barile and Brandon 2004; Beaudry 1996, 2004); structures and the habitus that look within and beyond the local site (Bourdieu 1977); and the material residue of the created memory associated with sites relating to popular people or events (Shackel 2000). The site is of interest in relation to Tubman's role as a leader in the African American community and her role as a woman who was also a head of household from the mid–nineteenth century through the early twentieth century (Agbe-Davies 2010; Battle-Baptiste 2011; Beaudry 2004; Mullins 1999; Spencer-Wood 2004; Stone and McKee 1998).

The Tubman farmstead is located on the edge of the Town of Fleming and straddles the line between the town and the City of Auburn (figures 1.6, 1.7, 1.14). Tubman's farm was at a point of interface between urban and rural.[12] The location was strategic and, I think, well thought out by both the buyer

10. Many of the ideas developed in this section were presented earlier in D. Armstrong 2015.

11. A growing body of literature deals with the archaeological investigation of late nineteenth-century farms and farmsteads (e.g., Beaudry 1996, 496; Groover 2008; Huey 2000; Pena 2000; Wurst, Armstrong, and Kellar 2000).

12. Most archaeologists discuss farms and rural life as a single concept (Groover 2008).

(Harriet Tubman) and the sellers (US senator William Seward and his wife, Frances). It interfaces not only urban and rural but also Black and white, rich and poor, large-scale and small-scale industries, and large-scale and small-scale farming.[13] Tubman's life and her deeds served to blur the "lines that divide" in a stratified society (Delle, Mrozowski, and Paynter 2000).

The farm's position on the interface of social action and social change is consistent with Tubman's position in a rapidly changing world. Her presence in this setting blurred divisions between economic, racial, and ethnic identities. Her death impacted the Home. With her passing and with intensified segmentation and segregation throughout the twentieth century, many of the intersections and bases for interaction faded to the background and became obscured by perceived veils of separation (Du Bois 1903). However, in her lifetime Tubman crossed these lines daily as she carried out her interactions and discourses on South Street, in the kitchens of neighbors, at public gatherings to articulate the needs of her Home, arm in arm with likeminded women on the stages of suffrage gatherings, sitting among affluent women in the parlors of their homes, and regularly stopping by their kitchens to sell her produce or to gather their garbage to feed her pigs. Tubman was a pragmatic farmer as well as a spiritual and free-thinking leader.

Tubman's farmstead can be considered a unit of production, which by its location intersected both urban and rural life. Tubman utilized its acreage and its proximity to the urban center of Auburn to facilitate its productiveness. The records of the William Seward house, also located in Auburn, document her walking up South Street selling the produce and the put-up glass jars of homemade canned goods from her farm and then, after resting in the Seward kitchen, returning down South Street to collect discarded food for her pigs from those same households to whom she had sold goods from her farm.

The household and domestic setting is the best place to find people on their own terms. It is here that they live out their lives and make their own choices. Moreover, households, broadly defined, are varied in composition but collectively make up the whole of any given community. Moreover, that which makes up a house and home is more than the area found between four walls of a house structure but also includes the yard garden, outbuildings, fields, and orchards, and so these areas have been included in this archaeological investigation. Historical archaeology can make a powerful contribution through its

13. Tubman's long life added a new dimension to these interfaces because it straddled the nineteenth and twentieth century.

ability to access household data and to interpret the complex composite array of artifacts left by women, men, old, and young within the same generalized spaces—be they called homes, houses, households, residences, compounds, apartments, or barracks (see Beaudry 2004, 255).

Harriet Tubman: Challenging Gender Assumptions

Harriet Tubman was not just a woman of note but also a resistor and activist in an era of social reform. It is appropriate to consider her role as a woman and the implications of her gender when investigating her life. Gender refers to the different ways that men and women are culturally defined and evaluated (Stone and McKee 1998, 4). Definitions of gender are fluid because "gender is a cultural construction, learned and institutionalized, often debated, and ever changing as human actors undergo life experiences and interact with one another" (Stone and McKee 1998, 4). How did expectations about gender influence Tubman's life, and how do they affect our interpretation of her today? In examining gender, Marie Sørensen challenges us to "translate theoretical and political convictions about the importance of gender into practical applications" (2000, 7). She argues that true gender archaeology should reject naturalized or restricting gender roles established over the past centuries and strive to open up a whole new understanding of culture and history. She notes that gender "is an inconsistent but permanent part of history and life" (7). The study of the role of gender in this more fluid sense, like other thematic frameworks or veils or patinas, provides a relevant lens through which we view people and society, their material record, and its contexts.

Harriet Tubman fascinated John Brown, and his view of her illustrates ways in which her actions challenged nineteenth-century gender roles. In 1863, Franklin Sanborn published a biographical article on Tubman and her deeds, indicating that John Brown referred to her as "him," called her "General Tubman," and stated that "he [Tubman] is the most of a man I ever met with" (Sanborn 1863). The perception of Tubman as either being gender neutral or assuming the role of a male is also conveyed by Sarah Bradford when in presenting Tubman's spirituality she wrote that Tubman regularly engaged in conversations with God, and "she *talked with God as a man talketh with his friend*" (1869, 23, emphasis in the original).[14] Tubman's nonconforming

---

14. During this era, the male pronouns *he, his, him* were commonly used as defaults and may not necessarily reflect intentional identification of Tubman as a person who blurred gender roles.

leadership, action, and advocacy placed her in what for the mid–nineteenth century constituted an array of gender-bending roles. She led people to freedom, solicited funds and resources for their sustenance in Canada, and appealed to the intellectual community of abolitionists and transcendental scholars of the Boston area to support her spiritually inspired mission. During the war, her role as a nurse fit the prescription of women's engagement with the Union's war effort, but her multivalent role as a spy and soldier and leader of troops transcended established gender lines of the era and later had to be painstakingly explained in efforts to gain her both credit for her deeds and duly earned military benefits. In Auburn, her roles as property owner, African American matriarch, supporter of women's rights, and founder of a home for elderly African Americans placed her outside of the established gender bound-aries of her day, and to the end she was always pushing for more.

The context of Tubman's farm and the Home that she founded projects her as a conduit of change. What role did gender play in a farm environment and for Harriet Tubman, who was not only a woman but an African American and a head of household? Many studies of farm life discuss the combination of male and female gender roles on the farm, stressing the mutual interde-pendence of all residing in the need for collective action in the production of goods on the farm. Diana Wall, who has stressed the presence of separate spheres of activities for women and men in the nineteenth-century middle- and upper-middle-class urban context in New York City, suggests that on farms men and women were more mutually dependent. With respect to dairy farms, she notes that "while dairy farming had a gender-based division of labor, men and women did not operate in 'separate spheres' as has been mod-eled for 19th century urban society in New York" (2004, 8). Suzanne Spencer-Wood (2009) advises us to critically examine the role of gender in relation to institutions such as Tubman's Home for the Aged. Gender roles were bent by Tubman's renown and by her role as the recognized head of household, but the household itself included family members (men, women, and children) as well as relatives and boarders. On her properties, one found African Amer-icans, Indigenous Americans, and white Americans, and both her farm and the Home were operated communally. Tubman procured a significant portion of the resources needed for sustenance, but she also relied on the goodwill of institutions such as the AME Zion Church and gifts from supporters and the local community.

Gender was an important issue on farms and continues to be for our interpretation of life within a farmstead. Spencer-Wood argues that "femi-nist theory and history are essential for fully defining and understanding the household and the family" (2004, 235). She suggests that power dynamics and social agency in households and families have been historically undertheorized because the latter have been undervalued as a "women's passive domestic sphere" (235). This undertheorization has led to a devaluing of household archaeology because it "concerns the domestic sphere that is traditionally identified with women" (235).

Harriet Tubman was an influential woman who was head of the household, the owner of the property, and a person with documentable continuity at the site over nearly half a century. However, she was only one of many who resided at the property. She cooked, ate, and interacted with others in the house, the yard, the garden, and the land that encompassed the farm. With guidance from feminist archaeologists such as Whitney Battle-Baptiste (2011), Mary Beaudry (2004), Marie Sørensen (2000), and Suzanne Spencer-Wood (2004), this study examines the complexity of the roles played by Tubman and by the other women, men, and children residing within these farmsteads. One aspect of this complexity is the interplay of the private and public nature of Tubman, the landscape of her properties, and the artifacts recovered from these contexts.

In many settings, one will find a power dynamic in which women's roles are controlled and circumscribed—but not here. Hence, even as I address gender issues, I caution against a priori gender stereotypes in defining Tubman's households (Spencer-Wood 2004, 239). Rather, like Sørensen (2000), I prefer to look toward a more engaging definition that accounts for and seeks out the specific roles of gender and many other variables, including age, ethnicity, economic condition, and belief systems, in explaining the complexity, diversity, and variability of household structures and interactions. The Tubman site lends itself well to questions about the impacts of Tubman's ownership of the property, her role as a leader in the African American community, and her role as an advocate of social justice. The material record documents lifeways and interactions among many within a place that was her residence and farm, settings that were and are viewed as both private and public.

Harriet Tubman was a woman who lived in both the public and private spheres, and in studying her life one should avoid assumptions of a dominant gender ideology that equates men with the public sphere and women with the domestic sphere. This would be a gross oversimplification not only of Tubman but of women in mid-nineteenth- to early twentieth-century Central New York. Permutations of such an ideology may have a root in specific middle-class households in places such as mid-nineteenth-century New York (Wall 1994), but such a construct arbitrarily restricts the role of women in a dichotomy that really does not conform well to the complexity of household structures or social interactions of the time. One could argue that Tubman was an exception to the rule (perhaps every rule!), but she also represents what I see as an accepted and acceptable variance in gender roles in both the private and public spheres. That Tubman owned her property and was the head of her household is a given, even when her parents resided there and later when she married Nelson Davis in 1869. She operated the household by inclusion rather than by exclusion or power broking. Hence, she was not relegated to her parlor but used her parlor and that of others to communicate her ideas to others in ways that blurred notions of the separation of private spaces and public spaces. In these actions, she was not alone: the parlors of homes in Central New York were regularly used by fellow women's rights activists to convene, discuss, and put forward women's issues. In the case of Tubman, her parlor was used for gatherings aimed at garnering support for her Home for the Aged. Thus, one can expect gender roles displayed in late nineteenth- and early twentieth-century Central New York to reflect variances advocated within sectors of society engaged in advocacy for social reform. Harriet Tubman thus breaks most if not all the stereotypes for women and women of color of the era if she is viewed from the broader context of the nation or of late nineteenth- to early twentieth-century women in general. However, within the social fabric of Auburn, New York, this variance fits definitively within the social constructs of a significant and vociferous segment of the population, including both men and women who advocated for social reforms (abolition, temperance, women's rights, health care, distributed property ownership, and voting rights).

The contexts of Harriet Tubman's properties allow us to look more closely into the intersection of gender, race, ethnicity, and identity.[15] From her home at 128 South Street, Tubman had to walk only a few hundred meters north to be welcomed into the parlor of Eliza Wright Osborne's home at 99 South Street, where on January 1, 1903, she joined a large number of women's rights advocates engaged in a formal "tea." Similarly, indicative of the importance of tea wares within Tubman's households, we found a set of tea wares, cups, and small saucers used to serve tea and coffee in the artifacts recovered from Tubman's personal house. Additional pieces of this matching tea set were also recovered from deposits at John Brown Hall and at three other locations

15. The notion of intersecting spheres deviates from notions of separate spheres often discussed in feminist archaeology as a means of defining a restricted place of their own for women and finding engendered spaces in the archaeological record (Spencer-Wood 2004; Wall 2004).

across the property. Our excavations recovered at least fifteen distinct cups and saucers that were part of what must have been a much larger set of "Lace" pattern, teal-blue, transfer-printed wares made by L. (Lazorus) Straus and Sons and sold at Macy's department store (figure 2.1). Other tea wares were also found at each site. Moreover, from historical records we know that Tubman hosted teas in her house and that she was invited into upper-middle-class and upper-class households for formal teas and conversations, like the one that Susan B. Anthony comments on in the frontispiece of her copy of Bradford's biography of Tubman and like the tea held to honor Tubman at the home of Mrs. Telford, announced in a local newspaper (*Auburn Bulletin*, April 6, 1888) (figure 2.2). In addition, a brass plate used to print calling cards displaying the name "Harriet Tubman Davis" was found in the wall of Tubman's house by Rev. Carter during architectural assessment (figure 2.3). The calling cards were used to respond to and make invitations to these formal social exchanges. The teas to which Tubman was invited were strictly woman's gatherings. In contrast, Tubman served tea to a mixed group of men and women in her home during early meetings of the Harriet Tubman Home Board of Directors.

Harriet Tubman was a nineteenth- and early twentieth-century feminist. Her actions sought opportunity and equality for herself, her family, and those around her. She was a person of action who would come to the podium to state her case and to advocate for her beliefs, but for the most part she demonstrated her beliefs in the actions she took, and so it would be others who would commemorate these actions in terms of their meaning to her selected causes. Unlike in the case of Jermain Wesley Loguen, an AME Zion bishop in Syracuse who espoused his beliefs from the pulpit and in public forums, including an autobiography, or in the case of Frederick Douglass, who was a great orator, motivator, publisher, and author, putting to pen both his beliefs and his autobiography, our knowledge of Tubman is more constrained. It has moved forward in time to us in fits and gaps, reflected upon in biographical form, first by Bradford and then by Conrad and now more completely by synthetic histories written by Kate Larson (2004), Jane Humez (2003), Milton Sernett (2007), and Joyce Stokes Jones and Michele Jones Galvin (2013) and then by the recovery of the physical and material record of her life from her properties.[16]

16. See Bradford 1869, 1886, 1901; Conrad 1943; Humez 2003; Jones and Galvin 2013; Larson 2004; Sernett 2007. See also the integrated archaeological and historical research in A. Armstrong and D. Armstrong 2012; D. Armstrong 2003b, 2003c, 2011, 2015; Ryan and Armstrong 2000.

Testing Power, Status, and Authority

Status is often equated to economic means or affluence, but it is also rooted in perceptions of where and how one relates to others in society. Tubman began her life as a slave, the legal property of somebody else. Later, after emancipating herself, she expressed her freedom by assisting others and acquiring two farms. Throughout her life, in economic terms she was a person who though not poor was also not affluent. Hence, she was of a marginally lower economic status than the persons of affluence with whom she drank tea. However, in another arena, that of social status and recognition for her abilities, efforts, and contributions, she transcended these devisors and attained a position of high if not exalted status and esteem throughout her life. Harriet Tubman was and is greatly admired by all, including Blacks and whites, rich and poor, both for what she accomplished and the steadfast manner of her pursuit of the principles of social justice and concern for others.

If one considers "power" to be defined as the ability to make people do what one wants and to acquire what one desires, then Harriet Tubman quietly became quite powerful. She freed at least seventy persons before the war and assisted in an effort that freed hundreds of thousands and changed the landscape of freedom and equality in the United States, if not the world. Authority projects an ability to gain "access to legitimacy" (Stone and McKee 1998, 8). Tubman had authority via her actions, the people with whom she associated, the changes that she brought about in institutions, and her iconic leadership role in society. Because of her actions, her causes, her risks, and her successes, particularly given the background and condition of her birth and the fact that she was a Black women and former slave in nineteenth-century America, she has been transported to mythical status, supernatural in influence and accomplishment. Yet even as much of her post–Civil War history has been forgotten, much of the strength of that myth rests in the fact that she lived a rather unassuming life on the edge of town, taking on the nonpresumptuous role of "Aunt Harriet" to more than just her immediate family.

An interesting aspect of Tubman's life is the way she gained symbolic autonomy or control over her own actions. Those engaged in the freedom movement were aware of the limitations on autonomy placed by the constraints of economic condition, employment, and ownership of property. Hence, one finds that Tubman was initially given a boost toward autonomy by her benefactors, the Seward family. The transfer of a seven-acre farmstead was critical to Tubman's symbolic and real autonomy. Ownership of the land provided her with a place to live for more than fifty years, a place to which she could invite others and protect them from hardship, and a place that she could use to generate the resources and produce the goods to retain her status as a self-sufficient member of several intersecting communities. Tubman and others used her autonomy as a symbol of the success of the concept of freedom for African Americans. In fact, Tubman's autonomy was built upon social networks of interaction and exchange that worked together to secure property for her, provide a market for her goods, and facilitate social discourse among and between many sectors of a stratified society.

Industrial Changes in the Cultural Landscape of Farming

Tubman's life on the farm coincides with significant changes in farming in America with the shift to industrial plows and steel farm implements. It is probable that Tubman did not fully see the changes in the scale and scope of farming in the late nineteenth and early twentieth centuries as she endeavored to work her farm and attempted to expand her production capacity in buying a neighboring farm in 1896.[17] Farmers pursuing the expansion of their farms in her region benefited from the new plows and technology to drain fields, but she, like many other small farmers in the region, was probably not completely aware of the long-term impact of what would become a dramatic shift in the scale and scope farming in the vast and expanding farmlands of the American Midwest and West. Many of Tubman's own friends and supporters in Auburn were facilitators of these changes. The Osborne family, who supported Tubman and had deep connections to both the abolition movement and the women's rights movement, also owned the Osborne Manufacturing Company. After the Civil War, this company, situated near the center of Auburn, grew dramatically, producing large-scale iron and steel plows that were part of a revolution in agricultural practice on a global scale. At the same time, one-piece iron water pumps, like those produced by Gould Pumps of Auburn and Seneca Falls, brought clean water to home and fields. By the turn of the twentieth century, Osborne plows were probably used to cultivate Tubman's fields, and two Gould pumps are present on the site. Tubman's own farm contributed to the industrial and technological shift in farming. Brick-yards on the property and on surrounding South Street properties produced

---

17. Though probably not fully recognized in daily life, the site represents "a tangible record of how people have adapted to environmental, social, economic, and technological change through time" (Bodner 1990, 76).

not only brick for homes (such as Tubman's brick house), civic buildings, and factories but also cylindrical clay tiles that were used to drain acreage and expand the size of farms.[18] The Tubman farmstead was thus involved in the changing forces of agrarian and industrial production and at once on the edge of and a part of changes in farming.

Country life has often been characterized as unchanging, particularly in contrast to the fast pace of urban life, but significant changes were taking place in the nature and scale of farming in the Tubman era. William Adams (1990) redefines farming environments to include elements of change and the necessity to adapt to a changing world. Though perhaps not fully recognized in the daily practice of farming in Fleming and Auburn, such change was occurring there. Even as Tubman seized upon this form of proprietorship to sustain herself and her family and did so relatively successfully over a period of more than fifty years, by the end of the nineteenth century farm life and the ability of a small farm to sustain its residents were under pressure. Tubman acquired the larger neighboring farm to expand her means of sustaining those who came to her for care. The goal was a cooperative farm that utilized the goods produced by the elderly residents to support themselves. The placement of her farm at the intersection of the rural and urban spheres made this change even more acute because this proximity led to challenges related to the myths and realities of country life. Hence, even as Tubman expanded her acreage, and as these farms entered the twentieth century, they were no longer self-sustaining. Unfortunately, the home for aging African Americans that she was trying to create would require more resources than could be generated by the farm; she therefore had to turn it over to the AME Zion Church, which in turn looked to the broader African American community for support.

18. The brickyard was a source of income, but on at least one occasion Tubman's fields were accidentally ruined when flooded by workers creating mud pits for brick production (see chapter 11).

2.1. Sherds from at least fifteen tea cups and saucers of a "Lace" pattern made and sold by L. (Lazorus) Straus and Sons, owners of Macy's Department Store in New York, were recovered during excavations at John Brown Hall (Locus 3). Sherds of this pattern and a second nearly identical pattern were recovered from several activity areas on the property: Harriet Tubman's brick house (Locus 1), the ruins of the basement of a house that burned in 1902 (Locus 4), excavated deposits associated with the roadbed linking John Brown Hall and Tubman's farm (Locus 5), and deposits associated with a brick kiln and brick-production area (Locus 6). Photograph by D. Armstrong.

A Tea for Harriet Tubman.

Mrs. W. H. Telford, of 8 Grant avenue, will give a tea party at her home Saturday afternoon in honor of Harriet Tubman. Harriet Tubman is an old colored lady ~ and quite a historical character. She acted as a spy for the Union army during the Rebellion and a book detailing her wonderful exploits during our "late unpleasantness" has been written and widely read.

2.2. "A Tea for Harriet Tubman," *Auburn Bulletin*, April 6, 1888. Public announcement of a tea held in honor of Harriet Tubman by Mrs. W. H. Telford at 5 Grant Avenue, Auburn, NY. Copy of article courtesy of Harriet Tubman Home, Inc., Auburn, NY.

2.3. Brass nameplate, "Harriet Tubman Davis," used along with ink and a rubber roller to produce calling cards. The nameplate was found behind a baseboard in Harriet Tubman's brick house. Photograph by D. Armstrong.

3

The Historical and Archaeological Landscape of the Harriet Tubman Home

I grew up like a neglected weed,—ignorant of liberty, having no experience of it. Then I was not happy or contented: every time I saw a white
man I was afraid of being carried away. I had two sisters carried away in a
chain-gang,—one of them left two children. We were always uneasy. Now
I've been free, I know what a dreadful condition slavery is. I have seen
hundreds of escaped slaves, but I never saw one who was willing to go
back and be a slave. I have no opportunity to see my friends in my native
land. We would rather stay in our native land, if we could be as free there
as we are here. I think slavery is the next thing to hell. If a person would
send another into bondage, he would, it appears to me, be bad enough to
send him into hell, if he could.

> —statement attributed to Harriet Tubman
> in Benjamin Drew, *The Refugee or the*
> *Narratives of Fugitive Slaves* (1856)

The Value of Archaeology:
Finding Missing Structures, Features, and Artifacts

The study of Harriet Tubman's properties projects the rich texture and
humanistic value of her legacy.[1] Careful excavation has yielded a wealth of new
information about Tubman's residence and her Home for the Aged. For any
structure and from almost any vantage point on the property, archaeology has
added new and important information on her life. From the rediscovery of John
Brown Hall to the recovery of personal items from her house and the discovery
of the ruins of a brick kiln, each find adds dimension to our understanding of

1. As a way of honoring Harriet Tubman, Syracuse University has maintained a strategy
of pro bono contribution during all phases of research of the Tubman properties. Research
was funded by grants from Syracuse University's Vision Fund and a Syracuse University Chan-
cellor's Community Engagement Grant.

Tubman's life. Individual items such as the heart-shaped pillbox recovered from John Brown Hall add a humanistic reality that allows to us re-create mental bridges to Tubman's deep concern for others (figure 1.15).

We initiated an archaeological investigation of Harriet Tubman's brick house in cadence with an architectural study of the structure to better understand Tubman's use of her house and adjacent yard before they could be affected by the restoration project. When we uncovered ash adjacent to her brick residence, it demonstrated the potential of archaeology to yield significant new information about her life (figures 1.2–1.3, 3.1–3.2). The discovery confirmed that the original wood-frame house occupied by Tubman was different than the brick house that she later occupied and that still stands at the same location on the property. Moreover, the abundance of artifacts associated with the house fire provided a detailed record of household goods from a specific event and a particular point in time. This information guided a careful search of historic records, which resulted in the identification of two newspaper accounts from February 10, 1880, that described the fire (figure 3.3). We were surprised at how much Tubman-era material and detailed context were recoverable as we continued excavating in the yard. These excavations identified a series of key artifacts, including a complete array of dining-room ceramic ware and glassware dating to the fire, a builder's trench associated with the fire that was filled with artifacts present in her house when it burned in 1880, and bricks that were deposited in the builder's trench during reconstruction of the house in 1881–82. Subsequent exploration in the basement of the standing brick house identified an old kitchen, a cistern, and the base of a staircase. Moreover, it told us that Tubman-era deposits survived at the site and confirmed the importance of archaeology as a means of testing, evaluating, and learning new things about the events, places, and things of her life.

Initial Survey and Excavations at John Brown Hall

The first archaeological survey conducted at the Home was an impromptu walk around the property that located the ruins of John Brown Hall in 1994. As described in chapter 1, this survey was quick and had positive results, which cemented an intellectual, spiritual, and personal relationship between the site, the researcher, and the Home's site managers. The rediscovery of John Brown Hall demonstrated to me that much more was present on the site and that archaeology could have a significant role in the preservation, restoration, and interpretation of the site (figure 1.9). The study at John

Brown Hall involved mapping of the ruins, systematic shovel tests of the surrounding yard, and excavation of the ruins. This phase of the project preceded and its positive results precipitated a formal survey of the entire property and excavations in numerous key areas of the property (Ryan 2000; Ryan and Armstrong 2000).

Without this ad hoc survey of John Brown Hall (Locus 3) and the demonstration of new and important findings at this site, I am not sure if the potential of archaeology would have been recognized or even considered in restoration planning. The excavation and popular public "dig days" at John Brown Hall, some with as many as three hundred visitors, demonstrated the value of archaeology, confirmed the importance of preserving, protecting, restoring, and interpreting the archaeological resources of the property, and emphasized that these resources had great value for the site's interpretation. This work also demonstrated the value of archaeology to the AME Zion Church's achievement and Harriet Tubman Home, Inc.'s long-term goal of educating the public and improving visitor experiences at the site to better project the positive values of Harriet Tubman's legacy.

Archaeological and Historical Site
Survey of Tubman's Properties

In 2002, we examined the entire property through a series of archaeological surveys. The surveys were carried out by faculty and students of Syracuse University's Anthropology Department and were done in conjunction with a broader cultural-resource assessment by Crawford & Stearns, Architects and Preservation Planners, of Syracuse, New York (Crawford & Stearns 2002). The surveys provided guidance for the restoration of structures and a plan for preservation of cultural resources.[2] A unique aspect of this project was the degree of cooperation and communication between the architects and preservation planners at Crawford & Stearns on the one hand and the archaeologists on the other. We shared historical maps and photographs, discussed findings and their implications, and on more than one occasion joined in combined surveys involving archaeologists, tree and vegetation specialists, architects,

---

2. The archaeological survey report (D. Armstrong 2003c) was submitted alongside a series of survey, site-treatment, and landscape reports by Crawford & Stearns (2002). New cultural-resource reports for the property are currently being completed. They include a cultural landscape report by John Auwaerter (2018) and a historic-structure report on the Thompson AME Zion Church by Rebekah Krieger (2018).

and historians—all traversing the landscape, crawling through the attics and basements of buildings at the Home, pointing out to one another features that we saw in the landscape and the design elements that we saw in the building.

The architectural reports made use of preliminary archaeological testing to define an architectural chronology of standing structures. For example, the architectural study incorporated archaeological findings such as evidence for repointing of stone and additions of cut block on top of an earlier fieldstone foundation at Tubman's brick residence (Locus 1, figure 3.4). In turn, the architectural report provided details on construction, including the positioning of a former stairway to the basement and the survival of part of the old stairway (figure 3.5). Later, when we excavated in the basement of the house, we used the architectural information to direct excavations that rediscovered the footings of the staircase in the basement.

To enhance information on the cultural landscape, surveys were done in the fall and the winter, when the site had far less foliage to block our view. In the process, we found features such as a series of pits dug to obtain clay for brickmaking in the wooded area on the north side of the property (part of Locus 6). The winter survey was designed to look for spatial patterning that could be highlighted by observation when leaves were off the trees and when snow had melted back to highlight features on the landscape. In this survey, I enlisted my son, Alan Armstrong, then in middle school. He became enthralled with the discovery process and has gone on to become an archaeologist who specializes in landscape archaeology. This survey and Alan's involvement in it were presented in a children-oriented article in *Dig* magazine (D. Armstrong 2003b).

The winter survey tested an idea that differential melting of snow on a sunny day after a snow fall would be useful in identifying the signature of past activity areas. The survey went well. Using this sun-melted-snow strategy, we identified a long-forgotten roadbed that extends from behind the barn at the rear of Tubman's brick residence straight back to the east end of the property (Locus 5). The road was forgotten because from the 1920s on the back of the property was unused and became reforested. It had not been seen because in the 1930s cinder block bus bays were added to the north and south sides of Tubman's old barn.[3] The barn's north bay was built atop the old roadbed,

---

3. From the 1930s through the 1960s, the barn was used as a garage for the Norris family's bus company. Cinder block bays were added to both the north side and south side of the barn, and the barn itself was modified to provide areas to house and work on school buses.

cutting off its use and blocking it from view. The roadbed begins on South Street and is still used as the driveway on the north side of Tubman's brick house. During the Tubman era, it extended west to east across the northern edge of Tubman's seven-acre farm. The roadbed even crosses a stream before ending very close to the south side of John Brown Hall. Access along the roadbed is limited in the summer, but with the leaves off the trees, and the berry vines beaten down by the snow, we found that the roadbed was accessible in the winter. The differential melting of snow on the south side of the raised roadbed made the roadway visible and led us on a path that allowed us to trace it through the woods.

We also carried out informal surveys of adjacent properties to better understand uses and modifications to the landscape. This survey identified a building that was nearly identical to the John Brown Hall structure, which was a building associated with a brickyard on a property about one hundred meters south of Tubman's farm.

Through the landscape survey, we found that portions of the property had been extensively modified during the late twentieth century due to the dumping of rubble and trash and the borrowing of soils for construction projects in the area. The far eastern portion of Tubman's seven-acre farm was used as the source of soil in the construction of Seward School. Clay had been extracted from this area during the nineteenth century, and the additional digging for clay fill for the Seward School resulted in an even deeper hole spanning the width of the property and partially filling with water in the spring and after heavy rains. The northeastern corner of the property borders a lot owned by the City of Auburn on which old concrete and road materials were deposited without much concern for the actual property line. Hence, much of the area that during Tubman's time was used to grow a variety of grain crops (wheat and corn) is now covered with layers of concrete and asphalt road-construction debris. Fortunately, although these alterations to the landscape modified the overall setting, for the most part they impacted areas that had been used for farming or extracting clay for brickmaking and did not directly affect standing structures or the ruins of past structures on the property.

While we proceeded with our walking surveys, the Tubman Home, Inc., had moved forward with a development plan for the property that featured an array of multipurpose uses (Beardsley Design Associates 2002). In comparing the development plan and our survey findings, we immediately realized that two areas of the property designated for development were places where we had found evidence of undocumented and as yet unknown anomalies, which were later confirmed as archaeological features or structural ruins. Because there were active plans for development, I took immediate action to organize the remote-sensing (magnetometer and conductivity instrument) surveys to evaluate these two features using grant funds I had generated.

Remote Sensing (Geophysical) Investigations

In the late spring of 2002, as I was initiating excavations at Tubman's farmhouse, I contacted R. Christopher Goodwin, a historic-preservation archaeologist based in Maryland who I knew had a team of remote-sensing specialists. I told him of the immediate need, and he agreed to send his team up to the Tubman Home to carry out a remote-sensing survey of the two areas.[4] This was an important step because we were able to rapidly generate critically important data that identified geophysical anomalies in both areas that ultimately protected two areas of significant ruins, including a brick kiln or clamp (Locus 6) and the ruins of a house, along with features associated with Harriet Tubman's barn (figures 3.6–3.7) (A. Armstrong 2011; A. Armstrong and D. Armstrong 2012; D. Armstrong 2003c). I was able to convey this significant information to the Harriet Tubman Home Board of Directors in time for their spring meeting, and the directors in turn acted to set these areas aside and protect them until they were fully evaluated.

The East Area Survey Block was situated in an open grass field northeast of the Home's museum (figure 3.7). Topography within the survey block was relatively flat, with a low rise in the middle of the grass field. The magnetic gradient survey identified two large clusters of anomalies. The findings led to this area being recognized as an area that should be set aside and not altered pending further investigation. In 2005, a series of shovel tests confirmed the presence of a brick kiln, or clamp, in this area. The full extent of this feature was exposed, uncovering a brick kiln in 2006 (Locus 6) (A. Armstrong 2011; A. Armstrong and D. Armstrong 2012; D. Armstrong and Hill 2009).

4. Earth conductivity and magnetic susceptibility surveys were undertaken with a Geonics Limited EM-38B Ground Conductivity Meter. A magnetic gradient survey was undertaken with a Geometrics G-858 Cesium Gradiometer. A total of 4,600 square meters (1.14 acres) were surveyed within the two blocks. Geophysical investigations were undertaken on May 22 and 23, 2002. Fortunately, I had funds remaining in the Vision Fund grant from Syracuse University, and I arranged for R. Christopher Goodwin & Associates to test these areas (see R. Christopher Goodwin & Associates 2002). The remote-sensing survey was carried out by William Lowthert, working under my direction and with the assistance of a rotating group of undergraduate and graduate student volunteers.

The second area, West Area Survey Block, was situated to the north and east of Tubman's house and barn (figure 3.6).[5] The remote-sensing surveys identified several anomalies, including an area that was later confirmed as the basement, foundation, and ruins of a house that burned in 1902 (Locus 4). A second area with anomalies within the remote-sensing block was located immediately behind Tubman's barn. The survey guided the positioning of a series of shovel test pits that revealed deep deposits of iron-rich cultural deposits and burned materials that suggested the accumulation of materials associated with a series of fires.[6] The depositional sequence identified through an expanded array of shovel tests and excavation units confirmed a series of burned deposits that were linked with earlier barn and shed structures (that had previously burned) as well as the practice of burning trash behind (east of) the barn during the period of Tubman's ownership of the barn.

Excavation Strategies and Data Recovery

Our initial studies at John Brown Hall, the remote-sensing tests, and test excavations across the property showed the value of archaeological excavations as a means of reconstructing the cultural landscape of the Tubman era and generating a rich material record of the things used in everyday life by Tubman and those whom she cared for on her properties. Excavation strategies at the Home varied according to the specific problem being addressed; however, across the site we excavated using either shovel test pits or one-by-one-meter excavation units (referred to as "one-by-ones").[7] The relatively small one-by-ones were dug in a series of levels, each dug down no more than ten centimeters. If we encountered a change in soil (color, texture, etc.) or a physical feature such as a brick walkway, we stopped and either left the underlying material in place or started a new level. The one-by-ones were dug in clusters to generate groupings of data. The excavation units were placed strategically to address specific

5. For example, see Coyle et al. 2000; Lowthert et al. 1999, 2002.

6. Findings related to this brick kiln were the focus of an honors thesis by Alan Armstrong and an article that describes the site and the importance of brick making on the property (A. Armstrong and D. Armstrong 2012). The brick clamp and the role of brickmaking at the Tubman Home and in the South Street brickyards is discussed in detail in chapter 11.

7. We used the one-by-one as our basic unit of excavation to generate refined data on the distribution of artifacts across the site. By joining together groupings of connected one-by-ones, we were able to map out features and to generate data related to areas of activity or focused accumulation of artifacts within an activity area, feature, or structure.

problems and questions. For example, we excavated a series of units to expose ash deposits associated with a house fire and rows of units along a builder's trench associated with the reconstruction of Tubman's house because the trench is where artifacts from her house at the time of the fire were redeposited when the house was rebuilt. Tubman's basement was excavated to recover information from her kitchen and to find room dividers and footings for her basement staircase, both excavations with positive results. As new features were recovered during excavations at each locus, problem-oriented strategies were developed for each feature. For instance, upon discovering the brick kiln at Locus 6, we stopped excavating when we reached the surface of the lines of brick that made up the clamp, then opened up a wide area of contiguous one-by-ones to expose the entire kiln, complete with sets of linear rows of brick that alternated with the burned ash base of a series of kiln ovens.

Although this study provides an abundance of archaeological and historical information for most of the structures and features identified at the site, our attention has focused on areas of immediate need. The study of Tubman's farmhouse was done in advance of its restoration; testing of the barn was done in cadence with its restoration; and the brick clamp was excavated to confirm its presence and to counter development plans for the site. However, there is still much that can be learned, and there are structures and features that should be explored. For example, we identified and tested the ruins of a foundation of a house that burned in either 1902 or 1904. However, this area is not slated for development or modification, so we simply dug two units to confirm the presence of a cellar and left it alone, simply documenting and preserving the ruins for future investigation.

Another area, defined as Locus 8, probably holds the stone footings of at least one barn, but this area is so full of mid-twentieth-century fill and debris, including roadway cement and asphalt, that the barn would be difficult to define and recover. Similarly, our efforts to identify the ruins of the small house once owned by Tubman's brother William H. Stewart Sr., tentatively defined as Locus 7, were hindered by the abundance of what appears to be sheet metal and plywood from a mid- to late twentieth-century trailer or mobile home. Also, a wooden barn structure is shown on the 1904 map of the area just west of John Brown Hall (figure 1.14), and a 1940s-era photograph of children of the Norris family shows what appears to be the corner of a barn roof on the south side of John Brown Hall (figure 9.2). However, no evidence of structural features or surface scatters of artifacts was found in this area. These areas may require further archaeological attention as plans move forward for additional restoration and interpretation of the Tubman properties.

3.1. Ash deposits associated with the fire that destroyed Harriet Tubman's wood house on February 10, 1880. Photograph by D. Armstrong.

3.2. Burned and melted artifacts (porcelain buttons, tobacco pipes, and ceramics) recovered from ash associated with the fire on February 10, 1880. Photograph by D. Armstrong.

Another Conflagration.

The residence of Harriet Tubman Davis, the once famous Union scout and spy,
located near the South street tollgate, was
entirely consumed by fire at an early hour
this morning. Only a small portion of
the household goods were saved. The
conflagration is said to have originated
from a defective stovepipe stuck through
a hole in a lintern and which was utilized
for a chimney.

3.3. "Another Conflagration," *Evening Auburnian*, February
10, 1880. Report on a fire at Harriet Tubman's house. Copy of
article courtesy of Harriet Tubman Home, Inc., Auburn, NY.

3.4. Builder's trench excavated showing two types of foundation stones. The lower
courses are irregular fieldstone. After the fire, the fieldstone foundation was repointed,
and cut limestone blocks were added to the top. The brick house was constructed on
this foundation. Photograph by D. Armstrong.

3.5. Stair steps leading to what had been Tubman's basement kitchen, found by Crawford & Stearns Architects during an architectural survey of Tubman's brick house in
2002. Photograph by D. Armstrong.

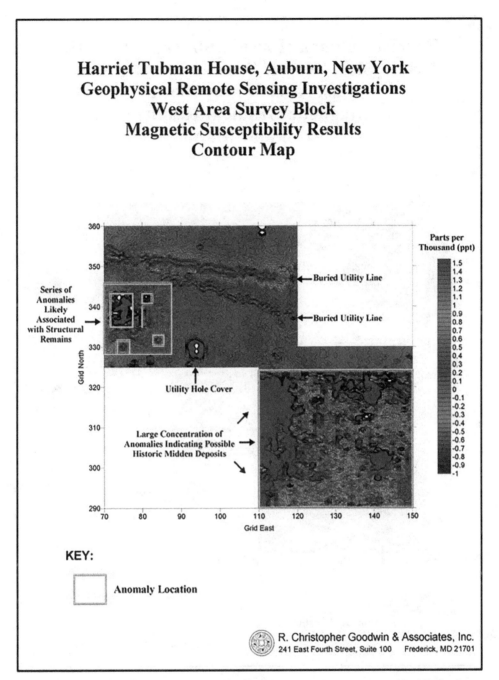

3.6. Remote sensing (magnetic susceptibility contour map) used to identify the location of foundation ruins of a house (Locus 4) and a dense pattern of metallic materials associated with iron, ash, and brick in the area behind (east of) the barn on Tubman's farm. From R. Christopher Goodwin & Associates 2002, 22.

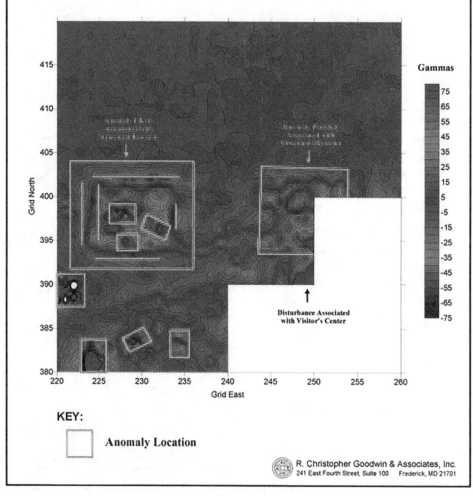

Harriet Tubman House, Auburn, New York
Geophysical Remote Sensing Investigations
East Area Survey Block
Magnetic Gradient Results
Contour Map

Gammas

KEY:

Anomaly Location

R. Christopher Goodwin & Associates, Inc.
241 East Fourth Street, Suite 100   Frederick, MD 21701

3.7. Remote sensing (magnetic susceptibility contour map) used to identify the brick kiln site (Locus 6). From R. Christopher Goodwin & Associates 2002, 23.

PART TWO

Historical Perspective
on Harriet Tubman

4

The Pursuit of Liberty
and a Life in Freedom

Four score and seven years ago our fathers brought forth on this continent, a new nation, conceived in Liberty, and dedicated to the proposition
that all men are created equal. . . . It is for us the living, rather, to be
dedicated here to the unfinished work which they who fought here have
thus far so nobly advanced. It is rather for us to be here dedicated to the
great task remaining before us—that we here highly resolve that these
dead shall not have died in vain—that this nation, under God, shall have a
new birth of freedom—and that government of the people, by the people,
for the people, shall not perish from the earth.

> —Abraham Lincoln, "Gettysburg Address,"
> November 19, 1863

An Activist for Freedom

There is no better starting place for explaining the significance of Harriet
Tubman's life's work than the powerful sentiment and philosophical view-
points expressed in Abraham Lincoln's "Gettysburg Address." Lincoln suc-
cinctly rededicated the effort to complete the "unfinished work" of a nation
conceived in the ideals of liberty and equality. Throughout her life, Tubman
engaged in the struggle for freedom. She quietly but assertively liberated herself from slavery and then engaged in an epic series of rescues as she escorted
others to freedom. She followed up these actions by consecrating her freedom and that of her extended family by establishing herself as the owner of a
farmstead, including a house and land on which she and her family lived and
shared with others.

For years, Tubman had moved enslaved people so that they could live
freely in St. Catharines, Ontario, Canada, but in the years immediately prior
to the Civil War she and her family chose to live in the United States. Therefore, she negotiated to acquire land, and she became a property owner, buying
a farm in Fleming, New York, just south of the Auburn city line. During the

war, she worked tirelessly as soldier, nurse, and spy to achieve the goal of liberation so that she, her family, and all African Americans could live their lives
in freedom. When fellow abolitionist Frederick Douglass spoke the words "If
there is no struggle, there is no progress" at an event in Canandaigua, New
York, on August 3, 1857, he addressed emancipation but also foretold a struggle for freedoms that would flash strong during the Civil War and would be a
longer, never-ending battle for social justice. In his speech, Douglass asserted:
"Power concedes nothing without a demand. It never has and it never will.
Find out just what a people will submit to, and you have found out the exact
amount of injustice and wrong which will be imposed upon them; and these
will continue till they are resisted with either words or blows, or with both.
The limits of tyrants are prescribed by the endurance of those whom they
oppress" (Douglass 1857). The study of Harriet Tubman's life in Fleming and
Auburn, New York, recounts the story of her ongoing, long-term struggle not
only to live her life in freedom but also to provide shelter and support to other
African Americans in need. She chose Central New York as her residence
because of local support and the opportunity to own a farm and provide for
herself and those around her.

In 1863, as the Civil War raged on inconclusively and Lincoln spoke so
eloquently at Gettysburg, Franklin Sanborn, one of Tubman's abolitionist
friends in Boston, wrote the first short narrative of her amazing story.[1] He
described her as a liberator who followed spiritual guidance to deliver "at least
fifty souls" to freedom on the Underground Railroad (Sanborn 1863).[2] Published in the *Commonwealth* (Boston), an abolitionist newspaper, Sanborn's
account attracted attention to Tubman by retelling the stories of liberation
and faith that she had told to captivated audiences in the parlors and meeting halls of prominent abolitionists and philosophers in the Boston area in

1. In 1856, Benjamin Drew, a Boston abolitionist, interviewed Harriet Tubman and a
group of "fugitive slaves" living in St. Catherines, Canada. In his book based on the interviews, Tubman describes slavery as a "dreadful condition" and compares it with "living in
hell" (Drew 1856, 30); see the chapter 2 epigraph.

2. Franklin Sanborn was a lifetime friend and supporter of Tubman. He was among a
large group of supporters she had inspired during the several trips she made to Boston before
the war. Sanborn was also one of John Brown's key financial supporters and co-conspirators.
He is one of the few abolitionists to outlive Tubman. His long-term concern for Tubman
is indicted by a letter he wrote to Thomas Osborne in March 1913 shortly before she died
(Franklin B. Sanborn, Concord, Massachusetts, to Thomas Osborne, Auburn, New York,
Feb. 3, 1913, Osborne Family Papers, Special Collections Research Center, Syracuse Univ.,
Syracuse, NY) (see chapter 9).

the years and months leading up to the war. By 1863, Tubman was deeply involved in the war effort, and she was beginning to take on mythological status as a heroine of the cause. After the war, her notoriety as an abolitionist, her legendary deeds as soldier, nurse, and spy during the war, as well as the reality of her need of financial resources and recognition of her military service during the war were chronicled in Sarah Bradford's biography *Scenes in the Life of Harriet Tubman* (1869).

Tubman repeatedly traversed roadways in the dark of night with the goal of living in freedom. This same goal can be seen in the tangible and symbolic meanings of her ownership of property. Her farms provided her a margin of self-determination and a space of security for herself, her family, and those who came to her for support. Her ownership of property was an essential means of sustenance to her and a mechanism by which she could extend communal assistance to others in need in her personal home and, later, in the Home for the Aged that she created.

Born into Landscapes of Slavery, Creating Landscapes of Freedom

Tubman was born into slavery in the slave state of Maryland on March 10, 1822,[3] and her early life experiences in bondage provided her with practical knowledge of the roads and landscape of her region as she was rented and lent out as a house servant and later a field laborer to several small farms and households. In the 1840s, it would have been common to see Araminta Ross, or simply "Minty," as Harriet Tubman was then known, walking from farm to farm on the country roads of Dorchester County, Maryland. As opposed to the larger cotton, rice, tobacco, and grain plantation owners of the Carolinas and Virginia, the slaveholders who owned Tubman's family engaged in a range of mixed farming practices, and Minty's tasks included everything from housework such as babysitting and weaving to field work—planting, harvesting, and at times checking animal traps (Larson 2004). Biographical accounts of her life as a slave note harsh treatment, whippings, and abuse. In her early teens, Minty was struck in the head by a "two-pound weight" thrown by an angry overseer; the injury nearly killed her and caused trauma to her head that resulted in lifelong spells of illness (Bradford [1886] 1993; Clinton 2004; Conrad 1943; Larson 2004, 41–44).

---

3. The actual date of Harriet Tubman's birth is well debated; for an overview of that discussion, see Larson 2004.

By the mid-1840s, Minty's father, Benjamin Ross, had bought his freedom and was working as a manager for a timber company. Minty took on the first name of her mother, Harriet Green Ross, and added the surname "Tubman" in 1844 when she married John Tubman, a free person of color (Larson 2004). Today we know her as "Harriet Tubman" even though she would separate from John Tubman when she decided to move to a place of freedom, but her husband was unwilling to do the same. He remarried and died before Tubman married Nelson Davis in Auburn after the Civil War.[4]

Despite the harsh conditions of slavery, during her early life in Maryland Tubman was surrounded by family. The threat that sparked Tubman's flight to freedom was the danger that members of her extended family would be sold "south" to planters in points unknown, a fear that was nearly a reality when she learned that she herself might be sold after the death of her owner. In 1849, after one aborted attempt with two of her brothers, Tubman made her way to freedom by escaping to Philadelphia. It is important to understand the changing geography of freedom during this tumultuous era. At the time of Tubman's initial walk to freedom, she had to get to Pennsylvania. In Philadelphia, she was afforded the security of an urban setting with well-established support networks for those seeking freedom. The initial acquaintances she made in the emancipation-friendly communities of Philadelphia would serve her well in her later efforts to free others. Her Pennsylvania connections included the free Black abolitionist William Still and the abolitionist and woman's rights activist Lucretia Coffin Mott.[5]

In the mid-nineteenth-century United States, the landscape of slavery and freedom was both contentious and fluid. Only a year after Tubman's escape in 1849, the battle over slavery and abolition became more acute with the passage of the federal Fugitive Slave Act, which included the Compromise of 1850. This law dramatically altered the landscape of freedom and slavery by allowing federal intervention in "free" states. Self-emancipated individuals

4. During her life in Auburn, Tubman went by a combination of names, including "Harriet Tubman Davis," simply "Harriet," and "Aunt Harriet." An excavated brass nameplate to make calling cards (figure 2.3) shows that at least for formal greetings she added her husband's surname and went by "Harriet Tubman Davis." This brass nameplate would have been used to produce calling cards by which Tubman could send and receive notes and invitations. Although Tubman was essentially illiterate, the nameplate's presence in her house shows that she was actively engaged in written communication with others.

5. Tubman would soon establish close ties with Lucretia Mott's family, including Mott's sister, Martha Wright, who lived in Auburn, New York.

who had taken up residence in states such as Pennsylvania, New York, Massa-chusetts, and Ohio were now subject to the threat of being legally captured by bounty hunters and turned over to US marshals for extradition to their "own-ers" in slave-holding states. The Fugitive Slave Act allowed for the admission of gold-rich California as a free state, but it escalated the battle over slavery and abolition across the country. Through the 1850s, territories such as Kan-sas were to become sites of civil unrest as slavery and antislavery interests wrestled for political and popular support.

The danger of the Fugitive Slave Act to self-emancipated individuals such as Harriet Tubman, Jermain Wesley Loguen, and Frederick Douglass was amplified by a shifted landscape in which the distance to freedom for some-one from Maryland grew from the border of Pennsylvania all the way north to Canada, which had abolished slavery in 1834. Tubman was no longer safe in Philadelphia, and the distance from her birthplace in Dorchester County, Maryland, to St. Catharines, Ontario, Canada, just north of Niagara Falls, was eight hundred kilometers, four times the distance to Philadelphia and thus an even greater amplification of the danger of capture.[6]

Definitions of citizenship, property rights, self-ownership of personhood, and ownership of property had much to do with Tubman's decision to acquire land. They also played a strong role in the decision made by her benefactors, then US senator William Seward and his wife, Frances, to sell to Tubman a seven-acre farm on South Street in Fleming, New York. This farm was on the same street as the Sewards' own home in Auburn. Tubman and others such as Frederick Douglass were deeply engaged in the philosophical, political, and physical battles for freedom (see Douglass 1852, [1855] 1994). In his speech "What to the Slave Is the Fourth of July?" in 1852, Douglass projected a lib-eral ideal relating to property ownership and natural rights and calls for slaves to be freed and to own the products resulting from their activities "plowing,

6. Borders, migration, and access to personal liberty were key issues of debate in the nine-teenth century and often determined life or death to those who attempted to self-emancipate by crossing borders. The Fugitive Slave Act made the road to freedom and life beyond the borders of slave states more difficult and dangerous to them. Today, the world has changed, but border crossings once again have taken center stage in social and political debate. Jason De León is currently using the methods of archaeological reconnaissance to bring public consciousness to the dire consequences of current US border policy for people from Mexico and Central American countries. In *The Land of Open Graves* (2015), he chronicles the tragic consequences for those "living and dying on the migrant trail." De León's study illuminates how today's structured policies force those seeking access to the United States to traverse extreme environmental conditions that often lead to their deaths.

planting and reaping, . . . [and], erecting houses." Tubman's acquisition of property in Auburn and Fleming, New York, allowed her to do these things as a free person and landowner.

The sale of the farm to Tubman in 1859 was legal in the State of New York, where African Americans had the right to own property and live in freedom. However, the transaction was in defiance of the Fugitive Slave Act. Under federal laws that defined Tubman as the property of a Maryland slave owner, she could not own property and was subject to capture and return to her owner in Maryland. There can be little doubt that this transaction was done in part to satisfy Tubman's desire for land and in part to declare personal freedoms through the assertion of citizenship rights as defined in New York State law.

The Tubman site and Tubman's life on her personal property make good the premise of the inalienable rights espoused by Thomas Paine in 1774: "life, liberty, and property" (Paine [1774] 2003; see also D. Armstrong 2010).[7] Although the American Revolution and ultimately the new nation were grounded in the notion of inalienable rights, from the nation's inception the issue of slavery was much debated. Leaders such as Thomas Paine, John Adams, and Alexander Hamilton believed that human rights extended

---

7. To fully understand the importance of Tubman's ownership of property in the mid–nineteenth century and its relationship to principles of freedom, one must step back in time and explore the changing definitions of laws governing slavery and citizenship in Pennsylvania, Delaware, and New York as well as in Canada. In the legal landscape of slavery and freedom, abolition was a point of contentious debate in Pennsylvania at the time of the American Revolution. One direct impact was the separation of a portion of Pennsylvania as the independent state of Delaware in 1776. As part of this change, three-quarters of Pennsylvania's slave population was shifted to Delaware. Hence, in 1849, when Tubman walked to freedom, it was a two-hundred-kilometer trek from Maryland to Pennsylvania and not simply a forty-kilometer walk to Delaware, for which statehood was tied to the continuation of slavery.

Debates concerning emancipation took place in the Pennsylvania Assembly in 1778. As in the Declaration of Independence, the Pennsylvania Assembly changed Thomas Paine's wording "life, liberty, and property" in his provocative pamphlet *Common Sense* ([1774] 2003) to the less contentious phrase "life, liberty, and the pursuit of happiness" (D. Armstrong 2010). Paine was an abolitionist, and his notion of property was limited to land and possessions and specifically omitted human chattel; he argued that all humans possessed the inalienable rights of ownership of oneself, one's land, and one's personal possessions. This idea of personal liberty and freedom was based on notions of rights to what one had worked to obtain and did not consider compounding issues of structured class difference or the large-scale ownership of properties and their potential abuse, which Karl Marx and Frederick Engels ([1888] 2004) would later define as "bourgeois property."

to all people—white or Black—and that slavery was unjust. However, from the Declaration of Independence forward, the new American government accepted a paramount paradox by professing human rights yet condoning slavery. This paradox would ultimately lead to conflict, resistance by people such as Harriet Tubman, and a bloody civil war before the founding documents were amended to uphold the fundamental human right to self-ownership of personhood—usually referred to as emancipation or the abolition of slavery. Hence, Lincoln emphasized "unfinished work" and the goal of "a new birth of freedom" as he addressed those gathered in the Union cause on the battlefields of Gettysburg (Lincoln 1863).

New York State, where Harriet Tubman ultimately acquired property and settled, began as a Dutch colony, New Amsterdam, with its own ambiguous history relating to slavery. Enslaved Africans were present in New Netherlands from the founding of the Dutch colony in 1626. In the mid–seventeenth century, through the West Indies Trading Company the Dutch were the dominant European slave traders in Africa (Klein 1999, 76–77). However, in New Amsterdam they were also interested in land-based farming as well as in trade, and so "slavery helped to prepare the way for this transition by providing the labor which made farming attractive and profitable to the settlers" (McManus 1966, 7). The Dutch interests, however, were primarily in trade and brokering of goods from farm provisions to furs. Hence, rather than establishing a complete hegemony, the Dutch took a somewhat laissez-faire approach. Free Blacks served in local militias, and Blacks who gained their freedom had coequal standing in colonial courts and could own property, including slaves. In 1664, the British took possession of New York from the Dutch when title was transferred to the duke of York. Under the British, the role of slavery was dramatically expanded, but the Dutch system survived in laws that recognized free Blacks' property rights and granted emancipation via matrilineal inheritance of property. Hence, the child of a male slave and a free woman was free; the child of a female slave and a free man remained a slave (McManus 1966, 7).

Following the American Revolution, the New York State Legislature banned the importation of African slaves in 1788 and in 1799 passed "an Act for the Gradual Abolition of Slavery," a law modeled after Pennsylvania law. This act provided for the eventual freeing of all children born to slave women after July 4, 1799: males were to be freed when they reached the age of twenty-eight, females when they reached twenty-five; those born into slavery before July 4, 1799, were to remain slaves for life but were reclassified as "indentured servants." In 1817, this act was modified to grant freedom to all slaves by July 4, 1827. However, it did allow for "nonresidents" to enter New

York with slaves for up to nine months and for part-time residents to bring their slaves into the state temporarily, an exemption that was not eliminated until 1841 (McManus 1966, 7).

After the creation of the United States, free Black males who owned property had the right to vote in New York, in continuity with earlier Dutch (not English) traditions. However, in 1815 the first of a series of New York laws was passed aimed at limiting voting by Blacks. This law required that Blacks get special passes to vote in state elections. In 1821, property qualifications were eliminated for whites but were raised from property valued at $100 to property valued at $250 for Blacks. The latter amount was equivalent to a small urban house or rural farm. Hence, even as the state moved toward emancipation, the rights of citizenship for free Blacks were being restricted, and ownership of property was being used as the demarcation line of full citizenship. Hence, ownership of land had become even more important to freedom, liberty, and the rights of free Blacks as citizens.

Finally, in projecting the geography of slavery and the world that Tubman had to navigate to deliver people to freedom, one must look north to Canada. Enslaved individuals accompanied the earliest French and English settlers to the region, but the numbers were always small, despite a significant influx with the arrival of British loyalists and their slaves during the American Revolution. Upper Canada became the first British territory to pass an antislavery act. In 1793, the Upper Canada Abolition Act freed any slave who came into Ontario (Upper Canada) and stipulated that any child born of a slave mother would be free at the age of twenty-five. In the other Canadian provinces by 1800, slavery was effectively limited through various court rulings. For instance, the chief justice of Montreal ruled in 1803 that slavery was not consistent with the laws of Canada. The courts put the burden on slave owners to provide proof of ownership, and this proof was rarely available. However, it was not until 1834 that slavery was formally abolished in Canada. This change occurred at the same time that Britain abolished slavery in its colonies, such as Barbados and Jamaica, though full emancipation in most British colonies would not come into effect until 1838. Another aspect of liberty and freedom revolves around the opportunity for social and economic equality. In 1776, Adam Smith wrote *An Inquiry into the Nature and Causes of the Wealth of Nations* (Smith [1776] 1909) in support of the opportunities of capitalism, while also espousing the responsibilities of those engaging in free markets. Yet his discussion omitted mention of the role of slavery and thus stood mute to this critical moral dilemma as well as to the limitations of purely economic-based policy without checks to ensure humane values and consideration of those impacted. In studies of the archaeological record of Annapolis, Maryland, the archaeologist Mark Leone examines the relationship between the social hierarchy and capitalism, a relationship that he sees as a requirement for capitalism to exist. As such, he sees the concept of individual liberty as being in competition with capitalism, the foundational element of democracy. His view is that the two are in competition and that "they never get along. Capitalism always wins" (2008, 102). Leone takes a pessimistic view, seeing "projections of individual liberty as an illusion" (102).[8] In framing a new constitutional government that retained systemic injustice by allowing the continuation of slavery and the omission of equal rights for women, the new nation fell short of the philosophical values of liberty and freedom.[9]

Both the North and the South proclaimed themselves practitioners of capitalism and democracy prior to the Civil War. The core difference was therefore not "capitalism" per say but the breadth of democratic inclusion (freedom versus slavery) and the philosophical notion of the importance of freedom and the extension of human rights to all—in other words, the ability and necessity to legislate controls aimed at protecting people, including the poor, laborers, and the enslaved, against unbridled, unregulated, and irresponsible forms of capitalism. Irresponsible capitalism of the mid–nineteenth century was perhaps most profoundly signified by the retention of enslavement and the institution of slavery.

Networks of Support in Auburn and Central New York

At the time New York State abolished the last vestiges of slavery in 1827, the core of the region's rapidly expanding economy was a mix of agricultural and industrial production linked by economically viable transportation systems by

8. In the years immediately following independence, this same pessimism was experienced by many who had fought in the revolution. The same group of yeoman Massachusetts farmers who in 1774 had written in opposition to the "terrors of slavery" rose up in what is referred to as Shays Rebellion against what they saw as a new tyranny of new forms of taxation that threatened their independence as farmers and property owners. Their actions had results that were both immediate and indirect. Not only did this rebellion and its concerns force action resulting in the Constitutional Convention, but the farmers' attack on the armory in Springfield, Massachusetts, was a model used in the conceptualization of John Brown's abolitionist insurrection and his raid on the armory at Harpers Ferry in 1859.

9. Women's rights were clearly not on the Founders' agenda. However, they would be part of the critical collective interests of social reformers engaged in social reform in mid-nineteenth-century America.

sea, river, and canal. In Central New York, the opening of the Erie Canal in 1825 provided a means to get goods to market. Auburn and its surrounding countryside were tied into this production and transportation web. In this region, agriculture and industry grew in tandem, and the population soared as farms were subdivided out of larger Revolutionary War–era land grants, and laborers came to work in the businesses and industries of the growing urban areas. The combination of exponential growth, radical changes in industrial production, and the steady demand for both farm and industrial products put a premium on labor. Yet in this setting the economy was structured on a combination of ownership of property and one's own labor on the one hand and the use of wage labor on the other—both of which were in direct competition with the system of slave labor in the American South.

The area of New York where Tubman found refuge and into which she settled was undergoing rapid change. Relatively small farms of 5 to 160 acres were common and grew out of a Revolutionary War land-distribution system. Farms with a few acres of grain, a small orchard, some hogs, and industrial production of brick, like the farms owned by Tubman and many others in her immediate neighborhood, were typical for this era in Central New York. Moreover, any one of the individual elements found on Tubman's farm or on a farm like it could easily have been replaced by another element; for instance, wheat could be replaced with teasels (a thistle used in industrial looms), and the farm would function essentially unchanged within the broader economic system.[10] Farms in the area were also engaged in alternative economic activities, including maple production (redefined during the pre–Civil War era as "free sugar"), wood lots for firewood and construction, and even small-scale seasonal ice-cutting industries.

New York farmers tilled their own fields, worked cooperatively in bringing in the crop, and paid room and board to laborers. Prior to 1827, farmsteads often included small numbers of enslaved laborers, and many of the farms of Cayuga County, where Auburn is located, included enslaved Africans within the households of founding farms. Later, these African Americans remained in the area as free persons working on farms and in the expanding industrial production centers and mills that grew along stream- and riverheads after the

10. The teasel is a thistle that was grown in Central New York for inclusion in the products made by flax and cotton mills. Naturally designed much like the nap of modern Velcro, this sturdy plant was used extensively in northeastern textile mills, such as those that grew to prominence along the riverine outlets of the Finger Lakes, including Owasco (Auburn) and Cayuga (Seneca Falls).

opening of the Erie Canal. Farms continued to require labor and often relied on extended families or the contracting of indentured laborers. In the pre–Civil War years, many of these indentured servants came from Ireland, and these laborers were not always satisfied with the conditions associated with indenture. Like their enslaved counterparts in the South, some fled to secure greater freedoms. For example, in 1835 a reward of $5 was advertised for information leading to the return of an Irish laborer from the Van Etten farm on Lake Skaneateles, about seven miles from what would become Tubman's farm.[11] Hence, although New York had abolished slavery, it did rely heavily on differential class structures associated with social categories defined by race and ethnicity that facilitated the availability of relatively inexpensive labor.

Farms varied in size from small parcels, like the one owned by Tubman, to tracts of many hundreds of acres. In the early 1800s, the number of acres of rich glacial soils available exceeded the capacity for production, and with a dearth of surplus labor there was an incentive to mechanize production. The opening of the Erie Canal made adjacent lands up and down the Finger Lakes region imminently viable. Exceptions to the basic pattern of relatively small-scale independent farming emerged in the region; for example, Rose Hill Plantation was established by Robert Rose, a Virginia planter who immigrated to the Seneca Lake area in 1803 with thirty-seven enslaved laborers (Delle and Fellows 2012). However, this type of plantation setting was not the norm. The legal system brought freedom to newborns, and ultimately the entire population gained freedom and redistributed themselves within the regional landscape (Delle and Fellows 2012).

New York State farms grew hand in hand with industry, and the combination of the relative scarcity of labor, deep soils, and flat open fields provided the perfect incubator for the invention of the all-steel plow and the production of a full range of mowers and reapers to harvest the expanding fields of grain. These industries initially utilized the region's hardwoods to stoke their furnaces and then utilized the region's relatively inexpensive canal, river, lake, and later rail transportation systems to access coal.

Perceptions of class, race, and gender infringed on the universal and equal application of inalienable rights, and opinions regarding "property" tended to align along divisions of wealth, although not exclusively. In time, such divisions were based at least as much on the politics of geography as on individual

11. "Van Etten Farm on Lake Skaneateles," 1835, newspaper clipping on file at the Onondaga Historical Association, Syracuse, NY.

or regional wealth. In the North, some of the leading proponents of aboli-tion in the second quarter of the nineteenth century emerged among a rising wealthy and landed class. In New York State, the Seward, Wright, and Osborne families of Auburn, the Smith family of Peterboro (Madison County), and the Fuller family of Skaneateles (Onondaga County) were typical of an emerging group of social activists with wealth and prominence in the fields of farming, land sales, and industry. There was, for at least a period in American history, a degree of altruism that transcended economic class in support of philosophi-cal and religious values based in notions of freedom and liberty.

The economic and social system that emerged in Central New York and the northeastern United States was in sharp contrast to the system built on enslaved labor in the American South. In contrast to "free states," slave states such as Maryland and Virginia had a different system of property and owner-ship and consequentially a different perception of human rights. In the South, there were lucrative financial rewards for those who could control sufficiently large labor forces and harvest labor-intensive crops such as cotton, sugar, tobacco, and rice.

The area where Tubman was born in Maryland did not conform to the large-scale ubiquitous plantocracy of some of that state's southern neighbors, but slavery prevailed there nonetheless. As noted earlier in this chapter, Tub-man herself was born into a setting dominated by smaller mixed-production farms. She was "shopped," or rented out, from home to home and plantation to plantation. In this setting, her movements between estates were virtually unnoticed and provided her with a base of knowledge of the roadways and overall landscape that was later to facilitate both her departure to freedom and her return trips to assist others in freeing themselves.

Opposition to slavery, most obviously manifest in regions such as Central New York in the northern states, provided an alternative ideal and a mechanism for freedom. Initially limited to those in residence or fleeing to these areas, this opposition ultimately grew into a movement that precipitated change that to Tubman and her family was not an illusion but a reality of such great value that many risked their lives to fulfill their dreams of liberty. Tubman and the many who made their way from slave states to free states helped to bring about the "new birth of freedom" (Lincoln 1863).

The social reform movements, which tended to vest themselves in the northeastern United States, were tied to progressive views toward social wel-fare and to deep-rooted belief systems. Within this social and religious envi-ronment, raw capitalist notions based solely on economics were incompatible with belief systems of social reform and justice. These ideas were professed by groups such as the Society of Friends (Quakers), Congregationalists, and Universalists (Sernett 2007). Religion was an important part of social life. Belief in equality under God had a profound impact on a range of social issues. Abolition, women's rights, temperance, and care for the indigent and infirm were nearly always fused as a common suite among the socially conscience of all economic classes. Even among the staidest religious organizations such as the Presbyterian Church, sectarian groups broke off from their core churches on the basis of human rights issues. Protestant reform groups, such as the Methodists, struggled with regional differences in social relations and labor structures and tended to splinter under conflicts that arose between beliefs and economics.

In Central New York, several decidedly abolitionist denominations emerged, including the Wesleyan Methodists, who tended to form integrated congregations, as well as African American–centered denominations such as the African Methodist Episcopal and the African Methodist Episcopal Zion Churches. Milton Sernett (2007) has written extensively about the religious callings of the "Burned-Over District" of Central New York, referring to the religious fervor that grew in the area during the second quarter of the nineteenth century. The strong spiritual beliefs and vivid description of flight to freedom under the guidance of God that Tubman expressed in her oratory in the parlors and meeting halls of New York and Massachusetts fit perfectly in this milieu of belief-based social reform.

In Auburn, a new Central Presbyterian Church was formed by abolitionists, many of whom were also strong supporters of the women's rights movement. Tubman supporter and biographer Sarah Bradford was the daughter of the president of the Auburn Seminary, one of the largest Presbyterian seminaries in the country. This was the church of the women's rights advocate Martha Coffin Wright of Auburn, co-organizer of the first women's rights convention in Seneca Falls, New York, in 1848. Although Frances Miller Seward, William Seward's wife, had a Quaker background, the Sewards, along with the Wrights, were members of the Central Presbyterian Church. Harriet Tubman and her second husband, Nelson Davis, exchanged wedding vows in its sanctuary in 1869,[12] a significant indication of the relative racial openness within the Auburn community at the time.

12. Charles Nelson Davis to Harriet Tubman, Mar. 18,1869, Marriage Register, Pauline Cope-Johnson personal papers, copy on file in the Harriet Tubman Home Collection, Harriet Tubman Home, Inc.

Support for abolition was explicitly manifest in religious doctrine and social networks, and many of these religious institutions professed equality. Abolition and free labor were also supported by the form of independent-owner and wage-based-labor capitalism that emerged in the Northeast. Freedom and free labor were essential to this form of capital economy; however, the system did not expect and was not inclined to support full economic equality. Rather, it was based on clear class divisions and notions of differentiation in race and ethnicity. The result was a structured inequality in the ownership and wage systems of the workforce. It was expected that a farmer could become wealthy and influential. Farmers working large tracts of land could and would hire laborers, while industrialists would hire labor from a lower social and economic class to work in their factories. Still, the ideal and the practice followed by wealthy and influential farmers and industrialists in Central New York were to reward labor with reasonable wages and to support educational institutions. Moreover, both the workforce and the basic education system were open to all. Abolition was consistent with the combined economic and social beliefs. The region was also known for its support of women's rights. However, even as reformers targeted both causes, abolition got a faster start and enjoyed greater traction in the mid-nineteenth century. Ultimately, women's rights and associated freedoms did not receive real legal support until the movement's revival in new forms in the early twentieth century.

In mid-nineteenth-century Central New York and in enclaves in Boston and New York City, civil liberties were being advocated by growing social reform movements. This assessment is in contrast to Mark Leone's (2005) characterization of the lack of change in mid-nineteenth-century America based on his study of urban Annapolis, a city in Tubman's home state of Maryland.[13] In 1849, Tubman fled Maryland and its institution of slavery and ultimately made her home in New York, whose social reformers had pressed forward their multifaceted agenda. Activists throughout the Northeast (William Seward and Gerrit Smith of New York and Thaddeus Stevens of Pennsylvania, among many) were engaged in pursuing legislation aimed at changing legal structures. By midcentury, activists such as the abolitionist William Lloyd Garrison and African American scholars and leaders such as Frederick Douglass and Jermain Wesley Loguen were making very public declarations of

13. I highlight the difference in perspective projected for Annapolis and Auburn because the two areas have been studied extensively, and they project what might be best regarded as divergent social settings. It is important to emphasize that both social settings coexisted in the United States.

human rights for African Americans.[14] Women's rights activists worked hand in hand with the abolition movement. Leaders such as Elizabeth Cady Stanton in Seneca Falls, Martha Wright in Auburn, and Wright's sister Lucretia Mott in Philadelphia joined forces to organize the first convention of women's rights at the abolition-centered Wesleyan Methodist Church in Seneca Falls, just west of Auburn. Frederick Douglass was among the attendees moved to sign the "Declaration of Sentiments." Many of the women and men present took active roles in assisting Harriet Tubman in her quest for freedom.

Working quietly behind the scenes were activists such as Harriet Tubman, who after liberating herself in 1849, repeatedly made trips from Maryland through Pennsylvania and New York to St. Catharines, Canada, spiriting people to freedom. By the time the Civil War broke out, the once invisible Tubman was becoming more vocal and visible and was directly engaged with abolitionists in the Boston area, where she stayed with several families and took part in abolitionist rallies (Sanborn 1863). Meanwhile, others took a different approach. Emily Howland, a life-long friend of Tubman who lived in Sherwood, a hamlet in the vicinity of Tubman's farm, stood behind her Quaker beliefs by taking on the task of teaching African American girls at places such as Miss Minor's Normal School on the outskirts of Georgetown, Washington, DC (Myers 1998, 31).

Great Britain emancipated enslaved laborers in its colonial holdings in the Americas between 1834 and 1838, and by the mid–nineteenth century France, Holland, and Denmark had prohibited slavery. Meanwhile, the United States was becoming more isolated and more polarized on the issue. However, if anything, slavery was even more entrenched in the American South due in part to the vast profits reaped by the expanding and labor-intensive cotton industry (Riello 2013). The admission of California as a free state was extracted at the price of the Fugitive Slave Act of 1850, which reiterated enslaved laborers as property and provided federal authority to capture and return persons who had fled enslavement, including those who had made new homes in free states. Hence, self-emancipated African Americans who had enjoyed freedom in places such as New York were now subject to being hunted down, captured, and returned to their "owners" under federal sanction. Making matters worse, the Kansas-Nebraska Act of 1854, pressed for by Senator Stephen A. Douglas of Illinois, was passed, which set the stage for

---

14. Significantly, the African Americans Frederick Douglass ([1855] 1994) and Jermain Wesley Loguen ([1859] 2016) published their views in memoirs and treatises challenging slavery.

years of regional conflict stemming from states deciding on their orientation toward slavery based on "popular sovereignty." Territories seeking admission as states had the right to decide if they would be "slave" or "free," so pro- and antislavery forces fought bitter and bloody battles for control, with the initial battleground focused squarely on the Kansas Territory.

Among those who went to free enslaved persons taken to Kansas by proslavery farmers were John Brown and his followers. Brown and his band were willing to confront and engage in violence associated with this struggle. Brown's group included brothers from the Osborne family of Auburn, who had ties with white abolitionists of the Wright, Mott, and Seward families as well as to Tubman.[15] Ultimately, John Brown and some of his followers moved their action to a more dramatic stage when they attempted to inspire an uprising and arm a rebellion by capturing the armory at Harpers Ferry in the Shenandoah Valley of West Virginia (Du Bois [1909] 2001; Sanborn 1872).

Tubman, while pursuing her activities as a conductor leading African Americans to freedom, was a supporter of action to achieve the goals of freedom. She met John Brown in April 1858 in St. Catharines, Canada, and helped him make connections with freed persons in Canada.[16] She also provided him with details of the Maryland landscape (Du Bois [1909] 2001, 120; Larson 2004, 159). Tubman did not take part in Brown's raid at Harpers Ferry, however.[17]

15. John Osborne was on the initial Harriet Tubman Home Board of Trustees, serving as its financial manager. Earlier in his life, he and possibly two of his brothers rode with John Brown in Kansas (Lithgow Osborne, handwritten note in the margins of Jane Abbey Osborne's Diary, Nov. 17, 1962, box 236, MSS 64, p. 49, Osborne Family Papers). While John Osborne was riding with John Brown, his brother David Osborne was expanding the Osborne Manufacturing Company's farm machinery business in Auburn. John later joined the Osborne firm and was an "office man" involved in the financial affairs of the company. He is known to have had an extensive collection of records and a printing press in his home. Unfortunately, these records were destroyed in two house fires.

16. Brown met self-emancipated AME Zion reverend Jermain Loguen in Syracuse and traveled with him to St. Catharines to meet Tubman and a large community of Black refugees. He sought to expand his army of "shepherds" with Tubman's support and recruits from this community (Du Bois [1909] 2001, 120; Renehan 1997, 148).

17. At the time of the insurrection, Tubman's whereabouts are not definitively known. She was variously reported to have been in New York "ill with fever" or in Canada recruiting for the rebellion (Humez 2003, 39). Other historians, such as Kate Larson (2004, 174), suggest Tubman may have been in Maryland rescuing more family members from slavery but perhaps also recruiting people for Brown's raid. Accounts of her presentations to abolitionist groups in the Boston area during this period describe her as raising funds for another campaign to bring people to freedom.

Frederick Douglass was at the time clearly calling for action, as expressed in his address in Syracuse at a commemoration of the "Jerry Rescue" two weeks before the raid. At this gathering, Douglass advocated insurrection as being best calculated to promote the emancipation of slaves in this country.[18] However, by the time of the actual raid, Douglass apparently had doubts about the viability of John Brown's specific plan for action and did not join him at Harpers Ferry (Larson 2004, 174). W. E. B. Du Bois suggests that Tubman also had her doubts ([1909] 2001, 176); however, it was in fact illness that prevented her direct participation. Although Tubman did not participate, throughout her life she embraced John Brown's actions as a catalyst to the freedoms that were ultimately won, and throughout their lifetimes both she and Douglass considered John Brown a prime martyr for the cause of freedom (see, e.g., Douglass [1855] 1994).[19]

Personal Property in a Setting
of Individual and Communal Freedoms

By the time of her arrival in Auburn in 1859, Harriet Tubman had through her activism become a heroine to the abolition cause and, conversely, a formidable antagonist to the interests of slavery. What better way to secure Tubman's position as a vested citizen with civil liberties than to acknowledge her personal liberty through landownership? Philosophically, the transfer of real property in Auburn to Tubman was designed to reinforce the trilogy of fundamental and inalienable rights and was done at a time and in a region where people were willing to stand up and speak out for these principles (D. Armstrong 2010).

The reasons that the well-traveled Harriet Tubman selected Central New York for her home can be linked to a combination of positive experiences and support. The choice correlates with the active nature of her interaction with like-minded freedom fighters of mid-nineteenth-century America. Certainly, the most obvious reason she selected Auburn was that Senator William

18. William Gould, a Wesleyan Methodist minister, recorded in his diary details of a speech by Frederick Douglass in Syracuse on October 1, 1859, commemorating the collective action to free William Henry in an event referred to as the "Jerry Rescue" on October 1, 1851 (William Gould Diary, entry for Oct. 1, 1859, Onondaga Historical Association).

19. When the dormitory was finally opened at the Harriet Tubman Home in 1908, Tubman chose to name it "John Brown Hall" in honor of Brown's service to the abolition of slavery (*Auburn Daily Advertiser*, June 23, 1908).

Seward and his wife, Frances, were supporters of her efforts and had land they were willing to sell her. By 1859, Tubman desired to relocate her parents from Canada to Auburn. The land represented a means to stand behind beliefs, and both the buyer and the seller saw it as providing her with security for her family. Tubman was not offered land in an abstract sense or at some distant place; rather, she was offered land on the Sewards' street and in their community. Although on the edge of the city, Tubman's farm was not isolated from the holdings of her wealthy white abolitionist and social activist friends. It was bordered to the south by a parcel that continued to be owned by the Sewards, and land two properties north of Tubman's was owned by the Osborne family into the twentieth century.

There is no doubt that the offer of a seven-acre farm at market value ($1,200) but on favorable payment terms was a reason for Tubman's choice to live in the Auburn area.[20] However, that offer and her decision to move to the region and to live there for more than half a century relate to a series of events and her linkages to complex social networks. These networks provided economic support and a social context for Tubman and her family. They included connections with the region's African American communities and active support from a broad base of activists engaged in abolition, women's rights, and temperance. However, the support Tubman had in the community was not universal, nor was it without the limitations of social prejudice based on class, race, and gender. The farm was located on the edge of town, and the ability of a seven-acre farm to provide the basis of sustenance for all the people who lived there was always a challenge. Nevertheless, beyond the simple transference of a title to land, there was a sense of acceptance of Tubman and her activities within the community of Central New York. Moreover, there was a mutual desire for Tubman to be a successful, self-sustaining landowner. This latter issue may sound a bit trite, but it was at the core of the philosophical convergence of Tubman and the greater Auburn community.

20. The price and the liberal terms are recorded in a ledger that was kept in William Seward's home office in his house on South Street. The ledger includes transactions beginning with the sale of the property on May 25, 1859. Accounts of payments and charges to the account span the period from 1859 to 1867. The initial ledger entry documents the transaction at $1,200 and then tracks what was essentially an open account of payments and extension of additional credit on what appears to be a very flexible basis (original agreement on the sale of the property is recorded in Harriet Tubman Ledger, 1859–67, entry dated May 25, 1859, microfilm reel 192, no. 6557, William H. Seward Papers, Seward House and Cayuga Community College, Auburn, NY).

Tubman's decision to settle her family on US soil came in 1859, at a point when the issue of slavery was coming to a head. Not only were Tubman and her family ready to settle down, but they were also no longer willing to settle for refugee status and freedom only outside the scope of the Fugitive Slave Act. It would take an additional six years and a civil war before the mission of freedom was achieved and Tubman allowed herself to settle down with her family in Auburn. Interestingly, during our excavations, we rediscovered an 1852 Canadian one-penny coin from the Bank of Quebec just outside the doorway of the north entrance to her brick house (figure 4.1). We do not know if this Canadian token was simply inadvertently lost by Tubman or a resident of her house as she or he prepared to enter the house or if it was placed in the ground to commemorate a link to Canada and a demarcation of the home as a place of freedom. However, the token shows an important link between the householders and their treks to Canada before they were able to secure a place to live in freedom in New York.

It must be emphasized again that the transfer of property to Tubman was also an act of civil disobedience because Tubman was at the time still considered a fugitive under US law.[21] The act of transfer of land from a prominent radical abolitionist US senator to a lightning-rod African American female leader in the antislavery movement was decidedly symbolic, even if it was done somewhat under the veil of secrecy. The transaction was known generally by the abolitionist movement but not initially publicized for fear of reprisal to all concerned. If this act was aimed only at providing a place for Tubman's family, the Sewards could have sold the property to Harriet Tubman's father, who was a free man. But they knew Tubman and chose to sell to her as a person who was legally free in New York State but not considered free under US law. Hence, they opted to risk legal jeopardy. In fact, the transfer was initially simply a ledger agreement and mortgage recorded in the Seward financial books. The transfer was not formally filed with the Cayuga County Records Office until well after the war.[22]

Those who knew the characters involved understood very well the symbolism of property ownership by an African American woman for both the white and Black communities engaged in a battle for human rights. I personally feel

21. However, she was a legal resident under New York State law.
22. The principal, interest, and additional drafts of the open line of credit were paid off with funds from the proceeds of Bradford's book (1869) and with the forgiveness of debt in 1873 by the Seward heirs upon the death of William Seward.

that the Sewards and Tubman knew exactly what they were doing and would have pressed the issue of Tubman's ownership of property under New York State laws and in opposition to the Fugitive Slave Act if they had been openly challenged. However, staged theatrics related to the selling of land to Tubman never came up as a political issue because within a few months of the purchase tensions between the North and the South escalated with John Brown's raid and congressional action that would certify admission of Kansas as a free state. Even before Lincoln effectively took office in March 1861, the lines of war had been drawn, and by the time the US census formally recorded Tubman in the register of property owners and heads of household in Fleming, New York, the first torrents of war were flooding the land.[23]

The transfer of land from Seward to Tubman was to members of the antislavery movement an act that demonstrated their belief in the importance of self-determination as expressed in the ownership of property. The basic philosophical issues of property ownership should not be overlooked or underestimated as an active expression of freedom and citizenship. During this era and most definitively earlier, in New York State law recognition as a citizen was defined in terms of a combination of self-ownership of personhood and the ability to own, control, and convey personal property, most specifically land (D. Armstrong 2010). In 1859, when this land was transferred to Tubman, the ambiguities were clear to all involved. What better way to challenge the institution of slavery than to create a setting where a formerly enslaved person not only was free but also recognized as the owner of real property? Those involved in the study of slavery and freedom at the time saw direct correlations between ownership of self (personhood), ownership of property (goods and land), and control of one's labor. For more than "four-score" years, they had witnessed the consequences of a lapse of fundamental judgment in the legal structures that had emerged with a new nation founded in opposition to colonial tyranny and the consequences of capricious governance.

Conveying land to Tubman represented an assertion of basic inalienable rights. In fact, although Senator Seward is usually credited with the sale of

23. Given this background, I wonder if the selection of a farm in Fleming, just outside of the City of Auburn, the city with which she and Seward were associated, was meant as a sleight of hand. Anyone searching for Tubman in Auburn would find no listing of her because the purchase of property was recorded in the lesser-known township of Fleming. Even to this day, historians sometimes miss records related to Tubman by searching for her in Auburn rather than in the Town of Fleming, where her farm was located.

the property to Tubman, the transaction took place while he was out of the country on a visit to England, and so it was probably facilitated by his wife, Frances. Likely, Frances approved and put forward the action. Since 1848, New York's Married Women's Property Act, as amended in 1849, had asserted a woman's rights to real property, including property gained through inheritance; hence, the farm was actually Frances's, not William's (Livingston and Penney 2004). There can be no doubt that Tubman's ownership of property was an important act targeting support of an inalienable right to property, but the conveyance of this property from one woman to another may also be framed as an important statement about women's rights.

Female Head of Household

So how and why did a refugee from slavery, a person who was legally a fugitive in the eyes of federal (not New York) law, acquire property in 1859, and what is the significance of that act? Jane Dabel suggests that Black women had a "strong presence in the labor market" (2008, 41). Moreover, as noted in the previous section, New York State laws provided a means by which women could own and inherit land and other property. However, Harriet Tubman's ownership of property and role as head of her household represent a special case related specifically to her role as a heroine of the cause of abolition. Hence, rather than saving up to earn funds to acquire property, she was offered property on special terms based on her demonstrated character and position in society. I argue that Senator Seward, Frances Seward, and other leading advocates of abolition recognized that to live free one needed to have an economic basis for autonomy and self-determination.[24]

African Americans had been among the initial settlers of Auburn at the beginning of the nineteenth century, and a substantial community of free Blacks was in residence in Auburn from at least the 1830s. By the 1850s, when Tubman was passing through the region guiding people to freedom, local Auburn corporations such as the Osborne Manufacturing Company (which was owned by abolitionists) were hiring Blacks, and the local brickmaking industry surrounding what would become Tubman's farm on South Street

---

24. I also note that Tubman had more in common with elite white women who were attempting to exert pressure for recognition and legal representation of African Americans than with poor white women. Hence, she was usually participating in activism with women in Central New York on an uneven field weighted down by issues of class and race.

employed primarily Black laborers from at least the mid-1850s (A. Armstrong and D. Armstrong 2012).

By 1850, when the federal Fugitive Slave Act was passed, a strong abolitionist coalition in Central New York operated counter to this law. Moreover, the political activists in this region had a long history of organized activities aimed at securing citizenship and even voting rights for Blacks, and ownership of land was a well-established means to this end. Decades earlier, Gerrit Smith, a Central New York abolitionist, had offered farm parcels to African Americans to secure their position as free voting persons of color under New York State law. Ironically, as the state moved to abolish slavery, it began to limit voting rights that had previously been enjoyed by free persons of color. In 1825, the requirement of property ownership was dropped for whites but was increased from property valued at $100 to property valued at $250 for Blacks. Hence, ownership of real property was paramount to expressed and lived freedoms.

Both Seward and Tubman recognized the importance of ownership of land as an expression of freedom, and it was Tubman who asked Seward for land. The correlation between landownership and living free is consist with the philosophy of freedom.[25] In the mid–nineteenth century, debates revolving around the means to achieve freedom raged in abolitionist circles but took on an activist tone in Central New York. I have no doubt that both Tubman and her supporters saw her ownership of land as a symbolic representation of freedom. Given the legal history of New York, there is reason to believe that both the Sewards and Tubman felt that freedom and ownership of self could be assisted and sustained by ownership of land.

Harriet Tubman had come to know Central New York during her travels to and from St. Catharines, Canada. Her contacts in Auburn, New York, included Martha Coffin Wright, to whom she was no doubt introduced by Lucretia Coffin Mott (Wright's sister), whom Tubman had known in Philadelphia. Moreover, Martha Wright's daughter Eliza had married David Osborne, a farm machine industrialist whose family was actively engaged in the abolition movement. David Osborne traveled frequently to Buffalo, and correspondence between him and his wife openly discussed assistance given by her to people moving to freedom, and she specifically asked that he keep an eye

25. Expressed in the inalienable right to property as defined by John Locke ([1690] 2012) and presented in an American Revolutionary context in Thomas Paine's pamphlet *Common Sense* ([1774] 2003).

out for persons heading to Canada while he was in Buffalo.[26] Ownership of land by an African American woman no doubt had special meaning to Tubman's local supporters, many of whom were also engaged in the struggle for women's rights. Not only did Tubman want to own land, but her ownership of land was also viewed as a symbolic representation of liberty for both Blacks and women.

There can be no doubt that the mortgage for the farm was sold to Tubman by Senator William Seward on favorable terms in part to recognize Tubman's service to the cause of abolition and in part to demonstrate a point regarding the role of African Americans and women as landowning citizens. Seward did not gift the land to Tubman; he sold it to her, in contrast to the land transactions made by Gerrit Smith from Peterboro, New York, who gifted land to Blacks in Timbuktu, a community located in and around Lake Placid, New York, as part of a scheme to assist African Americans toward financial independence and voting rights. James Fuller, a Quaker philanthropist from Skaneateles, the village immediately east of Auburn, also provided land grants to former slaves who settled in Canada. Fuller gave an outright gift of $800 to the British American Institute of Science and Industry to establish the Dawn Community for self-emancipated Blacks near Chatham, Ontario. Records of the Tubman/Seward transaction and follow-up financial dealings show that the Tubman house and farm were purchased for a price of $1,200, with a payment of $25 down to secure the deal, which was agreed upon on May 25, 1859, but not formally recorded until 1873, after Seward's death.[27] Unlike in the case of modern mortgage formalities, Tubman and Seward appear to have agreed on something more like a line of credit in that the account books show

26. Eliza Wright Osborne to David Osborne, Sept. 1, 1857, Osborne Family Papers. On September 17, 1857, David Osborne responded to Eliza from Pittsburgh indicating that his business in Buffalo had concluded and that he had moved on to Pittsburgh. He acknowledged her concerns but did not specifically address any interaction with the freedom seekers (David Osborne to Eliza Wright Osborne, Sept. 17, 1857, box 10, Osborne Family Papers).

27. According to Rebecca Green (1998), the initial purchase agreement was not recorded until the sale was recorded in the Cayuga County Clerk's Office on May 29, 1873, by Seward's son Frederick Seward. Frederick forgave the balance of the loan, which had grown to $1,500 (Frederick Seward to Harriet Tubman Davis, May 29, 1893, Cayuga County Deeds Book 169, p. 85, Cayuga County Clerk's Office, Auburn, NY; Tubman Accounts, "Minute on William Seward Ledger as to Terms of Settlement," reel 192, no. 6579, Seward Papers; see also William Seward, ledger inventory, "Mrs. Harriet Tubman holds Article from Estate of E. M [Elijah Miller] for 7 acre log Burton Farm with house thereon, May 25, 1859, $1200, interest payable quarterly," reel 193, no. 6579, Seward Papers).

relatively few payments in spite of documents whereby she agreed to pay $10 in interest per quarter.

Seward's financial ledger shows some small payments by Tubman but also a series of additional expenses by Tubman, so that the mortgage took on the functional form of a revolving line of credit.[28] Tubman used this line of credit during the Civil War, at which time her parents were among those in residence at the property while she engaged in the war effort. Tubman once used the line of credit in Washington, DC, to pay for a horse that cost $50. At the time of William Seward's death in late 1872, the balance of the loan had grown to $1,529.27 (Green 1998), and some of it was retired as a gift to Tubman by Seward's son Frederick in honor of Tubman's effort for the cause.[29]

Based on the archaeological and historical research on the property, we now know that this farm was situated squarely at the center of the South Street brickmaking industry (A. Armstrong 2011; A. Armstrong and D. Armstrong 2012). Not only were bricks made on the property, but Tubman's brothers, cousins, and many residents of the house were employed in the local brick-yards. The seven-acre farm produced an income from brickmaking as well as from the production of a range of food crops and livestock, in particular hogs. Although the importance of jobs and income deriving from the local brick industry has been omitted from formal histories of the area and has been over-looked in most examinations of Tubman's choice of property (A. Armstrong and D. Armstrong 2012), the economic viability of the land was probably well known by both Tubman and Seward and no doubt figured in Tubman's decision to purchase the property.

What better way to challenge the institution of slavery than to create a setting where the formerly enslaved not only was free but also recognized as the owner of real property? Philosophically, the transfer of real property in Auburn was designed to reinforce a trilogy of fundamental and inalienable rights and was done at a time and in a region where people were willing to stand up and speak out for these principles. Tubman's activities as a property

28. Later generations of the Seward family more firmly established a system involving a line of credit for individuals with the founding of what is now the American Express Corporation, best known for the American Express credit card.

29. Frederick Seward to Harriet Tubman Davis, May 29, 1893. Over the years, payments were made, and new debt accumulated, with the debt going as high as $1,604.36 on July 1, 1866 (reel 93, no. 6603, Seward Papers). The balance in December 1872 was posted as $1,509.27 (reel 93, no. 6614, p. 199, Seward Papers). However, upon William Seward's death the final debt was posted as $1,200.

owner and head of household as well as her role in the local brickmaking industry serve to challenge and disrupt more constraining expectations of gender roles and to break most stereotypes concerning women of color in this period.

Tubman's position as an influential African American woman imbues her properties and their material records with special meaning (D. Armstrong 2011).[30] I hope this archaeological study of Tubman's life achieves a degree of the discipline's potential to address what Paul Mullins has called "the transgressive history of race and diasporic experience." He argues that archaeology is "well positioned to weave an exceptionally complicated narrative of life along and across the color line that challenges racialized presumptions and fleshes out the genuine roots of diasporic heritage" (2008, 117).

Harriet Tubman in the Interplay of Race and Social Relations

Exploration of the Tubman site and of records relating to Tubman herself provide a basis for gaining a better understanding of the interplay of race and social relations revolving around Tubman, her farm, and her care facility in Auburn. Harriet Tubman was not without means, but they were limited, yet she nevertheless assertively used what she had to serve others. She held a place of special recognition in her community, as demonstrated by her being afforded a seat of honor at the front of the audience at a gathering commemorating the centennial of Lincoln's birth in 1909. Her honored position in the community resulted in her entertaining or caring for a bimodal stream of visitors. One group, comprising both Black and white, rich and poor, tended to make their way to her farm on the outskirts of town to pay homage to her for her deeds; the other came to her doorstep in need and sometimes desperation.

Tubman was a landowner, but she also had many people relying on her for support, which in her later years derived in part from rents, pensions, produce, and gifts. She always struggled to balance the need to pay off her mortgages with her desire to distribute whatever resources she had to those in need. On the one hand, certainly race, her lack of formal education and training, and, later in her life, her position as a female head of household served as limiting

30. Broader discussions related to African Diaspora contexts can be found in Battle-Baptiste 2011; Franklin 1997, 2001; Franklin and McKee 2004; Leone 2010; Sesma 2016; Singleton 1999; and Weik 2004.

factors financially. On the other hand, she was known to all as "Aunt Tub-man" or "Aunt Harriet," and the Auburn community regularly honored her with monetary gifts and baskets of goods and supplies.

In the late nineteenth century, long after most of her core abolitionist supporters had died, Tubman continued to retain support and special status based on her contributions and ideals. Financial support for her and her envisioned care facility came from both the African American community and the Anglo-American community. Most specifically, her efforts to establish a home for the aged were assisted by leaders and congregants of the AME Zion Church. Tubman had a long association with the Thompson AME Zion Church in Auburn, and she turned to the governing body of that church to achieve her goal.[31] She transferred ownership of her twenty-five-acre farm to the church in 1903, and finally in 1908, after twelve years of chartering and maintaining a less formal home in her house, she was able to open the Harriet Tubman Home for the Aged in a building she named John Brown Hall.

Tubman was not shy about reaching out to anyone who might provide support, and she had strong and long-term supporters in the Anglo-American communities of Auburn and Fleming (as well as of Central New York in general). Much of this support was tied to her special place in history and mutual bonds felt by people throughout the region. Individuals from Auburn's white community, such as the women's rights advocate Eliza Wright Osborne, be-friended and provided a margin of material and financial support to Harriet.[32] In a letter dated June 15,1906, Eliza describes bringing a woman named Mrs. Walling to Tubman's house and how Mrs. Walling bought a $2 book and then paid another fifty cents for a photograph.[33] Osborne's most telling words are in response to the visitor's inquiry about Tubman's financial

31. This structure as well as the structures on the Harriet Tubman Home properties and Harriet Tubman's gravesite and marker at Fort Hill Cemetery in Auburn are part of the multisite Harriet Tubman National Landmark (US National Park Service 2001).

32. The detailed manuscript records of the Osborne Family Papers, which are part of Syracuse University's Special Collections Research Center, provide an interesting portrait of the sisterly relationship between Eliza and Harriet. Eliza's personal letters, often to others engaged in the women's movement, such as Emily Howland, are personal in nature and detailed in social content and commentary. They also project the duality of respect interlaced with condescension and use of pejorative terms that probably relate to the economic, social, and ethnic gulf that existed between Eliza and Harriet.

33. Eliza Wright Osborne to Helen Osborne Storrow, June 15, 1906, box 220, Osborne Family Papers.

condition. Osborne assured Mrs. Walling that Tubman "had not anything but what people give her." Later in the letter she states: "She does not starve, but she lives very simple and cares for a great many people." Tubman told Osborne that she "wished she could paper her room over, so I suppose she want[s] me to do it for her. I don't know if I shall or not." Osborne goes on to provide a lengthy description of Tubman's house and a special relationship and basis for ongoing support:

> I fixed her house up last fall, so that it would be comfortable for the winter. I sent a carpenter, who stuck in shingles here and there, fitted the doors, had glass put in where it was out, and he charged me one hundred dollars, when he got through. He also put in a new cistern but did not put in the pipe to carry the water to the cistern, the pig, as I found out afterwards. I gave her a new stove; hers was in pieces, so she was quite comfortable off. I don't mean she want while she lives. She certainly has done enough in helping others and has earned the necessities of life, at any rate.[34]

This account offers details of the conditions of life at Tubman's farmhouse in the early twentieth century. It tells of replacing broken window glass and missing roof shingles, replacing a broken stove, and constructing a new water cistern in the basement of her house. In the archaeological deposits at the site, we found broken window glass and stove parts. We also rediscovered an old wooden water cistern in the yard and remains of the masonry cistern at the southeast corner of Tubman's basement (in an area that had previously been her kitchen). I was struck by the details and intimacy in Osborne's writing to her daughters about Harriet Tubman. The letters project a well-seasoned relationship and the common calling between these two activist women. However, the letters also show that there was a social gap between them based on class and race.

Amid discussion of a possible vacation to the West Indies in a letter dated February 14, 1911, Eliza writes to her daughters in Boston complaining of being charged an exorbitant rate for hospital care for Harriet Tubman. Though upset about the cost ($8 per week for four weeks), Osborne indicates that she agreed to pay half of the hospital bill if the Town of Fleming would pay the other half. She goes on to bemoan how much "poor folks are charged for health care and ponders why they charge it other than they figure I will

34. Eliza Wright Osborne to Helen Osborne Storrow, June 15, 1906.

4.1. Bank of Quebec one-penny coin (*front and back*), 1852, found in the pre-1880 fire deposits located just outside the door and under the north porch of Harriet Tubman's house (Locus 1). Photograph by D. Armstrong.

pay." Osborne concludes her discussion of Tubman by saying, "Dear me, she is one of the people who are living beyond all possibility, it is such a pity. She has been so wonderful in all the days she was helpful."[35]

With this background of the broader social context of Tubman's selection and retention of the Town of Fleming and the City of Auburn as her home, I move to a more specific history of Harriet Tubman and her social interactions in and around her farm as well as to events and interactions affecting her life and her efforts to establish a home for aging African Americans.

35. Eliza Wright Osborne to daughters Helen Osborne Storrow and Emily Osborne Harris, Feb. 14, 1911, box 87, Osborne Family Papers. Eliza Wright Osborne died on July 18, 1911, only a few months after writing this letter to her daughters expressing her concern for Tubman's welfare.

5

Harriet Tubman's Life
in Central New York

All these years her doors have been open to the needy, the most utterly
friendless and helpless of her race. The aged, forsaken by their own kith
and kin, the babe deserted, the demented, the epileptic, the blind, the
paralyzed, the consumptive all have found shelter and welcome. At no
time can I recall the little home to have sheltered less than six or eight
wrecks of humanity entirely dependent upon Harriet for their all.
                      —Mrs. Emma Paddock Telford, circa 1905[1]

Tubman's Life in New York

The farmsteads on which Harriet Tubman lived are hallowed lands because
they are where Tubman lived out her dream of freedom in her own way and
on her own terms. She had fought for freedom as a conductor on the Underground Railroad and as a soldier, spy, and nurse during the Civil War. The
story of her life in New York is less dramatic than the compelling story of
Tubman the tenacious Underground Railroad conductor to liberty, but it
embodies the fulfillment of her dream of freedom as well as the continuation
of her battle for liberty. Her life on her properties on the boundary between
Fleming and Auburn, New York, was vindication of her efforts to overthrow
the shackles of slavery that had gripped not only the enslaved but the whole
of American society.

The study of Harriet Tubman's life in Fleming and Auburn illuminates
her long-term struggle to live her life in freedom. She chose Central New York
as her residence because of the support and opportunity this setting provided
for her extended family and associates. Harriet Tubman was a strong, spiritual

---

1. Mrs. Emma P. Telford to Mrs. Mabel Evans (her daughter), "Harriet: The Modern
Moses of Heroism and Visions," dictated c. 1905, Cayuga County Museum, Auburn, NY.

believer in the cause of freedom not just for herself but on behalf of her family, community, and those in need. Many of her strongest supporters felt that by the end of the Civil War she had done enough for others and were willing to support her, but they were less supportive of her continued efforts on behalf of others. It was Tubman's outward-looking, communal perspective and her efforts to care for others that drove her and is the resonating theme of her life after the Civil War.

Broader Contexts of Family, Community, and Communal Support

The community and communal aspects of Harriet Tubman's ownership of land deserve attention. On the one hand, the properties are indelibly tied to the individual—Harriet Tubman—and to her roles as property owner and as caretaker of those who came to her for support and care. Her family was always present in her household and a core part of her life. However, there are communal implications in Tubman's view of her role as property owner. From the time of her acquisition of the seven-acre farm in 1859, she held the property not only as a personal possession but as a home to others, including family members and friends. The critical role of the surrounding Black community in Tubman's life in Fleming and Auburn is consistent with broader patterns of mutual support networks, cooperative organizations, and community formation within the settlements of those who made their way to freedom (LaRoche 2014b, 26). The free Black communities that Cheryl LaRoche studied in Illinois and Indiana (2014b, 26, 127) mirror the type of bonds seen within and around Tubman's house and later the Home for the Aged she established and in the generation of collective support around family, cooperative organizations, church, and community. Tubman selected a farmstead in close proximity to where other Blacks had settled. Her unifying and supportive presence then served as a magnet of collective support to an emerging African American community in Fleming and Auburn.

It may be that Tubman's communal use of her farms relates specifically to her personal interest in caring for others. However, it may also reflect a broader notion of shared property within the African American community of which she was a part. Collective ownership of property was (and still is) present in a range of traditional systems of land tenure. Communal use and operation of farms were typical of life on small farms in America during this era and were part of the cultural landscape of the Eastern Shore of Maryland from which

Tubman and her family came.[2] The breadth and scope of such practices make it difficult to attribute them to any one specific group but rather indicate that they are related to the general practices of many cultural groups.

In discussing the relationship of lands and notions of citizenship in many West African contexts, Simeon Onyewueke Eboh asserts that many African communities tie their identities to specific traditional lands, which are the basis for the maintenance and sustenance of the community (2005, 13–14). Examining Nigeria during the colonial era, he points to the disruption of traditional lands and land titles at the hands of colonial authorities and the consequent upheaval within communities when ownership was shifted from a collective community-based system organized through the chiefs and elders to a system of more arbitrary assignment to individuals, who often had connections to or were controlled by the colonial polity (78–79). The "traditional" notion of land ownership was linked with the authority of elders, who served as custodians for communal lands that were shared for the common good of the community. Land thus was cooperatively owned by the community, and individuals benefited from the mutual production of goods on communal lands.

In a study of a free Black community on St. John, US Virgin Islands, formerly Danish West Indies, collectivity and community in relation to property ownership by persons of African descent have been shown to have been of paramount importance (D. Armstrong 2003a).[3] The East End community was established on communally owned family lands by people of color nearly a century before the abolition of slavery in the Danish West Indies. The community was reliant on the stability offered by ownership of provision farming, homes, and land that provided a home base for craftswomen who worked as seamstresses and did needlepoint and that gave men a safe harbor and home port as they supported the community by fishing and transporting cargo among the Virgin Islands, Lesser Antilles, and Puerto Rico. This research moved me to see the tangible and symbolic meaning and importance of Tubman's property as a space of security for Tubman, her family, and the broader African American community with which she interacted.[4] Tubman's ownership of property was an essential means of sustenance to her and a mechanism

2. Kate Larson, personal communication to the author, Aug. 5, 2017.

3. The East End community was founded by five families in 1754 and continued to operate collectively through the transfer of the Danish West Indies to the United States in 1917, after which the community was gradually abandoned (D. Armstrong 2003a).

4. See also Groover and Wolford 2013; J. Scott 2018.

by which she extended assistance to others through the warmth of her house, the products of her farm, and ultimately through the Home for the Aged, which she created to care for elderly and infirm African Americans.

Similarly, Native Americans considered land and resources in Central New York to be for the collective use of the people rather than for individual ownership. West African and Native American concepts of communal land are in sharp contrast with landownership practices as defined in British, Dutch, and American laws. In New York State, individual ownership of land became the common practice. However, in Central New York, specific groups and individuals followed collective and communal practices in landownership and transfer. The Oneida Community founded by John Noyes adopted not only the name of the local Indigenous nation but built up a collective perfectionist society based on communal ownership and living (Klaw 1993; Oneida Community 2022). This decidedly capitalistic group enjoyed considerable agricultural success with the production of seeds and later industrial success with the production of flatware well into the twentieth century (Oneida Limited 2022). Closer to Auburn, the Skaneateles Community, located on the outlet of nearby Skaneateles Lake, was a short-lived utopian agricultural commune established by John Collins (who was also an abolitionist) and the Society for Universal Inquiry and Reform in 1843 (Wells 1953). The commune's farm, mill, and print shop yielded economic viability, but internal disputes associated with the shared living arrangements and authority within the group ultimately led to its abandonment in 1846 (Wells 1953). Although of decidedly different durations, these communities demonstrate economically viable models of communal ownership of land that were well known in the Tubman era, albeit at variance with common landownership and tenure systems in the Central New York region.

Harriet Tubman was the owner of her properties, but in both organization and action she shared her properties communally with family, friends, and those who came to her in need. One might ask if this communal sharing of personal property was completely understood by the broader Auburn community, in particular her sponsors and supporters. The answer appears to be both yes and no. If one contrasts Tubman's philanthropic use of her personal property with that of her neighbors' use of their property, one finds that although many within the white community of both the abolitionist generation and the next generation were quite generous, particularly regarding areas of social concerns and issues—donating money, chairing committees, and standing on the boards of a range of agencies, including those associated with the local orphanage, asylum, churches, and service organizations—they tended to keep their personal space and personal property separate from the groups and organizations to whom they donated. Thus, the personal homes of activist women such as Martha Coffin Wright and later her daughter Eliza Wright Osborne served as social gathering points for teas and fund-raisers, but they could also afford to build separate buildings or provide philanthropic support for their favorite charities and causes. For instance, to support her concern with women's rights, Eliza Wright Osborne spent $200,000 to build a separate women's building on South Street for one of her favorite charities, the Women's Education and Industrial Union.[5]

The Women's Education and Industrial Union was in principle open to and encouraged use by women of all economic classes and ethnic backgrounds. A distinction emerges, however, when one considers the scale of financial support given to Tubman. Even though Eliza Wright Osborne remained a supporter of and donor to Harriet Tubman throughout her life, her support was directed toward Tubman the individual rather than toward Tubman's causes and was always allocated on a limited scale. Moreover, even though they lived on the same street, their lives were very much separate, divided by race and class structures and bounded by specific visits and events.

There was considerable concern among Tubman supporters, including Eliza Wright Osborne, that in her later years people took advantage of her charity. In essence, many felt that people, including the elderly African Americans in her house and Home, took advantage of Tubman and used resources that were meant for her. In contrast, Tubman does not appear to have felt particularly taken advantage of; rather, she had a more ecumenical and communal view toward sharing her land and goods with others. The fact that she was willing to use her personal residence as the Home for the Aged projects a personal tolerance of others in her space and even an enjoyment of sharing. Thus, one difficulty connected to her operation of a charitable organization appears to be potential sponsors' willingness to assist her specifically but not

5. This building was later incorporated into the Auburn YWCA. Eliza Wright Osborne followed in her mother's footsteps and was very active in the late nineteenth- and early twentieth-century women's movement. She was vice president of the New York State Women Suffrage Association. The Women's Building that she had constructed on South Street was valued at $200,000 in 1911 (*New York Times*, July 19, 1911). One is left to contemplate the fact that although it is clear that Eliza Osborne was a long-term friend and supporter of Harriet Tubman, she did not fully understand or appreciate Tubman's goals for a home for the aged. Clearly, her philanthropy was focused in other directions, as witnessed by the funds she spent on the Women's Building in Auburn.

to offer their resources to assist her support for others.[6] This distinction is conveyed in an undertone in letters written by Eliza Wright Osborne, but it is also clear that Eliza respected Tubman for her generosity as well as her accomplishments.

In 1896, when Tubman acquired the farm adjacent to her seven-acre property with the objectives of generating a more formal place for her Home for the Aged and separating her private life from her public service to others, she engaged in an act that was more easily understood by the broader community. This action ultimately garnered formal support when the AME Zion Church took over the property. It also provided a more definitive division between gifting to Tubman and gifting to the Home, at least from the broader community's perspective. When in 1903 the AME Zion Church took over the ownership and management of the twenty-five-acre farm that became the Home, it did so with the support of people such as John Osborne, who had earlier ridden with John Brown in Kansas and who was very much engaged with Tubman's later charitable works.[7]

It was clear to all that Tubman viewed her properties as being something that should be shared with others. From her initial purchases of the two properties in 1859 and 1896 until her death in 1913, she offered use of these properties to others. The farms were operated communally by those in residence, and the twenty-five-acre property was formally consigned over for communal use as the Home for the Aged. Hence, these farms were an intersection of personal and communal property. Even as many of Tubman's strongest supporters in the white community did not understand her communal approach or those with whom she shared her possessions, they loved and respected her based on her deeds and generosity.

Acquiring a Farm but Staying Engaged in the Cause

During the period leading into the Civil War, Tubman became more publicly engaged with a spectra of abolitionist leaders and began to shift her roll from stealthy conductor, working under the cover of darkness, to vocal and public

6. This is made clear in the details of Eliza Wright Osborne's letters to her daughters. However, almost every time she stated her concern over Tubman's efforts on behalf of the Home for the Aged, she followed up with an acknowledgment of Tubman's generosity and accomplishments.

7. John Osborne was Eliza Wright Osborne's brother-in-law. His house was also on South Street between Eliza's house and Harriet's house.

crusader for the cause. In a relatively short period from 1857 to 1861, she became known for her colorful and spiritually powerful oratory in describing her rescues. She became a landowner and beginning in 1859 was openly raising funds for her rescue missions to the South and to support those she had brought north to St. Catherines, Canada. As a new landowner, she also had to raise funds to make payments on her farm and to support her family.

In 1859, when she acquired the "Barton Farm" from Frances and William Seward, the property included a wood-frame house, a barn, and a few small outbuildings. It was located on land that had been the territory of the Cayuga Nation of the Iroquois Confederacy. Much of the land in this region of Central New York was acquired by treaty from the Iroquois and distributed as military land grants to pay debts to soldiers following the American Revolution.[8] The parcel acquired by Tubman was part of a larger six-hundred-acre tract distributed as one of these military land grants. This parcel was initially set aside to support schools and churches, but by 1840 it was in the possession of William Barton, a farmer in the Town of Fleming.[9] William Seward's name begins to appear in the tax records for the property after his wife, Frances Miller Seward, inherited the parcel from her father. Reference to the seven-acre property under the ownership of William Seward began in 1853.[10]

This seven-acre farm was located in the Town of Fleming, just south of the boundary line between the City of Auburn and the Town of Fleming. The farm that Tubman then acquired to expand her Home for the Aged in 1896 was immediately north of her original seven-acre farm. The attribution of this twenty-five-acre property is a bit more complicated because twenty-one acres were within the City of Auburn but four acres within the Town of Fleming. The fact that these properties were on the far south edge of the City of Auburn and in the neighboring Town of Fleming has caused confusion with

8. Military Lot #66, Aurelius Township, recorded in Town of Fleming Tax Rolls, 1853, Cayuga County Clerk's Office, Auburn, NY.

9. US census, 1840, Town of Fleming, Cayuga County Records Office, Auburn, NY. Records define the Barton farm as containing between forty-seven and fifty acres.

10. Tract #66 was a six-hundred-acre tract of the military lands distributed after the American Revolution. This tract was specifically reserved for churches and schools within Aurelius Township (Cayuga County Deeds Book A, 1800, pp. 365–67, Cayuga County Clerk's Office). The land was sold off in parcels to various settlers, the proceeds presumably used in pursuit of the specified purposes. Records on the property include a listing in the Cayuga County *Balloting Book* (*Balloting Book* [1825] 1983, 1122). After 1887, tax records refer to the property as part of Aurelius Lot #65 rather than Lot #66 (Town of Fleming Tax Rolls, Cayuga County Clerk's Office).

respect to historic records. The census takers seemed not to make clear distinctions in regard to municipality as they worked their way south on South Street recording households on the border of the City of Auburn and the Town of Fleming.[11]

In 1859, after establishing her parents, family, and friends in her newly acquired house on the seven-acre farm in Fleming, Tubman resumed her abolitionist effort with travel aimed at securing funds for another trip to bring people to freedom. During this period, her brother John Stewart assumed the mantle of responsibility for caring for her parents and her farm. On November 1, 1859, John Stewart wrote a letter to her seeking advice concerning the care of their parents. This letter indicates that her father wished to travel to Canada to retrieve possessions that had been left there. Her parents were having trouble securing a stove, and the cold of winter was approaching. Brother James's wife, Catherine Stewart, who is later listed as being a resident in the house in the 1865 census (table 5.1), had not yet arrived from Canada, but John Stewart writes that "she wants to very badly." John is very concerned about financial affairs, indicating that William Henry [Seward] has "received nothing as Payment since the 4th of July that I knows of."[12] He goes on to say that he plans to write to Seward and asks Harriet to tell him, John, "what to do as I want to hear from you very much."[13] Kate Larson suggests that Tubman probably traveled to Auburn to address matters at some point after November 1 and that she was in New York City by midmonth (2004, 175).[14]

11. Town of Fleming Tax Rolls, 1896–1901, Cayuga County Clerk's Office.

12. In fact, there were three William Henrys in Tubman's life: her brother William Henry Stewart Sr.; her nephew William Henry Stewart Jr.; and William Henry Seward. By context, my assumption is that in his mention of "William Henry," John Stewart was referring to Senator Seward (who was soon to become secretary of state). In fact, William Seward's ledger sheet for Harriet Tubman shows that she did not make another payment until January 7, 1860, a payment of $174.81, part of a pattern of irregular payments that would characterize her long-term debt to Seward (Harriet Tubman Ledger, William H. Seward Papers, Seward House and Cayuga Community College, Auburn, NY).

13. John Stewart to Harriet Tubman, Nov. 1, 1859, Rochester Ladies Anti-Slavery Society Papers, vol. 1, p. 19, William Clements Library, Univ. of Michigan, Ann Arbor, reproduced in Larson 2004, 176. Catherine Stewart is the wife of James Stewart. She and two of their children are listed as in residence at Harriet Tubman's home in the 1865 census (New York State census, 1865, Auburn and Fleming, Cayuga County, NY, Cayuga County Records Office).

14. Larson indicates that on the day John Brown was hanged, Tubman was at Ednah Cheney's house in Boston (2004, 175). Ednah Dow Cheney (June 27, 1824–November 19, 1904) was an abolitionist, women's rights activist, and transcendental reformer. A strong supporter of Harriet Tubman, she wrote a biographical sketch of Tubman's life (Cheney 1865).

In April 1860, Tubman was en route to Boston to meet with abolitionists and raise funds when she became involved in one of the better-known rescues of a former slave. On the morning of April 27, she was in Troy, New York, visiting her cousin John Hooper when a refugee from slavery named Charles Nalle was arrested.[15] Hooper was involved in the effort to free Nalle, who was being held at the US Commissioner's Office. Tubman joined the action. She entered the office and monitored the situation, signaling others outside. When Nalle was moved to another building, a fight to free him began, with Tubman playing an active role in both the fight and the successful rescue before slipping out of sight (Bradford 1869, 90–91; Larson 2004, 180). In the wake of the raid on Harpers Ferry, this event raised the scale of fervor among abolitionists in Boston once Tubman arrived there, bruised, beaten, her clothes torn, but with a new and exciting story of Nalle's rescue. Ultimately, the abolitionist community raised money and purchased Nalle's freedom, enabling him to return from Canada to Troy (Bradford 1869, 103). In Boston, where abolitionists were in crisis mode, Tubman's vivid telling of this new event in Troy at abolitionist meeting halls attracted considerable attention and support. Moreover, her lively presentations describing the rescue of her parents at a women's suffrage meeting at Melodeon Hall on July 4, 1860, served to further cement her legendary status as a woman known for "fighting in a good cause" and as someone with an uncanny ability to pull off dramatic escapes ("Women's Rights Convention," *Liberator* [Boston], July 6, 1869).

Southerners were also taking notice of Tubman, with pro-slavery writer John Bell Robinson responding in horror to the applause given to Tubman at the Independence Day convention in Boston in 1860. Robinson argued that Tubman had taken her parents "away from ease and comfortable homes" and suggested that her "cruelty to her parents was a thousand times worse than to sell young ones away" (Robinson [1863] 2003, 322–23).[16] His critique of Tubman's actions project the paternalistic view that Tubman's parents were better off being "caressed and taken care of" by slave owners than they were

15. Charles Nalle was employed by Uri Gilbert, an abolitionist and wealthy industrialist, and was captured as he was walking to a bakery to buy bread for his family. His arrest involved a complex setting of intrigue in that his wife, a free Black, had been arrested for conspiring in his flight to freedom, and because he was illiterate, he had contracted an unscrupulous lawyer to write letters in an attempt to aid his wife and gain safe passage for his six children to Troy. The lawyer, Horace Avril, instead contacted Nalle's owner, Blucher Hansbrough, who took action that led to the arrest of Nalle.

16. Robinson's response to the applause for Tubman was written in 1860 but not published until 1863 in his book *Pictures of Slavery and Anti-slavery* (see Larson 2004, 183–84, 356).

living in freedom, a notion that Tubman and her family wholly rejected and that further energized the abolition movement.

Harriet continued to raise funds in Boston before heading to Maryland on a mission of freedom. She eventually made safe passage back through Philadelphia and Central New York, reaching Canada on December 30, 1860 (Larson 2004, 186–89). It had been a tumultuous trip south. She arrived in Maryland to find that her sister Rachel had died, and events prevented her from rescuing Rachel's children, but she was able to rescue the Ennals (a.k.a. Ennets) family.[17] On the final leg of her journey, she stopped at the house of Gerrit Smith in Peterboro, New York, arriving on a cold Christmas Day with seven refugees and "frosted feet."[18] She stayed five days at Smith's home, which she called "the Big House," to rest up and recover from the winter trek. While there, she was asked to go hunting with Gerrit Smith's son, Greene, but responded that she could not because her shoes were worn out. Years later, in 1911, when being interviewed by James B. Clarke, a Black student from Saint Vincent, British West Indies, who was studying at Cornell, Tubman recounted events of the day: "I remember once after I had brought some colored people from the South . . . Gerrit Smith's son Greene, was going hunting with his tutor and some other boys. I had no shoes. It was a Saturday afternoon and would you believe it—those boys went right off to the village and got me a pair of shoes so that I could go with them" (Clarke 1911, 115). According to Clarke, the Smiths considered Tubman "equally skilled with a gun or a hoe, in the laundry or the kitchen" (115).

After Tubman's departure from Auburn to Canada, Martha Coffin Wright wrote from Auburn to her daughter Ellen Wright Garrison in Boston on December 30, recounting Tubman's travels with seven charges whom she had just "pioneered safely from the Southern part of Maryland."[19] Another of Wright's daughters, Eliza Wright Osborne, wrote a letter describing how she and the women of Auburn had gathered together to sew clothing for infants who were en route to Canada.[20]

17. According to William Still, this family included Stephan and Maria Ennals and their three children, Harriet, Amanda, and a three-month-old infant (Still [1871] 1970, 554–55).

18. Gerrit Smith to Franklin Sanborn, Jan. 29, 1861, Franklin Sanborn Papers, Rare Book and Special Collections Division, Library of Congress, Washington, DC.

19. Martha Coffin Wright to Ellen Wright Garrison, Dec. 30, 1860, box 36, F. 948, Garrison Family Papers, Sophia Smith Collection, Smith College Library, Northampton, MA.

20. Eliza Wright Osborne to David Osborne, box 10, Sept. 1, 1857, Osborne Family Papers, Special Collections Research Center, Syracuse Univ., Syracuse, NY). It is likely that these letters describe events relating to the same group of refugees.

During this period, reports were circulating about increased slave-hunter activities in Central New York that may well have been aimed at capturing Harriet Tubman. David Wright in Auburn received a letter from Charles Mills, an abolitionist in Syracuse, cautioning him to warn Harriet. Wright responded by sending Mills's letter to Mr. Hosmer, the editor of an Auburn newspaper, who in turn rode out to Tubman's farm to warn her parents. In fact, Tubman was already in Canada, having been escorted there by Gerrit Smith, but her family had stayed in Auburn (Larson 2004, 191). To assist her family in Auburn during her absence, Tubman asked Martha Wright to send them flour.[21] Wright not only obliged by providing the flour but also took responsibility for getting Tubman's parents to Sunday school at the First Presbyterian Church in Auburn.

In early 1861, Catherine Stewart, James's wife, came to live in Tubman's home in Auburn. Sarah Bradford wrote in her biography of Tubman that during this period Tubman's mother, Ritta (also "Rit" or "Ritte"), "was querulous and exacting, and most unreasonable in her temper, often reproaching this faithless daughter as the Israelites did of Moses of old, for bringing them up into the wilderness to die there of hunger" (1901, 143). Ironically, this diatribe sounds eerily like that of pro-slavery commentator John Robinson ([1863] 2003) quoted earlier. Tubman's father, Benjamin Ross (listed as "Benjamin Stewart" in census records), had been a manager of a lumber mill in Maryland, but he was now in his late sixties, and finding work was probably difficult for him. He may have found work in the local brickyards, but he is not listed among the numbers of African Americans engaged in brickmaking. John Stewart, one of Tubman's brothers, does not show up on the 1865 census, but he is regularly listed in the *Auburn City Directory* from 1862 on as either a laborer or a teamster, and in some years he is listed as a laborer in the South Street brickyards.[22]

Meanwhile, Harriet, traveling throughout New England to raise money, was no doubt negatively impacted by mismanagement of relief funds by another abolitionist, Hiram Wilson. To avoid similar concerns, Tubman's supporters established a fund called the Fugitive Aid Society of St. Catharines. The organization was headed by Charles A. Hall, while Tubman, her brother William Henry Stewart Sr., John Jones, William Hutchinson (treasurer), and

21. Martha Coffin Wright to Lucretia Coffin Mott, Feb. 1861, box 37, F. 950, Garrison Family Papers.

22. See, for example, *Auburn City Directory*, 1862, Cayuga County Historian's Office, Auburn, NY.

Mary Hutchinson, his wife, served on its managing "committee."[23] Tubman had entered into a world of formal business dealings in her fund-raising efforts on behalf of refugees and with the purchase of her house and farm from William and Frances Seward. Although she was skilled at spiriting people to freedom, financial matters were something else altogether. We have already seen that after buying the house in 1859 and settling her family there, Tubman resumed her abolitionist calling and left her brother John Stewart to deal with unpaid house payments and support of her household.[24]

As early as 1861, some of her biggest supporters, such as Gerrit Smith and Franklin Sanborn, had begun to express concern over the way Tubman handled money. They were eager to assist her but tended to limit their assistance to small installments of $10 to $20. Their concern centered on her lack of control over how she handled money or, perhaps more specifically, her practice of passing it on to others. Later, Sarah Bradford would write that Tubman's "heart is so large, and her feeling are so easily wrought upon, that it was never wise to give her more than enough for present needs" (1901, 145). Unfortunately, this opinion was widely shared even among her most ardent supporters and tended to result in paternalistic gifting practices that addressed only immediate needs. Consequently, throughout her life Tubman was almost always having to ask for support, which she received in small, intermittent allotments. Later, this practice of limited gifting would have a dramatic impact on her ability to raise funds for the Home for the Aged. Ultimately, she would need to have the AME Zion Church take over fund-raising for her dream to be fully achieved.

In April 1861, shots were fired at Fort Sumter, South Carolina, and the Civil War began in earnest.[25] Harriet is reported to have spent time in Boston in early 1862, and through her abolitionist contacts she met John Andrew, the governor of Massachusetts, with whom she arranged to travel to Beaufort, South Carolina, to work at the Union's headquarters at Port Royal (Larson 2004, 196).[26] Before leaving for South Carolina, she sought funds to care for

23. "Relief of Fugitives in Canada," *Liberator*, Oct. 25, 1861, and "Relief of Fugitives in Canada: An Organization," *Liberator*, Dec. 20, 1861.

24. John Stewart to Harriet Tubman, Nov. 1, 1859, in Larson 2004, 176.

25. The initial shots in defense of the fort were fired by Abner Doubleday, who grew up in Auburn, New York.

26. To raise funds for this trip, Tubman addressed many abolitionist audiences, including the Twelfth Baptist Church in Boston. However, the *Liberator* reported on February 21, 1862, that donations were small.

her parents in Auburn. Ednah Dow Cheney, one of Tubman's early biographers and an activist in Boston's circle of abolitionists, wrote that the "only condition she made was that her old parents should be kept from want[;] . . . with what shred economy [*sic*] she . . . planned all their household arrangements. She concluded that thirty dollars would keep them comfortable through the winter" (1865, 38). Although this fund-raising effort covered the winter of 1862, the war would last another three years.

I will not cover the details of Tubman's exploits during the Civil War but concentrate on her family and her activities in relation to them at her house and farm in Auburn.[27] One of the most interesting and controversial events related to Tubman and the family members she had brought to Auburn occurred in the period prior to her leaving for the war and revolves around Margaret Stewart, one of those family members. Rather than taking Margaret to her own house, Tubman took her to live at the Seward house with Frances Miller Seward, and Margaret split her time between the Seward home and that of Frances's sister, Lazette Miller Worden, also of Auburn.[28] The story of Tubman's relationship with Margaret Stewart and the timing of Margaret's removal, or "kidnapping," from her home in Maryland is complicated. Based on communications with Margaret's daughter, Alice Brickler, Earl Conrad suggests that her removal from Maryland occurred between 1855 and 1856, when she was eight or nine (1943, 74). However, Kate Larson associates Margaret Stewart's arrival in Auburn with events of the spring of 1862, when Tubman was preparing to leave New York to support the Union forces in South Carolina (2004, 196).

A letter from Martha Coffin Wright to her daughter Francis places Margaret Stewart in Auburn with Lazette Worden. On May 28, 1862, Wright wrote that "Mrs. Worden . . . has taken a contraband 10 yrs. old to live with

27. Tubman's efforts as a soldier, spy, and nurse during the Civil War are dealt with in detail in Bradford 1869, 1886, 1901 and in Larson 2004. They took place well removed from the setting of her farm in Central New York.

28. Margaret Stewart is reported to have lived in Tubman's household in the years prior to Margaret's marriage to Henry Lucas in 1872 (Humez 2003, 78; Larson 2004, 361), after which she established her own home in the Auburn community. The 1880 US census lists her as "Maggie Lucus" (twenty-nine, who worked as a housekeeper), living in residence with her husband, Henry Lucas (a thirty-year-old laborer), son Allen (six), and one-month-old daughter (presumably Alice, who later married and was known as Alice Brinker) (US census, 1880, Auburn and Fleming, Cayuga County Records Office). In 1880, the Lucases lived on Cornell Street in Auburn.

her, a niece of Harriet Tubman."[29] Worden had her own home in Auburn, but she stayed in the Seward house with her sister when William Seward was serving as secretary of state in Washington, DC (Larson 2004, 197).[30] Alice Brickler's recollections suggest that Harriet Tubman "gave the little girl, my mother, to Mrs. William H. Seward, the Governor's wife."[31] She goes on to say that "this kind lady brought up my mother—not as a servant but as a guest within her home. She taught mother to speak properly, to read, write, sew, do homework and act as a lady. Whenever Aunt Harriet came back, mother was dressed and sent in the Seward carriage to visit her. Strange to say, mother looked very much like Aunt Harriet."[32]

It is probable that Conrad's timeframe is too early, but it is also possible that Margaret had been taken from Maryland well before 1862. Either the little girl had already been placed with the Worden and Seward households prior to Martha Wright's letter of late May 1862, or she had lived with Tubman and her extended family in Canada or Auburn for several years prior to her transfer to the Wordens' and Sewards' charge when Tubman took care of family matters before she left for war.[33] If Margaret Stewart did live with Harriet Tubman and her family in Canada during the period prior to her delivery to the Worden and Seward households, it would do much to explain the closeness of their long-term relationship.[34] The interaction between Harriet Tubman

29. Martha Coffin Wright to Francis Wright, May 28, 1862, box 41, F. 1028.22, Garrison Family Papers, at http://asteria.fivecolleges.edu/findaids/sophiasmith/mnsss175_bioghist .html.

30. Through careful unwinding of the story, including use of Conrad's papers and Wright family correspondence from the era, Larson presents the details of the known records, concluding that Margaret's parentage "remains a mystery." The correspondence between Alice Brickler and Earl Conrad suggest that Margaret's father was one of Tubman's brothers and that he and his family were free Blacks (Alice Brickler to Earl Conrad, July 19, 1939, Earl Conrad/Harriet Tubman Collection, Schomburg Center for Research in Black Culture, New York Public Library, New York). However, Larson wondered why Harriet did not simply leave this girl with other family members at her own home. Larson speculates that there is a remote possibility that Margaret Stewart was in fact Harriet's own daughter (2004, 198–99).

31. Seward had been a two-term governor of the State of New York earlier in his career.

32. Conrad 1943, 75; Alice Brickler to Earl Conrad, July 19, 1939.

33. Martha Coffin Wright to Francis Wright, May 28, 1862.

34. As indicated in note 30, Larson suggests the possibility that Margaret Stewart was actually Harriet Tubman's own daughter. Although evidence supports the idea that that Harriet had a particularly strong bond with Margaret, there is no evidence to support the conjecture that Margaret was her biological daughter other than the similarity of looks to be expected of a niece (see Conrad 1943, 75). Moreover, a critical evaluation of the timeline

and Lazette Worden, Frances Seward, Martha Wright, and Margaret Stewart is indicative of the complex network of women engaged in the Underground Railroad in Auburn.[35]

Life on a Farm in Fleming, New York

The census and tax records for the Town of Fleming and the City of Auburn provide a basis for understanding the demographic makeup of Tubman's household and its immediate surroundings. Census records also provide information related to the production of foods for consumption and sale on her farms. After acquiring the seven-acre farm in Fleming in 1859, Tubman brought her family there. In the aftermath of the raid at Harpers Ferry, Tubman's friends in Boston, including Franklin Sanborn, advised her to take her family back to St. Catharines, Canada, for fear of their prosecution as co-conspirators.[36] Accordingly, Tubman, returned from Boston and took her family back to St. Catharines, where they stayed through the beginning of 1861. Tubman, however, returned to Auburn in January 1960 and then continued her travels, with stopovers that included a visit to her cousin John Hooper in Troy, New York, in April 1860 before proceeding on to Boston. Hence, when the 1860 US census was conducted, no one was home at Tubman's house and encompassing farm in Fleming.[37] Then again, given their position as refugees or, in the eyes of Southerners, "fugitives," it is unlikely that they would have taken part in the census had they been present. There is little record of the livelihood of those living on Tubman's farm during the Civil War. As noted earlier, we do know that in May 1862, prior to departing for South Carolina, Tubman solicited and received $30 from her abolitionist friends in Boston to support her family in Auburn during the next winter (Cheney 1865, 38; Larson 2004, 196).

---

suggests that the girl was probably taken from Maryland well before the beginning of the Civil War and that there was considerable time for the two to develop a strong bond prior to Tubman's departure to South Carolina and the war effort.

35. Details of Lazette Miller Worden's radical abolitionist stance were recorded by her daughter Frances Worden Chesbro (Frances Worden Chesbro, untitled manuscript, Seward Collection, Rush Rhees Library, University of Rochester, Rochester, NY). She and her family lived at 2 Frederick Street in Auburn.

36. Franklin Sanborn to Friend, Dec. 20, 1859, MS E.5.1, pt. 2, p. 141, Anti-Slavery Collection, Boston Public Library. Larson notes that Tubman was back in Auburn by January 1, 1860, and was "settling some of her debts with Seward" (2004, 354).

37. US census, 1860, Auburn and Fleming, Cayuga County Records Office.

The 1865 New York State census lists nine persons in residence in Tubman's farmhouse. Tubman's father, Benjamin (Ross) Stewart, age seventy, is listed as the head of the household and is followed in order by his wife and Tubman's mother, Ritta, age sixty-seven (tables 5.1 and 5.2). Thomas and Ann Elliott are a second married couple in residence (ages twenty-five and twenty-two, respectively, from Maryland). A third adult male, Newton Thornton (age thirty-five, born in Virginia), is also present, along with three children, Margaret Stewart (thirteen, Maryland), Elijah Stewart, and Hester Stewart. All three adult males are listed as laborers, but with no mention of specific employment.[38] However, in later years Thomas Elliott is listed as laborer in the local South Street brickyards.[39] In the decade prior to Tubman's acquisition of her seven-acre farm, several brickyards are reported for the area surrounding what would be her farm.[40] No employment or occupation is listed for the adult women, and it appears as if the children, based on their literacy, were students in the Auburn public schools.

During the era following Tubman's acquisition of her farm and to the end of the nineteenth century, a number of African Americans are recorded as labors working in the South Street brick- and tile-making district that encompassed Harriet Tubman's farm.[41] The clay from this zone produced a

38. Thornton Newton remained in the Auburn area and provided evidence in support of Tubman's efforts to receive Civil War widow's benefits in 1893.

39. *Auburn City Directory*, 1867–68, Cayuga County Historian's Office.

40. Samuel and Lydia Wilcox (of Somersetshire, England) started a brickyard in the early 1850s and sold it to John Farmer by 1860 (Tucker 1973). An 1853 map of the Town of Fleming (Cayuga County Historian's Office) shows the Wilcox brickyard on the creek just east of South Street near the tollhouse. An 1859 map of the Town of Fleming (Cayuga County Historian's Office) indicates that J. Farmer had both a brickyard and a tile kiln and that the latter was positioned where the Wilcox brickyard was situated on the 1853 map. The US census of 1860 records the brickyard owned by John Farmer and indicates the industrial value of the brick and tile it produced as $4,000 in brick and $4,000 in tile per year, with an additional $2,000 assigned to the value of the property. Wilcox appears to have sold his brickmaking business to Farmer, but he and his family still had a house in the area (US census, 1860, schedule 5, p. 1, "Products of Industry," Cayuga County Records Office). In 1860, John Farmer employed eight brickmakers—Frank S. Collings, G. W. Beard, Barney Collings, Thomas Kenney, Cornelius Roin, John Flinn, George Fichunds, and John Camp (Tucker 1973). The 1860 census indicates that these eight brick laborers were paid a collective total of $160 a month (or $20 per person). No specific ethnicity is given for this group of laborers. They probably lived in the brick structure at the back of John Farmer's farm that would later be called "John Brown Hall."

41. The brickmakers listed for the 1860s include Flavel Danforth, who made hollow bricks associated with tiling fields (Danforth sold his interests to Sylvester Ross in 1874), William J.

TABLE 5.1

NEW YORK STATE CENSUS RECORD FOR HARRIET TUBMAN'S FARM, 1865, PART 1

Last Name	First Name	Age	Sex	Race	Relation to Head	Birthplace	# of Children	# of Times Married	Now Married	Widowed	Single	Occupation
Stewart	Benjamin	70	M	B	head	MD		1	X			laborer
Stewart	Ritta	67	F	B	wife	MD	9	1	X			
Newton	Thornton	35	M	B	boarder	VA					X	laborer
Elliott	Thomas H.	25	M	B	boarder	MD		1	X			laborer
Stewart	Catherine	27	F	B	boarder	MD					X	
Elliott	Ann M.	22	F	B	boarder	MD		1	X			
Stewart	Margaret E.	13	F	B	boarder	MD						
Stewart	Elijah	9	M	B	boarder	Canada						
Stewart	Hester A.	12	F	B	boarder	Cayuga [NY]						

Source: New York State census, 1865, Auburn and Fleming, Cayuga County Records Office, Auburn, NY.

The names listed in all tables are as recorded by census takers and published in the censuses. The categories listed in the headings and the abbreviations designating sex, race, marital status, home ownership, missing data, and so on are also from the censuses.

TABLE 5.2

NEW YORK STATE CENSUS RECORD FOR HARRIET TUBMAN'S FARM, 1865, PART 2

Last Name	First Name	Age	Sex	Race	Native	Naturalized	Alien	Colored Person Not Taxed	Owner of Land	Over 21 and Illiterate	Deaf, Dumb, Insane, etc.	Now in Army	Now in Navy	Formerly in Army	Formerly in Navy
Stewart	Benjamin	70	M	B				X	X	X					
Stewart	Ritta	67	F	B				X		X					
Newton	Thornton	35	M	B				X		X					
Elliott	Thomas H.	25	M	B				X		X					
Stewart	Catherine	27	F	B				X		X					
Elliott	Ann M.	22	F	B				X		X					
Stewart	Margaret E.	13	F	B				X							
Stewart	Elijah	9	M	B				X							
Stewart	Hester A.	12	F	B				X							

Source: US census, 1865, Auburn and Fleming, Cayuga County Records Office, Auburn, NY.

The language used to designate census categories, in particular "deaf, dumb, insane," is the original language used by the New York census and typical of the period.

distinctive-colored brick when aged, a variegated red to yellow color that is still seen in several buildings in and around Auburn. The brickyards produced hundreds of thousands of bricks used in construction of houses and industrial buildings. They also produced extruded hollow tiles of various sizes and shapes (round, round with a flat side, octagonal, etc.) that were used as drainage tiles in fields. The round tiles were part of an important transformation in farming by serving as conduits to remove surplus water from fields.[42] It is during the period after Tubman acquired her initial farm that African Americans began to show up as laborers in the South Street brickyards.

In the immediate aftermath of the war, Tubman was somewhat of a celebrity. However, she remained largely dependent on the goodwill of others in terms of her financial affairs. Although Union soldiers received veterans' benefits, Tubman's ad hoc albeit often chartered and sponsored roles in the war effort unfortunately did not garner her those immediate benefits. To support herself and her family, she returned to the "abolitionist" lecture circuit, including trips to New York and Boston, to tell stories of her activities as a conductor on the Underground Railroad and more recently in service to the Union army as soldier, nurse, and spy. The *Brooklyn Daily Eagle* announced on October 21, 1865, that she would be an honored guest at Rev. J. M. Williams's AME Church at Bridge, Brooklyn, the following Sabbath.

In 1867, Tubman and her many friends began to pursue a claim for back pay and military benefits related to her service during the Civil War. Sarah Bradford's biographical book *Scenes in the Life of Harriet Tubman* (1869) aimed not only to generate funds to pay down Tubman's mortgage but also to publicize her heroism and service and to support her claim for war benefits.

Hedger, Sylvester Ross, and Albert Watkins (who owned SE & A Watkins brickmakers) (*Auburn City Directory*, 1862–63, 1863–64, 1865, 1865–66, 1866–67, 1867–68, 1868, 1869, Cayuga County Historian's Office; see also A. Armstrong and D. Armstrong 2012).

42. More importantly, industrialists in the region developed steel farming implements that changed the scale of farming and greatly assisted farm production both on local farms and in the much larger farmlands that were opening up in the western United Sates. The local Osborne Manufacturing Company (now integrated into International Harvester) made a variety of plows and farm tools; the Austin Manufacturing Company (with ancestral roots in Skaneateles, New York) made grading machines to level the land; and Gould Pumps of Seneca Falls made steel water pumps. These industrial manufacturing companies had roots in Auburn and surrounding communities. Hence, even as Tubman started her small farm, the world of agricultural production was rapidly being revolutionized in ways that were probably difficult for her to see—even as field tiles were made from the clays of her property and her friends and benefactors expanded their industrial farming-implement businesses (see chapter 2).

Bradford described William Seward's efforts on Tubman's behalf: "Seward exerted himself in every possible way to procure her a pension from congress [*sic*], but red-tape proved too strong even for him, and her case was rejected, because it did not come under any recognized law" (1869, 4). Recognition of Harriet Tubman's service as a soldier (technically a nurse) would not be achieved until 1899, following a new effort in the 1890s that resulted in an act of Congress directed specifically at her service.[43]

When Tubman returned to her farm following the war, most of the neighboring households were engaged in family farming organized around the labor of couples and their children. In the 1860s, most of these families were relatively new arrivals. Some were from other parts of New York (Onondaga, Chenango, Oneida, and Saratoga Counties), but the majority were immigrants from outside the state and country (Pennsylvania, Connecticut, Massachusetts, New Hampshire, Maryland, Ireland, and Germany). Only one other household had more than one laborer in residence. Hiram Ingraham's household, located south of Tubman's farm, was being operated as a brickyard in 1865, although Ingraham is listed as a farmer. This property later became part of the Ross and Sullivan brickyard. Also on this farm were a group of men, including Ingraham's two sons and five boarders, all listed as laborers. The five nonfamily members are listed in the *Auburn City Directory* as having been born in Ireland, England, and Germany. It is highly likely they were brickyard workers.[44]

Harriet Tubman's brother John Stewart (also spelled "Steward" or "Stuart") is the first African American to be recorded as a brickyard laborer in the *Auburn City Directory*. He is identified as a laborer working in the South Street brickyards.[45] He first appears in Boyd's *Auburn City Directory* in 1863 and is listed annually as a brickyard laborer and teamster through 1876 and often as working for brickmaker Ira Swift.[46] Beginning in 1867, several other African American men began to be listed as laborers in the South Street brickyards,

43. In 1895, Tubman began to receive a widow's benefit, and in 1899 she finally was awarded veteran's benefits by a special act of Congress.

44. *Auburn City Directory*, 1865, Cayuga County Historian's Office.

45. John Stewart and others in Tubman's family made several trips back and forth from Fleming to St. Catharines between 1859 and 1861 to ensure that family members were not taken captive. He and his wife, Millie, are listed in the marriage records of Central Presbyterian Church in Auburn for 1863.

46. *Auburn City Directory*, 1862–63 to 1876–77, Cayuga County Historian's Office. Later records show John Stewart living in a house at the intersection of South Street and Swift Street in the City of Auburn. However, the 1880 US census lists a John Stewart employed as

including Jacob Jasper, Frank Brown, William Copes, Charles Harper, and Eli Rossum, along with Tubman's brother John Stewart, who is listed as a teamster rather than a laborer, his earlier designation. Of these men, William Copes and John Stewart continue to be listed in association with brickmaking through the mid-1870s, while the others drop from the record.

Nelson Davis (a.k.a. Charles Nelson), whom Tubman would marry on March 18, 1869, arrived in Auburn soon after Tubman's return from the war. He lived as a boarder in her house for three years before they were married.[47] A published announcement described the wedding scene at the Central Presbyterian Church, an integrated church populated by many of Tubman's white abolitionist friends.[48] The *Auburn Morning News*'s account of the wedding published on March 19 was written using a tone of familiarity, stating that Tubman, "the heroine of many a thrilling incident by fire and flood, the emancipator of a large number of her race and the faithful Union Scout, and Spy, took upon herself a husband and made one William Nelson [Nelson Davis] a happy man. Or at least that is the supposition. The audience was large, consisting of many of the friends of the parties and a large number of first families in the city." The article concludes: "We tender our congratulations to the happy bride and groom, and may they never see a less happy moment than when [Anthony] Shimer, that prince of a good fellow, spurred on by a prominent Democratic politician of the Third Ward, rushed frantically forward, and in an excited manner congratulated them on the happy event."[49]

Nelson Davis was active in Union veterans' organizations and a member of the Crocker Post of the Grand Army of the Republic (Storke 1879, 211). His name appears in the *Auburn City Directory* as a brickmaker working in

---

a grinder in a shop and a resident of Parker Avenue in Auburn (US census, 1880, Auburn and Fleming, Cayuga County Records Office).

47. Back in Maryland, Tubman's first husband, John Tubman, had been shot and killed by a neighbor, Robert Vincent, on September 30, 1867. Vincent was tried for murder but summarily acquitted in what at least one newspaper described in a headline as "An Outrage in Talbut County: A Colored Man Murdered" (*Baltimore News American*, Dec. 23, 1867; see also "Acquitted of Murder," *Baltimore News American*, Oct. 7, 1867).

48. The Wright family regularly provided transportation for Tubman's parents so they could attend Sunday school and church at Central Presbyterian Church in Auburn while Tubman was away at war.

49. Anthony Shimer would appear prominently in an infamous "gold swindle" in which Tubman was involved a mere four years later, in 1873. This story is recounted later in this chapter.

the South Street brickyards in 1875. He died of consumption in 1888.[50] In 1893, after Davis's death and the creation of a pension program for widows of Union soldiers, Harkless Bowley, Harriet Tubman's great-nephew, wrote an affidavit in which he asserted that he and Nelson Davis had been residents in Tubman's home, Bowley as a boarder for two years. Bowley also indicated that Davis was a brickmaker and that he, Bowley, had worked with Davis in a brickyard on Harriet Tubman's property (Humez 2003, 86). Davis was also active in the St. Marks AME Zion Church and served on its board of trustees from its founding in 1870 (Storke 1879, 211–12). He also was an active member of Auburn's Nehemiah Lodge 28 of the Colored Masonic Society.[51]

Davis first appears in the *Auburn City Directory* in 1871 in reference to his membership in the Colored Masonic Society, where he held the office of junior warden. "William Copes, (T) [tiler]," was also listed for the local Colored Masonic Society in 1871–72 and 1872–73, and Jacob Jasper is listed as tiler for 1873–74.[52] Both Davis and Copes worked in the South Street brickyards. By 1874–75, a much larger group of persons are listed in association with this chapter of the Colored Masonic Society, with Noah Gibbs serving as worshipful master,[53] G. S. Loguen as senior warden, H. S. Williams as junior warden, J. E. Smith as treasurer,[54] S. W. Johnson as secretary, W. F. DeWitt as

50. *Auburn City Directory*, 1874–75, Cayuga County Historian's Office; Nelson Davis, Record of Death, City of Auburn, Oct. 14, 1888, Health Department, Bureau of Vital Statistics, City of Auburn.

51. *Auburn City Directory*, 1871, 1872–73, 1873–74, Cayuga County Historian's Office.

52. Davis's and Copes's Masonic positions are listed in the *Auburn City Directory* for 1871–72 and 1872–73, with only Jacob Jasper (tiler) listed for 1873–74 (Cayuga County Historian's Office). As early as 1867, Jasper is listed as a brickmaker boarding in the tollhouse on the opposite side of the street just north of Tubman's property, where the creek crosses the road (running east to west). Jasper was still living at the tollhouse in 1874 and continued to work in the brickyards, but by 1888 he was listed as living at Harriet Tubman's residence at 176 South Street (*Auburn City Directory*, 1888). His last appearance in these records is in 1890 (*Auburn City Directory*, 1890).

53. In the US census of 1880 (Auburn and Fleming, Cayuga County Records Office), Noah Gibbs is listed as being sixty-six years old. He lived on Union Avenue (census house 30). He was the head of his household and worked as a cook. He was recorded as having been born in Vermont to a father from Maryland and a mother from Vermont. Gibbs was one of the largest contributors to Bradford's first biography of Tubman, contributing $100 (Kate Larson, personal communication to the author, Aug. 5, 2017).

54. In the US census of 1880 (Auburn and Fleming, Cayuga County Records Office), J. E. (John) Smith is listed as being thirty years old. He lived on Court Street (census house

senior deacon, Rev. William Bowman I as chaplain, Thomas Elliot as junior deacon,[55] and Jacob Jasper as tiler.[56] Many of these individuals had long-term relationships with Tubman and her family. For instance, Jacob Jasper lived for a time as a boarder in her house and worked in the South Street brickyards. He later bought a small property north of Tubman's, near the toll house on South Street, which he sold to Tubman and which she later transferred to her brother William.[57]

Money was a continual problem for the Tubman household, in part because of Harriet's communal philanthropic views and actions, whereby she was eager to support innumerable causes on behalf of African Americans in need. As noted earlier, she had many friends who were more than willing to support her but reluctant to assist in her many causes. This disconnect between Tubman's ideals and beliefs and those of her would-be sponsors shows up with consistency throughout her life. It is perhaps best expressed in a quote that Sarah Bradford credits to William Seward, who sometime in the late 1860s responded to Tubman's request for a contribution to southern freedmen, "You have worked for others long enough. . . . If you ask for a donation for *yourself* I will give it to you, but I will not help you rob yourself for others" (quoted in Bradford 1869, 112, emphasis in original). Seward's ideals projected a form of mid-nineteenth-century Republican support and reward for Tubman's individualism, self-sufficiency, and actions that was in sharp contrast with Tubman's far more communal form of philanthropy, which extended more broadly to many individuals and communities in need. Earl Conrad points out that Tubman did not follow Seward's advice and never

---

12). He was a boarder in the house and worked as a barber. He and his parents were from North Carolina.

55. In the US census of 1880 (Auburn and Fleming, Cayuga County Records Office), Thomas Elliot is listed as being thirty-eight years old. He lived on Union Avenue (census house 31), which means he was Noah Gibbs's next-door neighbor. He was the head of his household and worked as a laborer. He and both of his parents are reported to have been born in Maryland. He is probably the same person as Thomas H. Elliot (age twenty-five from Maryland) listed as a boarder in Harriet Tubman's house in the New York State census of 1865 (Auburn and Fleming, Cayuga County Records Office). That individual was married to Ann M. Elliot and was listed as a laborer in 1865. In this listing, his wife is listed as "Hellen," and she is recorded as having been born in Canada.

56. Neither Nelson Davis nor William Copes appears on this longer list of officers.

57. William came to Auburn from Canada to live with his son in 1889. He remained in Auburn and often worked for Tubman, assisting her with her hogs.

gave up in her appeals for a wide range of charitable causes, including freeman schools, the Salvation Army, and the Thompson AME Zion Church on Parker Street (1943, 211). Thus, although many of her supporters would continue to contribute to Tubman and provide for her personal needs, Tubman's appeals on behalf of others were often neglected and responded to negatively by even her closest personal supporters.

William Seward died on October 10, 1872. By the time his estate was settled on May 29, 1873, Tubman's irregularly paid debt on her house had grown to more than $1,500 (Green 1998). Seward's son Frederick forgave at least a portion of the loan; however, the balance was paid off with proceeds from Bradford's book.[58]

When William Seward died, the funeral for this former governor, US senator, and US secretary of state was a significant event in Auburn. In a later version of her biography of Tubman, Bradford wrote of Harriet at the funeral: "Just before the coffin was to be closed, a woman black as night stole quietly in, and laying a wreath of field flowers on his feet, and as quietly glided out again. This was a simple tribute of our sable friend and her last token of love and gratitude to her kind protector" (1886, 89–90).

Although cash funds were always in short supply, Tubman's farm produced grains and some milk and butter; she also raised hogs, and bricks were periodically produced on the back (east end) of the property. In addition, funds were generated through the antislavery network that extended from Auburn to Boston. Elizabeth Fitzhugh Birney, Gerrit Smith's niece, contributed an annual payment of $50, transmitted to Tubman through Martha Coffin Wright and later through Eliza Wright Osborne, who served as Tubman's patrons. The fact that Martha and Eliza were directly engaged in deciding how these funds would be dispersed is documented in Martha Wright's diary. An entry dated November 9, 1869, states, "I have to paddle down to Mr. Wise's and see what is needed most on the Mortgage or in the household. He has been so active in selling her *Life*, he may know."[59]

---

58. Frederick Seward to Harriet Tubman Davis, May 29, 1893, Cayuga County Deeds Book 169, p. 85, Cayuga County Clerk's Office. This document says that the transaction was completed "in consideration of $1500." Over the years, payments had been made, but Tubman had also drawn funds, thus adding debt to the account.

59. Martha Coffin Wright, diary, entry for Nov. 9, 1869, Wright Family Papers, Sophia Smith Collection, Smith College Library. Sarah Bradford's book *Scenes in the Life of Harriet Tubman* was published that year.

The US census for 1870 lists Tubman as age forty (she was actually forty-eight to fifty)[60] and as in residence along with her husband, Nelson Davis (forty), and her parents, Benjamin (eighty) and Ritta (eighty), along with William Leone, a twenty-two-year-old Black male who is listed as a laborer born in Canada. No children are listed, and no one in the household is listed as being able to read or write. Harriet's employment is given as "keeping house" (table 5.3).[61]

Tubman and her household continued to maintain themselves by growing a variety of garden plants, raising stock such as pigs and chickens, and growing grain on the farm. Numerous accounts describe her selling and bartering vegetables, fruit, and meat. Accounts in Martha Coffin Wright's diary for the 1860s and early 1870s mention several transactions with Tubman and details on social exchanges. On August 31, 1868, Harriet came to see Ellen Wright Garrison (1840–1931) and her babies and brought them some fresh eggs. Ellen had married William Lloyd Garrison Jr. of Boston. During the visit, Wright purchased some "late peas" from Harriet. Peas do not show up as a crop in the 1875 agricultural census for Tubman's property (see the later discussion of this agricultural census and table 5.5) but were among the kitchen garden plants grown for household use and informal sales. In October 1872, Wright bought a large basketful of pears and apples from Tubman, whose farm had both apple and pear trees.[62] Tubman and perhaps others in her household also made baskets, as evidenced by an entry in Wright's diary for January 14, 1871, that indicates that Harriet sold her a "hoop basket" for sixty-two and a half cents.[63] Harriet Tubman is known to have been involved in cleaning the homes of Martha Wright and Lazette Worden. Later, Eliza Wright Osborne employed her to care for Eliza's children. On May 2, 1870, Eliza hired Tubman for spring cleaning that included having her "help wash [clothes]," and

60. Tubman is generally referred to as someone who is older than her chronological age, but in this census, perhaps in contrast to the age of her parents, the census taker cuts about ten years from her age.

61. US census, 1870, Auburn and Fleming, Cayuga County Records Office.

62. William Seward is also likely to have planted the apple trees in the orchard on the twenty-five-acre farmstead because his wife (and her sister) had inherited that farm prior to it being sold to John Farmer and then to Tubman. Later, in 1881, the Seward family planted hundreds of pear and peach trees along with a few apple, apricot, and nectarine trees on the lot south of Tubman's farm; however, there is no indication of the productivity of these trees (Expense Ledger, Dec. 1881–Feb. 1882, Seward Papers).

63. Martha Coffin Wright, diary, entry for Jan. 14, 1871, Wright Family Papers.

TABLE 5.3

UNITED STATES CENSUS, AUBURN AND FLEMING, CAYUGA COUNTY, NEW YORK, 1870

Name	Age	Sex	Color	Profession	Value of Real Estate	Birthplace	Cannot Read	Cannot Write	Male Citizen, 21 years+
Davis, Nelson	40	M	B	laborer		VA	1	1	1
Tubman, Harriet	40	F	B	keeping house	$600	VA	1	1	
Stewart, Ritta	80	F	B			MD	1	1	
Stewart, Benjamin	80	M	B			MD	1	1	1
Leone, Wm.	22	M	B	laborer		Canada	1	1	1

Source: US census, 1870, Auburn and Fleming, Cayuga County Records Office, Auburn, NY.

Harriet Tubman was probably forty-eight years old at the time of the 1870 census, and Nelson Davis was probably twenty years her junior. Based on military records and later census records, Nelson Davis was probably younger than thirty rather than forty at the time of the 1870 census. Note that Tubman's parents, Benjamin and Ritta (Harriet, "Ritte," "Rit") are listed under the surname "Stewart" instead of "Ross." The Stewart surname was also used by Tubman's brothers John and William.

then "she and Mary cleaned the front parlor. . . . Frank Round's man helped Lawrence shake carpet and Mary and Harriet got it done in time for Mary and Lizzie to go to the wedding after the tea was ready." The following day, May 3, 1870, Eliza wrote that she "had Harriet Tubman to clean around front door & entry and steps & take nails out of the front chamber carpet."[64] These personal accounts describe Tubman assisting with the removal of the heavy winter carpets with the arrival of spring and as positioned working alongside Eliza's children. They provide a sense that Tubman was a familiar person at the Osborne home, which at 99 South Street was only a short distance from Tubman's farm. Tubman frequently cared for children and on occasion took pay for the boarding of children. Helen Tatlock described to Earl Conrad how Tubman would care for children of employed mothers, often receiving only a "trifle for their care."[65] Tubman also cared for the five children of Congressman Theodore Pomeroy (Humez 2003, 172).[66]

Many people who lived in Harriet Tubman's house were not recorded by census takers. One of these persons was Harriet Tubman's great-nephew Harkless Bowley. As an elderly man in 1939, Bowley was contacted by Earl Conrad, who was doing research on Tubman for his book (Conrad 1943). Bowley responded to Conrad's questions in a series of letters, where he indicated that he had lived with his grandparents and Aunt Harriet when they came back from Canada for a year or two before his family moved back to Maryland.[67] During this time, he knew Nelson Davis and John Stewart, one of Tubman's brothers. Bowley described his Uncle John as being afflicted with rheumatism and as having a bad hand, which meant he could not work. However, he recalled that John Stewart "had a fine team of horses and hired a man to drive them" and that "for a while Uncle John's youngest son worked his team." Bowley recalled a time when "I helped him load the wagon—both of us were quite young. Afterwards uncle William [William Henry Stewart Sr.],

64. Eliza Wright Osborne to Martha Wright, May 2 and 3, 1870, box 13, Osborne Family Papers.

65. Mrs. William Tatlock, statement to Earl Conrad, 1939, Earl Conrad/Harriet Tubman Collection, Schomburg Center.

66. Congressman Pomeroy later became mayor of the City of Auburn. His family was also associated with the abolition movement, and he was a law partner with David Wright (Martha's husband and Eliza's father). He was instrumental in finally securing Tubman's veteran's benefits through a special act of Congress.

67. Harkless Bowley to Earl Conrad, Jan. 4, 1939, Earl Conrad/Harriet Tubman Collection, Schomburg Center, copy on file in the Harriet Tubman Home Collection, Harriet Tubman Home, Inc., Auburn, NY.

who at the time still lived in St. Catherine[s], came to live with Aunt Harriet in Auburn and later died there."[68]

In the spring of 1873, the local press reported a light-hearted story involving a huge goose egg produced by one of Harriet Tubman's geese. The account projects the esteem for Tubman within the community while telling us not only that Tubman had geese on her property but also that they produced eggs of grand proportion. On April 4, 1873, a goose egg measuring "12 longitudinal inches and weighing ten and a half ounces" was astonishing the locals at George L. Parker's store on State Street. Typical of stories related to Harriet Tubman, the reporter wrapped the story of the egg around Tubman's heroic past: "This monstrosity was done by a goose owned by the celebrated Harriet Tubman, a lady renowned in the history of the late war, whose secret services in the Union cause were of immense value to our government." The report goes on to indicate that Tubman and the goose reside "on the South street road, near the toll gate," and concludes, "She certainly owns the boss goose of the continent, and for her sake we wish it might lay a golden egg each day, and never be killed" (*Auburn Morning News*, Apr. 4, 1873).

Later that year Tubman was involved in an unfortunate swindle. In October 1873, she and her brother John Stewart became involved in what became known as the "Gold Swindle and the Greenback Robbery," or simply the "$2,000 gold swindle." The story involved considerable intrigue in its day and was an event long remembered within the community. The intricacy of details reported provide insights into the social relations and interactions of Tubman and her surrounding community. As initially reported in the *Auburn Daily Bulletin* on October 6, 1873, and retold many times in many ways over the years, Harriet Tubman became enmeshed in a cash-for-gold deal in which $2,000 in cash, or "greenbacks" fronted by Anthony Shimer, were stolen. Shimer is the same gentlemen who had come forward so vivaciously with kind words at Tubman's wedding.

A man going by the name of Stevenson represented himself to Tubman's brother as having access to a large quantity of "Southern gold" valued at more than $5,000, which he would be willing to trade for $2,000 in paper money.

---

68. Harkless Bowley to Earl Conrad, Aug. 24, 1939, Earl Conrad/Harriet Tubman Collection, copy on file in the Harriet Tubman Home Collection. Tubman's brother William apparently returned from Canada shortly after 1890. He was present in her household for the 1900 US census and remained in residence until 1911. When Tubman became ill in 1911 and could not care for her household, her brother was removed to the Cayuga County Almshouse in Sennett, New York, where he lived until he died (see chapter 8).

John Stewart, unable to raise the money, asked his sister for assistance. Tubman took Stevenson and his partner, John Thomas, into her home while she tried to arrange funding from bankers. Once ensconced in her home, they further endeared themselves to her by convincing her that they knew her cousin Alfred Bowley. Tubman then approached many of her wealthy friends in Auburn, most of whom warned her that these people were most likely robbers. Neither David Wright nor John Osborne would have anything to do with the deal. Tubman's neighbor John Mead, a former sheriff, was concerned and came by to see Tubman in an effort to warn her off the deal.[69] But by then she had contacted another local businessman, Anthony Shimer, who had agreed to provide the money. Anthony Shimer was wealthy and known as a risk taker.

Shimer provided the money, and Tubman went with Stevenson into the woods to meet someone called Harris, who had a heavy box, while the others waited at a local tavern. From this point on, the accounts involve a convoluted tale of misadventure, including Tubman's fear of ghosts in the woods and her being chloroformed and losing consciousness, only to awaken to find herself bound, gagged, and bruised. Meanwhile, her brother, Shimer, and his banker, Charles O'Brian, became alarmed and set out to find her. By this time, Tubman had awakened and was making her way through the woods when they found her cut and confused, and together they went back to the meeting point to find a trunk full of rocks instead of gold. Tubman was then taken to the home of her friend Emily Howland in Sherwood to recuperate.[70] Shimer lost his speculative money and tried to pin the blame and the loss on Tubman. John Stewart told reporters that he was out the cost of the "hire of a livery rig, and this expense and loss of time," "with his after tribulation [sic] and fear of ruin are all that he has realized for his trouble." Ultimately, it was Shimer who in this and other actions lost his reputation.[71] Within weeks, the sensational reporting in the local Auburn press had spawned national headlines under the headline "A $2000 Gold Swindle—A Mysterious Affair—An

69. Mead lived on South Street, across the street from Tubman.

70. Emily Howland was a classmate of sisters Frances Miller Seward and Lazette Miller Worden.

71. Shimer publicly asked Tubman and Stewart for repayment, but Tubman and Stewart claimed that it was Shimer's deal. "They claim that if Mr. Shimer had lent them the money, he would not have carried it to Smith's Corners, or Poplar Ridge, in his own possession as they say he did" (*Auburn Weekly News and Democrat*, Oct. 9, 1873). Despite this setback, Anthony Shimer died a wealthy man.

Innocent Auburnian Robbed—No Trace of the Thieves" (*New York Evening Telegram*, Oct. 20, 1873).

Stories of the event provide considerable personal detail on Tubman and her relations with others in the Auburn community. Her brother John was described as an "honest and industrious man of 55 years" who was at the time employed as a teamster with the Osborne Manufacturing Company in Auburn. Nelson Davis, Tubman's husband, was employed not on Tubman's property but as a laborer and brickmaker in the neighboring Pierce brickyard on South Street (*Auburn Weekly News and Democrat*, Oct. 9, 1873). We see continuity in relationships with the Wright and Osborne families (who advised against the deal). Interestingly, in matters of family and care it was the women of those households who tended to interact most frequently with Tubman, but in matters of money Tubman turned to the men, and in this situation and several other interactions they tended to offer skeptical caution.

The story also projects information about movement within the region. John Stewart's position as a teamster put him on the region's roadways. He first encountered the swindling highwaymen in Seneca Falls through mutual acquaintances within the African American community.[72] Negotiations related to the transactions took place in Seneca Falls, at Tubman's home in Auburn, and in the hills of Fleming (between Owasco and Cayuga Lakes). At the end of the story, Tubman recuperated at the home of her friends the Howlands in Sherwood (midway between Owasco Lake and Cayuga Lake). The events initially shook Harriet Tubman; however, Emily Howland later commented that within a short amount of time Tubman was regaling her household with colorful tales of her travels and adventures.

Tubman appears to have been compromised by the very traits that were her strengths: her strong beliefs, compassion, and trust. She did not see the danger and did not heed the many explicit warnings. Once in the woods, she knew things were not right and in reviewing the situation commented on the fear of ghosts and spirits as she realized the dire trap into which she had been lulled. She retained much of her reputation, but numerous reports of the event describe her naïveté, gullibility, innocence, and trust. There is no indication that this event had any profound impact on her personal relations with families such as the Osbornes, Wordens, and Sewards. Records show that she continued to provide care for their children, cleaned their houses, and sold

72. This mirrors the type of free Black social networks described more generally for settlements across the Northeast in LaRoche 2014b.

provisions to them from her farm. Moreover, Tubman continued to receive small gifts from throughout the Auburn community as well as more broadly from her abolitionist friends in the Northeast. Meanwhile, John Stewart continued to work for the Osborne Manufacturing Company as a teamster. Still, one wonders if this event did not solidify concern about her care of funds and work against her later efforts on behalf of the elderly.

The New York State census of 1875 (table 5.4) scrambles family names and relationships and mixes up Harriet Tubman and her mother, who was also called "Harriet" or "Ritta" (Larson 2004, 80–81).[73] However, it provides important details on the construction of Tubman's house by defining it as a wood-frame structure, and it lists Nelson Davis's occupation as a brickmaker. In 1874 and 1875, New York State conducted detailed agricultural censuses that included considerable detail on the productivity of her farm. The agricultural census valued the farm at $1,400, while the tax register for that year listed the value of her house as $350. The value of buildings other than the farmhouse is listed as $100, stock at $250, and farm tools and implements at $25 (table 5.5). In 1874, two and a half acres of land were plowed, and four and a half were in pasturage. A half-acre plot planted in potatoes yielded fifty bushels. No peas, beans, or root crops were reported. The only orchard crops reported were apples growing on six trees. A few years later, records of the Seward family indicate that they planted a considerable number of trees on the property that they owned just south of Tubman's, and it is likely that she had access to the fruits from this orchard. Tubman's farm had two milk cows that produced 300 pounds of butter. Milk was produced, but none was formally sold at market. The farm also had one horse and one mule. Different figures were given for the number of pigs on the farm for 1874 and 1875. In 1874, only one pig is reported, but eleven had been slaughtered, producing 2,500 pounds of pork. The following year, 1875, there were seven pigs, and only one had been slaughtered. The value of chickens on the property in 1874 was listed at $30, while the value of chickens sold was $5, and the value of eggs sold was $5. For 1875, no values are given for poultry or eggs, apparently because the year was not finished when the census was taken (table 5.5).

As the years passed, the composition of Tubman's household changed. Tubman's father, Ben Ross, died in 1871. On October 14, 1879, the *Auburn*

---

73. New York State census, 1875, Auburn and Fleming, Cayuga County Records Office, including agricultural census. Even though Harriet Tubman was well known, on several occasions we find that her name is misspelled or listed incorrectly as "Charlotte Tubman" or "Tupman" or "Maryette Davis" or that, as in this case, she is confused with her mother.

TABLE 5.4

NEW YORK STATE CENSUS, 1875, AUBURN AND FLEMING, CAYUGA COUNTY, NEW YORK

Dwelling Material	Value	Name	Age	Sex	Color	Relation to Head of Family	Birthplace	Now Married	Now Widowed	Single	Profession	Place of Employment	Voter— Native	Over 21, Illiterate
Frame	$600	Nelson Davis	37	M	B	[head]	NC	1			Brickmaker	Fleming	1	1
		Maryette Davis	40	F	B	wife	MD	1						1
		Harriet Stewart	80	F	B	[wife's] mother	MD		W					1

Source: New York State census, 1875, Auburn and Fleming, Cayuga County, Cayuga County Records Office, Auburn, NY.

This census lists Harriet Tubman Davis as "Maryette Davis" and again underestimates her age. Even though Tubman was the owner of the property, Nelson Davis, her husband, is listed as the head of household.

TABLE 5.5

NEW YORK STATE AGRICULTURAL CENSUS, 1874–75

Year	Name of Owner, Agent, Manager of Farm	Acres: Improved Land	Acres: Unimproved Land	Farm	Farm Buildings Other Than Dwelling	Stock	Tools and Implements	Gross Sales from Farm
1874	Nelson Davis	7	0	$1,400	$100	$250	$25	$0
1875	Nelson Davis	7	0	$1,400	$100	$250	$25	$0

Year	Name of Owner, Agent, Manager of farm	Grasslands: Acres Plowed	Grasslands: Acres in Pasture	Grasslands: Meadow	Grasslands: Meadow, Bushels of Grass Seed
1874	Nelson Davis	2.5	4.5	0	0
1875	Nelson Davis	2.0	4.5	0	0

Year	Name of Owner, Agent, Manager of Farm	Orchards: Kinds of Trees	Orchards: No. of Trees	Orchards: Barrels of Cider	Maple Sugar	Maple Molasses	Grapes	Honey and Wax	Uncnumerated Produce
1874	Nelson Davis	Apple	6		0	0	0	0	0
1875	Nelson Davis	Apple	6		0	0	0	0	0

Year	Name of Owner, Agent, Manager of Farm	Potatoes: Acres Planted, 1874	Potatoes: Bushels Harvested	Peas	Beans	Root Crops
1874	Nelson Davis	½	50	0	0	0
1875	Nelson Davis	½	not harvested	0	0	0

(continued on following page)

TABLE 5.5 (CONTINUED)

NEW YORK STATE AGRICULTURAL CENSUS, 1874–75

Year	Name of Owner, Agent, Manager of farm	Heifer Calves	Bulls of All Ages	Milch Cows	Milk Sent to Factory	Cattle Killed for Beef	Butter: Pounds Made by Families	Cheese: Pounds Made by Families	Milk Sold in Market
1874	Nelson Davis	0	0	2	0	0	300	0	0
1875	Nelson Davis	0	0	2	0	0			0

Year	Name of Owner, Agent, Manager of Farm	Swine: Pigs	Swine: No. Slaughtered	Swine: Pounds of Pork	Sheep	Poultry: Value	Poultry: Value	Poultry: Value of Eggs Sold	Value of Manures and Fertilizers Bought
1874	Nelson Davis	1	11	2,500	0	$30	$5	$5	$0
1875	Nelson Davis	7			0				$0

Year	Name of Owner, Agent, Manager of Farm	Horses: Colts	Horses: Two Years Old and Over	Mules
1874	Nelson Davis	0	1	1
1875	Nelson Davis	0	1	1

Source: New York State census, 1874–75, including agricultural census, Auburn and Fleming, Cayuga County, Cayuga County Records Office, Auburn, NY.

News and Bulletin reported the death of "Harriet Steward," speculating that she might have been the oldest woman in New York State if not the entire country. The notice describes her as Harriet Tubman's mother.[74] According to the paper, Ritta's funeral service was held at the AME Zion Church on Washington Street. She had lived for nearly a century, and like the other elderly family and friends who came to reside with Tubman, she had been brought up in slavery but lived her final years in freedom in Tubman's household, surrounded by family and friends.

A Fire, a New Brick House, and a Place for Elderly African Americans

The 1880s began with traumatic events for Tubman and her family. Not only had Tubman's mother recently died, but a fire burned Tubman's wood-frame house to the ground on February 10, 1880. Details related to this fire were not known until excavations recovered remains from the fire. Archaeological artifacts from an ash lens indicated that the fire had occurred between 1880 and 1882, which in turn provided a timeframe that allowed for careful inspection of newspaper records. Two newspaper accounts of the fire were quickly found. The first, "Another Conflagration," details a fire at the home of Harriet Tubman Davis: "The residence of Harriet Tubman Davis, the once famous Union scout and spy, located near the South street toll gate, was entirely consumed by fire at an early hour this morning. Only a small portion of the household goods were saved. The conflagration is said to have originated from a defective stovepipe stuck through a hole in a lintern and which was utilized for a chimney" (*Evening Auburnian*, Feb. 10, 1880). A second newspaper account in the *Auburn News and Bulletin* provides more details on the fire but refers to Tubman as the renowned "Charlotte Tubman." It describes how the fire was first detected at eight o'clock in the morning and states that Tubman's house, "two doors beyond the tollgate was destroyed by fire." "The house which was of wood was small and dry, burning rapidly, and no alarm was given." It went on to indicate that the point of origin was in the rear or "kitchen part." Typical of reports dealing with Tubman, the account

74. The Ross-Stewart family tree indicates that Harriet Tubman's mother, Ritta (also "Ritte" or "Rit") was born Harriet Green around 1785 in Dorchester County, Maryland, and died in Auburn, New York, on October 8, 1880 (Larson 2004, 296). Ritta's death is recorded in "Record of Current Events—Local Necrology," Cayuga County Historical Society, Auburn, NY.

refers to her as "renowned in the history of the war for the Union as a scout and liberator of slaves." It also reminds the reader that a few years hence she had "achieved a still fresher notoriety from her supposed innocent connection with the party of colored confidence operators who robbed one of our prominent citizens of two thousand dollars, on pretense of exchanging confederate gold for his greenbacks." The mention of both events says much about how Tubman was viewed in the broader community. The fact that the reporter got her name wrong also suggests the impact of the passage of time since the Civil War. The article concludes by describing how the fire "renders the historic woman homeless" and recognizes that the damage to her house "is a severe blow to her in her old age" but positively suggests that "there is no doubt she will receive aid to enable her to regain a home" (*Auburn News and Bulletin*, Feb. 10, 1880). The latter statement projects her continued position of esteem. With her house burned to the ground, Tubman was effectively homeless for a short period of time until it could be rebuilt.

The US census of 1880 was made before Tubman's brick house was constructed. It lists Harriet Tubman as being forty-four, although she was nearly sixty. Her husband, Nelson Davis, is listed as forty. Gertie Davis is listed as their adopted daughter. It is probable that Gertie was informally adopted or taken in by the couple as a baby. Also present are Tubman's brother John Stewart as well as his wife, Millie, and their son, Moses. Nelson Davis was reported as a farmer, while John Stewart was employed as a teamster, and both adult women are listed as "keeping house" (table 5.6). Larson suggests that Tubman took shelter with her brother John after the fire, and it is perhaps his household that is recorded by the census taker in 1880.[75]

Harriet Tubman's new brick house on her farm appears to have been built quickly on the ruins of the site of her earlier wood-frame house. Construction of this new house was completed in late 1881 or early 1882, as indicated by a

75. It is unclear exactly what house John and Millie Stewart and their son, Moses, lived in during this period. The ordering of census records indicate that it was in proximity to Tubman's farm. It is possible that they were living in an outbuilding on Tubman's farm because there is a record of a second house burning on her property in 1903. The house that burned is likely to have been on John Farmer's farm, but it might have been used by Tubman. They could also have been in residence a bit farther north in a house that at the time was owned by Jacob Jasper, which was later sold to Tubman in 1890, apparently on behalf of her brother William Stewart Sr., who is later listed as the resident owner of this property through the 1890s and early 1900s. However, there is no record of a formal transfer of this property from Tubman to her brother.

TABLE 5.6

UNITED STATES CENSUS, 1880, AUBURN AND FLEMING, CAYUGA COUNTY, NEW YORK

Names	Color	Sex	Age	Relationship to Head of Household	Single	Married	Widowed	Profession
Davis, Nelson	B	M	40	[head]		1		Farmer
Davis, Harriet	B	F	44	wife		1		Housekeeper
Davis, Gertie	B	F	4	adopted daughter	1			
Stewart, John	B	M	65			1		Teamster
Stewart, Millie	B	F	61	wife [of John Stewart]		1		Housekeeper
Stewart, Moses	B	M	27	son [of John Stewart]	1			

Source: US census, 1880, Auburn and Fleming, Cayuga County, Cayuga County Records Office, Auburn, NY.

Both the 1870 and 1880 censuses indicate Nelson Davis was forty, but the 1880 census is far more accurate (see table 5.3 for the 1870 census). Harriet Tubman is listed as being forty-four in 1880, but she was probably about fifty-eight. It is interesting that most accounts of Tubman describe her as older than her actual age, but the 1870 and 1880 censuses significantly underestimate her age.

jump in the property value in the tax records of 1882, and by 1883 the value had more than doubled from its prefire value.[76] A handwritten note that is part of the Stewart Family Papers describes the Harriet Tubman Homestead as being "three story red brick dwelling of nine rooms: 1st floor—basement kitchen and cellar; 2nd floor—living room, parlor hall, two bedrooms; 3rd floor—family bed rooms."[77]

Although the land in the immediate vicinity of Tubman's farm remained in use as small farms or brickyards, the City of Auburn was growing. By the late 1880s, records begin to show plans for new roads and subdivisions in the area, and by the 1890s there are subtle indications of competition between urban and rural lifeways in the area. Houses were constructed on many tracts on the north side of Metcalf Avenue in the City of Auburn, and plans were made to begin subdivision of the former Danforth farm by the Osborne family, who had acquired the farm, located two properties north of Tubman's farm. An *Auburn News Bulletin* announcement on July 23, 1881, describes plans for the creation of a new street running east from South Street at the extreme south limit of the City of Auburn, which the report calls "Danforth Avenue."[78] A map from the era includes the name "Danforth Street" penciled in, but the street was never constructed.[79]

Tubman's house fire was not her only economic setback during the early 1880s. By this time, her hog-raising enterprise appears to have grown considerably. The agricultural census of 1874 and 1875 had shown that hogs were the most significant economic product of her farm (table 5.5). On July 11, 1884, however, the *Evening Auburnian* published an account of the traumatic poisoning of forty of her hogs. This notice brings to light the scale of Harriet Tubman's hog-raising enterprise as well as the complex social relations associated with her activities on the farm:

76. Town of Fleming, Cayuga County Tax Records, 1883, Cayuga County Clerk's Office.

77. Handwritten note, n.d. (c. post-1908), Stewart Family Papers, Harriet Tubman Home Collection.

78. This street would have run east to west from South Street along the boundary of the former Flavel Danforth farm located north of the city line.

79. Auburn city map, 1882, Cayuga County Historian's Office. During this period, a long formal driveway was constructed down the center of the property that Tubman would acquire in 1896 for her Home for the Aged. In the early 1900s, this driveway begins to be referred to as "Danforth Avenue" in the *Auburn City Directory* (even though it is well south of the placement of the planned Danforth Avenue).

Harriet Tubman's Hogs: Harriet Tubman was in the city yesterday. She is the chief of the garbage system in this city. She has a swine ranch just outside the city limits southward, and thither she conveys the garbage of the city, and the swine find substance on the refuse collected at the back doors of Auburn. Harriet was in the city yesterday, as before stated, and brought news that she is losing her hogs. Forty of them have already died, and she fears she will lose them all.

At the outset of her losses she feared hog-cholera or some other plague had attacked her herd. But the symptoms did not confirm this view, and indications pointed to some kind of poisoning.

And now Harriet has solved the mystery by simple process of reasoning. She cites the fact that in the spring time people clean house.

How many men there are who can bear sad testimony to that fact! And in cleaning house all the rat poison, all the bed bug poison, all the cockroach exterminators and all the fig poison—all these are swept up and then the house cleaner looks about in the dire confusion that attends these yearly crises, and wonders where she'll throw the poison fly papers and all the rest that has been swept up.

The slop pall or garbage bucket is nearest, and that's the safest place. And then the garbage that feeds Harriet Tubman's swine is cast into the same receptacle. So, Harriet reasons that the devastation of her hog herds is chargeable to that vernal night mare—house cleaning.

Harriet's garden is now being heaped with the city's refuse, because of decreased means of consumption and because of the increased quantity of the gatherings by the carts.

No doubt Mr. Anthony Shimer will sympathize deeply with Harriet who losses, because she at one time is said to have caused him to be an object of public sympathy to the amount of $2,000 good money.

This account provides evidence that Tubman's stock of hogs had grown significantly since the 1874–75 agricultural census (table 5.5). By July 11, she had lost forty but still had more, as indicated by the statement that "she fears she will lose them all." The article recounts how as the hogs started to die, she and others were at a loss as to why, thinking that perhaps they had encountered some form of hog cholera, but the symptoms were wrong. Ultimately, it was decided that the rat, cockroach, and fig poison as well as the fly paper thrown in household garbage that she had collected for her hogs from houses throughout Auburn were the probable cause. This story is indicative of a change in attitudes toward vermin among the people of the city as they procured a wide array of poisons to clear, clean, and sanitize their houses.

The article describes her farm as a "swine ranch" located just outside the city limits, to which she conveyed garbage from the "backdoors" of Auburn households. It notes that with the loss of these hogs "Harriet's garden is now being heaped with the city's refuse," indicating that people accustomed to delivering garbage to Tubman's farm continued to do so even though she no longer had enough pigs to consume it all. It also suggests a broader problem of garbage in a growing city by noting the "increased quantity of the gatherings by the carts." The story also revives memories of the gold swindle in 1873 by saying that "no doubt Mr. Anthony Shimer will sympathize deeply with Harriet."[80] The financial loss to Tubman and her household was significant, but it did not stop her from raising hogs, and they were to appear prominently in public accounts relating to her and her properties for the rest of her life.[81]

A very vocal and agitated Harriet Tubman made the local news only a few months later when she came to the county jail to demand the release of her nephew Moses Stewart (son of John Stewart), who "was doing a term of thirty days for pork stealing." This account defines Tubman as "the famed negress of the City" and describes how she was "attacked by the 'power' and began marching about the building, praying singing and shouting." It went on to tell how she "declared that she would keep it up until Stewart was released, but she was eventually persuaded to desist" (*Auburn News and Bulletin*, Oct. 13, 1884). This is one of several accounts of Tubman's very verbal role in protesting or celebrating in which praying, singing, shouting, and spirituality are mentioned. The article projects Tubman not only as a famous person but also as a person moved by spirituality. It could be viewed as projecting her either as a strong-willed and free-spirited person or as someone who when provoked was a bit out of control or acted beyond the norms of society.

In 1886, Sarah Bradford published a new version of Harriet Tubman's biography with the title *Harriet: Moses of Her People*. This version of the book was written to provide a new wave of financial support for Tubman. Bradford also specifically mentions her desire to assist Tubman with funding for her dreams of creating a home for the aged and a school for girls. The publication of Bradford's new volume renewed Tubman's public popularity, and Tubman was invited to many forums and events related to the publication of the book.

80. This correlation of past and current losses projects a rather cruel perspective on the loss by invoking the continued community memory of Tubman's and Shimer's involvement in the $2,000 "gold swindle" eleven years earlier, in 1873.

81. Although we cannot be certain that all of Tubman's hogs were market ready, the loss of forty hogs may well have exceeded ten thousand pounds of pork.

In October 1886, she traveled to Boston and was hosted by her longtime abolitionist friend Franklin Sanborn. During the visit, Sanborn also arranged for a photo session so that both the books and the photographs could be sold to raise funds.

In Auburn, Harriet Tubman was the guest of honor at "a tea for Harriet Tubman" hosted by Emma Paddock Telford (Mrs. W. H. Telford) on April 6, 1888 (figure 2.2).[82] The event illustrates the fact that Tubman recurrently interacted in the formal parlors of the wealthy white population of Auburn and was often a special, honored guest. This tea party appears to have been designed specifically to honor Tubman, to renew her acquaintance with the leading women of Auburn, and to sell copies of Bradford's biography for Tubman's benefit. She is described as "an old colored lady and quite a historical character. She acted as spy for the Union army during the Rebellion" (*Auburn Bulletin*, Apr. 6, 1888). During this era, tea parties were an important form of social engagement, particularly for women. They afforded an opportunity to gather and discuss the issues of the day. As indicated by this and the previously described tea party at Eliza Osborne's house in 1903 that Susan B. Anthony attended (see chapter 2), in this region tea parties were also often used to organize on behalf of women's rights and suffrage issues.

A photograph taken in 1887 or 1888 shows Harriet Tubman and the residents of her house (figure 5.1). The photograph was taken facing Tubman's barn. Harriet Tubman is standing on the left of the photograph holding a pan from which she had probably just fed her chickens. This photograph provides a glimpse of the range of people living in her household. Next to Tubman is her adopted daughter, Gertie Davis, and seated in the foreground is her husband, Nelson Davis. The other two seated adults are Pop Alexander and the elderly Aunte Sarah Parker, or Blind Aunty Parker—dressed in white, holding a cane, and seated next to the family dog and Nelson. The three children in the photograph are Lee Cheney, Walter Green, and Tubman's great-niece Dora Stewart. The presence of these children shows that although the household is generally referred to in regard to its more elderly residents, children were present and made up a significant part of the household. The ongoing role of children at the site was confirmed by the number of children's toys, marbles, doll parts, and miniature tea wares recovered from the site. A family dog

82. Emma Paddock Telford was a long-term friend of Harriet Tubman who wrote an extensive account of Tubman's life for the *Auburn Citizen* (June 11, 1914) about a year after Tubman's death.

is also present in the photograph. The tax records for Tubman's farm show that she almost always had at least one dog, and on occasion a second dog is attributed to Nelson Davis.

Davis was a part of the Tubman household from 1867 until he died at age forty-five of complications due to tuberculosis on October 18, 1888. The following year John Stewart died. He was a brother she had brought to Canada in 1854 and who came to live with her in her farmhouse in Fleming. The two had been very close since her move to New York.

Throughout the post–Civil War era, some members of Harriet Tubman's family remained in Canada but continued to interact with Tubman. Her nephew William Henry Stewart Jr. and his family were well established in the Auburn area, living at 64 Garrow Street.[83] In 1889, her brother William Henry Stewart Sr. came to Auburn from Canada to join his son's family. Initially, he lived with them, but then he moved in with Tubman and finally acquired his own house and quarter-acre plot of land. In the early 1890s, another of William Henry Stewart Sr.'s sons, John Isaac Stewart, came from Canada after his wife died giving birth. John Isaac Stewart's daughter Eva Katherine Helena Harriet Stewart was taken to Auburn to live with her grandfather, William Henry, after John Isaac's death left her an orphan. Eva Katherine remained in the Tubman household along with her great-aunt Harriet and her grandfather, William Henry Stewart Sr., into the early 1900s.

Activities within the Tubman household proceeded rather quietly through the early 1890s. However, typical for a household in which the elderly were residents, one of her elderly charges would die and be replaced by others who came to Tubman for support. Entering the 1890s, the oldest resident in the Tubman household was Aunte Sarah Parker.[84] A detailed obituary describing Parker's life stated that "for years she has been unable to assist herself and has depended entirely on the kindness of her benefactress who has been all that a daughter could be." The account states that "it was quite affecting to witness the grief manifested by Miss Tubman over the death of the old woman who was undoubtedly the oldest women in this part of the country." Attending the funeral were the AME Zion presiding elder John L. Thomas of Binghamton

83. US census, 1880, Auburn and Fleming, Cayuga County Records Office.

84. Sarah Parker is not listed for Tubman's household in any of the census records, but she is in pictured in the photograph taken in 1887 or 1888 at the Tubman residence (figure 5.1). Discussing the period of the mid-1870s, Larson describes Parker as being "a seventy five year old blind woman who may have been a longtime friend or relative from Maryland" (2004, 260).

and Rev. J. R. Dangerfield, pastor of the local AME Zion Church, with Mrs. Winslow and Miss Jackson singing "That Like a River" (*Auburn Bulletin*, Feb. 10, 1890).

Throughout her life, Harriet Tubman had strong spiritual and religious beliefs and engaged with many churches in the Auburn area.[85] In 1891, the local AME Zion Church was renamed the Thompson AME Zion Church when it moved to Parker Street in Auburn.[86] During the 1890s, her ties with this church became more apparent.[87] Through the 1890s, she was closely associated with the AME Zion Church leadership, and they were to play an important role in assisting with the creation of the Home for the Aged at her residence in 1895 and ultimately took charge of the Home. Her brother William Stewart Sr. and many other family members are listed in the Parker Street church register from the earliest records in the mid-1890s. They remained active members for the rest of their lives. Harriet herself is not listed among members of the congregation or any of its committees, though. Meanwhile, she was involved with a variety of philanthropic efforts on behalf of the broader African American community. These efforts involved the AME Zion Church and other congregations, including the Methodist Episcopal (ME) Church of Auburn. An example of her philanthropy can be seen in a letter she dictated to be sent to Mary Wright thanking Wright for the clothes that she had sent from Boston as part of the two churches' clothing drive on behalf of "destitute colored children."[88]

When the New York State census was taken in 1892, only two residents were listed for the Tubman household, Harriet T. Davis (listed as age sixty-seven) and Winnie Stewart (age seventy-four). Tubman's brother William Henry Stewart Sr. was apparently living in a house on a small parcel of land near her on South Street (table 5.7). City directories indicate that he retained

---

85. Tubman's complex personal beliefs and spirituality are a focus of discussion in chapter 12.

86. Harriet Tubman is reported to have pledged $500 to the building campaign for Thompson AME Zion Church (Larson 2004, 279). It is unknown if she actually made this pledge or, if she did, whether she was able to fulfill it. During this period, she expected to receive a Civil War widow's benefit that her friends and family had sought on her behalf. However, the benefits were delayed, and she did not receive them until 1895.

87. Nelson Davis had been active in the AME Zion Church and had served on the St. Marks AME Zion Board of Trustees since its founding in 1870 (Storke 1879, 211–12).

88. Harriet Tubman to Mary Wright, May 29, 1896, Ms. A. 10.1, no. 90, Rare Book Room, Boston Public Library. See also Jane Kellogg for Harriet Tubman to Ednah Dow Cheney, Apr. 2, 1894, Ms. A.10.1, no. 36, Rare Book Room, Boston Public Library.

TABLE 5.7

NEW YORK STATE CENSUS, 1892, TUBMAN FARM, FLEMING, CAYUGA
COUNTY, NEW YORK

Name	Sex	Age	Color	In What Country Born	Citizen or Alien	Occupation
Harriet T. Davis	F	67		United States	C	
Winnie Stewart	F	74		United States	C	

Source: New York State census, 1892, Auburn and Fleming, Cayuga County, Cayuga County Records Office, Auburn, NY. The 1890 US census was destroyed by a fire, so the 1892 New York State census provides important data for the era.

ownership of this property until 1902 but that he had moved back into Harriet's home by 1900.

By the beginning of the 1890s, the City of Auburn had expanded, and issues began to arise related to differences between urban and farm life. Issues of health were forefront in people's minds, and the City of Auburn often addressed disease, including an outbreak of typhoid fever, and assessed sanitary conditions in the area. On September 8, 1890, the Auburn City Board of Health passed an ordinance limiting the keeping of hogs to farms outside the city and required farmers to submit applications indicating the number of swine they would have and the period the swine would be kept.[89] Violators of the ordinance faced a penalty of $10 for each offense. Tubman's hogs on her farm in Fleming were not subject to this regulation, but the creation of the ordinance reflects an environment that was looking to restrict the raising of hogs in the vicinity of the city, and one can see the nature of this concern. At the meeting of the Auburn Board of Health, presided over by Mayor Wheeler, a house at 155 Perrine Street, where typhoid occurred, was found to be in violation of the ordinance. It had a "hen house and pigsty all in filthy condition" (*Auburn Bulletin*, Sept. 15, 1890). To correct the situation, the owners were ordered to move the pigs out of the City of Auburn. Elsewhere in the city, sanitation issues and the expansion of sewer lines were discussed. With this as background, we find that even though Harriet Tubman's hogs were raised on a farm in the Town of Fleming, how she fed them would soon be challenged.

89. Ordinance of the City of Auburn Board of Health, Sept. 8, 1890, minutes of the meeting published in the *Auburn Bulletin*, Sept. 15, 1890.

On November 11, 1890, the *Auburn Bulletin* reported that Sanitary Inspector Sisson went before the Auburn Board of Health and reported "two gentlemen in the hall waiting the pleasure of the Board to be heard regarding the privilege of gathering garbage in the city." One gentleman, Mr. (William) Stewart (Sr.), "an old colored man who gathers garbage for his sister Harriet Tubman," appeared before the board and stated that "Mr. Sisson had told him that he was in violation of the city ordinance in gathering garbage about the town."[90] He said he wished to know whether he was or not; "if he was he would stop." Mr. Stewart reported to the board that he "gathered garbage from a few private families besides removing the ashes from about the house and the manure from the barns, but he never knew he was violating the city law." His account projects what appears to have been a long-standing practice by Tubman of collecting garbage that is commented on by the Wrights in the early 1870s and discussed in relation to the poisoning of Tubman's pigs in 1884. Tubman's brother was not the only person representing small farmers to appear before the board; he was followed by John Brady, who indicated that he owned a small farm located about three miles outside of the city. In response to these inquiries, Mayor Wheeler read part of a city ordinance relating to the collection of garbage. Based on the ordinance, Commissioner Titus said that those people who were collecting garbage were trespassing on the contract made with the garbage collector and that they should make arrangements with Mr. Offenburg, who apparently held that contract. Then Commissioner Alexander noted the ambiguity of enforcement and stated that the board "ought to do one thing or the other, "abrogate the ordinance or see that it is enforced." To this, Mr. Stewart asked if the Board of Health "would rather allow pork to be sold in the city that was raised around here than the pork shipped from the west where they did not know what it was fed on." After a spirited discussion, the board voted to adhere to its ordinance. As part of the discussion, it was decided that the Osborne family house garbage was "not the ordinary and legitimate waste of the [Tubman] farm and they had no right to feed it." One commissioner, Mr. Murdock, however, voiced his concern, asking why you would want to cut off the poor farmer from "feeding garbage to his hogs." However, permission to procure any other garbage except for genuine farm waste was revoked (*Auburn Bulletin*, Nov. 11, 1890).

90. Stewart had only recently arrived from Canada to be near his son William Jr.'s family and Harriet Tubman in Auburn. This record shows that he worked for his sister and assisted her in collecting food for her hogs (minutes of the meeting published in the *Auburn Bulletin*, Sept. 15, 1890).

This report shows that the City of Auburn was formalizing its procedures regarding garbage and sanitation and that garbage was now a valuable commodity to those who contracted to collect it for the municipality. The decision acknowledged farmers' right to their own waste but not to the waste produced by ordinary household residents. Thus, Tubman had to find other ways to feed her hogs. Interestingly, the article shows that Tubman, her brother William, and the local farmers recognized the scale of competition from large midwestern farms and meat-packing plants, and they tried, although to no avail, to draw on sympathy toward local production. This was one more strike against local small-scale farmers heading into the last decade of the nineteenth century.

Through the early 1890s, Tubman continued to take in boarders and the needy, to grow fruits and vegetables in her garden, to raise hogs, and to generate small amounts of dairy products. In a letter from Jane Kellogg to Ednah Dow Cheney in 1894, Kellogg wrote that Tubman "is as busy as ever going about doing good to everybody—her house is filled with 'odds and ends' of society—and to many are outcasts."[91]

Beginning in 1890, two years after Nelson Davis's death, Harriet Tubman and her supporters worked to get Civil War widows' benefits for Tubman.[92] Unfortunately, approval was delayed due the fact that Nelson Davis was listed as "Charles Nelson" in the military records. As a result, Tubman's friends and associates had to file affidavits to confirm both Nelson Davis's identity and the fact that he had been married to and lived with Tubman. The petitions were ultimately successful, and on October 16, 1895, Harriet Tubman was granted a widow's pension of $8 per month and in late October 1895 received a lump-sum payment of $500 for the years in which she hadn't received the pension.[93] A positive aspect of this effort involved the formal written affidavits filed by friends and supporters, which include details of their relationships to Tubman from the Civil War era through the early 1890s. These records not only document that Nelson Davis had been listed as Charles Nelson but also include information on who was living in Tubman's house as well as their occupations. It is from these records that we find much of the detail related to Tubman's household and the South Street brickmaking industry. The effort

91. Jane Kellogg for Harriet Tubman to Ednah Dow Cheney, Apr. 9, 1894.

92. In June 1890, Congress passed a law providing widows of war veterans with a monthly stipend of $8.

93. Affidavits in support of Tubman's claim were submitted to the Eighth United States Circuit Court. These records ultimately satisfied the Pension Bureau, and her claim was approved. See US House of Representatives 1888.

5.1. Harriet Tubman with family, c. 1887. *Left to right*: Harriet Tubman, Gertie Davis (Tubman's adopted daughter), Nelson Davis (Tubman's husband), Lee Cheney, "Pop" Alexander, Walter Green, Sarah Parker ("Blind Auntie" Parker), and Dora Stewart (granddaughter of Tubman's brother John Stewart). Photograph courtesy of Judith Bryant, Stewart Family Collection, Auburn, NY.

to get Tubman her widow's benefits also revived interest in getting her benefits as a veteran of the Civil War. Earlier efforts by William Seward and others in the late 1860s and 1870s had not been successful. The renewed effort used a new tactic by Auburn congressman Sereno Payne, who introduced a bill to grant Tubman a pension at a rate of $25 a month for her services as a nurse in the army during the war. Finally in 1899, after the rate had been dropped to $20 per month, her military contribution was rewarded with a combined pension of $20 per month.[94]

94. An article published in the *Auburn Citizen* on September 27, 1907, under the title "Its' a Pension But: Not What the Services of Harriet Tubman Warranted" was written for two reasons. First, it corrected an assertion in the previous Sunday's *New York Herald* that Congress had not provided Tubman with a pension, which in fact it had granted in February 1899. Second, it cites the pension attorney for the City of Auburn, Mr. Orin McCarthy, who had represented Tubman in her efforts to gain a pension, as asserting that Tubman had received an initial check of $488.67, which included back payments.

6

A Second Farm and Dreams
for a Home for the Aged

There was all white folks but me there, and there I was like a blackberry in a pail of milk. . . . I was hid down in a corner. . . . Then others
stopped bidding, and the man said, "All done! who is the buyer."
"Harriet Tubman," I shouted. "What! . . . Old woman, how are you
ever going to pay for that lot of land?" "I'm going home to tell the Lord
Jesus all about it," I said.

—attributed to Harriet Tubman, in Sarah Bradford,
Harriet Tubman, the Moses of Her People (1901)

A "Home" in Tubman's Personal House

By the 1880s, Harriet Tubman had set her sights on the creation of a home
for the care of aging African Americans who were in need. She conveyed her
desire to Sarah Bradford, who wrote a new version of Tubman's biography in
1886, which states that funds raised from book sales would go toward Tubman's last work: "This work is the building of a hospital for old and disabled
colored people; and in this she has already had the sympathy and aid of the
good people of Auburn; the mayor and his noble wife have given her great
assistance in the meetings she has held in aid of this object" (1886, 78–79).[1]
Bradford goes on to state that "she only prays, the Lord to let her live till it
is well started, and then she is ready to go" (78–79). In fact, by the time this
book was written, Tubman had already blurred the line between private and
public by opening her own private home to those in need.

---

1. The mayor was David M. Osborne, who along with his wife, Eliza Wright Osborne,
was a long supporter of Tubman and her causes. David Osborne died in 1886, but his brother
John remained involved in and served on the Harriet Tubman Home Board of Trustees as
treasurer. John Osborne helped in the refurbishing and opening of John Brown Hall and was
a frequent visitor to Tubman's house.

In late 1895, the *Auburn Argus* printed a legal notice of the pending sale at auction of properties belonging to the estate of John Farmer. Farmer had lived on South Street to the south of Tubman and was the owner of the farm immediately north of Tubman's (*Weekly Auburnian*, May 13, 1887). At this point, Tubman had little cash on hand but was optimistic about negotiating a Civil War widow's pension. This twenty-five-acre farm had several residential structures and barns as well as an apple orchard and farmland. The idea was to draw from the productivity of the farm and solicit donations to pay for the care of elderly African Americans who were in need. Presenting the story of the acquisition of land from the AME Zion Church's perspective in 1974, Bishop William Walls wrote that "for years Harriet had looked from the porch of her residence over a 25-acre expanse of adjoining *terrain*, dreaming of what a fine community farm it would make. She was desirous of presenting this to the Negro church of Auburn, for that institution to operate collectively" (Walls 1974, 399).

At about that time, in late 1895, Tubman met in her home with supporters, including clergy and lay leaders of the AME Zion Church and other leaders in the Auburn community, such as members of the Osborne family, with whom she had a long association. Around tea and discussion, they drafted a charter for a home, formalizing the institution of care that she was already informally providing in her house.[2] On April 10, 1896, soon after this meeting, formal notice of the creation of the "Harriet Tubman Home for indigent colored people" was published in the *Cayuga County Independent*. Hence, at the time of its formal chartering, the Home was already existing in Harriet Tubman's personal residence on her farm in Fleming. The announcement of the chartering stated that it "has been incorporated with the presiding elders of five colored conferences as directors," elders who represented the region's AME Zion churches.[3] According to the announcement, the trustees included Harriet Tubman Davis; Mrs. Julia P. Clarke of Auburn; Rev. W. A. Ely, pastor of the AME Zion Church in Auburn; Rev. George C. Carter, pastor of the AME Church of Geneva; Rev. James E, Mason, pastor of the AME Church of Ithaca; and H. C. Calles.

2. Given that all of the other references to tea and teas related to Tubman were gatherings of women, it is important to note that this tea was organized by Tubman but involved both men and women.

3. A Certificate of Incorporation of "The Harriet Tubman Home," dated December 3, 1895, was recorded in the Cayuga County Clerk's Office, Auburn, NY, on April 6, 1896, at 12:10 p.m.

The announcement of plans for her new Home attracted a writer from the *Syracuse Sunday Evening Herald* to visit Harriet at her house, resulting in the most detailed and best-illustrated account of the Home for that period (figures 6.1–6.4). The article begins with the byline "Dreams Realized," "Crowning Effort of Old Harriet Tubman's Life" (*Syracuse Sunday Evening Herald*, Apr. 19, 1896). Significantly, the article describes the Home for the Aged in active terms as being operated in Tubman's personal residence, and it provides an overview of Harriet's dreams for the development of the Home. The article presents one image of Tubman, accompanied by an elderly person and a child, in front of her house with the caption "Harriet Tubman's Home for Aged Colored Persons." Another image is a close-up of Harriet's face, while another shows Tubman sitting on her porch with a younger woman and a child who is described as her "charge," alluding to the fact that Tubman was engaged in childcare as well as in care for the elderly.

The *Syracuse Sunday Evening Herald* article begins: "A modest announcement of the incorporation of Harriet Tubman Home for Colored People at Auburn last week had hidden within its theme one of the most remarkable stories of American history." The reporter went out to Harriet Tubman's "little cottage" in Auburn to hear the story from "the lips of old Harriet Tubman." The story told is one of "a life of sacrifice for her race." Typical of most interviews of Tubman, this one describes her early life on a plantation in Dorchester County, Maryland, and the horrors of slavery. It then recounts her escape, her work as an Underground Railroad conductor guiding pioneers through dangers seen and unseen, and her efforts during the war as a soldier scout and nurse for the Union army—efforts that contributed to her being called the "Moses of her people." The article shows the influences of having read the second version of Sarah Bradford biography not only in the biblical reference to Tubman as "Moses" but also in the overstated statistics of nineteen trips, three hundred liberated, and the price of $40,000 on her head. It includes references to white and Black abolitionists with whom Tubman was associated, including Frederick Douglass and John Brown, as well as to her many friends in Boston, including William Lloyd Garrison, Franklin Sanborn, Wendell Phillips, the Emersons, the Brooks, the Alcotts, the Whitneys, Governor Andrew, and Central New York's William Seward and Gerrit Smith. It then goes into detail related to Tubman's life in Fleming and Auburn and her plans for a home for the aged. The article concludes on the subject of her farm and her planned home. It describes how after the war she was about to lose her house and her near centenary parents were on the verge of being sent to the poorhouse when she turned to her friends and a "little sketch of her life was published and sold and the proceeds saved her house. In this house her parents were able to continue to live out their lives and died blessing Harriet for her devotion."

An Act of Faith: Bidding on a Dream
and Tubman's Campaign to Create a Home

At last, in June 1896, by sheer audacity Tubman acquired a twenty-five-acre farm to house her Home. When the farm immediately north of hers came up for auction on June 22, "Harriet appeared at the scene with very little money, but determined to have the land, cost what it might" (Walls 1974, 440).[4] Many have retold the story of the auction, including Sarah Bradford, who did so in yet another new revision of her biography of Tubman published in 1901. As she wrote, Harriet said, "There was all white folks but me there, and there I was like a blackberry in a pail of milk. . . . I was hid down in a corner. . . . Then others stopped bidding, and the man said, 'All done! who is the buyer.' 'Harriet Tubman,' I shouted. 'What! . . . Old woman, how are you ever going to pay for that lot of land?' 'I'm going home to tell the Lord Jesus all about it,' I said" (Bradford 1901, 149–50). When the bidding was finished, Tubman had won at a price reported in the papers as $1,215 (*Auburn Bulletin*, June 22, 1896).[5]

A few days later, on June 28, 1896, a highly optimistic story on the "Harriet Tubman Home" ran in the *Syracuse Sunday Herald*, describing a June 27 meeting of the Board of Trustees of the "Harriet Tubman Home Association." The article indicates that the title to the property had been formally transferred to the Home, but in fact the transfer had not occurred. The trustee group's corporation attorney, Judge George Underwood, was out of

---

4. A notice of the sale of John Farmer's properties at auction lists Harriet Tubman as the person who bought a parcel adjoining her farm for $1,215 (*Auburn Bulletin*, June 22, 1896).

5. The deed for this property transfer lists the sales price as $1,215 (Cayuga County Deeds Book 57, July 14, 1896, Aurelius 24, Cayuga County Clerk's Office). On June 22, 1896, the *Auburn Bulletin*, reported the price as $1,250. The deed describes a parcel in which the northern boundary ran from South Street east, adjoining or abutting on its north side the property of Flavel Danforth. There is no mention of any small parcel at the northwest corner of the property, as is later defined in a mortgage to Judge George Underwood and his wife (see Deed of Mortgage to George Underwood, Cayuga County Deeds Book 30, Oct. 2, 1900, pp. 628–29, Cayuga County Clerk's Office). A conveyance from Harriet Tubman Davis to the Harriet Tubman Home, July 14, 1896, is conveyed in Cayuga County Deeds Book 57, Aurelius 24, Cayuga County Clerk's Office.

town, and thus action to transfer the property could not move forward.[6] The persons present at the meeting reflect representation of AME Zion Church leadership from throughout the region. Bishop Alexander Waters came from Jersey City, New Jersey; the Rev. G. C. Carter from Wilkes-Barre, Pennsylvania; as well as the following from the New York congregations: the Rev. J. E. Mason, DD, from Rochester, Rev. S. L. Carruthers from Elmira, the Rev. B. F. Wheeler, DD, from Ithaca, and Rev. E. A. U. Brooks from Elmira.[7]

The initial group of trustees for the Home had a goal of establishing a $10,000 subscription fund. They indicated that the fund had already been started, that at least one $50 gift had been received, and a follow-up meeting was planned for July 4, 1896, to discuss funding.[8] No decisions were made regarding the specific uses of existing buildings or plans for either remodeling or new construction. However, they did discuss the fact that they needed to raise $1,225 to pay for the twenty-five acres that Tubman had purchased. Moreover, they set a very short deadline for this, indicating that it needed to be raised before the July 4 meeting, at which time they planned to transfer the property. Rev. G. C. Carter was charged with heading the fund-raising team, and W. H. Meaker, a cashier of the Cayuga County Savings Bank, was to act as custodian of the fund (*Syracuse Sunday Herald*, June 28, 1896). There is no formal report regarding the gathering scheduled for July 4, but an article on Tubman appeared in the *New York Sun* on July 5, 1896.[9]

The first of many nationally based articles describing Harriet Tubman's efforts to raise funds for her Home was published in the *New York Daily Tribune* on July 22, 1896. The previous day Tubman had addressed the National Federation of Afro-American Women in Washington, DC. Her presentation, "More Homes for Our Aged," made a case for the need for homes like the one

6. Ultimately, formal title to the property was not transferred to the AME Zion Church until 1903.

7. E. (Edward) A. U. Brooks, a lawyer and a minister in the AME Zion Church, and Rev. B. F. (Benjamin Franklin) Wheeler (both generally were referred to by their initials and not their full names) played key roles in the founding of the Home.

8. Rev. Carter had formerly been an AME Zion minister in Auburn, but he had been transferred to Wilkes-Barre.

9. The *New York Sun* article draws from Bradford's (1886) book and recounts the noble deeds of "A Female Moses," making specific reference to Tubman's actions in Troy, New York. It provides no new information on her life, but it does illustrate how information on her actions was still being brought forward and that she was being discussed publicly during the mid-1890s. Portions of this article were republished in the *Poughkeepsie Daily Eagle*, July 6, 1896.

she was trying to create. The gathering was opened with an address by Mrs. Booker T. Washington titled "The Progress of Women." Tubman's presentation was followed by a series of papers addressing issues such as segregation, temperance, and prison reform as well as topics such as "the Douglass monument" (by Mrs. Jerome Jaffrey) and John Brown (by Mrs. T. H. Lyles) (*New York Daily Tribune*, July 22, 1896).[10] Tubman's speech targeted the needs of her Home for the Aged and the need to shift the focus from the heroic acts of her past to the objectives for the Home in the present and for the future. Her presentation was well received, but it appears not to have attracted significant financial support. Accounts of the meeting indicate the funds raised were able to cover only the cost of "Mother Tubman's" trip to Washington, with no mention of funds generated for the Home (National Association of Colored Women's Clubs 1902, minutes). However, the message that she delivered in her presentation was picked up by the national press, as demonstrated by the article published in the *New York Daily Tribune* on July 22, 1896. Soon after Tubman returned from Washington, another family member died. On August 6, 1896, John Stewart's widow, Amilia "Millie" Hollis Stewart, passed away, and accounts describe Tubman's "deep grief over the loss of an old and dear friend" (*Auburn Weekly Bulletin*, Aug. 6, 1896).[11]

10. As Kate Larson points out, by the early 1890s a newly unified National American Woman Suffrage Association acquiesced to pressure from emerging white women's suffrage leaders in the South to adopt a platform that included resolutions supporting individual states' rights in relation to the qualification of voters. This acquiescence secured wider support for suffrage issues but at the cost of allowing states to opt for white supremacy and the alienation of African American women's rights. As a result, African American women saw the need to organize on behalf of their own interests and in 1896 created the consolidated National Association of Colored Women, a merger of two groups—the National League of Colored Women and the National Federation of Afro-American Women, which had formed in Boston in 1895. In spite of the national trend, the white Central New York suffrage groups retained former abolitionists, including Anne Fitzhugh Miller (1856–1912) and her mother, Elizabeth Smith Miller, of Geneva, all of whom had befriended and included Harriet Tubman. So not only did Tubman participate in the African American women's conferences, but in November 1896 she traveled to Rochester for the New York State Women Suffrage Association meeting, where she met with her longtime friend Emily Howland and then stood arm in arm on stage with Susan B. Anthony (*Rochester Democrat and Chronicle*, Nov. 18, 1896).

11. The obituary notes that Mrs. Stewart was born into slavery on the eastern shore of Maryland and that she came to live in Auburn and was there for many years. Mrs. Stewart's services were conducted at the Thompson AME Zion Church of Auburn.

AME Zion Church Support for Tubman
and the Home for the Aged

There was no immediate follow-up to the optimistic plan to raise funds to pay off the $1,225 mortgage debt on the newly acquired twenty-five-acre property; however, Tubman's supporters continued to pursue the matter. Rev. G. C. Carter was given the responsibility of raising the funds from his base in Wilkes-Barre, Pennsylvania. In early September 1896, he returned to Auburn and spent a few days "perfecting arrangements for a public meeting" that was formally announced for "Wednesday, evening, September 9, with the Rev. H. R. Bender of the First ME Church presiding" (*Auburn Bulletin*, Sept. 5, 1896). The plans included representation from both the AME Zion and the First ME Church, and several AME Zion leaders, including Alexander Walters, presiding bishop of the Western and Central New York Conferences, were announced as participants. It was noted that the Harriet Tubman Home Board of Trustees would also meet that morning at the home of Mrs. Harriet Tubman Davis. This article shows that Harriet was involved in the planning and that she was opening her house to those who were assisting her in the organization of the Home. The meeting was not limited to those in the AME Zion Church but extended more broadly to others in the community.[12]

Another meeting of the Home's trustees and interested parties was held at the First ME Church on Wednesday evening, September 18, 1896. The focus of this gathering was an address titled "Harriet Tubman Home for Aged Indigent Colored People" by Rev. Edward A. U. Brooks of Elmira. Rev. Brooks was also the attorney for the Home (*Cayuga County Independent*, Sept. 18, 1896). Others presenting oratory on behalf of the Home were Rev. H. R. Bender, DD, of the First Methodist Church, Rev. W. A. Ely, and Rev. J. E. Mason of Rochester. This public meeting was intended to "awaken public interest in the home." Earlier in the day there had been a meeting of the Home Board of Trustees, whose officers included Rev. W. A. Ely, president; Rev. M. H. Ross of Syracuse, first vice president; Rev. S. L. Corrothers of Elmira, second vice president; Rev. J. H. Anderson of Rochester, third vice president; Rev. E. A. U. Brooks, secretary and attorney; and Cyrenus Wheeler Jr. of Auburn, treasurer. The board reported that it was ready to receive contributions for the

---

12. Unfortunately, once again there was no published follow-up to this meeting, so we do not know specific plans and outcomes.

home, which it "expected to situate on the grounds north of Mrs. Tubman's home just south of this city. The money left by Mrs. Tubman and $1000 borrowed from the Cayuga County Savings Bank is the nucleus of this enterprise, which also hopes at some future time to establish an industrial school for colored youths" (*Cayuga County Independent*, Sept. 18, 1896).[13] This account of the meeting goes on to say that the Home Board of Trustees also included former Auburn mayor Cyrenus Wheeler Jr. and Drs. Brainard, Ives, Beecher, and Hopkins.[14] The evening meeting was open to the public, and the board of trustees had apparently been expanded to include key politicians and doctors in the Auburn area. The composition of the group projects an effort to reach out beyond the core AME Zion Church supporters. Also, although the concept of a school for colored girls had been Harriet Tubman's documented goal from the time Bradford wrote the second version of her biography of Tubman in 1886, this article is the first to mention the creation of a school as part of the Home.

Harriet Tubman was charged with energy and actively engaged in the effort to gain funds to pay down the mortgage on the new land and to fulfill the dream of her Home for the Aged. She set out to renew old ties with associates, traveling to conventions and gatherings with the aim of gaining financial support for her cause. On November 18, 1896, she traveled to Rochester for the meeting of the New York State Women Suffrage Association, where she was introduced as the "great Black liberator" by Susan B. Anthony as the two stood hand in hand on the stage. However, this introduction of Tubman focused on her iconic efforts on behalf of women and abolition, and she gained little traction for her Home. A detailed and sympathetic report on her presence characterized her as a person dependent on the "kindness of friends to assist her" but made no mention of her plans for a home (*Rochester Democrat and Chronicle*, Nov. 18, 1896).

Efforts to raise funds for the new Home may also have been subverted by the death of Mr. Andrew Shimer. His death and the press's coverage of it

13. Tubman had virtually no money, so it is unclear what actual funds they were referring to except perhaps the anticipation of a payment of Civil War benefits or perhaps expectations regarding the proceeds of her estate upon her death. The latter would have implied the proceeds from her farm; however, much later, when she died in 1913, the farm was left to two relatives and a care provider. In late 1896, Mrs. Tubman remained very much alive and active in the plans for the Home.

14. Cyrenus Wheeler Jr. served two terms as mayor of the City of Auburn, 1881–86 and 1889–90.

refreshed the community's memory of the 1873 "gold swindle." A lengthy article/obituary on Shimer published in the *Auburn Daily Bulletin* on October 8, 1896, recounted the events of the swindle. The article projected a surprisingly negative accounting of Shimer's life, especially considering it was a form of obituary. Unfortunately, for Tubman it also rekindled discussion of the saga of her involvement with the unfortunate affair and the loss of $2,000 just as she was trying to raise funds for her Home. Interestingly, by now much of the blame for the incident of 1873 was placed squarely on Shimer's greed, and Tubman was remembered as someone simply caught up in Shimer's caper. In fact, the swindle had little impact on Mr. Shimer's wealth, which had grown dramatically by the time of his death. Moreover, people's view of Shimer had not improved in proportion with his wealth, which by his death included an estate of between $300,000 and $750,000, with much of its value rooted in properties he held in Chicago, which "he has not been there to alter and ruin." Whereas his hands-on management of his Auburn properties resulted in damage and neglect, his Chicago real estate had "increased wonderfully in value." At the time of his death, Shimer's neglect of his Auburn properties and lack of concern for others received more attention than his wealth.

As an example of Shimer's miserliness and lack of concern for others, the paper presented a detailed narrative relating to his selection of poor-quality varnish for the seats of his opera house in Auburn.

SHIMER: "I want some varnish, but the cheapest you've got."
DUNNING: "What do you want if for?"
SHIMER: "To varnish the seats at the Opera House."
DUNNING: "Well, you can't use cheap varnish for that. It will slick to the clothes."
SHIMER: "I don't want nothing but the cheapest."

The story went on to say that Shimer would buy nothing but the cheapest despite Dunning's concerns. The seats were refinished with the low-quality varnish and left to dry. However, the cheap varnish remained tacky. At the next performance, "ladies in fashionable attire were everywhere. The varnish got its work. Many valuable gowns were ruined. From that time on the house went down, down, down in public estimation," and so too did Shimer's reputation (*Auburn Daily Bulletin*, Oct. 8, 1896). Whatever the opinion of Shimer, the more important issue was that the timing of his death resurrected his connection with Tubman and the gold scam. This was not good for Tubman and her dream because it raised doubt about her ability to handle money just as she began her campaign to pay off the new mortgage and to begin development of the Home.

The republication of Bradford's book combined with the renewed interest in Harriet Tubman in association with her efforts on behalf of her Home and her revived presence at women's meetings, such as the gathering in Washington, DC, in 1896, brought notoriety that reached across the Atlantic to Queen Victoria. A note in the *Union Spring Advertiser* on March 26, 1897, reports that a friend of Queen Victoria sent a gift from England on behalf of the queen. The gift was a silver medal that commemorated Victoria's jubilee and a white shawl, which were accompanied by a note that read, "From a friend of the Queen of England to Harriet Tubman, having read her life [Bradford 1886] with great Interest and read it to her majesty."[15] Neither of these gifts

15. The shawl is now on exhibit at the Smithsonian's Museum of African American History in Washington, DC. The medallion has been lost through time, although perhaps it is buried with Tubman, but we know that it was a special medal honoring Queen Victoria on her Jubilee and was given to Tubman in honor of her efforts on behalf of the cause of freedom and humanity. This mention in the *Union Spring Advertiser* on March 26, 1897, is the only account from the year of the gift that I have found. Most accounts indicate that Queen Victoria read Bradford's book on the life of Tubman and that through an intermediary sent Tubman the silver medal commemorating Victoria's sixty years as queen of England, along with the white shawl (Clarke 1911; Humez 2003, 254–56; Larson 2004, 281). James B. Clarke's account describes conversations between Anne Fitzhugh Miller (granddaughter of Gerrit Smith) and Harriet Tubman concerning the gift and the attached note. Clarke reported that Miller inquired about the story of Queen Victoria's gifts to Tubman. Tubman responded to Miller: "It was when the queen had been on the throne sixty years, she sent me the medal. It was a silver medal, about the size of a dollar. It showed the queen and her family." Clarke also read the letter, which said, "I read your book to Her Majesty, and she was pleased with it. She sends you this medal." Tubman told her guests that the queen "invited me to come over for her birthday party, but I didn't know enough to go. The letter was worn to a shadow, so many people read it. It got lost, somehow or other. Then I gave the medal to my brother's daughter to keep" (Clarke 1911, 116). This version of the note from the queen is a bit different than the note published in the *Union Spring Advertiser*. According to Clarke, Miller's conversation regarding Queen Victoria was initiated by a request by Tubman to send a note of congratulations to King George V on his coronation in 1910, an assignment that they agreed should be delegated to Clarke based on his knowledge of protocol as a British West Indian (Humez 2003, 255–56, citing Clarke 1911). Milton Sernett also discusses the gifts from Queen Victoria, citing a letter from Earl Conrad (under his given name Earl Cohen) to Henry Johnson in which Conrad wrote: "Mrs. Carter tells me that Queen Victoria sent Harriet a shawl along with a letter and a medal. I am particularly familiar with the episode through the Clarke memoir, but I have not heard that she was given a shawl, and I also understand that the shawl disappeared" (June 29, 1939, in Sernett 2007, 361).

found its way into the material record of the Harriet Tubman Home site, but they do become registered in history as symbols of the breadth of respect afforded Tubman during her later life. Milton Sernett cites a report in the *Auburn Daily Advertiser* for March 13, 1913, that says that mourners saw the medal in Tubman's coffin when they passed by as she lay in state (2007, 361).

Personal and Public Life Intertwined

In April 1897, the *Women's Journal*, a suffrage newspaper, reported several receptions in Tubman's honor in Boston sponsored by former abolitionists and current suffragists, including Ednah Cheney (see Cheney 1897).[16] Tubman was invited to be present for the opening of a center named in her honor. In order to get to Boston, she sold a cow to pay for her train ticket.[17] However, one goal of the trip was to raise funds, and so she was feted at a fundraiser in her honor at the offices of William Lloyd Garrison Jr., where the latest edition of her biography was sold.[18] While in Boston, Tubman renewed her friendship with Franklin Sanborn and the children of William Lloyd Garrison. While she was staying at the home of Dr. Harriet Cobb, she spent time detailing her Underground Railroad exploits to Wilbur Siebert in Cambridge, who was writing a manuscript of what would later be published as a detailed study of the Underground Railroad (Larson 2004, 283).[19]

While in Boston, Tubman suffered from a severe headache, as she had many times since sustaining a head injury as a child. Her friends took her to Massachusetts General Hospital, where doctors performed brain surgery on her (Bradford 1901, 151–53). Regarding an interview with Tubman conducted in preparation for what became the last version of Tubman's biography,

16. Ednah Cheney is the same woman from Boston who interviewed Tubman and wrote a biographical sketch of her in 1865 (Cheney 1865). By the end of the nineteenth century, women's groups had begun to define themselves as "white" and to distance themselves from Blacks. This account projects a bit of an oddity: an announcement of events honoring a Black woman, Harriet Tubman, in a journal written for white women.

17. Larson 2004, 281, citing Helen Tufts Bailie Journal, 1886–1936, Helen Tufts Bailie Papers, Sophia Smith Collection, Smith College Library, Northampton, MA, at http://asteria .fivecolleges.edu/findaids/sophiasmith/mnsss175_bioghist.html.

18. William Lloyd Garrison Jr. was the husband of Eliza Wright Osborne's daughter Mary, for whom Harriet Tubman had been a babysitter and with whom she had carried out spring cleanings at the Osborne house when Mary and her sister Helen were children.

19. See Wilbur Siebert, "The Underground Railroad: Manuscript Materials Collected by Professor Siebert," Houghton Library, Harvard Univ., Cambridge, MA.

published in 1901, Bradford wrote, "Harriet's friends will be glad to learn that she has lately been for some time in Boston, where a surgical operation was performed on her head." Tubman told Bradford that before the operation her head hurt so that she could not sleep at night, but after the operation they sent her home in an ambulance, and her head improved so that "it feels more comfortable" (Bradford 1901, 153).

On February 3, 1897, Emily Howland wrote to Eliza Wright Osborne from her home in Sherwood. Along with the letter, Howland sent a check for $12.50, "which she [Tubman] may credit to the Lord if she wishes." Howland sent the check to Osborne because "she [Tubman] may not know what to do with it," and Osborne was one of Tubman's "guardians." By way of apology, Howland wrote, "I hope that I am not assigning you a task that will be a potter." After discussing several other matters, including conditions in penitentiaries, Howland concludes with the hope that "Harriet will have a visit that will refresh and restore her."[20] Thoughts of Tubman were often included in casual mentions in Osborne family letters. As an afterthought, attached to the end of a letter to her daughter Helen Osborne Storrow of Boston, Eliza Wright Osborne noted, "Oh, Harriet came in to see me yesterday—and was most enthusiastic over your hundreds to her. She said you were a star by name and a shining star really. I wish I could remember all her queer expressions she used."[21]

A Union Pension Granted, but the Challenge of Debt Remains

During this period, there was occasional recognition of Tubman's past service, and events such as Memorial Day celebrations often included the honoring of Tubman and the dead of the Civil War.[22] Through 1896, the only military

20. Emily Howland to Eliza Wright Osborne, Feb. 3, 1897, box 37, Osborne Family Papers, Special Collections Research Center, Syracuse University, Syracuse, NY.

21. Eliza Wright Osborne to Helen Osborne Storrow, n.d., last page only, box 57, Osborne Family Papers. Helen Storrow (born September 22, 1864) was the youngest daughter of Eliza Wright Osborne and David Osborne. Storrow was a founder of the Girl Scouts of America, and her husband, James J. Storrow, a banker, was the second president of the Boy Scouts of America. Today the Storrow name is perhaps best known in the Boston area for the road that flanks the Charles River, a designation bestowed in honor of James Storrow's contributions to the restoration of the Charles River Basin.

22. In 1897, Nelson Davis is listed among the dead soldiers who are buried at Fort Hill Cemetery in Auburn; he had died on October 14, 1888. Again, the following May, the local

benefits that Tubman had received was a lump-sum payment of $500 in 1890 from her accrued Union soldier's widow's pension. Plans for her Home continued to be hindered by the debt incurred in buying the property and the cost of care for the elderly in her charge. By the end of the nineteenth century, many of Tubman's most ardent supporters had died, and others were dubious of the drain on Tubman's own health and well-being caused by her insistence on caring for others (Humez 2003, 110).

In 1898, after several years' effort, Congress went forward with a special act to compensate Tubman for her service during the Civil War. After considerable debate and objections, particularly from the South Carolina delegation because the special act concerned a woman who had assisted the Union, a reduced total compensation package was agreed upon in 1899 that granted Harriet Tubman Davis a $20 per month benefit (US Congress 1899). This package allocated $12 per month for her military service (as a nurse) and $8 as her widow's benefit (Conrad 1943, 220).

As the older generation of abolitionists passed on, their grown children began to return to Auburn to pay homage to Tubman. In 1899, Agnes Garrison, whose mother had grown up in Auburn and had been cared for by Tubman as a child, came to Auburn to visit her aunt, Eliza Wright Osborne. While in Auburn, she encouraged Tubman to "tell stories of her youth with a stenographer taking down as best she could." At the time of Agnes's visit, Tubman was caring for three "adopted children," two of whom were "half-white" and one little boy who was "half-Indian and half-Spanish."[23] That same year, Tubman's exasperation over her inability to generate support surfaced when she traveled to Chicago to attend the second conference of the National Association of Colored Women in Chicago in August 1899. At the meeting, Tubman offered her twenty-five-acre property to the organization, but the offer was declined because of its mortgage encumbrance (Sernett 2007, 25).[24]

---

paper notes Davis's name in connection to one of the gravesites to be decorated as part of Memorial Day festivities (*Auburn Bulletin*, May 25, 1898).

23. Agnes Garrison to Ellen Wright Garrison, Nov. 25, 1899, Garrison Family Papers, Sophia Smith Collection. No doubt one of these children was Kate Stewart, the daughter of John Stewart and a grandniece of Harriet Tubman, recorded in the US census, 1900, Auburn and Fleming, Cayuga County Records Office, Auburn, NY.

24. However, this effort and her exposure among leading African American businesswomen at the conference may well have led to the Empire State Federation of Colored Women's Clubs adopting Tubman and her Home as its charity. Years later, when the Home had closed, that group offered to fund its restoration. See also Anna Agbe-Davies's (2011) study of the Phillis Wheatly Home for Girls in Chicago.

Tubman's Farm, Home, and Community
at the Turn of the Twentieth Century

By 1900, Tubman was being threatened with foreclosure on her twenty-five-acre farm. An auction was scheduled for March 27, 1900, but she managed to get it postponed until the following Saturday. At the time, the debt included a mortgage of $1,000, a mechanic's lien for $500 and interest, and "other things," all of which brought the amount up to $1,700, with the first mortgage being held by the Cayuga County Savings Bank (*Auburn Weekly Bulletin*, Mar. 27, 1900). The property was saved when Tubman refinanced it with the assistance of Judge George Underwood and his wife, Grace. They paid off Tubman's debt in exchange for a mortgage of $1,650 on the property.[25] Yet even with a new mortgage on the twenty-five-acre property, Tubman's financial situation was strained. In mid-May 1900, Sarah Bradford wrote to Franklin Stanford, "I have been to see Harriet & found her in a deplorable condition, a pure wreck . . . surrounded by beggars who I fear fleece her of everything sent her—She drew all the money I had sent for her, & I fear had little good of it—I am keeping the money I get for her now & will pay her bills & I send her a little at a time as she needs it—If I could only get her into a *home* where she would be well cared for I should be so glad, but she will not leave her beloved darkies."[26]

Harriet Tubman and later the Home rented houses on the property in order to generate income (*Auburn Bulletin*, Nov. 22 and 24, 1900). For Tubman, these rents meant an income of between $20 and $30 dollars a year. The US census for 1900 records a white family of eight in residence in the then

---

25. Mortgage to George Underwood and wife to Harriet Tubman, Cayuga Count Deeds Book 30, Oct. 2, 1900, pp. 628–29, Cayuga County Clerk's Office. The mortgage to Underwood also provided some details on the small one-quarter-acre parcel that had been sequentially owned by Jacob Jasper, Harriet Tubman, and then her brother William Stewart Sr., noting that the twenty-five-acre property excluded about one-fourth of an acre of land "heretofore sold to Jacob Jasper" at the northwest corner of the property (Sheriff Wood to George Underwood, Cayuga County Deeds Book 30, Apr. 30, 1900, p. 12, Cayuga County Clerk's Office). Thus, in 1896 this small parcel was part of the larger tract but was sold by Tubman to Jasper at some point after her acquisition of the property.

26. Sarah Bradford to Franklin B. Sanborn, n.d. (May 11, 1900 or 1901?), Franklin B. Sanford Collection, Special Collections, Boston University Library, cited in Humez 2003, 320–21. Bradford was concerned about Tubman's financial condition. However, though a longtime supporter of Tubman, she projects a very ethnocentric view of people of color in this letter. As in this letter, in her books she speaks of African American children using terms that by today's standards would be considered at best insensate.

red-painted wood-frame house (tables 6.1 and 6.2):[27] Charles and Caroline Sincerbeaux (head of household and wife) as well as two sons and four daughters ages five to twenty-one. Charles worked for the Osborne Manufacturing Company "setting up mowers," while his twenty-one-year-old son worked for the same company "setting up reapers and mowers."[28]

At the beginning of the new century, the brick house at the back of the property, later known as John Brown Hall, was also rented out to Alexander Steel (thirty, head of household) and his wife, Cora (twenty-six). He was from Iowa, and she was from New York. They had three daughters, all of whom had been born in Iowa. Their youngest daughter was two years old, so they had been in New York for only two years or less. Alexander Steel was listed in the 1900 census as a laborer in the brickyard. In addition, the family had a boarder named George Phillips (twenty-seven) from Ohio, who was employed as a "stationary engineer." All of the residents in this house were literate except for the youngest child. All the residents of both houses were white. Each family was recorded as renting the house only, not the attached farm.[29]

When Sarah Bradford published the last edition of her Tubman biography in 1901, the new version had twenty-one pages of new biographical information, including details from earlier notes and recent interviews. The book was aimed at providing a renewed source of income for Tubman, and Bradford defended the $1 price of the book in correspondence with Franklin Sanborn, saying, "It should be looked upon as charity."[30]

On December 9, 1902, a fire started in the "rear of the Harriet Tubman Davis property, just outside the city limits on South Street in a one and a half story frame structure." John James, age sixty-five, died from smoke inhalation. A team of firefighters from the "chemical company" "prevented spread of the fire to nearby buildings, but the house was totally destroyed" (*Auburn*

27. This house (which I have called the Legacy House, Locus 2) was part of the Home but was not used to house the elderly until after Tubman's death. Because of its use after 1914 as a dormitory for the Home, it has often been referred to as *the* "Tubman Home."

28. Several of the younger children were listed as being "at school" (US census, 1900, Auburn and Fleming, Cayuga County Records Office, with the house listed in the margins as "Tubman House"). The census taker wrote the family's name down as "Sincerbox," but other records for Auburn spell the name "Sincerbeaux." This family later moved to Moravia Street in Auburn, next to the bridge.

29. US census, 1900, Auburn and Fleming, Cayuga County Records Office.

30. Sarah Bradford to Franklin Sanborn, n.d. (May 11, 1900 or 1901?), in Humez 2003, 320–21.

TABLE 6.1

UNITED STATES CENSUS, 1900, TUBMAN FARM, FLEMING, NEW YORK, PART 1

Name	Relation to Head of Family	Color	Sex	Date of Birth	Age	Marital Status	# Years Married	Mother of How Many Children	Number of Children Living	Birthplace	Father's Birthplace	Mother's birthplace
T. Davis, Harriet	head	B	F	April 1813	87	Married		1	0	MD	MD	MD
Stewart, William	brother	B	M	August 1829	70	Married				MD	MD	MD
Wright, Mary	boarder	B	F	September 1845	54	Married				Washington, DC	SC	SC
Shaw, Max	boarder	B	M	February 1892	8	Single				NY	VA	VA
Stewart, Kate	granddaughter of brother William's son John	B	F	January 1894	6	Single				Canada	Canada	VA

Source: US census, 1900, Auburn and Fleming, Cayuga County, Cayuga County Records Office, Auburn, NY.

TABLE 6.2

UNITED STATES CENSUS, 1900, TUBMAN FARM, FLEMING, NEW YORK, PART 2

Name	Naturalization	Occupation	Attended School	Can Read	Can Write	Can Speak English	Owned/ Rented	Mortgaged	Farm or House	Number of Farm Schedule
T. Davis, Harriet		farmer		no	no	yes	owned	mortgaged	farm	172
Stewart, William		teamster		no	no	yes				
Wright, Mary		boarder								
Shaw, Max			8 mo.							
Stewart, Kate			8 mo.							

Source: US census, 1900, Auburn and Fleming, Cayuga County, Cayuga County Records Office, Auburn, NY.

TABLE 6.3

NEW YORK STATE CENSUS, 1905, FLEMING AND AUBURN, CAYUGA COUNTY, NEW YORK

Name	Relation to Head of Household	Color	Sex	Age	Nativity	Citizen	Occupation
Davis, Harriet T.	head	B	F	90	United States	C	X
Stewart, William H.	brother	B	M	70	United States	C	teamster
Stewart, Katy	niece	B	F	16	United States	C	at school (9)
Knight, Mary	boarder	B	F	80	United States	C	X
Blane, Caroline	boarder	B	F	90	United States	C	X
Newburg, Robert J.	boarder	B	M	28	United States	C	day laborer
Newburg, Anna	wife [of boarder]	B	F	30	United States	C	servant

Source: New York State census, 1905, Auburn and Fleming, Cayuga County, Cayuga County Records Office, Auburn, NY.

Democrat Argus, Dec. 9, 1902).[31] People reported that James had a "habit of drying kindling wood on top of the stove in the kitchen, and it was supposed that the stove became over-heated, setting fire to the kindling and the blaze communicated to the walls of the building" (*Auburn Democrat Argus*, Dec. 9, 1902). James reportedly had relatives in New York who were to be contacted; his funeral was held at the AME Zion Church in Auburn.[32] The combination of sources and archaeological findings suggest that this house was located either about twenty meters east of Tubman's barn or near the southwest corner of the twenty-five-acre lot in what is now an open field just north of Tubman's brick house.[33]

The 1905 New York State census indicates that Harriet Tubman was living in her house with six relatives and boarders (table 6.3). Tubman's age was listed as ninety, although she was actually only eighty-three. Her brother William H. Stewart (seventy), a teamster, was living with her along with her niece Katy Stewart (sixteen), who was attending school. Boarders included Mary Knight (eighty), Caroline Blane (ninety), and Robert and Anna Newberg (twenty-eight and thirty).

Pleas for Support for Tubman's Home for the Aged

During this period, the AME Zion Church had a strong affiliation with Booker T. Washington, best known for his school at Tuskegee and his advocacy of an industrial education movement for African Americans. The tie between Tubman and Washington was solidified by an annual visit for six years by Washington's financial officer, Robert W. Taylor, to Tubman. Following his visit in 1901, Taylor wrote a letter summarizing Tubman's goals for her

31. John Lane, a neighbor, "peered through the window and saw John James lying on the floor of his sleeping apartment." He then broke in the door, pulled James from the house, and took him to Tubman's house (*Auburn Democrat Argus*, Dec. 9, 1902). The account of the fire went on to describe how James had been in residence at the place for only about three months. It is possible that this structure was the building located on the lot north of Tubman's house. The ruins of a structure (Locus 4) found through survey and excavations date to this era.

32. John James was buried in Soule Cemetery.

33. A map of the City of Auburn shows a wood-frame house on that site in 1904 (Cayuga County Historian's Office, Auburn, NY), and we identified the footprint of its foundation through a combination of surveys, remote sensing, and excavation. It is probable that the map maker used information that dated to before the fire and was not aware that the house had burned when he completed the map in 1904.

Home, stating her recurrent financial troubles, and asking that donations be sent to support her fund-raising effort for her Home.[34]

Meanwhile, Harriet Tubman's brother William H. Stewart Sr. was also in financial trouble due to a series of doctor bills. In 1900, he is recorded as living with Harriet in her house on the farm in Fleming. He also owned a small, quarter-acre property adjoining the northwest corner of the twenty-five-acre farm. On February 19, 1903, William wrote a personal letter on Home stationery to Thomas Mott Osborne describing how he would like to see Osborne about some business, but he was sick and could not get out of the house. William noted that Osborne's mother and father have "been a friend to our family and I think you are one to [sic]." William Stewart had seen two or three doctors and needed money to pay them. He described how he owned two lots, one on South Street and one on Union Avenue, and he asked Osborne if he could take out a mortgage on one of the plots until he got better, "or if you can't do it mabie you know some body that will."[35] Two days later Thomas M. Osborne responded: "I do not see how I could help you in the matter you write about as I should not care to buy or take a mortgage on the lot you have."[36] He suggested that William should bring the matter up with John H. Osborne, the Home's treasurer, who was also Thomas's uncle.[37]

The AME Zion Church Steps Forward

Tubman remained in financial trouble and was in continued conversations with Robert W. Taylor about more formally entrusting the AME Zion Church

34. The letter was published in the *Christian Recorder*, July 25, 1901; see also Humez 2003, 113.

35. William H. Stewart to Thomas M. Osborne, Feb. 19, 1903, box 50, Osborne Family Papers. This is the earliest use of the new Harriet Tubman Home stationery that I have found. Thomas Mott Osborne was the only son of Eliza Wright Osborne and David Osborne. He was born September 23, 1959, grew up in Auburn, attended Harvard, and returned to Auburn after graduating. He became president of the Osborne Manufacturing Company in 1887 after his father's death. He held this post until he sold the company to J. P. Morgan, at which time the company became part of International Harvester Company. He also was the publisher of the *Auburn Citizen*, a newspaper that regularly published accounts of events associated with Harriet Tubman and the Harriet Tubman Home.

36. Thomas M. Osborne to William H. Stewart, Feb. 19, 1903, box 50, Osborne Family Papers.

37. Tubman had periodically cared for Thomas when he was a child and had been a regular visitor to his parents' house as both a guest and as someone hired to assist with seasonal housekeeping chores.

with the property and the project.[38] A plan to convey the property to the AME Zion Church in 1902 was held up by two key factors. Before the first mortgage could be transferred to the church, there was the problem of paying off a second ($575) and a third mortgage ($371). The church also had to deal with concern among some, including several of Tubman's prominent white friends, that she not be taken advantage of and that any transaction should include a guarantee of use of the property for life and a stipend for Tubman from the proceeds of rents until the Home was established. The AME Zion leadership interpreted Tubman's misgivings as having been generated by "white friends [who] were bitterly opposed to her deeding the property" (B. F. Wheeler, quoted in Humez 2003, 405, and Walls 1974, 441–42). Through the efforts of Rev. Dr. J. E. Mason and Professor Taylor, $200 was secured from the Church Extension Society, and additional funds were raised, including $161 by Taylor, from the sale of *A Brief Sketch of the Life of Harriet Tubman*, which Taylor had published for a personal expenditure of $96. The balance of the second mortgage was paid by a personal loan of $64 made by Rev. J. E. Mason and donations of $50 each by Rev. C. A. Smith, Rev. B. F. Wheeler, and Mr. R. J. Frazier (*Auburn Argus*, Mar. 2, 1902).[39]

With the issue of the second and third mortgages settled, Rev. Wheeler indicated that Tubman desired to have the deed transferred to Professor Taylor but that both he and Taylor urged her to deed the property over to the AME Zion Church. Wheeler wrote, "I urged her to deed it to the AME Zion Church, this she refused to do at first, but finally upon my telling her that in case she did deed it to the church, I would superintend it until other arrangements could be made, she reluctantly consented to do so. . . . When she became willing that I should select my own lawyer, I telegraphed to Utica to Rev. E. U. A. Brooks, who was also a lawyer, to come at an early hour next morning." The next morning Wheeler went to see Harriet with Rev. C. A. Smith and lawyer Brooks. He noted that "as some of Aunt Harriet's white friends were bitterly opposed to her deeding the property to us, we had to make generous provisions for her in drawing the deed. I stipulated in the deed that she had a life interest in the property. That is to say, she is to have

38. Walls indicates that Taylor secured a deed to the property on behalf of the Western Conference of the AME Zion Church in 1902 (1974, 440). Rev. Wheeler also used the date 1902 in a note to Thomas Osborne (B. F. Wheeler to Thomas Mott Osborne, Aug. 19, 1903, Osborne Family Papers, copy on file at the Cayuga County Historian's Office). Taylor did play a role in his conveyance of Booker T. Washington's and the AME Zion Church's support.

39. Wheeler provided each of these individuals with notes setting interest at a rate of 6 percent for a one-year term (Walls 1974, 440).

a life interest in all money accruing from rents, on condition that she pay the taxes and keep up the insurance, but that these rents would cease when we needed the property"[40] (as reported in Walls 1974, 441). When the deed was drawn up and signed over, "we hastened it to Little Rock, Arkansas, where the [AME Zion Church] Board of Bishops was in session." The deed transferred the property to the AME Zion Church but also assumed the balance of indebtedness on the property. This included a balance of $1,000 on the first mortgage, $575 on the second mortgage (held by George F. Ball), the payment of which had been secured, and $371 on the third mortgage (with interest for one year), which was held by William H. Stewart Sr. (Wheeler, as reported in Walls 1974, 440–42).

When the deed was sent to Arkansas, it went with the stipulation that the AME Zion Church arrange to pay off the third mortgage to William Stewart, which it agreed to do.[41] The agreement was made, and title to the property was formally transferred to the church on June 4, 1903, with the deed filed on June 11, 1903.[42] On April 10, 1903, the Church Expansion Society met in Philadelphia, and the AME Zion Board of Bishops appointed the following trustees to serve until the General Conference: Bishops James Walker Hood, Alexander Walters, George Wylie, J. B. Small, Hon., and J. C. Dancy; Rev. Drs. Martin R. Franklin, J. S. Caldwell, James E. Mason, and C. A. Small; Prof. Robert W. Taylor; John H. Osborne; R. J. Frazier; and Revs. E. U. A. Brooks and B. F. Wheeler.[43] When this group met, Bishop Walters served as president; Rev. B. F. Wheeler, the local AME Zion minister, was elected secretary; and John H. Osborne of Auburn's Osborne Manufacturing Company was elected treasurer.

40. There was concern that Tubman be provided for in her old age, and this effort was aimed at ensuring that she have means of support.

41. It is unclear how the property became indebted to William Stewart Sr. It is possible that Tubman had arranged to acquire his one-quarter-acre parcel at the northwest corner of the Home property. See the description of William's illness and correspondence with Thomas Osborne earlier in this chapter.

42. Harriet Tubman Davis to AME Zion Church, Cayuga County Deeds Book 33, June 11, 1903, Cayuga County Clerk's Office.

43. In his discussion of the history of the Home, Walls indicates that the date of transferring the deed was 1902, but the records indicate that it was done in 1903 (1974, 440). See note 44.

TWO OF AUNT HARRIET'S YOUNGER CHARGES.

6.1. Harriet Tubman sitting on the porch of her brick home at the announcement of the opening of the Home for the Aged, coinciding with the purchase of the twenty-five-acre farm. Illustration from the *Syracuse Sunday
Herald*, April 19, 1896.

HARRIET TUBMAN.

6.2. Harriet Tubman at the opening of the Harriet Tubman Home. Illustration from the *Syracuse Sunday Herald*, April 19, 1896.

HARRIET TUBMAN HOME FOR AGED COLORED PEOPLE.

6.3. Harriet Tubman standing with a child in front of her brick house at the opening of the Harriet Tubman Home. Illustration from the *Syracuse Sunday Herald*, April 19, 1896.

6.4. Harriet Tubman, c. 1896. This photograph was probably used for the illustration of Tubman in the *Syracuse Sunday Herald* on April 19, 1896. Item C8D00181-155D-451F-67528C91B231E573, courtesy of the Library of Congress, Washington, DC.

PART THREE

Integrating Historical and Archaeological Contexts

7

The Tubman Farmstead

Archaeological and Historical Contexts Uncovered

Another Conflagration—The residence of Harriet Tubman Davis, the
once famous Union scout and spy[,] located near the South street tollgate, was entirely consumed by fire at an early hour this morning. Only
a small portion of the household goods were saved. The conflagration is
said to have originated from a defective stovepipe stuck through a hole in
a lintern and which was utilized for a chimney.
                                    —*Evening Auburnian*, February 10, 1880

Archaeological Explorations of Tubman's
Personal Residence and Farm

Excavations at Harriet Tubman's farmhouse (Locus 1) began with a series of
one-by-one-meter units placed just outside of the southwest corner of the foundation (figures 1.2–1.3, 7.1–7.2). This area was selected to assess the potential
of archaeological reconnaissance and to answer questions concerning the age
and construction history of the house.[1] Census records indicate that when Tubman bought the property, the house was made of wood, but the house at the
site is made of brick, and records as early as the 1890 US census indicate a brick
structure. Moreover, an interview with Harriet Tubman by a reporter from
the *Syracuse Sunday Herald* in 1896 included illustrations of the brick house
(figures 6.1–6.3). An initial question that we wished to address through excavations was if the house purchased by Tubman in 1859 had in fact once been
made of wood. If so, what had happened to the house and when?

---

1. This study was undertaken in conjunction with an architectural assessment of Tubman's brick farmhouse by Crawford & Stearns, Architects and Preservation Planners. It was
carried out simultaneously with an archaeological survey of the entire thirty-two-acre Tubman complex (D. Armstrong 2003c). It was initiated to provide guidance for restoration of
the brick house, which began in 2003 and is still ongoing.

As described in chapter 3, we found evidence of a house fire at Tubman's residence on the first morning of excavations at the site. As we finished digging our second ten-centimeter level, we began to find burned and broken domestic ceramic and glass fragments mixed with topsoil and ash. Then at a depth of only twenty-five centimeters, we encountered distinct layers of gray then black ash (figures 3.1–3.4, 7.2). Together these deposits made up a total of not more than four to seven centimeters of soil. However, they provided evidence of burned wood, and the resulting ash contained a dense array of artifacts, including nails, broken glass, and pottery, some of them showing distinct evidence of melting and burning (figure 3.2). We stopped digging at the ash levels of the first units and expanded excavations laterally across the area, digging until we had exposed the ash layer; then we excavated through that layer and into the deposits below.

Out of the Ashes: Devastating House Fire and Reconstruction

By the end of the first week of excavation, we had recovered an abundance of information that demonstrated that the ash layer was the result of a house fire. The materials recovered, including an array of late nineteenth-century ironstone pottery with pottery maker's marks reading "O. P. Co.," for Onondaga Pottery Company (figure 7.3).[2] Collectively, the most recently manufactured materials from the ash layers suggested a date in the late 1870s, so I set a probable date for the fire at between 1880 and 1882 and began looking for accounts of the property related to this period. I passed this conjecture on to Beth Crawford of Crawford & Stearns Architects, who at the time was searching for records relating to Tubman in newspaper files at local archives. Using this information, she narrowed the range dates of her search for information and in the *Evening Auburnian* found a report of a fire at Tubman's residence that had occurred in the early morning hours of February 10, 1880 (figure 3.3). The short newspaper account described the cause of the fire as a faulty "stove pipe stuck through a hole in the lintern," presumably a wooden lintel above a window or door. Later, I found a second news report of the fire in the *Auburn News and Bulletin* for the same date.[3] According to the second

2. Onondaga Pottery, located in Syracuse, New York, changed its name to Syracuse China in 1895. The pottery line at Onondaga Pottery included Rockingham ware (Reed and Skoczen 1997).

3. The *Auburn News and Bulletin* account on February 10, 1880, indicates that the fire destroyed the home of the "renowned liberator of slaves and Union scout" but refers to her as

account, the fire began in the kitchen or back of the house. Neither report mentions any injuries, but both describe the destruction of the house. The second article notes that the fire left Tubman homeless, "a severe blow to her in her old age" (she was only fifty-seven at the time), but it also optimistically states that there "is no doubt that she will receive aid to enable her to regain a home" (*Auburn News and Bulletin*, Feb. 10, 1880). The archaeological evidence—literally thousands of artifacts and fragments from personal possessions, clothing, and furnishings that had been in the house—confirms the destructive nature of the fire.

We continued to dig next to the foundation and found that the ash layer disappeared as we approached within fifty to sixty centimeters of the structure. As we dug down, exposing the stone foundation, we found a change in the type of stone used in the foundation at a depth of about thirty centimeters. The stone changed from large blocks of Onondaga Limestone above the surface to smaller sheets of Marcellus Shale below the surface (figure 3.4). Seeing this, we went into the basement and found that the change occurred throughout the foundation. As we continued to dig near the foundation, we found out why there was no ash abutting the foundation wall. When the fire occurred, and as debris from the house was cleared out, an ash layer built up all around the house. Then when the new brick structure was constructed on the old foundation base, a forty-to-fifty-centimeter-wide trench was dug around the house. This builder's trench was dug down to a depth of about 1.2 meters. The old wall had been repointed then capped with new cut limestone blocks. The two-story brick house was built on this foundation. As the new brick house was constructed, bricks and fragments of brick used to construct the house were deposited in the bottom of the builder's trench. When the house was complete, the trench was filled using soils that contained a mix of artifacts burned in the fire and ash. In this way, the yard of the new house was cleaned up, and important and meaningful artifacts were buried in the trench.

By the end of the first week of excavations, we had also found ash deposit associated with the fire, complete with wood ash, nails, and burned artifacts, in the yard near the house. The red bricks found at the bottom of the builder's

---

"Charlotte Tubman." It also makes note of her recent notoriety and "her (supposed innocent) connection with the party of colored confidence operators who robbed one of our prominent citizens of two thousand dollars, on pretense of exchanging confederate gold for his greenbacks." This con and robbery occurred in 1873 (*Auburn Morning News*, Oct. 4, 1873). It is clear from the reference to Tubman as "Charlotte" in this article that this report of the fire was rapidly written by someone who really did not know who she was.

trench are compositionally the same as those found in the walls of the house, although those in the walls have been exposed to the weather and have taken on a modeled red-yellow-orange coloring (figure 1.3). The builder's trench is an important archaeological feature that served as a receptacle for Tubman's personal and household goods damaged by the fire. Debris cleared from within the foundation were reburied in the trench when it was refilled. For this reason, in the next several summer seasons we excavated sections of the trench on the north and west sides of the house and found clustered deposits of thousands of broken ceramics, glass, glassware, buttons, and personal items—all of which were part of the assemblage of furnishings and personal items in the house at the time of the fire.

The fire was a traumatic event in the life of Harriet Tubman and for those living in her household. However, from the standpoint of archaeological reconnaissance, the fact that the fire occurred and that evidence of it was retained undisturbed in layers of ash deposited in the surrounding yard was an unexpected windfall. Excavation of these deposits uncovered all sorts of significant personal possessions and household goods dating to the era of Tubman's life that would otherwise have probably been lost.

Over the next several seasons, excavations were conducted in yard areas on all sides of the house. Attention was paid to defining and excavating the builder's trench. We also excavated in the yard behind the house, in the basement of the house, and in and around the barn. In the process, we identified significant quantities of materials dating to the period before the fire, more evidence of the fire, and materials from the period after the fire. We also rediscovered a wooden cistern and explored a well in the yard near the house and in the area of a chicken coop south of the barn. We defined Tubman's house as Locus 1 for the Tubman properties and divided the area in and around the house into nine subloci to facilitate comparisons of material findings from each distinct area associated with the farmstead (see the identification and description of all loci in chapter 1).

Under the Porch: Uncovering a Deposit
of Tableware and Personal Possessions

The master plan for restoration was designed to restore Tubman's house first, then her barn. Restoration of the property would then be expanded to the white house and other parts of the property, including, perhaps, John Brown Hall. Part of the plan for restoration of Tubman's brick farmhouse included replacement of post-Tubman-era porches with versions emulating those present in the Tubman era, as shown in the illustration of the house done for the *Syracuse Sunday Herald* in 1896 (figure 6.3). Having found that the builder's trench contained materials that were in the wood-frame house and burned in the house fire, seeing in later photographs that the large porch on the north side of the brick building had been constructed in the 1920s, and surmising that the porch had essentially covered and protected that area for more than eighty years, we removed the floorboards to the north porch and began excavation along the north foundation wall and under the porch (figure 7.4). This was a fortuitous decision because the subsurface deposits had in fact been protected, and we quickly recovered evidence of the ash levels associated with the house fire and found the builder's trench, which was rich in burned and broken household and personal items and had piles of brick at the base of the trench. The well-stratified deposits under the porch also had distinct soils containing materials dating to Tubman's pre-1880 activities at the site and even a level that probably predated Tubman's acquisition of the property.

A wide range of materials representing each time period was recovered under the porch, including thousands of artifacts that had apparently been in Tubman's living and dining rooms, which were located adjacent to this area. We reconstructed more than a dozen plain ironstone plates and serving bowls (figure 7.5). Cutlery was also present, including a pair of bent spoons as well as bone-handled knives and forks (figure 7.6). A large group of glass stemware fragments from glass goblets may have served as ice cream or dessert goblets (figure 7.7). The possibility of the latter use derives from records of similar items defined as ice cream goblets in the household records of Eliza Wright Osborne.[4] A bud vase probably once held flowers from Tubman's garden (figure 7.7). Other artifacts present include fragments of a glass oil/vinegar decanter, cut- and pressed-glass candy jars, porcelain figurines, and glass lampshade fragments (figure 7.8). Materials from this assemblage might also have come from the adjacent living room or the basement kitchen below it. These items may have been given to Harriet and Nelson on their wedding day, gifted to them over the years, or simply acquired by Tubman or others in her household. This assemblage, which was found tightly grouped in the trench just outside of the doorway on the north side of the house, suggests that the materials had been in the dining room, perhaps on tables or in china or curio cabinets, for which a variety of furniture hardware was recovered. After the

4. Eliza Wright Osborne, household records, June 6, 1906, box 60, pp. 1–5, Osborne Family Papers, Special Collections Research Center, Syracuse Univ., Syracuse, NY.

fire, the burned artifacts were removed from the burned house to the yard, perhaps even sorted through for surviving whole items, and then, upon completion of the construction of Tubman's new brick house, were shoveled into the trench to clear the yard before the new porches, illustrated in the 1896 *Syracuse Sunday Herald* article, were constructed.

In addition to materials suggesting a dining and living room (or parlor) assemblage, there were a wide array of buttons (figure 7.9) and fasteners that could have come from the same rooms or, more likely, from second-story bedrooms above them. These items were made of a wide variety of materials and project a diverse collection of clothing items, from shoes to blouses, shirts, and jackets. They also suggest the presence of clothing that had some age. This is not altogether surprising given the advanced age of many of the residents living at Tubman's personal home, which was serving as an ad hoc location for the Home for the Aged. It might also relate to the presence of hand-me-down clothing. Among the buttons were many small burned and melted porcelain buttons that may have been used to fasten everything from shirts to shoes. Also present were bone buttons, cufflinks, and studs from women's and men's clothing. Coat or outer-garment buttons varied in size and composition. Among the metal buttons were four with a six-pointed star pattern, three of which are identical and the fourth with the same pattern but larger (figure 1.4).[5] The presence of matching buttons suggests that they were attached to items of clothing that had burned. Certainly, the presence of stars on buttons associated with people who had followed the North Star to freedom is an association worthy of consideration. A button identical to these was found by archaeologists from the University of Massachusetts, Amherst, during excavation of the boyhood home of W. E. B. Du Bois, the Burghardt house, now a National Historic Landmark in Great Barrington, Massachusetts. Interestingly, both the Burghardt family and Tubman were affiliated with the AME Zion Church, and the archaeologists working at that site also took pause to consider the possible correlation between the button star and the North Star as a symbol of the path to freedom.[6]

5. The design of the star buttons has been engraved into the buttons on Harriet Tubman's clothing on the anticipated Harriet Tubman $20 bill approved by Congress and the Department of the Treasury.

6. A W. E. B. Du Bois collection website describes a button with a six-pointed star as being found at the W. E. B. Du Bois House along with two other artifacts, a young bear's tooth and a polished stone, and suggests that the grouping of these objects might be connected to some sort of spiritual practice: "Certain combinations of objects have been used for

Among the intriguing artifacts found in the area under the north porch was an 1852 half-penny trade token from the Bank of Quebec (figure 4.1). This Canadian coin was found right outside the front door in pre-fire-era deposits. The fact that it is from the region of Canada from which Tubman and her family had moved to Auburn projects an active tie between the people and their movements. Was it simply lost as someone in the household went through his or her pockets to retrieve a key to open the door, or was it purposely dropped in the doorway for luck by Tubman, her parents, or others for whom the movement from Canada had great meaning? A key was found in the same deposits (figure 7.10), and both it and the coin may simply have fallen between the floorboards of the porch to the ground below, unretrievable to its owner.

The Front Yard and the Rediscovery of a Brick Walk

We initiated excavations on the west side of Tubman's brick residence in anticipation of the removal of the west porch. Our excavations tied into the grid of units initiated in 2002 and extended out three meters from the house. We began by digging down to expose the gray ash level across the front of the house (figure 7.2). The ash level in this area was undisturbed and indicated little modification of this area after the fire other than the buildup of sod and grass. Plantings of bridal veil spirea (*Spiraea prunifolia*) were found along the west side of the house.[7] The roots of these plants were limited to the area of the builder's trench. However, the *Syracuse Sunday Herald* illustration of this side of the house done in 1896 (figure 6.3) shows no plantings in this area, so they were probably added in the post-Tubman era.

As we extended excavations north along the west side of the house, we uncovered a previously unknown brick walkway extending out from the porch to South Street (figure 7.11). The walk was made of bricks identical to those

---

African spiritual practices in Hoodoo bundles and as symbols of the universe (cosmograms)" (James Aronson Collection of W. E. B. Du Bois, Robert S. Cox Special Collections and University Archives Research Center, University of Massachusetts, http://scua.library.umass.edu /category/du-bois-web/; see also the Du Bois National Historic Site, https://www.duboisnhs .org, and Muller 1994). The symbolic meaning of these stars is discussed in detail in chapter 12 and in relation to their selection for the new US $20 bill in chapter 13.

7. This plant is also known as bridal wreath spirea. It grows into a hedge and has abundant small white flowers that bloom in the late spring in this part of New York. The plant became a popular hedge shrub in the region beginning in the 1870s.

used to construct the house, suggesting that the walkway was added when the brick house was built in the early 1880s.[8] We exposed the brick walkway, found at an average depth of ten centimeters (A. Armstrong 2011), from the bottom step of the porch to the edge of South Street. After finding the walkway, we reexamined the illustrations in the 1896 article about the opening of the Home and found that the two images with Tubman and a child show a brick pathway (figures 6.1 and 6.3). Among the artifacts found on the walkway were a scattering of seven clay marbles, all within two meters of the steps. The presence of the grouping of marbles indicates use of the walkway and perhaps the porch by children for games involving marbles. The two sources of information—the marbles and the illustrations—work together to show the importance of children at a site usually most closely associated with Tubman and aging African Americans.

In all, a dozen clay marbles were found during excavations of the yard surrounding Tubman's brick farmhouse (figure 7.12). We thought the marbles were probably either made locally as an informal practice associated with brickmaking or brought to the site by children who had broken them out of stoppered soda bottles, like "Cobb Stopper" soda bottles (Elliot and Gould 1988), although the marbles in such soda bottles were made of glass (figure 7.13). The composition of several of the clay marbles were tested using Neutron Activation Analysis. Results indicated a wide range of compositions; however, it is possible that the clay used for the clay marbles was different than that used for the bricks or that various clays were mixed to create a range of colors for the marbles.

An array of damaged yet recognizable artifacts preserved after the fire reflect a range of items for play. In addition to the marbles, toys present include doll parts and miniature porcelain tea wares from play tea sets (figure 7.14). A thimble indicates that someone at the site was engaged in sewing, and a jaw harp is suggestive of an individual playing a personal musical instrument (figure 7.15). Tobacco pipes were present at the site in forms that are consistent with those used in the later nineteenth century (figure 7.16). A total of twenty-eight tobacco pipes were recovered from all areas associated with Tubman's house, barn, and yard. Glass beads constitute another group of items used for personal adornment and in apparel. We did not find them in abundance, but those recovered represent an array of forms and colors (figure 7.17).

8. Confirmed through chemical characterization using Neutron Activation Analysis; see A. Armstrong 2011; A. Armstrong and D. Armstrong 2012.

Canning jars were found in the burned and refuse deposits in Tubman's yard. The bottles represent a range of manufacturers, including well-known Atlas and Ball jars as well as jars from lesser-known companies (figure 7.18). The presence of the jars at her house correlates with numerous accounts that describe the gifting of canned goods to Tubman and the Home. The jars point to the importance of canned goods as a source of food as well as to community-wide gifting and support.

A slate pencil was found among the burned materials in the trench outside of Tubman's house (figure 7.19). Harriet Tubman was illiterate, but others living in the house, including several children, were able to read and write. Several household items associated with the Tubman-era use, including brass picture hangers, brass curtain-rod holders (for a one-and-a-half-inch-round rod), and brass curtain-rod ring, were found in middens behind her barn.

Consistent with Tubman's beliefs and the practices of the AME Zion Church, alcohol bottles are virtually absent from the site; however, we did find one cluster of bottles that may have contained beer in the backfill of the builder's trench by the door on the north side of Tubman's residence.[9] These bottles are dark-green cylindrical bottles with "JPS" embossed on the side. The context and the bottles' positioning in the upper level of the back-filled trench suggests that those who constructed the house may have paused to celebrate the completion of the house construction and yard clearing with some liquid refreshment (figure 7.20).

Most of the artifacts recovered from the site date to the Tubman era (1859–1913), but the pre-1880 era (before the house fire) is less well defined in deposits than is the time associated with the fire and later periods at the site. The 1840 US census shows no buildings on the property, but by 1850 the land had been inherited by Frances Seward from her father and was occupied by the Barton family. There is no marked division between pre-Tubman-era and Tubman-era use prior to the house fire ash and materials. However, the lower levels project a date earlier in the nineteenth century, and the upper levels contain materials spanning the prefire Tubman era and suggesting a gradual accumulation of materials between the 1860s and 1880. Artifacts from the oldest levels include varieties of hand-painted polychrome creamware

9. Tubman was known to have acquired wine and whiskey from her neighbors and supporters "for medicinal purposes" (Kate Larson, personal communication to the author, Aug. 5, 2017).

and pearlware ceramics, almost all of them small-bowl forms (figure 7.21). Also present were US half pennies from 1804 and 1807 (figure 7.22). It is common to find coins of considerable age that were in continued use in the nineteenth century. It is possible that the ceramic wares were part of the initial household assemblage present when Harriet Tubman first bought the farm from the Sewards. The fine line designs represent relatively expensive wares if purchased in the initial decades of the nineteenth century, but these wares may also have been hand-me-downs from supportive community members or items purchased secondhand.

A Cache of Pharmaceutical Bottles
and Health and Hygiene Items

The builder's trench on the west side of the house (facing South Street) matches the trench found on the south and north sides of the house (figures 1.3, 3.4, 7.4). Along the west wall on the south side of the porch, we found a tightly packed cache of pharmaceutical bottles and other items suggesting that the contents of a medicine cabinet or table used to hold medicine were dumped into the trench together (figure 7.23). The mass of items included fragments from more than two dozen pharmaceutical bottles, four of which remained intact (figure 7.24). One retained part of its content, glycerin.

One of the most telling and personal items found with this group of pharmaceutical and personal hygiene artifacts was a toothbrush made of bone and boar's bristles (figure 7.25). Charring of the bristle area indicate that the toothbrush was burned and that the fire had lingered as the bristles burned down, causing greater damage to the bone in this area of the bristles than on the handle. Looking closely at the brush, I noticed what I thought at first might be a maker's mark impressed into the bone. Under magnification, we found that it was not a maker's mark; rather, the letter H had been scratched into the surface along with a second less well-defined letter, possibly a J, and a dot with a circle etched around it. It is tempting to think that the H represents "Harriet," but the presence of the second letter leaves the identity of the owner a mystery.

Nearby we found a fragment of a bottle of Dr. Marshall's snuff, a medicine used to relieve headaches (figure 7.26). At least three identical bottles, including two whole bottles, were found in the builder's trench and post-fire deposits on the south side of the house. Tubman suffered from chronic and sometimes debilitating headaches, so it is likely that she used some of

Dr. Marshall's snuff.[10] At least one person at the site wore eyeglasses because glass lenses were found in the deposits outside Tubman's house as well as in deposits at the post-Tubman-era dormitory of her Home.

The Backyard and the Rediscovery of a Wooden Cistern

The area on the east side of the house (away from South Street) was significantly modified by the Norrises after they bought the property from Tubman's estate in 1913. The Norris family tore down a Tubman-era shed behind the house and built a new structure in the 1920s. This new structure had a stone foundation and a basement level as well as a first-floor porch that allowed people to enter the first floor of the brick house through a door that was part of the construction of the house in the 1880s. Before removing this porch, we explored the area east of this structure as the possible site of a privy.[11] Our testing of the blacktop-covered parking lot area behind this structure proved negative; however, we did define several layers of blacktop and mixed ash and rubble fill that had been spread across the area to provide a stable surface for the many buses that the Norris family parked in the area beginning in the 1920s for their business (D. Armstrong 2008). Our shovel tests yielded a mixed assemblage of artifacts from the late nineteenth and early twentieth centuries.

When the 1920s-era porch structure behind the house was removed in November 2008, the demolition produced a hole that was a little more than one meter deep, so I had little hope of finding anything. However, as we scraped off the loose debris, we found a definitive black discoloration in the soil as well as two distinct circles (figure 7.27). The outer circle, spanning a 2.4-meter-diameter area, was defined by soils that were darker than the surrounding subsoil. This circle was 1.2 meters from the back wall of the house's

---

10. Tubman had worked for Dr. Anthony C. Thompson in an apothecary for years in Maryland before heading to New York. She also worked as a nurse during the Civil War. Hence, she was familiar with a range of health-care practices of the era.

11. We considered the Tubman-era shed-roof structure in this area to have served several possible uses, including the storage of wood or coal and possibly as a privy. The speculation regarding the latter use was based on Dorris Norris's discussion of early use of the yard by the Norris family. Dorris lived at this site and in a house on an adjacent property from the time of her marriage into the family in the late 1940s (Alice Norris, personal communication to the author, May 22, 2002).

foundation. We considered the possibility that this feature was a privy, but its shape was wrong. As we exposed it, we found that it was a large wooden cistern, with its side walls and bottom intact. Its wooden top was missing, but the top's presence was indicated by the iron ring. We excavated a quarter of the interior of the feature (figure 7.28). The cistern contained a wide range of artifacts, including ceramics that date to the turn of the twentieth century (figure 7.29). The cistern was constructed using five-quarter (5/4) thick oak of varying board widths (twelve to twenty-two centimeters). The boards were joined with wooden pegs. There was no definitive evidence for exactly when the cistern was constructed, but it probably dates back to the wood-frame house and continued to be used after construction of the brick house.

After the excavation of this feature, I found correspondence between Tubman supporter and guardian Eliza Wright Osborne and her daughter Helen O. Storrow written in 1904 that provides a date for the replacement of this wooden cistern with a masonry cistern in the basement (figures 7.28 and 7.30), which Osborne had paid for the previous year. The letter discusses many things, including the cost of health care for Tubman and a request made by Tubman for new wallpaper.[12] The timing of this new cistern fits well

12. Eliza Wright Osborne to Helen Storrow, Dec. 16, 1904, box 220, Osborne Family Papers. In this same handwritten letter to Helen Storrow, Eliza indicates that she had just returned to Auburn by train. She said that it looked as if it was ready to snow, and the "mercury is at zero." She therefore "sent Mrs. Lami out to Harriet's this morning to see if they were *freezing*." She found a pretty forlorn state of things. The cook stove was burned out and didn't look as if a fire could be made in it. "When she [Tubman] came to see me right after I got home I asked her about her stove and she allowed the cook stove wasn't much use. I have ordered one sent to her and put up in shape. I got it off Nill Metcalf and told him to see that a good fire was made before he left. I asked him to look at her other stoves to see if anything was needed for the other two stoves she has." She also notes, "Harriet is very miserable. I am having a basket of provisions got ready to send out after dinner. A big stash of pork, potatoes, bread, etc."

In another letter to Helen dated April 11, 1911, Eliza complains that the doctors attending "Mrs. Harriet T. Davis" had billed her (Eliza) for medical services, but since she had never sent Dr. Hudson to Tubman, she "should not think of doing it." She goes on to call Dr. Hudson a "low down Doctor who resides in this town and practices in an unspeakable way when asked to, just as if I would have anything to do with him."

Eliza, like Tubman, was in poor health, and her doctor thought she should have a nurse, but she notes that "I don't believe it will be necessary." She comments that "Harriet Tubman is here at the hospital, she has been there some three weeks I think, or four." "I tried to get word to the manager it was mighty silly for them to be enlarging the bill with the possibility

with the shift of Tubman's kitchen from the basement to the first floor of the house. Osborne complains that the contractor had failed to connect the new cistern to the downspouts that were designed to gather water from the roof. A hole in the east foundation wall fed water to the cistern from these downspouts. Based on Osborne's letter, we know that later versions of these downspouts were supposed to be tied into the internal cistern, and one can surmise by Osborne's vehement complaint that a contractor was put to work to correct the problem.

As part of the restoration of Tubman's house, new sewer and water lines were dug in 2011. While the excavation of the sewer line was being monitored, a clay tile water pipe was found that once connected the wooden cistern to a well behind the house. A late nineteenth-century Guild's cast-iron hand pump is still present on the property. It is possible that water was pumped from the cistern by this pump or a similar hand pump in a shed positioned above the wooden cistern.

Significantly, the archaeological record and the Osborne letter indicate an important reconfiguration of Tubman's house in 1903 and 1904 with the movement of Tubman's kitchen from the basement to her main living-floor level. The movement of the kitchen out of the basement shows a shift toward a twentieth-century living style. The new cistern with its focus on water from the roof rather than from the ground suggests a concern for water purity, health, and hygiene, which was also taking on greater importance during this era.

---

of not getting any of it. If the Fleming people, she lives in that district, will pay half I will pay half. I wonder what the charges are for poor folks with you, I think $8.00 a week is perfectly enormous for Harriet. That is what they are charging her thinking I will pay it but I won't. I will help. She really ought to stay there longer but she doesn't want to, and she has a niece here in town who wants to get her providing she can have some money to pay for her. Dear me, she is one of the people who are living beyond all possibility, it is such a pity. She has been so wonderful in all the days she was helpful" (Eliza Wright Osborne to Helen Storrow, Apr. 11, 1911, box 88, Osborne Family Papers). In the same letter, Eliza goes on to comment on the fact that "Helen is getting to be quite noted, who would ever have thought it." She says, "I am so interested in all this party business where blacks and whites join and have a good time. When you have your party the 25th. I am going to try to come to it but it does not seem as if it would be possible from my standpoint now, but I would like to see the combination of black and white, if there is to be such a combination. I suppose all your classes are to be asked are they not? I will send a little contribution which I hope will help a tiny bit. I am glad to help such a cause, anyway I want a ticket if I go, and I suppose $1.50 is reserved seats, so I will take that kind, and I will take two because I would like to bring Mrs. Kellogg."

The Kitchen Basement and Changes
in Lifestyles Entering the Twentieth Century

When Crawford & Stearns Architects (2002) did a building assessment of Tubman's house, we shared information linking archaeological contexts and elements associated with the standing structure. Physical evidence in the basement provided information related to its use and its connections to the floors above. The first critical piece of information from the basement was evidence that during the Tubman era the basement was divided into two rooms. The wood-frame wall had lath and plaster only on its east side, and the stone in the east room was covered with mortar. Nearly all of the lath and plaster has been removed, but a few laths remained attached to the ceiling, and one could see hundreds of nail holes and evidence of a light cover of plaster on the north wall of the finished room on the east side. After the Tubman era, the entire floor of the basement was covered with Portland cement, which was added after the dividing wall between the two rooms was removed.

We excavated several test units through the cement in each of these rooms and dug a one-meter-wide trench bisecting the rooms. Our initial tests were at the base of windows, doorways, and stairways. In the west room, we found a very shallow profile of cultural deposits atop a red-brown clay substrate. In contrast, units in the east room revealed a dense layer of burned coal ash that had been distributed across the floor, creating a hard surface, and twenty to twenty-five centimeters of black ash, slag, and burned rock from the coal that had been used to heat the house. Under this layer, we found the same red-brown clay. When we removed the old furnace, we gained access to a larger area on the southeast side of the east room, an area that had been the former basement kitchen. We excavated a trench that cut from east to west from the internal cistern into the unfinished room on the west side of the building, which allowed us to clearly demarcate the difference in accumulation between the two rooms (figure 7.31).

In excavating the basement, we were interested in testing for any unusual clustering or groupings of artifacts along each wall and at doorways and stairways, which might have projected behavior practices that we might otherwise have missed.[13] Moreover, we felt that the basement might provide evidence of

13. Selection of test units was aimed at seeing if any materials were present that would relate to religious practice associated with African American contexts from sites in Maryland, as reported by Mark Leone (2005) and others. We felt it was important to test these areas because of Tubman's and her family's ties to Maryland and her definitive record as an

pre- and post-1880s Tubman-era use of the property. Although we recovered surprisingly few artifacts or dietary remains in the basement, we found an abundance of data related to house construction and use.

We knew from the presence of debris in the yard and the abundance of materials in the builder's trench that the basement had been dug out after the fire in 1880 and before the new brick structure was built in 1881–82. Still, we were surprised that there was no evidence of any pre-1880s deposits left in the basement. The bulk of the material that accumulated on the floor of the east room was coal ash, with rocky impurities.

When the kitchen was moved from the basement in the 1880s, the stairs down to the basement were also removed up to the floor joists, and a closet was created under the stairway, which was rebuilt to connect the first and second floors. Two steps from the basement stairway survived, indicating the slope/pitch and the probable placement of the staircase's footing. A trench cross-cutting the basement exposed brick footers for the staircase in the basement (figure 7.31). After the kitchen was moved from the basement, the only access to the basement was through the exterior doorway located at the north side of the east wall of the basement (stonework indicates that this doorway dates to the rebuilding of Tubman's house in 1881–82). Elements of the early steep stairway between the first and second floors also survive under the current staircase leading to the second floor of the structure.

The South Yard: Pasts Disturbed and Preserved

The southeast corner of Tubman's house underwent a series of mid- to late twentieth-century water- and sewer-construction activities that disturbed the Tubman-era soils and thus prevented our recovery of undisturbed contexts. A water pipe in the basement dates to the 1950s, and a sewer line was added in the 1960s, when the house was finally tied into the Town of Fleming sewer system, the line cutting through the house's iron septic tank.[14] In 2011, the trench dug for new water and sewer lines provided us additional information

individual who had strong spiritual beliefs. Even though we did not find anything similar to material reported for African American contexts in Maryland, we felt that not testing would have left the issue unaddressed. In fact, there is an abundance of material evidence related to Tubman's belief systems present at the site, just not of the type projected by Leone. Moreover, materials from excellent contexts outside the house could quite easily be interpreted as bridging several levels of meaning, including the spiritual.

14. The septic tank had been installed by the Norris family.

on use of the yard, exposing some previously undisturbed Tubman-era soils that allowed us a glimpse of the continuation of the builder's trench east along the south side of the house. Also, the new sewer line cut a new path that ran between the wooden cistern and the well. We found evidence of clay tile piping running toward the well on an angle that would have connected the cistern to the well.

The Well behind the House

After the AME Zion Church purchased Tubman's house and farm from the Norris family in 1990, it planted a tree in the open well behind the house to prevent children from falling into the well. In 2012, with the sewer line trench still open, we focused our attention on explorations of the well.[15] To dig the well, we first had to remove the tree (figures 7.32–7.33). We excavated the area around the well to a depth of one meter. In the process, we found that the well was lined with brick for about thirty centimeters, after which it was lined with irregular shale fieldstones, but no mortar. We also exposed a round clay pipeline that ran from the well to the cistern at a depth of eighty centimeters. On the south side, we found another tile line at a depth of ninety centimeters that ran from the well in a southeasterly direction and was probably used for water runoff.[16] The lower stone of the well is consistent with the stone from lower levels of the foundation of Tubman's house and thus consistent with the construction of the 1850s-era wood-frame house that Tubman purchased from the Sewards. The upper courses of brick were probably added in the 1880s, when Tubman's brick house was built. We dug the well to a depth of two and a half meters with the assistance of a sump pump because it was below the ground waterline. However, even at that depth we were still finding a mix of Tubman- and post-Tubman-era materials, which indicated that we were still digging through fill and that throughout Tubman's lifetime the well was clear to a depth of greater than two and a half meters. The excavation of the well

15. One objective of the study of the well was to gather organic materials for a dietary study that was part of Jessica Bowes dissertation research at Syracuse University.

16. The relative placement of the tile lines suggests that the line from the cistern was meant as a water runoff from it to the well, and the line from the southeast side of the well was used as a general runoff for both. This same pattern of runoff of cistern water to a well in the yard was observed at a nineteenth-century farm site in Skaneateles, New York, about fifteen miles from the Tubman site.

provided important information on the construction and changes to the property and an explanation of the use of water at the site during the Tubman era.

Tubman's Barn and Farmyard

The barn located in the yard behind Harriet Tubman's brick residence is one of the three Tubman-era structures on the Home properties that is still standing. However, when we began work at the site, the barn was enveloped by more recent cinder block garage structures, and the old barn itself had been significantly altered (figures 7.34–7.37). Its western wall had been cut away to accommodate tall buses that were parked in the garage as part of the Norris Bus Company. The construction of additions to the north and south side of the barn dramatically changed the appearance of the barn and access to the lands behind it. The cinder block addition on the north side of the barn blocked access to the roadbed that extends all the way back to John Brown Hall (D. Armstrong 2003b, 2003c). The cinder block garage on the south side of the barn had changed the appearance of the barn but had also provided a weather guard for the south wall of the old barn. When the barn was restored, this wall was the best-preserved section of it and was used as a model to reconstruct the barn's board and baton siding.

Remote sensing in the area behind the barn (east side) showed high concentrations of iron (figure 3.6). In 2004, we carried out shovel tests in this area and uncovered a series of ash layers. The lower layers of ash corresponded with the period of the Tubman house fire and may represent a place where some of the materials from Tubman's house fire were deposited in 1880. Materials recovered from behind the barn included an array of household hardware, such as window latch parts, brass hangers, and rings for curtains used between rooms for privacy and to prevent drafts, particularly in the winter (figure 7.38). They indicate that some of the rooms in Tubman's house had finish details, such as crown molding with picture railings.

As restoration of the barn began, the cinder block garages were removed, as were the shed-roofed structures to the rear. Original parts of the barn were retained (figure 7.35). As the restoration proceeded, a trench for a new foundation was dug, and we examined soil profiles beneath the barn (figure 7.36). We also excavated units under the barn. The deepest cultural materials included artifacts that were either from the house that burned in 1880 or from another possible fire from the same period. Deposits from test units and units under the barn had nineteenth-century plain white ironstone dinner plates like those found in the builder's trench around Tubman's brick house. The soil profile below the barn included a wide range of iron fragments, nails, and items most closely associated with barn and farm-related activities. These materials suggest that the barn on this site is from the 1890s or later. There were several barns on Tubman's two properties. The foundation of this barn was made of two courses of brick of the type made in the South Street brick-yards. The upper levels contained Tubman-era materials that were probably removed from the house when the Norris family remodeled the house. Excavations indicated that the barn that was restored had originally had a brick footing; however, in an effort to protect the barn's siding when the barn was restored, a cement foundation was poured and then lined with stone. The barn was then lowered onto this new foundation, and new siding was used to supplement surviving framing and board and batten lumber. The barn restoration was completed in 2009 (figure 7.37).

From census records, we know that Tubman usually had at least one horse and a cow, along with several dozen hogs (table 5.5). Although the barn on the site probably dates to the late nineteenth century, it possibly was rebuilt on the site of a fire reported in 1911.[17] A report in the *Auburn Citizen* on March 4, 1911, describes how a "small barn on the Home estate in Fleming just outside the city limits in South Street, burned to the ground early this afternoon with the contents consisting of a few tons of hay and some farm implements." No cause is reported for this fire. It occurred at a time when Tubman was sick with pneumonia. When she returned home from the hospital, she was admitted as a resident and patient in John Brown Hall.

This barn fire on Tubman's farm was part of a much-discussed arson spree reportedly carried out by George Mountpleasant. Defined as an "Indian,"[18] Mountpleasant had applied to live in the "red house," referred to here as the Legacy House (Locus 2), which at that time was painted red, but he was turned down by the Tubman Home Board of Trustees, who "decided not to rent the premises."[19] It was reported that "soon after a barn on the premises was burned to the ground . . . those on the property are unanimous in declaring that there was absolutely nothing in the barn that could cause a fire

17. However, the barn described in the *Auburn Citizen* report of March 4, 1911, may have been an earlier version of the barn now standing behind (to the east of) Tubman's brick house or possibly a barn located about twenty meters east of the current barn.

18. Mountpleasant is also described as a graduate of the Carlisle Indian School of Pennsylvania (*Auburn Bulletin*, March 13, 1911).

19. This house had been rented out but had recently been vacated.

without incendiarism." The report goes on to say that "Mountpleasant was familiar with the vicinity and had loitered there at various times" (*Auburn Bulletin*, Mar. 13, 1911). Rev. E. U. A. Brooks, president of the Tubman Home Board of Trustees, reported to the *Auburn Bulletin* that Mountpleasant had come to him several times during the past week for assistance. He added that he had aided "the Indian," but the latter had been so unpleasant on Friday, using an unusual method to persuade the clergyman that he ought to assist him. Mountpleasant told Brooks, "You are a friend and I'll give you a tip. I know of a plot to burn your home and the church and if anything happens you want to look out for _____," giving a name that was not disclosed by Rev. Brooks but referring to someone who Brooks said was supposedly associated with the AME Zion Church. Rev. Brooks said he gave the conversation little consideration until Mountpleasant's name was associated with the burning of St. Alphonsus Catholic Church in Auburn. He reported that Mountpleasant had always included fires in "strange stories used to obtain money from persons who have been in the habit of assisting him" (*Auburn Daily Bulletin*, Mar. 13, 1911). The article describing the barn fire goes on to link Mountpleasant to at least three other fires in Auburn: a fire at St. Alphonsus Catholic Church, one at a barber shop, and another at a boardinghouse and laundry owned by Hattie Stout. The March 13, 1911, account of the fire on the Tubman farm does not give specific details of the location of the barn. However, excavations beneath the current barn when it was being restored in 2010–11 included evidence of a fire at the site. Hence, it is probable that the barn standing on this site was at least partially reconstructed after a fire, and that fire may have been the one reported in 1911.

Tubman's Yard, Chicken Coops, Gardens, and Hog Pen

Tubman and her family engaged in a variety of farming and gardening activities in the areas south and east of her house. In the 1940s, a chicken coop still stood about twenty meters south of her house. This area was excavated in 2012, and a variety of domestic artifacts and dietary remains were recovered. However, we did not find any direct evidence of the wood-frame and wire chicken coops that appears in photographs from the 1940s. Numerous accounts describe Tubman growing vegetables and flowers in a kitchen garden. It is likely that this garden was in proximity to her house. However, the survival of a distinct ash layer indicates that the area within five meters of the house was not dug deep enough for the garden, so the garden was probably a bit farther to the south or perhaps east.

The 1874–75 New York State agricultural census tells us that two and a half acres of the farm were plowed and that fifty bushels of potatoes were grown on a half-acre of this plowed land (table 5.5). Several accounts describe the growing of wheat and other grains on the farm. Therefore, it is probable that the hogs were kept in a restricted area near Tubman's barn. No direct archaeological evidence of the hogs' pen was found. However, the archaeological dig did recover numerous pig bones and teeth from the full range of temporal contexts associated with Tubman's ownership of the farm. These data provide additional confirmation of the importance of hogs in the Tubman household's diet.

Historical accounts provide considerable information about Tubman's raising of hogs. The 1874–75 agricultural census indicates that in 1874 she sold eleven hogs that yielded 2,500 pounds of hog meat and retained one hog and that in 1875 she had seven hogs (table 5.5). A decade later, her passel of hogs had grown considerably. Even with the loss of forty hogs to poisoning in 1884 (see chapter 5), she still retained a significant passel. A question that is more difficult to answer is exactly where her hogs were kept. It is possible that they were in the yard on the south side of the farm. A photograph shows that this area was fenced in, and hogs could have been placed here. However, it is more likely that this area served as her kitchen garden area and that the hogs were corralled farther back on the property, probably behind and to the south and east of the barn and behind the area of the chicken coop.

Tubman continued to raise hogs on her farm until the end of her life, and on more than one occasion she was injured while feeding and attending to them (see, for example, a report in the *Evening Auburnian* on July 11, 1884). Hogs represented a significant and continual source of income. They also provided food for Tubman's table. Chickens were another important source of food in the form of both eggs and meat. Excavation in the yard included the shovel tests behind (east) of the barn and the area where a chicken coop was in the late nineteenth and early twentieth centuries. Although no foundations or indications of fence lines were found, data from these areas provide details related to the broader distribution of artifacts in the yard of Tubman's farm.

She usually kept at least one cow in her barn. The presence of cows is confirmed in the New York State agricultural census of 1875 that describes two "milch [milk]" cows and the production of a quantity of butter, some of which had been sold (table 5.5). Cows also show up in relation to other activities and social interactions. On one occasion, she sold a cow to pay for a trip to Boston, and on another she spent funds aimed to assist her in order to pay for a cow for the Home instead.[20]

Tubman enjoyed raising animals and had both pets and farm stock. Her raising of geese might have escaped notice if not for the report of an enormous goose egg that she sold to George L. Parker's grocery store in Auburn (*Auburn Morning News,* Apr. 4, 1873; see chapter 5). Tubman usually had at least one dog. Her dog was present in a group photograph taken by her barn (figure 5.1), and tax records show that she paid an annual fee of fifty cents for a dog license. For many years, both Harriet and her husband, Nelson Davis, had dogs, each of them paying for a dog license. Tubman once kept a young bear in her yard, relinquishing it only when it became too big to manage.

Tubman's Farm in Perspective: Comparison with Other Farms in Central New York

Small farms like Tubman's farmsteads represented an important component of the nation's social and economic core from the mid-nineteenth through early twentieth centuries, yet relatively few have been studied in depth. In 2000, a comprehensive study of archaeological sites in Central New York indicated that farms and associated farmsteads were being systematically omitted from recognition as significant historic properties (D. Armstrong, Wurst, and Kellar 2000; Wurst, Armstrong, and Kellar 2000, 21). Ironically, the abundance of farms on the landscape has mitigated against the designation of a specific farm's historic significance, resulting in the exclusion of farmsteads from the National Register except under special circumstances, such as ownership by a particularly well-known personality such as Tubman (D. Armstrong, Wurst, and Kellar 2000; Groover 2008, 26–30; Hardesty and Little 2000, 7–9, 119–31). Certainly, Tubman's farms would never have attracted attention if not for her prominent position in history, yet it represents not only a significant record of her life but also an important look into aspects of diversity and variation in farm life in America.

Indigenous peoples of the region had engaged in agriculture for centuries, with the local Iroquois planting a variety of crops, including corn for food and tobacco for religious practices. During the historic period, people

20. Thomas Osborne to Emily Howland, Feb. 19, 1913, box 97, Osborne Family Papers; see also Larson 2004, 281.

were drawn to the Central New York region for the relative abundance of its farmlands. After the American Revolution, the distribution of military land tracts as payment to soldiers encouraged the expansion of settlement in places such as Auburn and its surrounding environs. Settlement involved many persons of Dutch descent moving west from Orange County, New York. These settlers brought with them small numbers of enslaved African Americans, such as the Freeman family, whose descendants remained in the area and later rented the land of Tubman's farmstead as well as that of the Home for the Aged in the early twentieth century.

Through the nineteenth century, a virtual revolution occurred within farming in Central New York. The Erie Canal provided rapid conduit of goods to the growing urban areas of the East and opened expansion of lands in the West to settlement. Industrial production of steel plows and harvesting equipment expanded the ability to cultivate. These tools and innovations such as clay drainage tiles to dry fields allowed farmers to modify the landscape by leveling and draining fields. These innovations expanded the capacity of small farms and lent muscle to farmers, making small farms like Tubman's viable for successful mixed-product farming.

The period in which Tubman owned and operated her farms was an era of dramatic expansion of farms and farmland in American (Groover 2008, 3; US Department of Agriculture 2014). When Tubman purchased her farm in 1859, there were approximately 2 million farms in the United States, but by the time of her death in 1913 there were more 6 million, with the number peaking at 6.4 million in 1920. Much of this increase was associated with the opening of vast new tracts of land in the West, infilling and division of farms in the Northeast, and restructuring of former plantation lands in the South.

Unfortunately for Tubman and many small-scale farmers, by the end of the nineteenth century the dramatically changing scale of farming and farm production gradually made small-scale farming less viable, even as the number of farms continued to increase (Groover 2008, 97). Small farms were made obsolete by the ability to clear and till more acres with new steel plows and large-scale harvesters, the opening of vast tracts of western farmlands, and the ability to transport goods greater distances by rail. Recognizing that she needed to produce more on her farm to sustain a home for the aged, Tubman bought the adjacent twenty-five-acre farm in 1896. However, even the combined resources from planting crops, raising pigs, selling dairy products, and renting out houses on the combined thirty-two acres of the two farms were never sufficient to sustain her expanded household of aging persons.

Tubman probably realized aspects of the problems associated with the shift in scale of production that was part of a technological revolution in agriculture and farm production in the era. However, the scale of newly opened farmlands in the West and the broader economic implications of these changes were probably beyond her knowledge because she pursued farm production and cottage industries simply to sustain her household and support the local Black community. Ironically, the changes in scale and the mechanization or industrialization of farming beginning in the late nineteenth century had been initiated in part, within her very community by farm-implement companies such as Auburn's Osborne Manufacturing Company, a company owned by her longtime friends the Osborne family. As the net number of farms increased in the first two decades of the twentieth century, the viability of small farms, even those with mixed produce and production aimed at extending seasons and supplying local needs for produce, meat, and cottage industry products, could not match the scale of the change under way.

By the early years of the twentieth century, the production of farm goods on Tubman's farms did not come close to providing the type of communal self-sufficiency that such a farm may have produced at the time Tubman first bought the land. By the 1930s, farm production on the small scale afforded by these farms had become less viable unless the farms were converted to more intensive agroindustries such as dairy production, subsumed by expanding urban sprawl, or combined with new industries. After her death, Tubman's lands ceased to operate as farms, although fields continued to be rented out to local farmers, who grew crops on the lands of many farms. Meanwhile, Tubman's barn was converted to a shelter for buses, and her yard was used to maintain the buses of the Norris family's company.

Mark Groover suggests that although the American family farm may never disappear, its gradual decline represents a significant change in the American landscape (2008, 4; see also Friedberger 1988). Archaeological studies of farms have recognized their importance to the rural landscape of past times and as sources of information on past ways of life (Paynter 1982; Yamin and Metheny 1996). Studies of farms have ranged from examinations of pioneer settlements and homesteading by yeoman farmers to analyses of large-scale plantations and the rise of the plantation system and slavery, most notably in but not exclusive to the American South.[21]

21. Slavery was part of the cultural landscape of New York from the early days of Dutch control and was not completely eliminated until 1827. Moreover, from the 1790s until about 1820 a series of Southern planters brought their enslaved laborers from Virginia and Maryland

In fact, although farms in regions such as Central New York have been virtually ignored despite their past significance in the landscape, settings associated with enslavement in rural plantation (farm) contexts in the South may now be the best-studied farm setting. This emphasis on the antebellum South's farms is in part due to the recognition of the utility of such studies to counter the lack of historic detail recorded for enslaved African Americans. Given the paucity of plantation records and the recognition that Blacks were systematically omitted from the historic record, archaeological studies have long been recognized as a key and imperative source of information related to the African American experience during enslavement. More recently, these studies have also extended to the postemancipation period, in particular the Jim Crow era, which provided legal sanction for the silencing of details related to African Americans' lives and experiences (Barnes 2011). Studies of Southern plantations have provided important details on housing, material use, dietary practices, belief systems, and spirituality among African Americans that simply were not readily available in the historic record. These details and knowledge of the social changes in America coinciding with the beginnings of civil rights movement provided a basis by which archaeologists were able to define significance and to carry out extensive research (Battle-Baptiste 2011; Franklin 2001; Singleton 1999). More recently, this same absence of parity in historical documentation has led to the recognition of a wide range of farm-based African American contexts, as in the study of New Philadelphia in Illinois (Fennell 2011; Shackel 2000) and in this study of Harriet Tubman's farmstead. Archaeological studies of farms in North America have been used to show the relationship between wealth and material conditions: "Several key studies in rural archaeology indicate that differences in the living condition experienced by different tenure, racial, or ethnic groups were usually most pronounced or visible in the built environment and domestic dwellings" (Groover 2008, 17). Studies have also shown correlations between consumerism and scales of production and consumer choice in the archaeological record.[22]

The layout and foundations of Tubman's and her neighbors' farms were based on the distribution of land as part of military land grants following the Revolutionary War. The process of settlement was spotty and gradual,

---

to clear land and produce goods on plantation farms such as Rose Hill on the shore of Lake Geneva (Delle and Fellows 2012).

22. See Rafferty 2000 on consumerism and Spencer-Wood 2004 for studies focusing on consumer choice.

and the land tended to fall quickly from the hands of the veterans, many of whom had economic interests elsewhere or were simply not inclined to take up the parcels. There was a significant amount of land speculation as individuals accumulated parcels and redistributed them to prospective settlers. Tubman's farms appear to have undergone a multiphase shift from grantee to settler/speculator to land accumulator. In this case, it was William Seward's father in-law, Judge Elijah Miller, a banker and practicing Quaker, who accumulated these lands in this area, along with large tracks of land in western New York State. The small farms were sold or rented out to farmers and in this area also to brickmakers, who sold their products to expanding markets in the region in the era following the construction of the Erie Canal in the 1820s.

The farms surrounding Auburn benefited from the growth of canal and road systems in the first half of the nineteenth century and of canal and railroad systems in the second half of the nineteenth century and the early twentieth century. The region included a wide variety of farms, but the division of land as part of the original military land tracts generally kept farms within the range of from generally smaller parcels of about 5 or 6 acres to larger parcels at a maximum of 160 acres. Hence, Tubman's 7-acre farm was not atypical for the region in the second half of the nineteenth century. It was bordered by several farms of similar acreage on the east side of South Street and by larger farms on the west side of South Street. As one moved south to the gently sloping hills between the finger lakes, the farms got larger and had a more decided focus on the production of corn and grain rather than on the mixed production of the small farms located at the edge of the growing city of Auburn. This pattern is consistent with broader trends in farming described for the United States for this period (Groover 2008, 96).

The intersection of urban and rural can be seen in the fact that electricity made its way to Tubman's farms early in the twentieth century, and the Norris family updated the electrical system following their purchase of her farm in 1913.[23] Still, being on the edge of town and just outside of the City of Auburn and in the Town of Fleming, the farm was a relatively late recipient of municipal water and plumbing. Neither was present at Tubman's house on the farm during her ownership of and presence on the property.[24]

23. Alice Norris, personal communication to the author, May 22, 2002. Ms. Norris's identification of the update is confirmed by the presence of electrical wire, insulators, and porcelain electrical switches dating to the early twentieth century.

24. For a discussion of the role of public utilities versus local wells and outhouses on farms, see Groover 2008, 97.

Sean Rafferty's (2000) archaeological investigation of the Porter farm in Chenango County, New York (near Binghamton, New York, and about fifty miles southeast of the Tubman property), provides a basis for comparison of both scale and outcome with respect to farming and changing practices in New York State.[25] Differences in the materials recovered from deposits excavated at the Porter farm show a marked shift in both farming practice and the economic condition of the farmers living on the property (Groover 2008, 101). At about the same time that Tubman was establishing her farm in Fleming, the Porters were operating a larger but still middle-class farm that was assessed at $2,000, or about twice what Tubman paid for her farm a decade later. The assessment of $900 at the time she purchased the farm was about average for farms in the region (Groover 2008, 10).

The two farms project contrasting goals as well as outcomes. By the late 1800s, the Porter family became part of a rural upper-middle class when they shifted agricultural practices from general mixed grain-and-livestock farming to commercial dairying, a capital-intensive farm regime (Groover 2008, 101). Even as Tubman's acquisition and expansion of her land holdings in the last decade of the twentieth century could be considered consistent with trends moving toward consolidation of farming, her basic economic situation did not improve. In contrast, the Porter farm grew to 215 acres and was valued at $9,500 as early as 1875 (Rafferty 2000, 127). One can see two important shifts taking place at the Porter farm that did not occur at the Tubman property: first, the shift to intensive production of dairy products and a cash-based market economy and, second, a dramatic increase in the scale of production.

In contrast to the Tubman site, when the Porter farm was studied by archaeologists, it had no surviving structures, and much of the landscape had been modified. Fortunately, however, like at the Tubman sites, there were definitive middens that yielded materials relating to specific periods of site use. Whereas the discrete temporal differences at the Tubman site were obtained from stratified deposits, those at the Porter farm were derived by contrasting material data from sheet middens from different parts of the site. This distinction corresponds with the fact that the spatial layout of the Porter farm shifted along with a shift from grain production to industrial-scale dairy farming. At the Tubman site, even though the farmhouse on the seven-acre property

25. The study of the Porter farm was conducted by the Public Archaeology Facility of the State University of New York at Binghamton as a means of testing the "agrarian myth" of farming as an idyllic way of life (Rafferty 2000).

burned, resulting in the construction of a new house, the form of farming and the economic activities of the Tubman farm were more conservative and remained in the realm of mixed agriculture and industrial production. Hence, there was little movement or change in the layout of the principal structures on the property, and, consequently, there is no appreciable shift in the economics of the material record from the earlier to the later period of occupation at the Tubman site. In contrast, the shift to dairying on the Porter site was associated with not only an expansion of the farm but also a steady increase in mechanization and commercial agricultural practices through the final decades of the nineteenth century. In the last quarter of that century, the Porter farm became a medium- to large-size commercial dairying operation, which was supplemented with poultry, syrup, and orchard products (Groover 2008, 102; Rafferty 2000, 127).

Artifacts from the Porter farm reflect midden shifts corresponding to changes in the internal organization of the household as well as in economic practices. Patterns found include increased consumerism and material discard. Early materials include transfer-printed ceramics and high proportions of tableware, tea wares, and redware ceramics for food preparation and storage. The vessels were expensive but exhibit low vessel-form diversity, limited to plates, teacups, and saucers. The transfer-printed wares were not from matched sets, and the transfer prints were of a similar color (Groover 2005, 104). Rafferty (2000) felt that this pattern might reflect the availability of goods purchased over time at a country store. In contrast, the Tubman's household had access to an array of stores nearby in the heart of urban Auburn, a city fed by the Erie Canal and rail lines, the nineteenth-century functional equivalent to a superhighway. Thus, availability was probably not an issue, nor was the opportunity to buy in quantity if one wished to or could afford it. However, this is not what was recovered at the Tubman farmstead. Rather, the material remains from the Tubman property show an abundance of relatively inexpensive wares in regular use along with a few higher-cost items that may well have been gifts to Tubman as tributes to her services to society.

The next generation at the Porter farm corresponds directly with the shift to more intensive commercial dairy farming, expansion of lands, and greater wealth and cash flow on the farm. The midden shifted location, also suggesting a reorganization of functional spaces utilized within this reconfigured household. During the late nineteenth century, the house's occupants acquired and discarded "greater amounts of less expensive items than used during the first half of the site's occupation. There were also greater amounts of glass containers and decreasing amounts of food preparation and storage containers. From the 1870s, people living on the Porter farm appear to have purchased more processed food items from merchants rather than consuming their own foodstuffs. This suggests that increased commercialization encouraged consumerism" (Rafferty 2000, 142). Instead of relying on a more generalized array of farm products for both consumption and sales, the family focused production on dairy products and became consumers of other goods and goods produced by others (Rafferty 2000, 142). Hence, they were both self-sufficient in production and acquisitive in terms of consumption, opting to purchase nondairy goods as well as ceramic and glass products with the proceeds of their dairy products. Rafferty points out that this farm increased in size from 50 to 215 acres between 1850 and 1875, during which period the value of the farm rose from $2,000 to $9,500 (2000, 127). He suggests that the Porter family initially appears to exemplify middling farmers, but they gradually increased their holdings and productivity to "become one of the most successful family dairy operations in the area" (128).

Rafferty notes that the Porter farm had a significantly higher proportion of transfer-printed wares than five other farms reported for the period. In his comparison of the Porter farm to other sites in the region, he found that the forms of wares present were similar, but there was a noticeably higher proportion of more expensive wares on the Porter farm (2000, 139). They also had twice the number of food-preparation vessels than the other five farms. Rafferty argues that the large amount of preparation and storage vessels may have been related to the shift to commercial dairying on the farm as well as to the relative affluence of the Porter family compared with the other farming families in the area (139). However, Rafferty did report the presence of only an average proportion of tableware and tea ware. This may simply be a function of the relatively small size of the Porter household and hence of less breakage. At the Tubman site, we find one interesting contrast that would at first glance appear at odds to the relative marginality of the residents' economic condition. Whereas the relatively affluent Porter family had few tea wares, a variety of wares that generally are associated with affluence, at the Tubman property tea wares took on what appears to be special social meaning. They are represented by a large set of matching transfer-printed teacups and saucers found across the property. These tea wares reflect significant gatherings for social discourse.

With respect to material analysis focusing on the relative costs of different decorative styles, Mary Beaudry argues that these stylistic variations and cost of items may not completely characterize status, "for [they] fail to account for economic and symbolic use of the landscape as a means of social reproduction and production" (1996, 40). Moreover, in specific reference to farm settings, it can be argued that the need to invest in buildings and stock may have taken precedence over the purchase and even choice of domestic items such as pottery.

When examining the material remains at a farm site, one must consider that items manufactured for one purpose may well have been reused for another functionally related purposed. According to a model of self-sufficiency and account production on the farm, jars and bottles containing one product when bought were no doubt refilled with the products of the farm. This is specifically the design of some items such as canning jars and stoneware crocks, both of which were designed for use and reuse, but it may have also occurred with other containers, such as pharmaceutical bottles.[26]

26. In fact, this raises the question as to the material record and archaeological footprint of other small farms in the region, which would be important to understand these sites in terms of the similarities and diversity that might be expressed within them. For this reason, we have initiated an in-depth study of a farm located about ten kilometers from the Tubman sites, with living contexts inclusive of those found at the Tubman site but associated with Dutch settlers to the region and their descendants as well as to laborers in the region (including indentured persons from Ireland).

7.1. Harriet Tubman's brick house. Photograph attributed to Jane Searing in the 1940s but probably from an earlier date in the twentieth century. Photograph courtesy of Harriet Tubman Home, Inc., Auburn, NY.

7.2. Ash layer from fire on February 10, 1880, and brick walkway in front (west) of the house exposed. Photograph by D. Armstrong.

7.3. Ironstone ceramics with the maker's mark "O. P. Co.," made by Onondaga Pottery Company of Syracuse. This company later became Syracuse China. Photograph by D. Armstrong.

7.4. Stratigraphic profile showing lens of ash layer from the fire on February 10, 1880 (*black band*), builder's trench, prefire deposits, and red-brown clay (*at bottom*). Photograph by D. Armstrong.

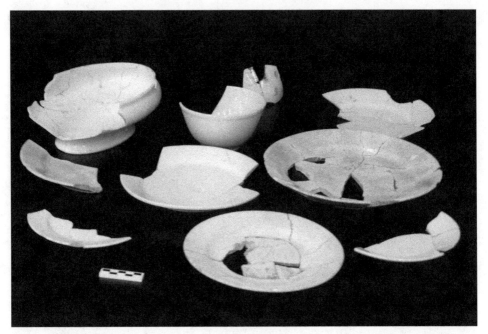

7.5. Plain white ironstone ceramic plates, bowls, and serving vessels. Hundreds of sherds representing at least thirty plain-white vessels from the builder's trench were found on the north side of Tubman's residence. Photograph by D. Armstrong.

7.6. Pair of identical silver-plated spoons found in the builder's trench on the north side of Tubman's residence. Photograph by D. Armstrong.

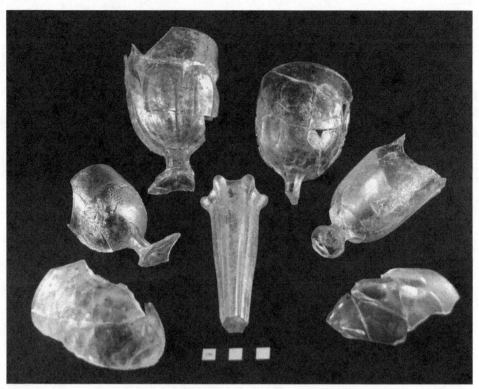

7.7. Glassware dessert goblets and bud vase (*center*) found in the builder's trench on the north side of Tubman's residence. Photograph by D. Armstrong.

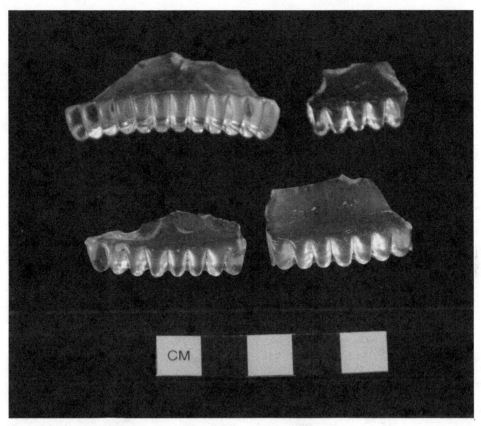

7.8. Glass lampshade fragments found in the builder's trench on the north side of Tubman's residence. Photograph by D. Armstrong.

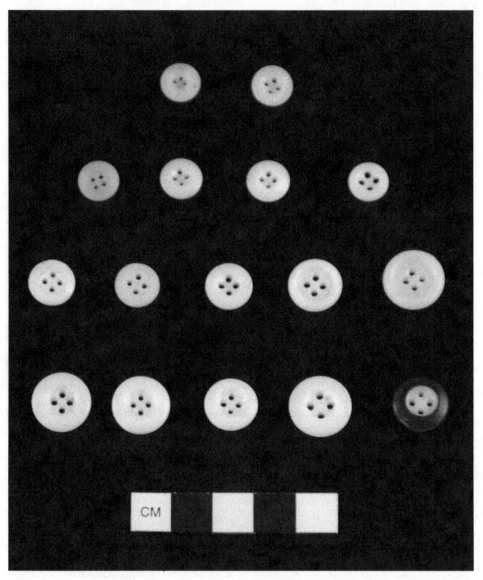

7.9. Selection of porcelain buttons found in the builder's trench on the north side of Tubman's residence. Photograph by D. Armstrong.

7.10. Key found in pre-1880 fire deposits in area of doorway and north of the builder's trench at Tubman's residence. Photograph by D. Armstrong.

7.11. Brick walkway rediscovered during excavations on west (South Street) side of Tubman's residence, 2009. Neutron Activation Analysis shows that the bricks have the same composition as bricks used to construct the house (A. Armstrong 2011; A. Armstrong and D. Armstrong 2012). Photograph by D. Armstrong.

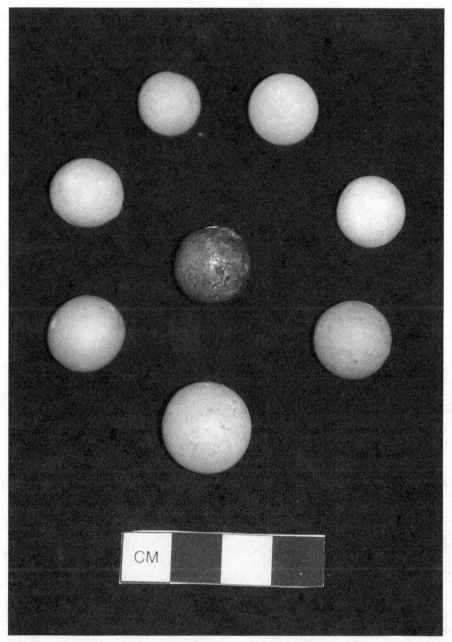

7.12. Clay marbles found on and near the brick walkway on the west side of
Tubman's residence. Photograph by D. Armstrong.

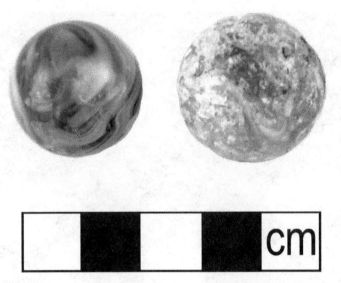

7.13. Glass marbles found at Harriet Tubman's residence.
Photograph by D. Armstrong.

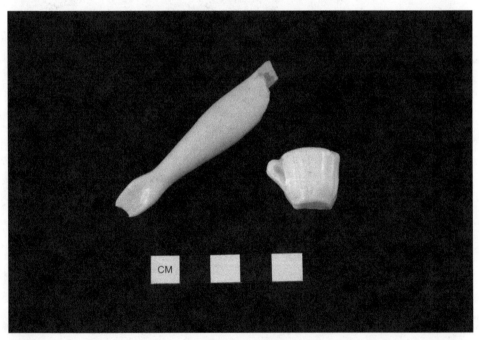

7.14. Toys, including porcelain doll (arm) and tiny teacup, found at Harriet Tubman's
residence. Photograph by D. Armstrong.

7.15. Jaw harp found in the builder's trench on the north side of Tubman's residence. Photograph by D. Armstrong.

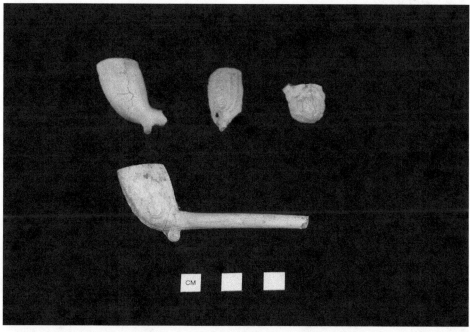

7.16. White-clay tobacco pipes found at Tubman's residence and yard. Photograph by D. Armstrong.

7.17. Glass beads found in the builder's trench at Tubman's residence.
Photograph by D. Armstrong.

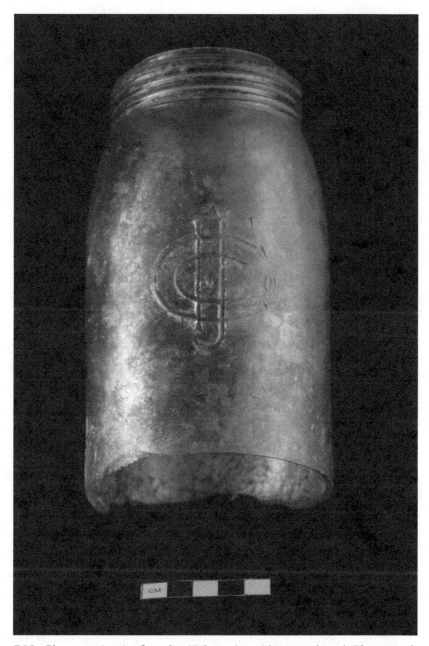

7.18. Glass canning jar found at Tubman's residence and yard. Photograph by D. Armstrong.

7.19. Slate pencil found in the builder's trench on the north side of Tubman's residence. Photograph by D. Armstrong.

7.20. Glass bottles recovered from the top or capping level of the builder's trench on the north side of Tubman's residence. The position and grouping of the bottles suggest beverages were consumed upon the completion of filling the trench after construction of Tubman's brick house. Photograph by D. Armstrong.

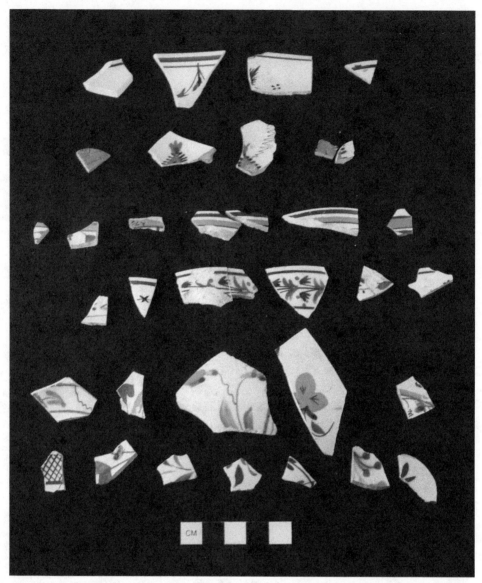

7.21. Hand-painted polychrome creamware ceramic bowl fragments deposited prior to the fire at Tubman's residence in February 1880. Photograph by D. Armstrong.

7.22. Half pennies from 1804 and 1807 found at the lowest cultural levels of Tubman's residence. Photograph by D. Armstrong.

7.23. Cache of pharmaceutical bottles and health- and hygiene-related artifacts found in the builder's trench on the west side of Tubman's residence. Photograph by D. Armstrong.

7.24. Unbroken pharmaceutical bottles, including one containing glycerin, found in the builder's trench on the west side of Tubman's residence. Photograph by D. Armstrong.

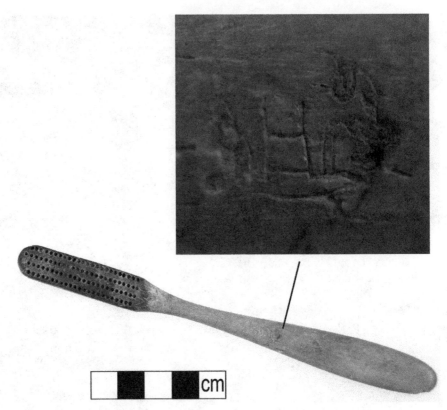

7.25. Bone toothbrush with burned boar bristles and etched personalizing artwork found among a group of pharmaceutical bottles in the builder's trench on the west side of Tubman's residence. Photograph by D. Armstrong.

7.26. Dr. Marshall's snuff bottle (headache medicine) found in the builder's trench on the west side of Tubman's residence. Photograph by D. Armstrong.

7.27. Wooden cistern located under the 1920s-era porch immediately behind (east) of Tubman's house. It was a source of water for both the wood-frame house and later the brick house. The wooden cistern was replaced by a masonry cistern in the basement of Tubman's house when her kitchen was moved upstairs in 1904. This home improvement was paid for by Eliza Wright Osborne, along with other improvements, including replacement of Tubman's stove, repairs to windows, and replacement of roofing shingles (Eliza Wright Osborne to Helen Storrow, Dec. 16, 1904, box 220, Osborne Family Papers, Special Collections Research Center, Syracuse Univ., Syracuse, NY). Photograph by D. Armstrong.

7.28. Quarter section of the wooden cistern excavated. Photograph by D. Armstrong.

7.29. Green transfer-print plate found in fill in the wooden cistern along with quantities of coal ash. Photograph by D. Armstrong.

7.30. Brick and mortar-masonry cistern built in 1904 when the kitchen was removed from the basement and rebuilt on the first floor of Tubman's house (Eliza Wright Osborne to Helen Storrow, Dec. 16, 1904, box 220, Osborne Family Papers, Special Collections Research Center, Syracuse Univ., Syracuse, NY). Photograph by D. Armstrong.

7.31. Excavated cross-section of the former kitchen area of the basement of Tubman's house (area with deeper deposits of coal ash) and into the room on the west side of the basement. Bricks used as a footing for a staircase to the basement are present at the west side of the metric measuring rod. The wall dividing the two rooms is immediately west of this cross-section and is indicated by a decrease in the depth of the cultural deposits. The soil below the cultural deposits is made up of a uniform red-brown clay of the type that was used in the local manufacture of bricks. Photograph by D. Armstrong.

7.32. Well southeast of Tubman's house (*view to south*). In the 1990s, the well was capped with cement, and a tree was planted when the hole was filled. Under the cement collar, we found several layers of brick. Beneath the brick, the well is lined with unmortared stone. Photograph by D. Armstrong.

7.33. Stones from the well exposed (*view to south*). Ceramic field tiles were used as an overflow drain for the well. Also present is a smaller round field-tile drain for the wooden cistern. Photograph by D. Armstrong.

7.34. Harriet Tubman's barn on the seven-acre property before restoration, c. 2000. Bays on north and south sides were added for use by the Norris Bus Company in the 1920s. Modifications were also made to accommodate buses in the older part of the barn (*center area*). Photograph by D. Armstrong.

7.35. Harriet Tubman's barn was raised off the ground, and a trench was dug to construct a new cement-and-stone foundation. The older foundation was simply two courses of local brick. Excavations were conducted along sections of the trench and within the barn. Photograph by D. Armstrong.

7.36. Profile of exposed foundation trench of barn. Note several layers of burned ash and cultural materials. The artifacts in these deposits suggest a sequence of at least two and possibly three fires (or possibly deposits of burned material). Some of the materials may have come from the fire at Tubman's house, but it is likely that there were two fires at the site of the barn. The most recent fire may be one described in an account in the *Auburn Citizen*, March 4, 1911. Photograph by D. Armstrong.

7.37. Harriet Tubman's barn after restoration, 2009. Photograph by D. Armstrong.

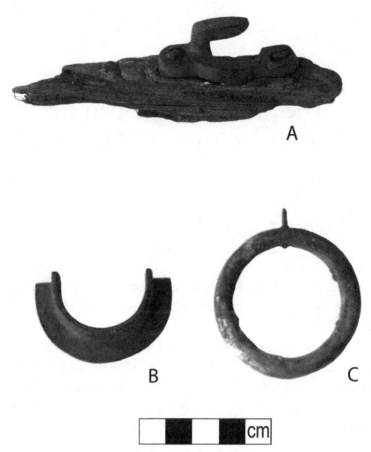

7.38. (A) Window latch, (B) brass curtain-rod holder, and (C) curtain ring from cultural deposits behind Tubman's barn. These items may date to Tubman's house fire in 1880. Photograph by D. Armstrong.

8

The Struggle to Open the
Harriet Tubman Home

Transfer of the Harriet Tubman Home
to the AME Zion Church

In 1903, when Tubman handed off primary management of the plans for the formal Home for the Aged to the AME Zion Church, she was eighty-one years old and in declining health. On June 19, 1903, the board of trustees met on the site of the proposed Home. A newspaper account of this meeting describes it as taking place in "the large brick house setting back in the orchard from South Street" (*Auburn Daily Advertiser*, June 20, 1903). At this meeting, Harriet Tubman named the building "John Brown Hall" in commemoration for her fellow abolitionist John Brown.

At this meeting, Superintendent Rev. B. F. Wheeler and Treasurer John Osborne read their reports (figure 8.1). Superintendent Wheeler asserted that his responsibilities as pastor of the Parker Street AME Zion Church required "all my time" and that it was "difficult to collect funds from the public for the home." He went on to state that "he sacrificed his Tuesdays and Wednesdays each week visiting neighboring towns and soliciting interest in the home" (quoted in Walls 1974, 440).[1] He indicated that he had found interest and suggested that if the AME Zion General Conference "let the superintendent give his whole time to the work, this home will soon be developed into a great institution for the aged and infirm colored people, who are constantly seeking shelter under its roof. It is not intended by the superintendent that this home

---

1. Rev. B. F. Wheeler is well documented in the records of the local church register, "Conference and Thompson Memorial, Parker Street AME Zion Church Register, Auburn, 1892–1938," hereafter Auburn Thompson AME Zion Church Register, 1892–1939, Harriet Tubman Home Collection, Harriet Tubman Home, Inc., Auburn, NY. Tuesday and Wednesday would normally have been his days off from primary pastoral duties at the church (Walls 1974, 440).

8.1. *Left to right*: Rev. Benjamin F. Wheeler, superintendent of the Harriet Tubman Home; Harriet Tubman; and John Osborne, treasurer of the Home Board of Trustees. These images and a short summary of the role of each of these individuals were circulated on a fund-raising flyer in 1903 soon after the transfer of the twenty-five-acre farm to the AME Zion Church for the purpose of opening the Harriet Tubman Home for the Aged. This photograph of Tubman was also published in an article highlighting Tubman's presentation at the AME Zion Conference meeting in Syracuse, New York, on June 6, 1903 ("Harriet Tubman, Noted Colored Woman, in the City: Speaks at AME Zion Conference," *Syracuse Post Standard*, June 6, 1903). Photographs courtesy of Judith Bryant, Stewart Family Collection, Auburn, NY.

shall be a heavy expense to the church; it simply needs a start and it can live and thrive by the help that comes from the public" (quoted in Walls 1974, 440). In his history of the AME Zion Church, Bishop William Walls mentions that the trustees agreed to pay Rev. Wheeler a salary of $400 per year as superintendent of the Home (1974, 440).[2] The trustees present at the meeting contributed $110 in cash, and a "goodly sum was subscribed." The granting of a salary to Rev. B. F. Wheeler was related to his assertion of the difficulty in generating funds for the project while also serving as pastor to the local church, particularly given the fact that no money was coming from the church, and none could be expected until the General Conference in 1904.

The superintendent's report also noted that the deed conveying the property stipulated that when the trustees were able to do so, they should establish

2. However, a letter from Rev. B. F. Wheeler to Thomas Mott Osborne (discussed further later in this chapter) indicates a salary of $300 (Aug. 19, 1903, Osborne Family Papers, Special Collections Research Center, Syracuse Univ., Syracuse, NY).

on the grounds "a school of domestic sciences where girls may be taught the various branches of industrial education" (quoted in Walls 1974, 440). This school was to be modeled after domestic education programs popularized by Booker T. Washington. Wheeler noted that such institutions are "particularly popular with the white people in this western part of the state of New York." The twenty-five-acre property is described elsewhere as a property on South Street, "the most aristocratic street in the city. It consists of 25 acres of land, with a large orchard, two houses and ten rooms each, one brick and one frame, together with two large barns and other out-houses."[3]

At the time of this meeting, Harriet Tubman appears to have been optimistic about the completion of the transfer of title and the Home's future and so traveled to Syracuse to speak in support of the project at the AME Zion General Conference and to raise funds. A newspaper account of Tubman's trip provides details about the Home Board of Trustees, including the roles of national leaders from the AME Zion Church, and John Osborne's involvement as treasurer (*Syracuse Post Standard*, June 16, 1903).[4]

With the formal transfer of the property to the church, things were looking up for Tubman and her dreams for the Home; however, her life did not get any easier. On the morning of July 15, 1903, the eighty-one-year-old Tubman was quite badly bruised and shaken up in an accident. She was thrown from her carriage in a collision with a lumber wagon on South Street. She was taken into the Thorne residence, in front of which the collision had occurred. Her injuries included a "severe jarring and some slight scratches," and she was attended to by Dr. E. G. Woodruff ("Harriet Tubman Hurt," *Auburn Bulletin*, July 15, 1903). Fortunately, Tubman recovered, but this event was only one of a series of injuries and illnesses that would collectively act to slow her down over the next few years.

Superintendent Rev. Wheeler was an engaging and dynamic leader who was well liked in the local community. He was responsible for significant growth of the local Thompson AME Zion Church on Parker Street. Records show that under his leadership church membership increased 65 percent between

3. AME Zion Church General Conference, Minutes of the Twenty-Second Quadrennial Session, 1903, cited in Walls 1974, 441. At the General Conference, the ten AME Zion bishops were elected to the Tubman Home Board of Trustees. Apparently absent from this list of confirmed trustees was the board's former treasurer John M. Osborne.

4. A second account of the evening placed the attendance at the conference as 860 people (*Syracuse Evening Telegram*, June 16, 1903).

1904 and 1905 from thirty-eight to sixty-three.[5] The church registry shows a strong financial growth, with an operating budget of $1,261.65, including $600 for the pastor's salary, $260 for repairs, and $212 used to pay debts.[6]

Thompson AME Zion Church records show that the Home itself was considered a separate enterprise and that Harriet Tubman herself was never a member of the church or on any of its committees. Moreover, mention of Tubman or the Home occurs very rarely in the church's minutes. When Tubman is mentioned, it is only in terms of the church's outreach and philanthropy. However, her brother William Stewart Sr. and his son were active members, and virtually all the people who served as local members of the Home Board of Lady Managers were AME Zion Church members. Nearly all of the superintendents, matrons, and leadership of the Home's management were active members of the Thompson AME Zion Church.

Under Rev. Wheeler's leadership, the church and plans for the Home moved forward, and demographic and statistical records recorded in the Thompson AME Zion Church register during this period show an interest in the broader social and economic affairs of the African American community. They include a summary of statistics for "Colored persons" in the City of Auburn, recorded on November 12, 1904, projecting the area's African American population at the time the church took over the twenty-five-acre Home:[7]

African Americans in the Auburn area in 1904.
Number Colored persons: 458
Number of former communicants that are not church members: 218
Number of Colored persons who are church members at present
    Baptists: 16
    Methodists: 96
    Episcopal: 28
    Congregational: 21
    Salvation Army etc.: 12
    Total: 173

5. Auburn Thompson AME Church Register, 1892–1939, 66.

6. Auburn Thompson AME Zion Church Register, 1892–1939, 66.

7. Auburn Thompson AME Zion Church Register, 1892–1939, 66. The register does not provide information on the source of these data or how they were collected, but they can be considered a useful guide to aspects of life within the African American community of Auburn as responsibility for the Harriet Tubman Home was signed over to the AME Zion Church.

Colored persons owning homes: 12
Colored persons buying homes: 10
Average daily wages of colored persons 20 years or older: $1.1
Colored graduates of Auburn High School in 1904: 6[8]
Number in business (Barber): 1
Number in Corporations: 0
Number in secret society or social organizations: 192
Number carrying life insurance: 68

Unfortunately, the transfer of the Home to the AME Zion Church did not go smoothly. One point of contention revolved around the makeup of the Harriet Tubman Home Board of Trustees, which changed dramatically after the AME Zion General Conference of 1904. Tubman herself had never been shy about engaging the white community in any of her efforts, from fund-raising to public events and even collection of garbage to feed her hogs. She held a special place in Auburn that cross-cut racial barriers. She saw value in soliciting support from the white community and was a friend of many white people of financial means. Rev. Wheeler and Tubman advocated for a board that included both AME Zion leadership and white civic leaders from Auburn.

On August 19, 1903, Rev. Wheeler wrote to Auburn's mayor Thomas Mott Osborne, requesting that Osborne agree to serve on the Home Board of Trustees.[9] The note calls on Osborne to reflect upon his family's long relationship with Harriet Tubman, dating back to the period of abolition, and goes on to say, "To be brief, for I do not want to take up any more of your time than is absolutely necessary, you know Harriet Tubman and her efforts to establish a Home for Aged Colored People, for she tells me that it was in the parlor of your father's that the very first meeting in the interest of the Home was held over 30 years ago."[10] The letter describes how Tubman had for years sheltered and cared for aged and unfortunate colored persons in her own private house "but had not given up the idea of establishing a Home on a larger

8. Harriet Tubman's grandniece Gladys Stewart Bryant, the daughter of William H. Stewart Jr., graduated from Auburn High School in 1903 (Judith Bryant, personal communication to the author, Aug. 10, 2017).

9. Rev. B. F. Wheeler to Thomas Mott Osborne, Aug. 19, 1903, Osborne Family Papers; all quotations come from this original handwritten copy of the letter, composed on Harriet Tubman Home stationery.

10. Wheeler is referring to the home of David Munson Osborne and Eliza Wright Osborne.

plan for that purpose."[11] Rev. Wheeler reviews the history of Tubman's acquisition of the twenty-five-acre property at auction, the difficulty that she had raising sufficient resources, and the fact that she deeded the property and its contents over to the AME Zion Church to be used as "a Home for Aged and Infirm Colored People and for a School of Domestic Science where colored girls may be taught cooking, needlework, hand laundering, and the like."

Rev. B. F. Wheeler's letter to Thomas M. Osborne provides important social and financial information on planning for the Home. Wheeler indicates that in March 1903 the debt on the property had stood at $1,950 but that since that time it had been paid down to $1,200 and that the treasury held about $100.[12] Wheeler states that until recently he had received no salary or money for travel for his role as superintendent or service on behalf of the Home but that the trustees had voted to give him a salary of $300 plus traveling expenses at the board's meeting on June 10, 1903. The letter notes that the Home, currently operating in Harriet's personal residence, was "helping four inmates now," regarding whom Rev. Wheeler added that "we care for one whole, the others partially." As superintendent of the Home, Wheeler was responsible for leasing out the Home's land "by the year—the money going for the personal support of Harriet Tubman. The total income from the rents being about $20 to $30 per year."[13] Wheeler also provides a description of the twenty-five-acre property as having two houses with ten rooms each.[14] He notes that John H. Osborne was "the current treasurer and the person to whom all moneys are sent and directed" and that at present John Osborne and Wheeler were the only trustees living in Auburn but that his plans for a new board would include six persons from the Auburn community.[15]

11. The Osborne family correspondence shows that Tubman frequented Thomas's mother's home and that she had babysat for Eliza Wright Osborne's children. When plans for the Home were being made, Thomas Osborne's mother was Tubman's primary sponsor.

12. This figure is consistent with what's given in AME Zion Church General Conference, Minutes of the Twenty-Second Quadrennial Session, 1903, 97–102, cited in Walls 1974, 441.

13. This information is consistent with the stipulation of the agreements associated with the deed (Harriet Tubman Davis to the AME Zion Church, Cayuga County Deeds Book 33, June 11, 1903, $1,575, pp. 410–11, Cayuga County Clerk's Office, Auburn, NY).

14. The two buildings referred to were the brick structure that would soon be renamed John Brown Hall, which would serve as the initial dormitory for the home, and the wood-frame building that at the time was rented out but would become the primary dormitory for inmates of the home after Tubman's death in 1913.

15. John Osborne was an executive of the Osborne Manufacturing Company, then headed by his nephew Thomas.

Rev. Wheeler indicates that the AME Zion Church Board of Bishops had given him "the privilege of nominating most of the board of trustees":

The Board of Bishops will be members of the board of trustees, 9 in number, and the other members if I can induce them to serve will be:

Honorable T. M. Osborne
Judge Underwood
Mr. Meeker [Meaker], Cayuga County Savings Bank
Dr. Stewart of the Seminary[16]
Mr. John H. Osborne

With this information on the Home, its financial status and its current operations, Rev. Wheeler asks Osborne's permission to include Osborne's name on the list of trustees for the Home, with the list to be put forward at the AME Zion General Conference in early 1904. He states that he had already met with Mr. Meeker (Meaker) and that Mr. Meeker had promised to serve as a trustee. "No name I could get would be more helpful to us in our work than yours. Some day when you are not too busy, I would like to take you over the entire property of the home. Your letter of endorsement I will use when I go out to solicit money for the Home—all of which is sent directly to Mr. J. H. Osborne by check."

Rev. Wheeler closed with his respects, then added a postscript stating that "there is no Home between here and greater New York that colored people can enter. This makes our home a necessity." In making this point, Wheeler is referring to a basic inconsistency between ideals and actions in Auburn in the early 1900s. Whatever its history of integration and abolitionist fervor may have once been, social and economic segregation had taken hold in Auburn by 1903. Auburn's Home for the Friendless had provided a private, church-sponsored home for women in need since the later years of the Civil War. Its charter stated a goal of providing homes to women in need and never indicated any restrictions based on race or ethnicity, but by the early 1900s it was a segregated institution. The confirmation of this fact shows up in census data for 1910. A report on benevolent organizations published by the US Bureau of the Census indicates that the Home for the Friendless did not admit "colored persons" into its facility and that there were no similar facilities opened to African Americans in the Central New York region (US Bureau of Census 1910, 210).

16. Dr. George B. Stewart, DD, was the president of the Auburn Theological Seminary.

Rev. Wheeler's letter shows that he was reaching out to a group that had social and economic means and who were well established in the field of charities aimed at providing support to the needy. This group included John Osborne, the Home's current treasurer and only member of its board in 1903 who was white; Judge George Underwood, who was one of the early organizers of the Home and had served as Tubman's legal counsel; and Rev. E. A. U. Brooks. Underwood and his wife had rescued the Home from a sheriff's tax sale in 1900.[17] They were also contributors to many local philanthropies, including Auburn's Home for the Friendless. William H. Meaker was an executive at the Cayuga County Savings Bank and had long held mortgage papers for Tubman despite irregular payments.[18] For whatever reason, none of these men was listed among the trustees accepted by the AME Zion Church Board of Bishops at the General Conference in 1904. The acceptance of these local leaders in Auburn would have retained a majority vote by the AME Zion leadership but would also have drawn in a broader cross-section of the white, financially influential, and politically progressive community in Auburn. Those proposed by Wheeler in his letter to Thomas Osborne (including Thomas himself) represented a cross-section of persons of means who might have been important to the financial success of the Home, and their makeup represented a structure very similar to that already in place at Auburn's Home for the Friendless (Home for the Friendless 1866, 1899, 1904). Thomas Osborne's collected correspondence does not include a response to Wheeler's request, but Wheeler's letter indicates that both John Osborne and Mr. Meaker had already confirmed their willingness to serve.

According to Earl Conrad, Tubman herself wanted a board of trustees that combined members from both the white and the Black communities, but the Black advisers of the AME Zion Board of Bishops overruled her and Rev. Wheeler and instead set up a directorship for the Home that kept the board "exclusively in Negro hands" (1943, 221).[19] For whatever reason, Rev.

17. Sheriff Wood to George Underwood, Cayuga County Deeds Book 30, Auburn, Apr. 30, 1900, p. 412, Cayuga County Clerk's Office.

18. William Meaker was the original secretary of the Home for the Friendless Board of Trustees. He was also one of the original group that served as trustees for the Harriet Tubman Home.

19. It would appear that the "colored advisors" to whom Conrad was referring were the men on the AME Zion Church Board of Bishops, which had the ultimate authority to make decisions regarding the formation of the Tubman Home Board of Trustees and the operation of the Home.

Wheeler's efforts did not gain the Board of Bishops' support, and he was ultimately replaced as superintendent of the Home and reassigned to another church. Certainly, there was a record of mistrust with respect to the white community, but there can be no doubt that the exclusion of both men and women who might be willing to help and who had the means to provide financial sponsorship made the effort to secure the structure and finances of the Home more problematic.

Over the years, Tubman was frustrated as the opening of the Home continued to be delayed, and she was upset over AME Zion plans to charge a fee of $150 for admission to the Home ("Dedication of the Harriet Tubman Home," *Auburn Daily Advertiser*, June 24, 1908; *Auburn Citizen*, June 24, 1908).[20] Conrad notes that Tubman was not always satisfied with AME Zion management of the Home, and "for a period she broke off active participation with it" (1943, 221). "When I gave the Home over to Zion Church, what do you suppose they did? Why, they made a rule that nobody should come in without a hundred dollars? Now, I wanted to make a rule that nobody could come in unless they had no money. What's the good of a Home if a person who wants to get in has to have money?" (quoted in Conrad 1943, 221). Bishop Walls would later reflect that even after the Home was established in 1908, "Aunt Harriet was up against a condition which she could not control. Her despair elicited a repining statement to her friend Dr. (Rev.) E. U. A. Brooks, 'If I had the privilege of bequeathing my property again. I would not give it to my church.'"[21]

Delays and a Decision: A Home for the Aged or an Industrial School for Girls?

Another issue that had to be resolved was the direction and purpose of the property. Would it be a home for the aged or an industrial school for girls or both? Care for the elderly and education of the young had long concerned both

20. The only exception would have been Harriet Tubman, who had negotiated her admission to the Home as a condition of transfer based on the strong recommendation of her friends in Auburn. Significantly, William Stewart Sr. was not granted similar terms of admission, and when he became ill in 1912, he was sent to the Cayuga County Almshouse in Sennett, which must have been troubling to Harriet because the two were very close and had lived with and relied upon one another for years.

21. Walls 1974, 443, relating a letter by Rev. E. U. A. Brooks before his death. Jean Humez presents issues relating to a power struggle in the AME Zion Church that took place with respect to fund-raising and the formalization of the Home between 1903 and its opening in 1908 (2003, 110–26).

Tubman and the AME Zion Church. During the planning and fund-raising period from 1903 to 1908, John Brown Hall, the ten-room, two-story brick structure at the back of the property (also known as 2 Danforth Street in *Auburn City Directory*) was designated as the primary dormitory of the Home for the Aged, and the red, wood-frame house at the front of the property (also known as 1 Danforth Street in the directory) was designated as the projected site of an industrial school for girls.[22] John Brown Hall was a large and substantial brick building and simply needed to be furnished. However, it was felt that additional space needed to be added to the wood-frame house to make it serviceable as a school for girls, so plans included moving to the site an old tollhouse building located across the street and just north of the Home property.[23]

The concept of a school for girls on the property dates back to the 1880s and was supported by Harriet Tubman. She was intrigued by Emily Howland's sponsoring of schools for African American girls in Washington, DC, Virginia, and Georgia.[24] Howland was also a strong supporter of Booker T.

22. In the early twentieth century, many African Americans in the South looked north for opportunity and joined the Great Migration to cities such as New York, Detroit, and Chicago, seeking new opportunities (Agbe-Davies 2011, 70–71; Dodson and Diouf 2004; Scott 1919). The idea of training schools and safe homes for African American girls and women that was explored for the Harriet Tubman Home took actual form at places such as the Phillis Wheatley Home for Girls, which was opened by the Phillis Wheatley Association in 1908 on the 3200 block of Rhodes Avenue, Chicago. This house was one of a series of homes sponsored by Black women's clubs in cities such as Chicago throughout the nation through the National Association of Colored Women's Clubs. The Phillis Wheatley Home for Girls operated from 1908 to the 1960s. Prior to the opening of the Harriet Tubman Home for the Aged, the backers of an "industrial" school at the Home envisioned it as a center to train young women for employment as private house servants and cooks. In contrast, the Phillis Wheatley Home was more of a protective boardinghouse used as a safe collective space for girls and women, many of whom worked as servants in private homes (Agbe-Davies 2011, 73).

23. This plan may be one of the reasons why the Tubman Home Board of Trustees turned down a request to rent the wood-frame house by George Mountpleasant, a Native American later implicated as an arsonist in a series of fires, including the burning of a barn on the Tubman property (*Auburn Citizen*, Mar. 4, 1911). Reverend E. U. A. Brooks, president of the board of trustees, reported to the *Auburn Citizen* that Mountpleasant had come to him several times for assistance and had previously asked to rent the house. Based on the reporter's account of Brooks's conversation, there can be little doubt that in addition to whatever plans the Home's board members had for the property, they did not feel comfortable renting the house to Mountpleasant (see chapter 7).

24. Emily Howland (1827–1929) was a longtime supporter of education for African Americans. She was a Quaker and a member of an activist abolitionist family from Sherwood,

Washington's efforts and was a financial supporter of the Tuskegee Normal and Technical Institute (Humez 2003, 110). Sarah Bradford (1886) wrote of Tubman's interest in starting a home for girls in the second edition of her biography of Tubman, and the idea continued to be considered up until the opening of the Home for the Aged in 1908.

In 1903, at the time the twenty-five acres was acquired by the General Conference of the AME Zion Church, the local Auburn church under Rev. B. F Wheeler's leadership was growing and had many members interested in supporting the effort. However, it took five years to open the Home, in part because of turmoil within the local church after Rev. Wheeler's departure in 1905 and before the arrival of Rev. George Carter in 1906. During the interim period in which Rev. J. C. Roberts served as pastor and superintendent, the local church was thrown into disarray, and plans for the Home floundered. Although the Home was organizationally separate from the local church, the two were closely tied, with the local pastor generally serving as overall superintendent of the Home and with an active local Board of Lady Managers, which provided assistance to the Home, organized dinners and events, and was made up primarily of women from the local AME Zion congregation (appendix G).[25]

The brief period in 1905 in which Rev. J. C. Roberts served as pastor resulted in a series of charges and countercharges and even a short period of expulsion of nearly all of the lay leadership from the church, including the women who made up the bulk of the Board of Lady Managers.[26] Fortunately, in 1906 Rev. George Carter arrived, restored order, and provided leadership. Soon after his arrival, the lay leaders were reinstated, and efforts on behalf of both the church and the Home were restored. Rev. George Carter was a dynamic leader of the congregation who served many roles, including

---

New York. Before and during the Civil War, she was a teacher at several schools, including Myrtilla Minor's school for free Black girls in Washington, DC. After the war, she bought a plantation in Virginia using funds from her father and distributed the lands to freed Blacks in a settlement called "Arcadia." She also provided funds for the Emily Howland School on the property and over the years provided funds for more than thirty schools for Black Georgia (Hazzard 1971; Humez 2003, 381). Howland was also close friends with Eliza Wright Osborne and Frances Miller Seward, with whom she worked to support the Woman Suffrage Association. Howland would often stop to visit Tubman on her way home from visits to the Seward house.

25. Auburn Thompson AME Zion Church Register, 1892–1939, 270–75.
26. Auburn Thompson AME Zion Church Register, 1892–1939.

superintendent of the Home from 1906 through 1916. He remained an influential leader even in his retirement and until his death in 1923.

During this period, Tubman continued to open her own house to both old and young. Helen Tatlock, a friend and neighbor, recalled that Tubman "had a great number of young and old, black and white, all poorer than she. There were children that she brought up . . . also a blind woman."[27] Tubman was traveling less than in earlier years, but on May 30, 1905, she went to Boston with her great-niece Alida Stewart to attend a reception in her honor at the Harriet Tubman Christian Temperance Union at Parker Memorial Hall. The newspaper notification of the reception speaks in superlatives about her role as a conductor and spy and of the much-exaggerated bounty of $40,000 offered for her capture by slaveholders in Maryland during the latter days of slavery. The article notes her early visits to Boston, stating that "she returned to the city and lived here a number of years before the war, during which time she devoted all her energies to aiding slaves escape and became friends of Wendell Phillips, William Lloyd Garrison, and Fred Douglass, Governor John A. Andrew, John Brown and many other noted abolitionists" (*Auburn Bulletin*, May 29, 1905).

A local newspaper reported that the AME Zion Church hoped that the Home would be opened by May 1, 1906 (*Auburn Democrat Argus*, Jan. 1906, no specific date available). To prepare, a meeting of the Home Board of Lady Managers was held at the home of Frances Smith (wife of Charles A. Smith) at 65 Fitch Avenue. The committee then "visited the home at Mrs. Harriet Tubman's and arranged to assist Aunt Harriet in the care of Mrs. Johnson, a blind woman out there. Active preparations are being made to formally open the home in the brick house which is to be fitted up for that purpose. It is expected that the home will be opened about May 1. There is to be a meeting for all who are interested in the home at the Zion church, Parker Street, next Friday evening" (*Auburn Democrat Argus*, Jan. 1906). Despite the desire to open the home in John Brown Hall in May 1906, it would not be opened until the spring of 1908. This gathering of lady managers included not only planning for the future home on the twenty-five-acre property but also the process by which one of the inmates, Mrs. Thomas Johnson, then age eighty, was taken in by the home (*Auburn Citizen,* Feb. 16, 1909). Mrs. Johnson

27. Mrs. William (Helen) Tatlock, statement to Earl Conrad, Earl Conrad/Harriet Tubman Collection, Schomburg Center for Research in Black Culture, New York Public Library, New York.

would be a resident in the home during the period of transition and one of the first residents of John Brown Hall.[28]

A report titled "Plans for Tubman Home" published by the *Auburn Daily Advertiser* on February 9, 1907, describes how for years "Harriet Tubman and her friends have been waiting for the home and school for colored people to materialize." An article in the *Auburn Citizen* published the same day projects an opening of the Home for the Aged on May 1, 1907, and goes so far as to provide details related to the renovations to the ten-room brick building known as John Brown Hall. Rev. G. C. Carter reported that the building would have "room enough to accommodate 10 persons" and that the president of the Board of Lady Managers, Mrs. C. A. Smith, had appointed a "soliciting committee to solicit articles to furnish the rooms." Unfortunately, even as things were looking up for the Home, Harriet Tubman was ill, suffering from pneumonia, and so was removed from her own home on South Street and admitted to the Auburn Hospital. The report on her health indicated that she was "convalescing very satisfactorily," and a short time later she returned to her house (*Auburn Citizen*, May 4, 1907).

Tubman recovered from pneumonia but continued to encounter a series of problems. In November 1906, she broke her foot while feeding her hogs (*Auburn Citizen*, Nov. 9, 1906). Then one of her horses died, "which was quite a loss to her" because she and her brother William H. Stewart Sr. relied on the horse, which "draws boxes and rubbish from some of the stores, and thereby earns a living for himself, and the horse is quite essential" (*Auburn Semi-Monthly Journal*, Apr. 5, 1907). In an effort to get someone to donate a horse, a notice was posted in a local paper indicating that "Aunt Harriet will be glad to receive whatever her friends desire to donate from another home, they can send it to Mrs. D. M. Osborne [Eliza Wright Osborne]" (*Auburn Semi-Monthly Journal*, Apr. 5, 1907). This notice illustrates Tubman's tenacious and straightforward ability to solve problems by drawing in the support of her broader community. During this era, Eliza Osborne had emerged as the go-to person for Tubman in relation to her personal needs. She contributed to the reoutfitting of Tubman's personal home, including expenses of at least $100 in moving her kitchen upstairs from the basement and building a new cistern in the basement as well as the costs of repairing her roof. On

28. Mrs. Thomas Johnson died on February 16, 1909, at age eighty-three. Her obituary in the *Auburn Citizen* that day describes her as a blind, colored woman who had been cared for at the Tubman Home. She was buried at Fort Hill Cemetery in Auburn.

another occasion, Eliza sent Tubman a care package of food including a side of ham and coal for her stove. When it became apparent that the stove needed to be replaced, she arranged for a new one to be delivered.[29]

Eliza Osborne's letters to her daughters indicate her willingness to pay to put Tubman in a care facility, but Tubman wanted to stay in her own home and see her dream through to fulfillment.[30] Although Eliza had great respect for Tubman and would do almost anything for her personally, she drew the line on the Home and Tubman's communal approach to helping others. That being said, in fact it was Eliza who contributed hundreds of dollars to restore Tubman's personal residence, even knowing full well that Tubman was using it as the Home. With assistance from the Osborne family as well as from others, including Emily Howland and Sara Bradford, Tubman retained her personal home and farm with free and clear title for the rest of her life.[31]

As the leadership of the AME Zion Church pursued fund-raising for John Brown Hall, the wood-frame structure at the front of the property was being promoted as the site of a proposed school for African American girls.[32] The plan assumed support from the broader white community, which was considered to have both the means and the desire to hire domestic servants in their homes. By tapping into this interest, the trustees of the Home hoped to expand and increase their fund-raising efforts on behalf of both the Home and the school.

Although African American boys and girls in the Auburn area had access to public education, their inclusion and issues pertaining to the type of

29. Examples of Eliza Wright's efforts on behalf of Tubman have been discussed in chapters 1–3 and 7, with details related to Eliza's willingness to do almost anything to help Tubman personally, including the restoration of her residence and the payment of her hospital bills. See Eliza Wright Osborne to Helen Storrow, Dec. 16, 1904, box 220, and Eliza Wright Osborne to Helen Storrow, Apr. 11, 1911, box 88, Osborne Family Papers, and the quotations from these letters in note 12, chapter 7.

30. Note that both Eliza Wright Osborne and Emily Howland felt it would be best for Tubman to be placed in a home where she would be cared for without the burden associated with opening a home on behalf of others. Neither of these women completely understood Tubman's communal perspective and drive to care for others, perhaps because they saw her as a person in need whom they were assisting.

31. Mention of Tubman's profuse thanks to Eliza Wright's daughter in various letters provides strong evidence that Helen Storrow, too, had made significant financial contributions to Tubman's well-being during this time. However, all indications are that virtually all of these contributions were directed to Tubman personally or to fix up her personal residence.

32. At this time, the wood-frame house was rented, not occupied by Tubman or others connected to her.

education they should receive were being debated within the African American community in the early twentieth century. Booker T. Washington tended to favor vocational and skill-based training. Washington was a phenomenal orator and fund-raiser and traveled the country drawing upon his ties to the AME Zion Church and Tuskegee University in Alabama.

In contrast, W. E. B. Du Bois took exception to the limitations of "industrial" education (see Du Bois 1903, [1903] 1994; Humez 2003, 103, 379). Du Bois instead called for expanded opportunities in more intellectually motivated formal academic, or "classical," education. Both Du Bois and Washington had long family ties with the AME Zion Church. Each wrote of Harriet Tubman and honored her for her efforts on behalf of African Americans. In his biography of John Brown, Du Bois ([1909] 2001) discussed Tubman's efforts with respect to abolition, and in an article in the NAACP publication *Crisis* written shortly after Tubman's death in 1913 he compared her service to that of David Livingstone's missionary work in Africa, noting that "both these sincere souls gave their lives for black men" (Du Bois 1913, 18).[33]

Between 1906 and 1908, local newspapers were relied upon to heighten community awareness and to generate donations.[34] In an article in 1906, plans for the Home and school are reported. It is noted that there was a reorganization of the Home Board of Trustees and most specifically with respect to fund-raising efforts under the direction of Rev. G. C. Carter. The article goes on to indicate that plans for the addition of a school for girls was discussed at a meeting at the Thompson AME Zion Church (*Auburn Weekly Bulletin*, Feb. 7, 1906).[35] This report clearly links the goals for the school with the infrastructure of education advocated by Booker T. Washington. Another article written later in 1906, titled "For the School," describes a meeting in Seneca Falls where Rev. G. C. Carter gave a presentation in the interest of the "Harriet Tubman School which has as its object the training of colored girls in domestic service." Carter describes three buildings on the property where

33. This comparison derives from an era in which David Livingstone was popular as a humanitarian. From today's perspective, his missionary efforts might garner more of a critique from Africanists and cultural theorists. This tribute to Tubman is in the May 1913 issue of *Crisis* rather than the March 1913 issue, as commonly attributed.

34. As indicated by the mentions of Thomas Osborne in this chapter, who owned the *Auburn Citizen*.

35. The article notes "plans for the establishment of an industrial school for both sexes on the lines of Tuskegee," "but pending the reorganization of the work now being done by the home the matter was left for the future."

the school can be established and indicates that he planned to call on "all of the large manufacturers" for support (*Auburn Citizen*, Nov. 15, 1906). Each account was presented with positive tones and indicated both funds obtained and more money needed to finish the task. However, as one traces the public fund-raising effort for the Home, one sees a pattern of dates pushed back and more funds needed.

On December 26, 1906, a public announcement in the *Auburn Citizen* stated that the Home Board of Trustees would hold its annual meeting on December 28, at which it was expected that action would be taken to open the Home "in one of the buildings on the 25 acres" and that the board would discuss "preparations made for the opening of the Domestic Science training school." The notification indicated that "a treasurer will be elected in the place of John H. Osborne."[36] The board meeting was to take place at ten o'clock and be followed by a public meeting at three o'clock, which would be presided over by Rev. Bishop A. Walters, DD, of Jersey City, who was board president. No report was made on the specific outcomes of this meeting.

Between February and April 1907, a series of articles updated the community on progress toward the opening of the Home and suggested that the Harriet Tubman School for Domestic Science "will be opened about May 1" (*Auburn Citizen*, Feb. 9 and Apr. 22, 1907). The article on February 9, 1907, indicated that "the work of the Harriet Tubman Home and Domestic Science school begins to take on definite shape." And in the report on April 22, with respect to the school for girls Rev. Carter repeats plans for the Home that had been promised over the previous five years: "The red house will be fitted suitably for the Domestic Science school work and the old toll gate that has stood there for so many years will be moved over to the red house and fitted up as a dormitory for the girls. As soon as the work is completed the school will be opened." According to the article, Rev Carter claimed, "It is believed that such a school as is contemplated will be well received in this city. In fact, the great demand for competent domestic help makes such a school a necessity. The aim is to fit colored girls in every way for domestic service, not merely how to do the work, but their responsibility and deployment in the house and what is expected of them as regards conduct. A full program of the course of training will be given in due time." The article concludes with a statement of financial need and support, declaring that "the amount needed to pay off the

36. It thus appears that John Osborne had been reinstated as treasure of the Home, most probably at Harriet Tubman's insistence. However, he was now stepping down.

mortgage, repair the building and fix up the place and meet other expenses will be $5000 and as soon as sufficient amount is subscribed to warrant work, it will begin." The question remains whether sufficient funds were ever raised and to what extent, if any, the work on this part of the project was actually undertaken. Certainly, the effort on behalf of the Home was ongoing, and the Home's completion was likewise uncertain.

In April 1907, Rev. Carter attended a meeting of the Auburn Businessmen's Association to report plans for the creation of a school to train colored girls "in domestic science." The objective was to bring "girls here from the South and teaching them all manner of house work, cooking, etc."; "they are also to study the properties of food and the care of the home." Carter told the group that "there are several available buildings on the land" (*Auburn Citizen*, Apr. 9, 1907).[37]

The local businessmen, however, responded that they saw no need for a school because any girls brought to the area could be placed directly in homes (*Auburn Citizen*, Apr. 9, 1907). Later in April, an article in the *Auburn Citizen* addressed "the domestic question," stating, "There has been such a demand for domestic help that Mr. Carter has decided to try and furnish a limited number of colored girls from the south." However, he had found that the "draft has been so great the past few years that the nearby cities like Baltimore, Washington and Richmond, have been pretty well cleaned for competent girls" and that he had found a "party in Atlanta, Ga, who has promised to look up and send to Auburn and elsewhere colored girls who will go in the families at once" (*Auburn Citizen*, Apr. 22, 1907). This shows a shift in plans as the demand for domestic help seems to have been so great that the

---

37. The reporter projects the sense that members of this group of Auburn businessmen was very positive about the need for domestic labor and the potential of employment for such girls, and no one questioned the idea that the school should focus on domestic services rather than on some more formal educational objectives. This attitude indicates the underlying class structure of the time as well as assumptions regarding education for African Americans. However, some present at the Auburn Businessmen's Association meeting questioned if a school was necessary for employment. One member, Secretary Adams, suggested that "they would not be able to keep the girls in the school a week if they were at all competent." It thus appears as if some of the fund-raising efforts were inadvertently at cross-purposes: the school may have drawn on Washington's ideals for industrial education, but potential employers did not perceive it as necessary. Hence, the efforts on behalf of the school only diluted the base of support for the Home, and supporters in the white community remained concerned that their efforts to support Tubman were being sidetracked by both the Home and the school. Issues of class and race were amplified as concern for Tubman's welfare.

girls could just bypass the proposed domestic-training school and go straight to work.[38]

Even as there appears to have been a shift away from using the Home also as a training school, in May 1907 Rev. G. C. Carter was still campaigning throughout the region for the planned Home and school (*Cayuga Chief* [Weedsport, NY], May 25, 1907). An account of the annual meeting of the Home for Aged in June 1907, however, describes only the Home and provides an update on the effort to refurbish the brick building (named John Brown Hall in 1908), including details of two rooms that had been completed (*Auburn Citizen*, June 15, 1907). Despite projections to open the Home and the school on May 1, neither were opened in 1907.

The announcement for the Home's annual meeting on June 12, 1907, described the gathering as "the annual meeting of the Harriet Tubman Home and Training School" (*Auburn Citizen*, June 8, 1907). However, the report on the actual meeting omitted mention of the school and went into details on specific plans for the brick building as the residential Home for the Aged inmates (*Auburn Citizen*, June 15, 1907). An effort to reach out once again to the broader community of Auburn can be seen when the Central New York Conference of the First ME Church provided assistance to the fund-raising effort for the Tubman Home with a fund-raiser highlighted by a presentation by Rev. M. C. B. Mason, DD, secretary of the Freedman's Aid Society and Southern Educational Department of the ME Church, who was described as "one of the most eminent speakers of the negro race" (*Auburn Citizen*, Oct. 22, 1907). Tickets to the November 15 event were on sale for fifty cents at several regional drug stores, including Hamilton's, Winegar's, Smiths, Remington's, Sagar Companies, and Walley & Co. (*Auburn Citizen*, Oct. 22, 1907). Advertising for the event stated that Rev. G. C. Carter was the superintendent of the Home and "is endeavoring to have everything in readiness for the reception of a large number of inmates at the earliest possible date." This account varies a bit from others in that it indicates that the Home planned to "train negro boys in the trades and negro girls will be taught domestic science" (*Auburn Citizen*, Nov. 7, 1907). Finally, by the spring of 1908 John Brown Hall had been made ready to receive its charges, some of whom would be moving from Harriet Tubman's personal residence, which had for so long

38. The article concludes with Rev. Carter's home address (18½ Parker Street, Auburn, the parsonage for the Thompson AME Zion Church) for those wishing to secure "colored girls" as domestic laborers.

also served in the capacity of the Home. On May 1, 1908, Mrs. Smith, president of the Home's Board of Lady Managers, announced in the *Auburn Citizen* that the Home would be open as soon as an inspection of the property was completed in the middle of May. Mrs. Smith asked assistance from the community with final furnishings for the Home: "Anyone having a table or chairs, or lamps, or pictures, or bedding, or groceries, in fact anything to donate, if they notify the officers or committee of lady managers, due credit will be given and an account kept of each one's gifts."[39]

Tubman's Household: Gifts Received, Thefts, and Generosity Extended

By this time, it had become a well-established tradition for the community to give Harriet Tubman gifts during the holiday season. Unfortunately, some of the most specific details of gifting and gifts received come from reports of Tubman repeatedly being robbed after Christmas, when everyone knew she carried coin and cash gifts in her clothing. On December 26, 1906, for example, "the founder of the Harriet Tubman Home for Colored Girls, was robbed of about $40 in gold and paper yesterday afternoon." Tubman reported that the money was in a stocking and comprised gifts donated for Christmas. She reported the theft to the Auburn police, but because her house was in Fleming, her case was turned over to the justice of the peace (*Auburn Weekly Bulletin*, Dec. 28, 1906).[40]

This was not the only time that Tubman was robbed. The practice of giving to Tubman during the holiday season was widely known and publicly encouraged by the press and the local school system. Hence, a year later, on Christmas Day 1907, Tubman was once again robbed. This time $30 was reported stolen.[41] Tubman told a reporter that she had carried the money

39. When the home opened on May 18, 1908, credit was given to several women for their contributions of furnishings.

40. The article mentions a warrant for the arrest of John Peterson, a seventeen-year-old Black youth, on the charge of grand larceny and concludes by indicating that Patterson protested his innocence but was committed to the county jail pending further investigation. This article also projects a bit of confusion related to the Home, focusing on the opening of a school for girls but also mentioning the Home for the Aged.

41. Octavias Phillips pleaded guilty to the theft of $9 of the $30 that Tubman reported taken. Phillips testified that he had stolen the money while Tubman was in a stupor and that he had spent $4 of the money and hidden away the rest, but when he had returned to get it, it

home on Christmas Day, safely hidden in her clothing. The next morning while her brother William was eating breakfast, Harriet showed him her presents (*Auburn Citizen*, Jan. 25, 1908).[42] Hearing the approach of someone at the outside door, she gathered her purse up in her apron and went upstairs. "At the head of the stairs, she was overcome by a sort of dizziness and sat down to recover herself. When she came to, her money was gone. Harriet thinks that she dropped her purse from her apron as she went upstairs, and someone passing through the hall picked it up. She has suspicions as to who the guilty one is and came to town early today to see if steps could not be taken to have her money returned" (*Auburn Semi-Weekly*, Dec. 31, 1907).

Private and Public Homes of Charity in the Auburn Area

A review of other charities serving Auburn's needy provides perspective on the problems faced in opening and maintaining the Harriet Tubman Home for the Aged. Auburn's Home for the Friendless, also known as "the Home," stands out for its longevity and well-orchestrated support. It was formally incorporated in the City of Auburn in July 1865 as a home for widows and orphans of the Civil War.[43] Like the Harriet Tubman Home, the Home for the Friendless was organized under a provision of New York State law passed in 1848 that provided for the establishment of charitable institutions.[44] This home was created for women who were made widows by the Civil War and older women who were in need, including those whose sons were killed in the war. It remained open after the war and in time shifted to a home for the aged.

Unfortunately, even though the Home for the Friendless was chartered to care for all women in need, by the late nineteenth century it was de facto a home only for white women and their dependents, and by the time Tubman began to organize her Home, the Home for the Friendless had become

---

was gone. Phillips was sentenced to serve eight months in the Onondaga County Penitentiary (*Auburn Citizen*, Jan. 25, 1908; *Syracuse Post-Standard*, Jan. 7, 1908).

42. This citation also serves as a reference to the presence of William H. Stewart Sr. as a resident in Tubman's house.

43. The Home for the Friendless was located at 45 Grant Avenue in Auburn. The original articles of incorporation were considered "in some respects defective," so a more formal certificate of incorporation was formulated in December 1865 (Home for the Friendless 1866).

44. This same law was the basis for the founding of the Harriet Tubman Home as a charitable institution.

an openly segregated institution. Hence, its trajectory provides an important contrast to that of the Tubman Home and illustrates the difficulties faced by persons of color who were in need of support during this era. It also highlights the financial limitations that Tubman and the AME Zion Church confronted in establishing and maintaining the Tubman Home for the Aged.

Whereas Harriet Tubman and the AME Zion Church had a very difficult time raising funds for her Home for the Aged, the Home for the Friendless was far more successful, garnering much more financial support and demonstrating an ability to transform itself in response to the community's changing needs and demands.[45] The Home for the Friendless was part of a broader movement to care for the needy resulting from the casualties of the Civil War. A report on its founding states that it grew out of "the actual wants of the population" and was a direct result of the efforts of the Auburn Female Bible Society to assist the "poor and destitute persons of Auburn" (Home for the Friendless 1866, 1–9). Plans were formulated at a meeting in 1864 at the Cayuga Orphans Asylum, an institution that was also supported by the Bible Society. At that time, a subscription was circulated, and sufficient funds were raised to purchase a home and grounds. The entire amount of the subscription was filled by December 1864, and the Home for the Friendless was chartered the following year. Part of this home's success was the timing of its inception at the height of the Civil War in a society where nearly everyone felt the pain of loss associated with soldiers who had died or were injured and those losses' impact on wives, children, and mothers left behind. Hence, we find the Home for the Friendless fully subscribed and expanding in a short period of time, in contrast with the process for the Tubman Home, which languished for years under the burden of debt from the point of its creation in 1896 to the formal opening of John Brown Hall in 1908 and on through the end of its trajectory as a care facility in the late 1920s.

The Home for the Friendless was open to "persons of good character, who may be in reduced and dependent circumstances" (Home for the Friendless 1866, 1–2). The original board of directors included a body of twelve civic

45. The Home for the Friendless on Grant Street was able to build and rebuild itself by generating adequate resources, including a substantial endowment. Over the years, its charter changed so that by the late 1800s it had shifted from a facility for widows and their children to a home for elderly women. The Home for the Friendless still exists as a pay-for-residency facility for elderly women called the Faatz-Coufut Home. It describes itself "not as a nursing home, but as an adult residence affording quality care supervised living and assistance" to its residents (http://www.thehomeauburn.org/).

leaders headed by Theodore Pomeroy and Dr. Sylvester Willard.[46] In addition to the board, the charter assigned management of the home to a board of thirty-three women, each of whom was to donate at least one dollar each current year, up to a total of $10 over time. The original group of women managers included Mrs. Pomeroy, Mrs. Willard, Mrs. Worden, Mrs. Meeker (Meaker), and Mrs. George Underwood (Home for the Friendless 1866, 6–7).[47] The articles of incorporation defined who would be accepted at the home: "Aged, infirm, or invalid who are homeless, those in search of employment, without the means of paying their board, or such as having means, require a temporary home, and are willing to conform to the rules and regulations of the family. Widows of soldiers, having infants, desiring a temporary home, may be received until a place may be procured for them, Also the invalid mothers of soldiers, who, by the death of their sons, have been deprived of a home and support" (Home for the Friendless 1866, 6–7). The articles of incorporation make no mention of any distinction in relation to race, ethnicity, or religion. The inmates were simply required to have "good moral character," "accept cheerfully such places of service as may be suitable for them," and be willing to devote a portion of their time employed in housework as "may be apportioned to them" (Home for the Friendless 1866, 16).

The first person to subscribe as a supporter of the Home for the Friendless was Mrs. Frances Seward, who made her donation shortly before her death: "She gave her name and her sympathies with it because she cared for the

46. Theodore M. Pomeroy (1824–1905), the president of the Home for the Friendless, was a Republican member of the US House of Representatives from 1861 to 1869 and served a short stint as Speaker of the House. He was later the mayor of Auburn and a member of the New York State Senate. Pomeroy was also the first vice president and general counsel of the American Express Company in 1868, a position that shows a business affiliation with the Seward family of Auburn. Dr. Sylvester Willard (1798–1886) was married to Jane Case and lived in a mansion at 203 Genesee Street, Auburn. He was one of founders of the Oswego Starch Factory and served as its president from 1848 until his death in 1886. He was associated with many philanthropic causes, and in addition to being a founding director of Auburn's Home for the Friendless, he was the first physician at the Cayuga County Almshouse. His nephew Willard Case inherited the mansion, and his son Theodore Willard Case built the Case Research Laboratory on the property, where the first commercially successful method for recording sound film was developed. This technology was purchased by Fox Films in 1926 and became the basis for "talkie" movies. The mansion house is now the Cayuga Museum.

47. "Mrs. Worden" is Lazette Miller Worden (1803–75), the sister of Frances Miller Seward and a person to whom Harriet Tubman turned to take care of her niece Margaret Stewart when Tubman left Auburn to assist in the Union cause during the Civil War.

poor, and her contribution was the offering of her heart to the homeless and desolate" (Home for the Friendless 1866, 16).[48] The initial report from 1866 notes that the home was still in its infancy but was already expanding, and "to this purpose Mr. Hayden made a donation of one thousand dollars to add a number of sleeping apartments and to make improvements" (Home for the Friendless 1866, 16). During the first year of operations, the treasurer, Jane Frances Case Willard, reported a strong outpouring of support from the citizenry of Auburn, with contributions totaling $5,419.67 and representing a range from fifty cents to $1,000 (Home for the Friendless 1866, 16–17). Among the people and families who had regular interactions with Harriet Tubman and who contributed to the Home for the Friendless were Mrs. David M. Osborne and Company ($100), Mrs. William Seward just before her death ($100), Mrs. Charlotte Underwood ($100), Mrs. Elizabeth Pomeroy ($50), Mr. John Farmer ($16), and Mrs. Anthony Shimer ($1).[49] The annual report on the Home published in 1889 indicated that there were currently seventeen inmates living in the building and that over its twenty-five year history 175 women "have found a home within these walls. 76 were from Auburn. 39 had gone onto their resting place, while others have found a home among friends" (Home for the Friendless 1889, 14).

The Home for the Friendless was remodeled in 1871 and was quickly rebuilt again after a fire in 1882. In 1889, it had a board of forty-five managers. That year the total balance of funds and endowments for the Home was $8,346.25, including a gift of $4,000 from the estate of William M. Gibson (Home for the Friendless 1889, 14). The annual report published in 1899 discusses plans for construction of a new building, with each new room being furnished by sponsors. The report includes considerable detail on the many donations made by the various sponsors, who outfitted dozens of rooms in

48. Frances Miller Seward (1805–65) was the wife of William Seward. She was a strong supporter of Tubman and was instrumental in the transfer to Tubman of a farm that she had inherited from her father. Mrs. Seward's unfortunate death prior to Tubman's return from activities associated with the Civil War was a significant loss to Tubman and her charitable causes. One wonders to what degree she might have contributed to Harriet Tubman's home if she had lived longer.

49. John Farmer was Tubman's next-door neighbor. She later bought a twenty-five-acre property from his estate to establish the Home for the Aged. Mrs. Shimer's husband, Arthur Shimer, was at Tubman's wedding and lost money in the gold scandal in which both he and Tubman were involved in 1873.

the house. For example, a set of bay windows for the front of the building was added to the architect's plans when Miss Willard ordered them, thus expanding the Willards' existing gift to the building fund. The treasurer's report published in 1899 shows a capital balance of $15,579.62, along with expenses of $14,995.41 associated with construction and outfitting of the new building (Home for the Friendless 1899, 15).

In 1904, there were thirty-three residents, and the Home's third floor, including five new rooms and a bathroom, had been finished with the "generous donations of Mrs. David M. [Eliza Wright] Osborne and Miss Caroline Willard" (Home for the Friendless 1904, 14).[50] Three of these rooms were outfitted by the Hon. George and Mrs. Underwood. The point of including this information here is to show a contrast between the scale of support for the Home for the Friendless and the support for the Tubman Home for the Aged even among persons who were known Tubman supporters.

In 1908, the year that John Brown Hall was finally opened at the Harriet Tubman Home, the Home for the Friendless was efficiently filling specific needs, including the purchase of a new mangle to assist with laundry and ironing flat items such as tablecloths and napkins (Home for the Friendless 1908, 16). Three years later, in 1911, the annual report for the Home for the Friendless espoused "an empathic desire to cherish and promote the spirit which is essential to every true home and is necessary to an institutional home, where the ties are not those of nature" (Home for the Friendless 1911, 16). In 1913, the year of Tubman's death, the Home for the Friendless reported on forty-five years of operation and chronicled changes from small beginnings associated with serving the needs of women caused by "the vicissitudes of the Civil War" to a much-enlarged home of charity. The report notes the assistance of several doctors, including Dr. Sincerbeaux.[51] It indicates that the parlors were painted and that new curtains presented "a general fresh and cherry appearance." In the kitchen, there was a new combination gas-and-coal range, and many new gas jets had been added to the building

50. Catherine Willard was the daughter of Dr. Sylvester Willard; she and her sister contributed money in 1892 for the construction of the Willard Memorial Chapel on the campus of Auburn Theological Seminary, located a few blocks from the Home for the Friendless and built in honor of Dr. Sylvester and Jane Frances Case Willard. Louis Comfort Tiffany designed the interior of the chapel.

51. Dr. Sincerbeaux's parents had for many years rented the wood-frame house at the front of the twenty-five-acre property from Harriet Tubman (see chapter 6).

to "lighten the dark corners."[52] The endowed legacies had reached a total of $10,000. The list of donors to the Home in 1912 and 1913 include Mr. and Mrs. W. H. Seward ($15 each year), Mrs. Josephine Osborne (worsteds and clothing, twelve glasses of jelly and canned fruit), and T. M. Osborne ($5) (Home for the Friendless 1912–13, 10–11).

In 1912–13, the by-laws for the Home for the Friendless were redefined, emphasizing the acceptance of women of "good character who are homeless, and willing to conform to the rules and regulations of the family." There is still no mention of race or ethnicity, and although no specific mention is made of religion, the by-laws do indicate an expectation that inmates will be present at "family worship." The cost of admission had been reset to $3 per week, and much of this funding continued to be sponsored through the support of local churches (Home for the Friendless 1912–13, 33). A review of annual reports published by the New York State Board of Charities shows a sharp contrast between the data collected on the Tubman Home and the data collected on other homes in the area, such as the Home for the Friendless, the Auburn Orphans Asylum (124 North Street), the Cayuga Asylum for Destitute Children (66 Oswego Street, Auburn),[53] and the Cayuga County Almshouse (Sennett, New York).

The Harriet Tubman Home, operating out of Tubman's residence, is listed as a charitable institution in the New York State Board of Charities annual report for 1899, but no specific information is provided on it.[54] This was the only year in which the Tubman Home was even mentioned in state reports until the report for 1921 (New York State Board of Charities 1922), where the number of its inmates and financial figures are given. Although the Home reported to the state only in 1899 and 1921, other homes for Blacks located in Brooklyn and New York City were consistently listed, so it is more likely that the Tubman Home did not supply information and did not conform with

52. Electricity was not added to this building until 1915 (Home for the Friendless 1915, 12).

53. An interesting side note about the Cayuga Asylum for Destitute Children is that Harriet Tubman signed its ledgers on July 28, 1891, when she took into her care a blind teenager who had been living at the asylum off and on since she was four years old (Messineo 2017).

54. This is in contrast to the details on the people whom each of the other homes served, the mission of each organization, the numbers of residents served, along with details on building values, available funds and expenses, and even who carried out the yearly inspection (New York State Board of Charities, 1899, 204; see also New York State Board of Charities 1904, 1910, 1914, 1915, 1917, 1918, 1919, 1922).

care-facility practices of the day, including annual inspections and reviews, than that it was simply omitted from the record.

The New York State Board of Charities reports show that the only place available to men in need in the Auburn area was the Cayuga County Alms-house. This facility was on a ninety-six-acre farm in Sennett. Not surprisingly, it served twice as many men as women. In 1898, it had seventy-two inmates (forty-four males and twenty-eight females), and it was open to all county residents regardless of race or ethnicity. That same year the Home for the Friend-less cared for nineteen women (three were supported by public funds and sixteen by private). The Auburn Orphans Asylum cared for 198 children (132 with public funds and 66 with private funds). The orphanage was open to children from ages two to sixteen who were free of contagious disease. A second institution for children was the Cayuga Asylum for Destitute Children, which cared for 145 children (New York State Board of Charities 1899, 4). The 1904 report of the State Board of Charities includes several Tubman supporters on its Cayuga County Visiting Committee: Miss Emily Howland (Sherwood), Miss Isabel Howland (Sherwood), Mrs. D. M. Osborne, Mr. Thomas Osborne, the Hon. George Underwood, and John H. Osborne. The structure of the State Board of Charities included a provision that the mayor of Auburn was authorized to appoint the chair of the Board of Chari-ties, so Mayor Thomas Osborne would have done this. Importantly, Thomas Osborne and half of the men on Rev. B. F. Wheeler's list of recommended board members for the Tubman Home were on the Cayuga County Visit-ing Committee of the State Board of Charities. One can easily see that their knowledge of institutional structures and charitable organizations could well have contributed to the support and operation of the Tubman Home. More-over, three women on the visiting committee were well-educated, knowledge-able supporters not only of charities for the needy but of Harriet Tubman. The inclusion of any of these women on the board of the Tubman Home would have been of assistance to it.

In 1904, the Board of Charities reported that the state legislature had authorized the established provisions for the New York State Training Schools for Girls (New York State Board of Charities 1904, 4). The objective was con-sistent with the stated objective of the school for girls proposed by the Tub-man Home Board of Trustees at the same time. This similarity and Booker T. Washington's influence on the Tubman Home board may have helped keep the idea of creating a school for girls alive.

During the era of the founding and establishment of the Tubman Home, changes in state laws governing charitable organizations resulted in the closure of the Auburn Orphans Asylum in 1909 and its merger into the Cayuga Asylum for Destitute Children as well as the reorganization of the latter institution to create the Cayuga Home for Children in 1913 (New York State Board of Charities 1913). There were also competing needs within the community related to nationwide epidemics. One acute need was to address the problem of consumption, now defined in epidemiological terms as tuberculosis. In 1913, Sunny Crest Sanitarium was founded to care for persons who had contracted tuberculosis (New York State Board of Charities 1913, 1914, 104). A national tuberculosis epidemic had struck all ages and classes, so a care facility drew broad public support. This facility was open to all, regardless of class or race. By 1914, the Sunny Crest Sanitarium was well established in buildings on a property valued at $34,547 and had receipts of $22,463 associated with operations. The Auburn facility's sixty-three patients included "10 paying and 53 public charges." This facility was supported by the City of Auburn as a means of both treating the sick and separating them from wider society with the aim of controlling the disease. It was a high-cost facility, but the fear of the spread of the diseases and the need for isolating those with tuberculosis from the general population gave it wide support and allowed inclusion of all, including African Americans (New York State Board of Charities 1914, 104).[55] Thus, while the Tubman Home struggled for support, other institutions targeting the needy, sick, and infirm were doing relatively well, and new organizations such as Sunny Crest Sanitarium were attracting wide public support to avert a widely perceived health problem in the region.

The only year for which any detailed records about the Harriet Tubman Home were reported to the State Health Department was 1921 (New York State Board of Charities 1922, 398, 402, 410). This report indicates that there were five inmates at the Home at the end of 1921, and during the year it had served a total of seven women. Two were paid for with public funds, and five were provided for with private funds. During the year, one person left the Home, and one died (410). Revenues and expenses for the Home included $15.59 spent on travel, $55.52 on garden and farm expenses, $65.18 on ordinary repairs, and $1,330.49 on total maintenance and operational expenses. Total receipts for the year were $1,455.01, with the Home holding $166.52 cash in hand on June 30, 1921. The value of the land was assessed at $10,000

---

55. The cost of the tuberculosis facility was $10 per week for those who could pay and nothing for those who could not. The facility also accepted patients from outside Auburn, all of whom were required to pay the $10 per week fee.

and of the furnishing and equipment of the home at $700, with zero indebt-edness, for a net total value of $10,700 (398).

Differing Perspectives: Tubman the Individual versus Tubman's Communal Orientation

Tubman's life on her farm epitomized the ideals of individuality, an ethos of hard work, and strong independent spiritual belief. All of these characteris-tics were understood and heralded by her many supporters—Black and white. However, in addition to her distinctive individualism, she was also strongly community oriented. Her wealthy and influential white supporters were eager to assist her and ensure her maintenance because they liked and respected her personally and because she represented a personification of their ideals for a free African American and an independent woman. However, many did not understand or support the more communal orientation and use of her per-sonal property or her objective of opening a home dedicated to the care of elderly African Americans.

It is in her communal efforts that divisions in class and race are most pronounced. As discussed in previous chapters, in the early twentieth cen-tury, as Tubman struggled to open her Home, Eliza Wright Osborne served as her benefactor and as an informal trustee through whom gifts from local donors as well as supporters in places such as Boston were distributed to Tub-man. Osborne was a generous friend who made sure that Tubman's house was updated and repaired, including a new stove, cistern, kitchen, and roof shingles as needed. Moreover, when Tubman was ill and in the hospital, Osborne negotiated her hospital bills, paying half and organizing support for the remainder. Decades earlier, Osborne had hired Tubman to assist with the cleaning of the Osborne home, and Tubman had babysat Osborne's children. On other occasions, such as a tea in Osborne's parlor with leading suffragists including Susan B. Anthony, Tubman sat as an equal. However, Osborne felt that Tubman should be looked after and did not support her more commu-nally minded effort to open a home for other African Americans in need. At times, Osborne was exasperated with Tubman. Rather than provide support for Tubman's Home, she offered to sponsor Tubman in a care facility. No doubt, her intention was to sponsor a room in the Home for the Friendless, to which Osborne made regular contributions. This offer would have fulfilled a commitment to care for Tubman, but it would have done nothing for other elderly African American women who were excluded from the Home for the Friendless based on a combination of race and class.

Ironically, however, Eliza Wright Osborne was willing to support other institutions that provided for communal needs: not only the Home for the Friendless but also the Women's Union, making good on her commitment to women's rights with a $200,000 donation for the construction of the Women's Union Building on South Street, a few blocks north of Tubman's properties. It was a communal building dedicated to women, women's workplace rights, and suffrage. It was open to all women regardless of race, background, or economic condition. Hence, Osborne knew Tubman well, looked after her, and was willing to support her financially as an individual. She was also willing to provide financial backing to communal charitable homes and to an inclusive Women's Union. However, she never responded to Tubman's quest for support for her Home, which was dedicated to communally oriented support of elderly African American women in need.

9

A Dream Fulfilled

The Opening of the Harriet Tubman Home in John Brown Hall

> The Tubman Home . . . was for many years an asylum for the needy, the oppressed and unfortunate, irrespective of nationality. Generous to a fault, boundless in her sympathies, who can tell how many wounds she mollified with ointment, or how many hearts alleviated of pain?
>
> —James Edward Mason, Secretary, Livingston College, Salisbury, North Carolina, quoted in *Auburn Advertiser-Journal*, June 6, 1914

History and Archaeology of John Brown Hall

The AME Zion Church officially opened the Harriet Tubman Home for the Aged in John Brown Hall on June 24, 1908, a dozen years after Harriet Tubman had stepped forward to buy the twenty-five-acre property for the Home (figure 1.9). This building is now in ruins at the back of the twenty-five-acre farm. Detailed newspaper reports on the opening provided details related to each room and its furnishings as well as information on the Home, its supporters, and the events of the day.[1] Interestingly, although both a home for the aged and a school for domestic science had been discussed for years, on the day the Home was opened, there was no mention of the school for girls (*Auburn Citizen*, June 24, 1908). From this point forward, plans for a domestic school for girls simply was dropped from the agenda, and energy was focused on one thing—the Harriet Tubman Home for the Aged.

On May 18, 1908, in advance of the formal open house, the *Auburn Semi-Weekly Journal* provided a detailed account of the facility:

---

1. "Dedication of the Harriet Tubman Home," *Auburn Daily Advertiser*, June 24, 1908; *Auburn Citizen*, June 24, 1908. See also *Auburn Citizen*, May 19 and June 17, 1908.

The Harriet Tubman Home: "How much meaning is contained in these three words? Harriet Tubman the grand and noble Christian woman for whom the institution is named needs no introduction. The public knows her—her race respects and honors her—and for founding the home we quote the words of St. Marks, 14th chapter, ninth verse: "this also that she has done shalt be spoken in memorial to her."

The Harriet Tubman home is truly a place in which can be found all that goes in to make a home—comfort, rest, beauty, and neatness. The corridor landing east from the large sitting room off from which are the sleeping rooms is light and warm. The room furnished by Mrs. George Brown of Schenectady, called the Brown room, is pretty, the predominating colors being white and maroon. The room furnished by Mrs. Thomas Freeman of Auburn is in white and gold.

The spacious sitting room, mainly furnished by the indefatigable Mrs. Cregor of Geneva [New York] and Mrs. Lee should be seen to be appreciated. The Brussels carpet, the exquisite lace curtains, the upholstered furniture, and the many small articles. Two other rooms are to be furnished by Mrs. Charles Goodow and Mrs. Edwards.

The visitors who called on inspection day were welcomed by the matron and ladies, escorted to the ledger on which each one registered, and then made a tour through the building and from the upper floor to the living rooms, dining rooms, the furnace, purchased by the lady managers, the spacious kitchen and cellar and so on.

This account projects the long-awaited opening of the Harriet Tubman Home and provides details on furnishings, the organization of space, and the involvement of specific donors who assisted in outfitting the house. The structure of the campaign to gain sponsorship with the outfitting of each room appears to parallel the type of fund-raising campaign successfully used by the Auburn Home for the Friendless during this period (Home for the Friendless 1904, 1912–13).

Twenty days prior to this momentous event, several of Tubman's friends spoke about equal rights for women at a Cayuga County Political Equality Club convention held in Auburn (*Auburn Citizen*, June 4, 1908). The gathering included papers by Emily Howland (president) on women's suffrage, and a paper written years earlier by Martha Coffin Wright that was read by Eliza Wright Osborne.[2] The delegation was entertained at the Auburn

---

2. The text of Martha Coffin Wright's paper (as presented by Eliza Wright Osborne) was included in the newspaper account, noting that to the homes of David M. Osborne, Gerrit

Women's Union Building (a.k.a. Educational and Industrial Building), with a dinner in the cafeteria. The gathering discussed women's contribution to the abolition movement and "the women's rights movement growing naturally out of the anti-slavery struggle." As part of the gathering, Eliza Osborne's "Auburn home welcomed to its fireside the brave women pioneers Elizabeth Cady Stanton, Susan B. Anthony, Lucy Stone, Antoinette Brown, Ernestine L. Rose and their worthy compeers, and every summer for many years like a blessing came the visit of the beloved sister, Lucretia Coffin Mott. In this communion of spirit was a joy of life" (*Auburn Citizen*, June 4, 1908). Although on the surface Tubman's objectives for her Home for the Aged appeared to be in sync with those of the Cayuga County Political Equality Club convention, the two exhibited a growing distance centering on a combination of race and class. Ironically, this gathering of scholarly women presented reflective papers to celebrate their antislavery role in the grand Women's Union Building, while only a few blocks south on South Street Tubman and her AME Zion supporters prepared to celebrate a much smaller home for elderly African Americans in relative isolation; despite the close proximity, there was virtually no financial outreach from the Political Equality Club to the Tubman Home.

On occasions, however, the Auburn community came together as a whole to celebrate the common cause of the Union. On February 12, 1909, the City of Auburn held a celebration in honor of Abraham Lincoln's one hundredth birthday (*Auburn Citizen*, Feb. 12, 1909). The Lincoln celebration at Osborne Hall, another public building funded by the Osborne family, was hosted by the Cayuga County Historical Society, with General William H. Seward Jr. contributing the plenary speech. The packed house included several veterans' groups and bands. Harriet Tubman, "wearing many small American flags crossed in her bonnet and on her dress, and carrying a larger flag that she waved continuously," was given a seat of prominence on the stage. "As the speeches concluded Harriet Tubman waved her flag enthusiastically and then joined with the glee club and the audience to sing the *Battle Hymn of the Republic*. Near the end of the ceremony Tubman was honored for her service to the cause of freedom by Doctor Ives who went into detail regarding

---

Smith, Samuel May, and their wives had come the "despised anti-slavery lecturers. The Garrisons, Phillips, Pillsbury, the Fosters, Douglass, Higginson, Conway and others" (*Auburn Citizen*, June 4, 1908). The presentation describes the burdens on the women of each household in "entertaining such souls" as well as "getting up meetings and circulating tracts and petitions among the indifferent or hostile people."

her role in the Underground Railroad, for which she received an ovation" (*Auburn Democrat Argos*, Feb. 13, 1909).

In May 1909, the *New York Sun* printed an article in tribute to Harriet Tubman.[3] The article projects support for Tubman and calls for community support of the Home: "As a memorial to her it is proposed to expand this home into an industrial school of the type of Tuskegee and Hampton." The article projects Tubman's responses to a series of questions asked by the reporter, who visited her at her farmhouse in Fleming. When asked her age, she responded: "Deed I don't know, sir. I'm some'eres about 90 or 95. I don't know when I was bo'n, but I'm pretty near 90."[4] The reporter noted the high regard of her in the Auburn community: "When she was placed on the platform with Gen. William H. Seward [Junior] when he narrated his reminiscences of Lincoln at the recent centennial celebration, she was greeted with enthusiasm as she came on stage decked from head to foot with miniature American flags and joined in singing '*The Battle Hymn of the Republic.*'" With regard to the Home, the reporter noted, "she looks with satisfaction on the prospect of having her last ambition gratified in the establishment of these premises of the Harriet Tubman Home for the Aged and Infirm Negroes, which she started alone six years ago by simply taking in several old members of her race and going around Auburn begging for food and money for support."[5] The reporter caught her in a candid moment, and when she responded to a question about tensions between herself and the AME Zion Church, Tubman explained: "W'en I gave the Home over to Zion Chu'ch, w'at you s'pose dey done? Why, dey made a rule dat nobody should come in 'dout dey have a hundred dollahs. Now I wanted to make a rule dat nobody could come in 'nless they had no money 'tal."[6] In spite of some misgivings,

3. The article was reprinted in the *Auburn Citizen*, May 19, 1909, and quotes come from this reprint.

4. If born in 1822, she was about eighty-seven at the time of the interview in 1909.

5. In fact, Harriet Tubman had opened the Home in her personal house at least thirteen years earlier and six years earlier had turned the project over to the care of the AME Zion Church. The article suggests that she had turned the Home over to the AME Zion Church at the time of the formal opening of John Brown Hall in 1908, but the church had taken charge in 1903 and was actually responsible for the fund-raising effort that resulted in its formal opening in May 1908.

6. This same quote is given without grammatical inflections in Conrad 1943, 221. Earl Conrad included another line that did not follow directly in the text of the *Sun* article, at least as it was reprinted by the *Auburn Citizen*: "What's the good of a Home if a person who wants to get in has to have money?" The *Auburn Citizen* article appears to borrow liberally from

Harriet Tubman remained involved with the church, and in early December 1909 she spoke at an event held at the Thompson AME Zion Church marking the "fiftieth anniversary of the martyrdom of John Brown" (*Auburn Citizen*, Dec. 2, 1909). Also speaking were Rev. C. A. Smith, who had been a private in the Fifty-Fourth Massachusetts Infantry, and A. E. Rankin of the Auburn Seminary. Typical of such gatherings, the program included music and a dinner prepared by the church's Stewardess Board.[7]

By 1910, when the Home was in full operation and a special meeting was held on January 10 to report on its progress and plans to retire the mortgage on the property, Harriet Tubman was present; she participated in deliberations and was honored by those at the gathering. By this time, Rev. E. U. A. Brooks was president of the board of trustees as well as special agent and financial agent to the Home (*Auburn Citizen*, Jan. 29, 1910).[8] His report included a description of the Home building as an eleven-room brick structure (John Brown Hall) and a total of two inmates, Mrs. Maria Jones of Oswego and Mrs. Rebecca Cross of Elmira, and mentioned that funding was in place to pay the remaining mortgage ($1,000) in full (*Auburn Citizen*, Jan. 29, 1910).[9] Later in the year at the regular annual meeting for the Home on June 7, 1910, Rev. Brooks provided details of expenditures and planning for the Home in his annual report (*Auburn Citizen*, June 10 and 11, 1910).[10]

At a meeting on June 11, 1910, Rev. Brooks in his role as treasurer (employed by the Western New York Conference of the AME Zion Church) reported that the Home's account had received from the various churches in the conference $186.98 for the mortgage fund (to which ten cents was added at the meeting). Of this amount, $24 had been invested in young pigs, leaving a total of $163.03 in the fund. "The Home now owns 17 small and four large pigs," he stated (*Auburn Citizen*, June 11, 1910). This shows that the Home had assumed management of Tubman's hogs and that it was continuing what

---

a number of sources and at one point refers to Tubman's "recent" marriage to Nelson Davis (they were married in 1869), who, it says, died a year earlier (he had died in 1888).

7. I point out the role of women on the Stewardess Board at the seminary to project the similarity in gender roles played by the women of the Board of Lady Managers in support of the Tubman Home.

8. Brooks had a long association with Tubman and the Home that extended back to the early days of its operation within her house.

9. Other accounts described John Brown Hall as a ten-room structure. No mention was made of a school for girls.

10. Once again, there was no mention of the school for girls.

was now a long tradition of raising hogs on the property. It is probable, given ordinances limiting the raising of swine within Auburn's city limits, that these hogs were, as in the past, actually being raised on Tubman's personal farm, just across the city line in the Town of Fleming.

Mrs. H. T. Johnson, secretary of the Board of Lady Managers, read a "splendid report of the year's work showing the affairs of the Home to be in excellent condition" (*Auburn Citizen*, June 11, 1910). Based on the accounts, this appears to have been a very optimistic time for the Home and its governing board. The financial report on the Home was made by Mrs. James Dale, treasurer for the Board of Lady Managers. The report showed receipts of $383.85, expenditures of $321.43, and a cash balance of $37.42 in the treasury. Mr. Dale made a parallel report for the local board of trustees, which showed receipts of $277.07, expenses of $266.88, and cash on hand of $10.19. The Home's matron, Mrs. Donas Griger, indicated that she had $91 on hand for the erection of a porch on the home. The census records for 1910 show that she and her husband were in residence in John Brown Hall and that he was a carpenter (tables 9.1–9.4).[11] The meeting confirmed the continuation of Mrs. Griger as matron of the Home and elected William Freeman as its superintendent.[12]

Mr. William Freeman was also given a two-year contract to work the land, for which he agreed to pay the Home $100 per year. As part of this agreement, he would also care for the passel of hogs belonging to the institution and be responsible for "supervision of the Home, except the brick cottage [Harriet Tubman's house] and the land enclosed about it" (*Auburn Citizen*, June 11, 1910).

11. It is therefore probable that Mr. Griger constructed the porch later in 1910. Photographs of John Brown Hall show the hall before and after the porch was constructed. Hence, one was from before June 1910 (it probably commemorates the opening of the Home), and one was taken after that date, when Tubman was being cared for in the Home.

12. William Freeman had been elected superintendent of the grounds of the Harriet Tubman Home at a joint meeting of the board of trustees and managers held at the residence of Mr. and Mrs. James Dale. Freeman succeeded John A. Lewis, who had held the office for nearly two years and whose term would soon expire (*Auburn Citizen*, Mar. 25, 1910). The election was confirmed at the annual meeting held on June 11 (*Auburn Citizen*, June 11, 1910). During the previous year, Mrs. Griger had raised $40 and donated $39.48 more for moving expenses and improvements. The combined total of all income received in 1910 was tallied at $807.50. From their fund, the trustees paid expenses for coal, repairs, livestock, and food, a total of $268.88. The Board of Lady Managers paid the salary of the matron and for provisions, clothing, and other supplies, a total of $321.42. Mrs. Griger paid $30.48 in miscellaneous repairs. The Home had total cash on hand of $301.55.

TABLE 9.1

UNITED STATES CENSUS, 1910, TUBMAN RESIDENCE, FLEMING, NEW YORK, PART 1

Name	Relation to Head of Household	Sex	Color	Age	Marital Status	Years Married	# Children Born	# Children Living	Birthplace	Father's Birthplace	Mother's Birthplace	Citizenship	Language
Stewart, William H.	head	M	B	90	married	60			MD	MD	MD		English
Davis, Harriett T.	sister	F	B	97	widow		0	0	MD	MD	MD		English
Smith, James E.	boarder	M	B	63	widow				NC	unknown	NC		English
Whitman, James	boarder	M	B	85	married				NY	NY	unknown		English
Printey, Margarette	servant	F	W	70	widow		9	4	Canada-English	England	England	1860	English

Source: US census, 1910, Auburn and Fleming, Cayuga County, Cayuga County Records Office, Auburn, NY.

TABLE 9.2

UNITED STATES CENSUS, 1910, TUBMAN RESIDENCE, FLEMING, NEW YORK, PART 2

Name	Profession	Place of Employment Business	Out of Work?	Can Read?	Can Write?	Attended School?	Owned/ Rented?	Mortgaged/ Free?	Farm or House?	# Farm Schedule	Military?	Blind	Deaf and Dumb
Stewart, William H.	none			No	No		O	Free	H				
Davis, Harriett T.	own income			No	No								
Smith, James E.	none			Yes	Yes								
Whitman, James	none			No	No								
Printey, Margarette	servant	private family worker	No	No	No								

Source: US census, 1910, Auburn and Fleming, Cayuga County, Cayuga County Records Office, Auburn, NY.

TABLE 9.3

UNITED STATES CENSUS, 1910, HARRIET TUBMAN HOME, JOHN BROWN HALL, AUBURN (FLEMING), NEW YORK, PART I

Name	Relation to Head of Household	Sex	Color	Age	Marital Status	Years Married	# Children Born	# Children Living	Birthplace	Father's birthplace	Mother's birthplace	Citizenship	Language
Griger, Shaburn	head	M	MU	72	married	48			NY	Spain	NY		English
Griger, Donas	wife	F	MU	60	married	48	5	1	NY	NY	NY		English
Leiss, Rebecca	boarder	F	B	70	widow				PA	West Indies	MD		English
Jones, Maria	boarder	F	MU	74	widow		1	1	NY	NY	NY		English

Source: US census, 1910, Auburn and Fleming, Cayuga County, Cayuga County Records Office, Auburn, NY.

TABLE 9.4

UNITED STATES CENSUS, 1910, HARRIET TUBMAN HOME, JOHN BROWN HALL, AUBURN (FLEMING), NEW YORK, PART 2

Name	Profession	Place of Business	Employment	Out of Work?	Can Read?	Can Write?	Attended School?	Owned/ Rented?	Mortgaged?	Farm or House?	# Farm Schedule	Military?	Blind	Deaf and Dumb
Griger, Shaburn	carpenter	Tubman Home	no	o	yes	yes		R		H				
Griger Donas	matron	Tubman Home	no	o	yes	yes								
Leiss, Rebecca	none				yes	no					3	3	7	
Jones Maria	none				yes	no								x

Source: US census, 1910, Auburn and Fleming, Cayuga County, Cayuga County Records Office, Auburn, NY.

One of the fund-raising efforts planned was the publication of Harriet Tubman calendars.[13] There was also a "rally day" scheduled for the second Sunday of July, on which "collections for the Home should be taken in the churches of the Western New York conference."[14] During this period, the Home and visitors to the Home were well covered by the local press; for example, on July 9, 1910, Mr. and Mrs. Andre Dunkle "and Mrs. Saltsman of St. Johnsville were the guests of Mr. and Mrs. Griger" at the Home (*Auburn Citizen*, July 9, 1910).

Tubman's Residence after the Formal Opening of the Home

The 1910 US census provides details for both Harriet Tubman's personal farm and residence and the newly opened Home dormitory called John Brown Hall (tables 9.1 and 9.2). Harriet Tubman's personal brick house had five persons in residence: Harriet Tubman, her brother William Henry Stewart Sr., two boarders, and a nurse or house servant who was white, Margarette Printey, a seventy-year-old Canadian with English parents.[15] Only James E. Smith, a sixty-three-year-old boarder, could read and write. The composition of Tubman's own home show that it was still serving as part of the Home for the Aged through the care of elderly boarders. Also, it is notable that the elderly male boarders or inmates remained in Tubman's residence, while the females were in residence at John Brown Hall. Finally, in contrast to earlier years, there were no children or young adults in the household. By 1910, Harriet Tubman was wheelchair bound. Her niece Alice Brinkler later wrote that Tubman had lost the use of her legs and that "she spent her time in a wheel chair and then finally was confined to her bed."[16] This is confirmed by the presence of Tubman in a wheelchair in photographs of this period.

For John Brown Hall, the 1910 US census shows that the building was serving as the dormitory for the Home. This ten-room brick structure was

13. Rev. C. L. Harris reported on the calendars. The plan was to have them ready for January 1, 1911. I have not found one of these calendars. Please let me know if you find one!

14. Funds from the rally were to be "forwarded immediately to Rev. Brooks in Auburn" (*Auburn Citizen*, June 11, 1910).

15. US census, 1910, Auburn and Fleming, Cayuga County Records Office, Auburn, NY. Pitney is listed in the 1910 census as a servant and in the 1910 *Auburn City Directory* (Cayuga County Historian's Office, Auburn, NY) as a nurse.

16. Alice Brinkler to Earl Conrad, Aug. 14, 1939, in Conrad 1943, 74–75, recorded by Conrad as "Letter to the Author from Mrs. Alexander D. Brinklery [*sic*], Wilberforce, Ohio, August 14, 1939."

occupied by Donas Griger, matron for the Tubman Home, along with her husband, Shaburn Griger, a carpenter, both defined as "mulatto" ("MU" in table 9.3). None of the residents, including Mr. and Mrs. Griger, was listed as being employed, but based on accounting in annual financial reports, both of the Grigers were employed by the Tubman Home. Two elderly women were residents at John Brown Hall: Rebecca Leiss was blind, "deaf and dumb" (as worded in the census), while Maria Jones was recorded as engaged in agricultural production for the property. The *Auburn City Directory* for 1910 indicates that Shaburn Griger was in residence at 2 Danforth Street, the building called John Brown Hall.[17] In 1910, the wood-frame building at the front of the property—the "Legacy House" (Locus 2)—is listed in the directory as both 176 South Street and 1 Danforth Street. The Legacy House is listed as vacant in the 1910 census.

An example of the difficulty of dealing with health and mental conditions of the elderly is seen in the story of Mrs. Susan Van Schaick, an old Black woman. Because Van Schaick was a widow and had a pension, the New York State Board of Charities tried to provide her with an alternative to the Cayuga County Almshouse by sending her to the Tubman Home. However, she had a history of violence and behaviors that today might be recognized as age-related dementia. Relatives had tried caring for her, but she had insisted on leaving them. She had been arrested several times and was repeatedly reported for begging. Earlier she had been sent to the Women's Relief Corps Home in Oxford, New York, but "her unruly conduct there had already brought

17. US census, 1910, Auburn and Fleming, NY, Cayuga County Records Office; *Auburn City Directory*, 1910, Cayuga County Historian's Office. The link between the census records and the city directories is important as it clearly defines the three-way correlation between the listing of the broader property of the Harriet Tubman Home as 176 South Street and the fact that at this time the driveway on the property was being considered Danforth Street, a road that was never built but that was used as a means of distinguishing the houses at the front and back of the Harriet Tubman Home property. John Brown Hall, at the back of the property and actually in the Town of Fleming, was listed as 2 Danforth Street and was included in the census records of the City of Auburn, but the majority of the Home property was in Auburn. The wood-frame building at the front of the Home property was listed as 1 Danforth Street; both the census records and the *Auburn City Directory* indicate that this house was vacant in 1910. In the early years of the 1900s, it had been rented out to the Sincerbeaux family (see US census, 1900, Auburn and Fleming, Cayuga County Records Office), but up through at least 1908 plans for the Harriet Tubman Home included a school for girls in this building, and it was no longer rented out. After Tubman's death, the Home was reconfigured, and the wood-frame house at 1 Danforth began to be used to house the Home's inmates.

some physical damage to several of the nurses." She did not get along well at the Tubman Home and was therefore sent to the Cayuga County Almshouse (*Auburn Democrat Argus*, Nov. 21, 1910).[18]

The US censuses of 1900 and 1910 and the New York State Census of 1905 indicate that Tubman's brother William H. Stewart Sr. was a resident of Harriet Tubman's brick house on her small seven-acre farm. He had owned a small parcel on the north side of Tubman's twenty-five-acre property but had moved in with Harriet. In 1903, he was looking to get a mortgage on his property in order to cover medical bills. It is possible that he sold the property to Harriet and/or the Home in 1903. This would explain why the Harriet Tubman Home had a $371 third mortgage that was not recorded anywhere other than within the family and between him and the Home. The mortgage does not show up in county records, but the financial transaction was part of the transfer of Tubman's property to the church in 1903.[19]

Although the Tubman Home operated separately from the Thompson AME Zion Church on Parker Street, the Tubman Home occasionally shows up in the church meeting minutes. Church records include a report from the Harriet Tubman Committee on August 10, 1911. Mrs. James Dale, president of the Board of Lady Managers, reported on behalf of her committee that the July 4 picnic at the Home had generated $20.02 for the Home.[20]

Harriet Tubman Living in John Brown Hall from 1911 to 1913

Early in 1911, Harriet Tubman Davis and her brother William were living in her residence in the brick farmhouse at 184 South Street, but she became ill and was sent to the hospital. Florence Carter, the wife of George Carter, the local AME Zion minister and superintendent of the Home, recalled that Eliza

18. Another event like this had occurred in 1907 when Sheriff Ferric sent Undersheriff Walker to respond to a request to deal with a Black woman who was creating a disturbance at Harriet Tubman's house on South Street. Undersheriff Walker found that the woman had calmed down; he was able to get her to promise to move out of the house, and no arrest was made (*Auburn Semi-Weekly Journal*, Mar. 23, 1907).

19. Harriet Tubman Davis to the AME Zion Church, Cayuga County Deeds City Book 33, June 11, 1903, pp. 410–11, $1,575, Cayuga County Clerk's Office, Auburn, NY.

20. "Conference and Thompson Memorial, Parker Street AME Zion Church Register, Auburn, 1892–1938," Harriet Tubman Home Collection, Harriet Tubman Home, Inc., Auburn, NY.

Wright Osborne and Jane Seward "helped get her to the hospital."[21] We know from Eliza Osborne's correspondence that Eliza paid for at least half of Tubman's medical bills in this instance. On Valentine's Day, Eliza was also taken ill with a cold, and both she and Harriet Tubman were in Auburn's hospital.[22] She included mention of Tubman in a letter addressed jointly to her daughters, Helen Storrow and Emily Harris.[23] Mary Talbert of the Empire State Federation of Colored Women's Clubs also helped raise funds for Tubman's care.

When Harriet Tubman was well enough to return from the hospital, she was placed in John Brown Hall (2 Danforth Street) with other resident inmates of the Home. It was reported by the press that "the most noted conductor of the Underground Railroad was taken to the home last Thursday ill and penniless" (*New York Age*, June 8, 1911). During the early months of her stay in John Brown Hall, she was visited by Anne Fitzhugh Miller and James B. Clarke. Miller had known Tubman all her life. She was the granddaughter of Gerrit Smith and the daughter of longtime women's right advocate Elizabeth Smith Miller and had grown up with the Smith family in Peterborough before moving to Geneva, New York, where she and her husband lived at Lockwood Estate with her suffragette mother. Anne F. Miller and Harriet Tubman spoke on a range of subjects, including Queen Victoria's gifts of a silver Jubilee medal and shawl to Tubman (described in chapter 6). They also discussed women's rights issues, in which Miller was deeply involved.[24] On

21. Eliza Wright Osborne to H. [Helen Osborne Storrow] and E. [Emily Osborne Harris], Feb. 14, 1911, box 87, Osborne Family Papers, Special Collections Research Center, Syracuse Univ., Syracuse, NY.

22. Based on a hospital bill and receipt defining costs associated with Tubman's hospital stay, it is likely that the William Stewart Jr. family paid part of the bill or conveyed this bill to supportive friends (Stewart Family Papers, Harriet Tubman Home Collection).

23. Eliza Wright Osborne to H. [Helen Osborne Storrow] and E. [Emily Osborne Harris] Osborne, Feb. 14, 1911. In the letter, Osborne attributed her own illness to too many hot baths while vacationing at Clifton. She notes that due to her illness she would probably cancel her scheduled West Indian trip by boat from New York.

24. The scrapbooks that Anne Fitzhugh Miller (1856–1912) compiled on women's suffrage between 1897 and 1911 include numerous photographs of Harriet Tubman as well as a rich body of information on the era's women's rights movement. These scrapbooks were later donated to the Smithsonian. Some of the images of Tubman utilized in this study were part of the Miller NAWSA (National American Woman Suffrage Association) Suffrage Scrapbooks, 1897–1911, Elizabeth Smith Miller and Anne Fitzhugh Miller Collection, Rare Book and Special Collections Division, Library of Congress, Washington, DC, at http://memory.loc .gov/ammem/collections/suffrage/millerscrapbooks.

her return to Geneva, Miller sent Tubman a life membership in the Geneva Political Equality Club and a postcard referring to their recent meeting.

> Dear Harriet,
>   Here is your club badge—you know the face. The wedding cake was—Sally Hazard's of Syracuse—a grand-daughter of Ms. Sedgwick. We saw your Jubilee medal in honor of the 60th year of Queen Victoria's reign. I think James Clarke will write the letter to King George the V for yall—I hope to call you soon again.
>   A. F. Miller[25]

The postcard had an image of a woman carrying the banner "Votes for Women" (figure 9.1).[26] Miller refers to having seen Tubman's Jubilee medal from Queen Victoria, which caught the interest of her British West Indian guest, James Clarke, who, Miller indicated, would write a note of congratulation to King George V on his coronation on behalf of Tubman. It is not known if Clarke ever wrote to King George V. After he visited Tubman with Anne Fitzhugh Miller, though, he did write an account of their conversation, "An Hour with Harriet Tubman" (Clarke 1911).[27]

During this period, gifts given to the Home were often acknowledged in the local press. An article titled "Harriet Tubman Home Grateful" describes thanks given by the matron and the Board of Lady Managers to the St. Peters Guild and Associated Charities for their organized efforts on behalf of the Home as well as to "all friends who so generously remembered the Home. The inmates enjoyed one of the best Christmas dinners since the opening of the Home. They were kindly remembered by Mr. and Mrs. John M. Brainard by a fine turkey and boxes of candy and Herrling Bros, sent a chicken." It goes on to give "thanks to all friends and thanks all, especially Mrs. J. W. Martin of Willow Brook for a robe, Miss A. F. Miller of Geneva for gowns and a check of

25. Anne F. Miller (Lockland, Geneva, New York) to Harriet Tubman, postcard, dated July 1, 1911, but not sent through the mail, Harriet Tubman Home Collection.

26. This was an era of the passing of the older generation of abolitionists and women's rights activists. Anne F. Miller died in 1912, shortly after the death of her mother, Elizabeth S. Miller, in 1911.

27. James B. Clarke was a Cornell University student from St. Vincent who spent the summer of 1911 with the Millers in Geneva, New York. A short biography of Clarke is given in Easton 1911.

$15 to the fund, and Mrs. William Hills, a basket of fruit" (*Auburn Citizen*, Jan. 12, 1912).

When Harriet Tubman was taken into the Home in the spring of 1911, the Home assumed primary responsibility for her care, while Tubman retained financial responsibility for expenses related to her residence and farm. Her residence in John Brown Hall is confirmed by the *Auburn City Directory* for 1912, which lists Harriet Tubman Davis as a resident at 2 Danforth, and George Miller is listed as in residence as a renter in Tubman's personal brick home at 184 South Street.[28]

During this era, as in the preceding decade, the public and private interface between her personal residence and the Home were closely interwoven. With Harriet Tubman no longer able to care for herself, the Home published in local papers a plea for support for the Home and Tubman's. It also sent out a press release that was broadly published and received considerable notice among her supporters in New York and Boston.

Tubman never fully recovered from this illness. She remained in the Home and was confined to a wheelchair for the rest of her life. However, she outlived two of her supporters. While Tubman left the hospital and returned to the Home, Eliza Wright Osborne succumbed to her illness on July 19, 1911. This was a great blow to Tubman because Eliza had served as a personal trustee, ensuring her care and stepping forward when needed to take care of Tubman's personal needs.[29] Another of Tubman's long-term supporters died that

---

28. *Auburn City Directory*, 1912, Cayuga County Historian's Office.

29. Eliza Wright Osborne contributed to the Auburn Home to the Friendless and was on the Cayuga County Board of Charities. Her obituary states, "The beautiful building upon South street stands as a noble and enduring monument to her wise charity on behalf of working women of every race, and the Tubman home, to the south of this city, substantial and useful as it is, is but an incident in a long life of effort in behalf of the colored people. We give brief mention of these only because they are matters of common knowledge. To gain added beauty and significance as public illustrations of the character of Mrs. Osborne, and a visible and material evidence of a long life devoted to benevolence in the cause of those whose lives have been made unhappy through poverty, suffering, or the influence of unjust and unequal social, political, or economic conditions" (*Auburn Semi-Weekly Journal*, July 19, 1911). As indicated throughout this volume, Eliza Osborne was an active and willing contributor to Harriet Tubman and right up until her own death served to ensure that Tubman's personal needs were taken care of. While the obituary credits her for her contributions to the Tubman Home, Osborne's personal correspondence indicates that her effort was targeted squarely on the needs of Harriet herself and not so much on the Home. The facts that the Home was in Tubman's house until near the end of her life and that Eliza Wright Osborne was perhaps most

summer: John Henry Osborne, Eliza Osborne's brother-in-law and longtime Home treasurer, died on August 17, 1911, at age seventy-nine. His obituary makes the clearest statement about his involvement in the abolition movement: "In his youth he was attracted to the work of John Brown and became a bitter foe of the institution of slavery. He went to Kansas with the hero of Ossawat-omie and engaged in border warfare for a time to prevent that territory from becoming slave soil" (*Auburn Democrat Argus*, Aug. 17, 1911). After riding with John Brown, John Osborne returned east and took up employment with his brother's farm machinery firm in Auburn, the Osborne Manufacturing Company, rose to the position of secretary of this rapidly growing company, and remained with it until it was sold to International Harvester in 1903 (*Auburn Democrat Argus*, Aug. 17, 1911). He was a social reformer and collector of books, documents, and prints. Unfortunately, his house at 130 South Street, just a few blocks from Tubman's residence, burned in a fire on January 2, 1904, and his entire collection of saved documents was lost. This was a significant loss to our efforts to reconstruct the history of the Home because, excepting Tubman herself, John Osborne was perhaps the person most closely associated with the financial management of the Home from its inception, and he was known as a keeper of notes and records.

As had become a well-established custom within the Auburn community, the holiday season of 1912 saw an outpouring of support for Harriet Tubman and the Home, in which she was now a resident "inmate." The Board of Lady Managers sent a note of thanks to the community that was published in the *Auburn Semi-Weekly Journal* on January 24, 1913.

> The Board of Managers of the Harriet Tubman Home begs to acknowledge with many thanks, the Christmas donations consisting of the following: From Mrs. Brainard,[30] candy for inmates and basket of fruit; Mr. Wm. Hills, pork roast, oranges, oysters, cake; Mr. Letchworth, potatoes, candy; Mrs. Dale, candy and handkerchiefs; Dr. Stough and party, potted plant for each inmate: basket fruit; East Auburn W. C. T. U., three pairs stockings, shawl, hood, night gown, 11 boxes candy for inmates; Associated Charities, meat

---

responsible for that house's upkeep (along with perhaps funds received from Eliza's daughter Helen Storrow) mean, however, that Osborne was by these actions a major indirect contributor to the Home. The local suffrage club, which met in the Women's Union Building funded by Osborne, was renamed the "Eliza Wright Osborne Club" in her honor and continued to pursue the cause of women's suffrage (*Auburn Citizen*, Feb. 11, 1914).

30. Mrs. Brainard is probably the wife of John M. Brainard.

and groceries; Herrling Brothers, chicken; Mm. Belcher, pair pillows and pillow slips, ten pounds sugar.

This notice of thanks provides an important window into the range of persons who had the Tubman Home in their thoughts during the Christmas season. The gifts came from individuals, charitable organizations, and businesses. The Women's Christian Temperance Union's gift reflects a contribution in respect to Tubman's long-standing solidarity with the cause of temperance. The Associated Charities raised funds and provided gifts to many organizations throughout the region, and this gift acknowledged the work of the Home.

The gifts project the Auburn community's desire to ensure a festive occasion for the Home inmates on Christmas. The donated food items included both basic foods such as chicken, potatoes, fruit, and general groceries as well as more extravagant items such as better cuts of meat, imported oranges and oysters, as well as cakes and candy.[31] The Women's Christian Temperance Union also provided practical items of women's clothing, some of which may have been made by members of the organization.

Although virtually nothing in the way of records from this era survived in the Home's archives or library, a descendent of persons involved with the Home visited the site around 2015 and then sent a collection of correspondence written to the Home during the era of Tubman's stay at John Brown Hall from 1911 until her death on March 10, 1913. These letters were addressed to Harriet Tubman Davis, the Harriet Tubman Home, and Rev. Charles A. Smith, chaplain of the Harriet Tubman Home.[32] They show that during this period several persons, such as Miss Elizabeth C. Carter, president of the National Association of Colored Women in New Bedford, Massachusetts, sent small donations.[33]

31. The Tubman Home raised and sold hogs, as did Tubman for decades prior to the formal opening of the Home. The gifting of pork is consistent with food associated with seasonal meals and recognizes what people probably saw as a preferred meal for this occasion at the Home. The presence of oyster shells was documented in the excavations of both Harriet Tubman's personal residence and John Brown Hall.

32. The correspondence mentioned here also includes the postcard from Anne Fitzhugh Miller quoted earlier, who wrote regarding her recent visit, as well as some newspaper clippings related to events associated with the Harriet Tubman Home during this era.

33. Miss Elizabeth C. Carter, President, National Association of Colored Women, 211 Park St. New Bedford, MA, to Mrs. Harriet Tubman Davis, July 12, 1911, Harriet Tubman Home Collection.

A letter from Mrs. W. A. Jackson, a woman Tubman had assisted when Mrs. Jackson was a girl, thanks Tubman for taking her in and provides details of Tubman's household during her visit at a time in which Tubman's parents were still alive and living in her house:

Mrs. Harriet Tubman—Dear Aunt Harriet you will no doubt be more than surprised to receive a letter from me. When you know who it is who is writing to you after so many years. I am going to try and make you remember who I am. I am the little girl who came to your door one cold winter's day and asked if I might come in and get warm. You were sitting by the fire asleep. But woke up and said, yes come in and sit down. I had come from Buffalo and had an Aunt who lived very near your House, her name was Josephine Cole, and she lived in the house with a family named Dale.

At the time you took me to live with you. You also had a girl by the name of Mary Ellen Stewart and another by the name Ella Mills and a boy of the name William Lane and another by name of Edward Woods.

My name was Eliza Williams and my name now is Mrs. W. A. Jackson and seeing an appeal in the Amsterdam News for aid for you I wanted to do something for you to show that I have not forgotten your kindness to me and though I did not know enough then to appreciate what was done for me I have never forgotten you and have often told my children about you and how I came to you and you took me in, hoping that you will remember me and that I shall hear from you soon so that I can do what I can for you and will come and see you soon Oh yes I forgot to say, your mother and father were living at the time I was there and occupied the front room upstairs in your house which stood on the south side of the street—I can't remember the name of the street. But it was out by the West Toll gate.

Hoping you will—[illegible] this and remember who I am, I want an answer.

Yours Truly Mrs. W. A. Jackson, 11½
West 137th St., New York City.[34]

34. Mrs. W. A. Jackson to Harriet Tubman, n.d. (c. 1913), Harriet Tubman Home Collection.

In addition to describing Tubman's kindness and consideration in taking her in as well as a setting in which Tubman sat dozing in her rocker by the fireplace on a cold winter's day, the letter writer mentions some of the people living in Tubman's house during the time of her stay there, including the four other children. Although much that is written about Tubman's household focuses on its relation to aged and infirm persons, this account reflects on a child's experiences in the house and brings attention to the children with whom she interacted.

Julius Heiman of New York City sent a note along with a copy of the newspaper clipping of the call for help, which he attached with a straight pin to his note: "Please give me full particulars, should be happy to assist if needed—Julius Heiman."[35] Another note sent to Mrs. Harriet Tubman Davis in 1912 was from Charles E. Lawrence, keeper of the Cayuga County Almshouse. He enclosed $5 that had been given to him by James E. Smith, a former resident in Tubman's house, who had died the previous week, to pay back a sum Smith owed to Tubman.[36] It appears as if all of the men were removed from Tubman's own brick farmhouse during this period and that the house was rented out to George Miller in early 1912. The 1912 *Auburn City Directory* lists George Miller as renting Harriet Tubman's house at 184 South Street, Fleming.[37] There is no correspondence from the keeper of the Cayuga County Almshouse regarding Tubman's brother William Henry Sr. He had been ill for some time and in 1912 was moved to the almshouse in Sennett. The Home had made provisions for Harriet Tubman, but not for her brother. He died in Sennett later in 1912 after a lingering illness.[38]

35. Julius Heiman, Heiman and Lichten, 315 West 105th Street, New York, to Harriet Tubman Home, June 4, 1911, Harriet Tubman Home Collection.

36. Charles E. Lawrence, Keeper, Cayuga County Home, Sennett, NY, to Mrs. Harriet Tubman Davis, Auburn, NY, Nov. 3, 1912, Harriet Tubman Home Collection. James Smith is listed as a sixty-three-year-old in residence at Harriet Tubman's personal home in the 1910 census (US census, 1910, Auburn and Fleming, Cayuga County Records Office). At that time, the male inmates of the Home lived in Tubman's house, and the women lived in John Brown Hall. James apparently was removed from Tubman's house and sent to the Cayuga County Almshouse sometime between late 1910, when the census was taken, and early 1912, when the keeper of the county facility sent $5 to Tubman to pay off James's debt to Tubman.

37. *Auburn City Directory*, 1912, Cayuga County Historian's Office.

38. It is probable that due to a combination of William Henry Stewart Sr.'s chronic illness and a desire to rent out Tubman's personal residence to cover costs of the Home that he was placed in the Cayuga County Almshouse (along with James Smith), where he died in 1912. As early as 1903, William had illnesses that required treatment by three doctors and probably

On March 3, 1913, Franklin Sanborn sent a letter to Rev. C. A. Smith at the Home in response to Rev. Smith's request for support for Tubman. A carbon copy of Sanborn's letter survives among Thomas Osborne's correspondence along with a second letter to Osborne asking about Tubman's condition and the state of her affairs. In response to Rev. Smith, Franklin Sanborn wrote:

> Your note of 29th ult., only reached me yesterday by reason of my two-day absence from the house, and I sadly comply with Harriet's wish to hear from me. She and her friends in Auburn have long known my address, and could have reached me by letter long ago. Since the death of Mrs. Osborne, with whom I used to communicate in regard to Harriet I had heard nothing about her until your note came. The slip accompanying it is full of gross exaggerations concerning Harriet's age, and history. The true facts are given in a little volume written by Mrs. Bradford more than 50 years ago, or about that time, which we twice had printed and sold for Harriet's benefit. What has become of that book? Does Harriet know anything about it? About 1860 I went over her recollections with Harriet and we settled the date of her birth as not earlier than 1820. I printed in the Boston Commonwealth, which I then edited, in the weekly of July 17, 1863, a sketch of her life up to that time, which afterwards went into Mrs. Bradford's book. She was born about 1820–1821, married John Tubman, a free colored Maryland man in 1844, escaped from slavery in 1849, returned to her old home in 1851, found her husband married to another man [*sic*] and gave him up as hopeless. She then continued bringing away slaves and aiding them to escape, and finally brought off her father and mother in 1857—at first to Canada, and then to Auburn, where she had bought a home for them of Gov. Seward. Please read the above to Harriet and tell her that I and her friend[s] hereabouts who are living, remember her well, and wish to know that they can do for her now. Most of her friends here in Boston are dead—the Emersons, Thoreaus, Whitings, Brooks, Cheneys,

---

resulted in his selling his quarter acre at the northwest corner of the Harriet Tubman Home property (which constituted the third mortgage that needed to be paid off before the title of the property could be transferred to the Harriet Tubman Home and the AME Zion Church). While Tubman was able to oversee her brother's welfare, she had taken him into her own home, but after she herself was placed in the Home, she lacked the ability to take care of him. William's son was still living on Garret Street but may not have been able to take care of his father. William Jr.'s wife died at about the same time, in 1912, as her father-in-law.

Clarkes, etc. But F. J. Garrison is living and Mrs. Storrow and others have appeared here in later years.

And may I hear from you in regard to the matters in this letter. Who wrote the printed article and where did it get printed? What supports the home, and is there any separate fund for Harriet's support? Who own and manage the Home? What is the amount of its property, and how much of it is under Mortgage.

Truly your Friend, F. B. Sanborn[39]

Before sending the letter to Rev. Charles A. Smith, Sanborn wrote a second letter to Thomas Osborne, to which he attached a copy of his letter to Smith:

Concord, Massachusetts, Feb'y 3, 1913

Dear Mr. Osborne:

You will remember me as the old friend of Mrs. Osborne and of Harriet Tubman, whom I met in Boston about 1857, recommended to me by Gerrit Smith. I had heard nothing about her of late till yesterday I received a note from Rev. C. A. Smith, Chaplain of the Tubman Home in Auburn, saying that Harriet is lying helpless at the Home, and has been trying to hear from me for months, and desires me to write her a line, which I will gladly do. But along with this note came a printed article about Harriet, full of mistakes and exaggerations, which ought not to be allowed to circulate. It states that she was born in 1807, which exaggerates her age by some 13 years. When she was first with me here in Concord, about 1861, I went over her early recollections with her, and we fixed her date of birth as not earlier than 1820, so that she is now probably about 92 years old. She was married about 1844 to a free colored man named John Tubman. Had she been born in 1807 would she have waited til the age of 37 for her first marriage? I trow not. There are many other exaggerations in the article. What has become of the biography of Harriet which has been twice printed and sold for her benefit? Would it not be well to have it again printed and sold for her profit? Or has it disappeared?

---

39. Franklin B. Sanborn, Concord, Massachusetts, to Rev. C. A. Smith, Chaplain of the Harriet Tubman Home, Auburn, New York, Feb. 3, 1913, Harriet Tubman Home Collection, copy also in Osborne Family Papers.

Will you not write me in the enclosed envelope what Harriet's actual condition is, and what in your view ought to be done for her now?

Truly Yours—F. V. Sanborn

I have written to Mr. Smith as enclosed[40]

In addition to enclosing a copy of his letter to Rev. Smith, Sanborn sent Osborne $10 to assist Harriet Tubman. In both letters, Sanborn refers to a "printed article . . . full of mistakes and exaggerations," dated 1901, possibly by Robert Taylor, a biography for the Tuskegee Institute to raise funds for Tubman. Sanborn is clearly upset that the story of Tubman's contributions was being diluted by unnecessary and inaccurate hyperbole and wanted Smith to know that a more detailed and accurate biography had been written (Humez 2003, 378; Taylor 1901).

It is clear that Thomas Osborne knew of Sanborn's important role as an abolitionist, historian, and friend of Tubman. Osborne responded to Sanborn in a letter dated March 5, 1913, indicating that he had asked his cousin Josephine Osborne to call on Tubman. He also had his personal secretary look into Tubman's financial affairs and then responded to Sanborn:

Mr. Sanborn:

Your letter of February 3 is received. I have heard that Harriet Tubman is ill, but noting further since my Mother's death there has been no one that I know with sufficient interest in Harriet to look after her, but when my Mother was living it was difficult to do much for her as anything given her would be stolen by the worthless living there who misused her kindness.

I will have someone see Harriet soon, and will write just how she is. The colored church take an interest in her and I do not think she is suffering.

About the printed article you mention, I know nothing of the book of which you speak, "Harriet, the Moses of her People" is on sale here at our book-stores. I don't know it is of much use to have a new edition printed.

Very Sincerely yours—Thomas Osborne[41]

40. Franklin B. Sanborn, Concord, Massachusetts, to Thomas Osborne, Auburn, New York, Feb. 3, 1913, Osborne Family Papers.

41. Thomas Osborne, Auburn, New York, to Franklin B. Sanborn, Concord, Massachusetts, Mar. 5, 1913, carbon copy, Osborne Family Papers.

A few days later, under instructions from Thomas Osborne, his secretary wrote a follow-up letter to Mr. Sanborn, with an update pertaining to Harriet Tubman:

F. B. Sanborn, Esq.
Concord, Mass.

Dear Sir:

Mr. Osborne wished me to write you regarding Harriet Tubman. His cousin, Miss Josephine Osborne, went to see Harriet the other day and found her very ill. She has pneumonia, I believe, and is still in a very weak condition, although she may live all summer.

Regarding her expenses. Miss Osborne says that they amount to $31 a month—$16 for the nurse, $12 for the board, and $3 for washing. Then of course her doctor's bills are additional. She gets a pension of $20. a month and she has an annuity of $50 per year. There is to be a meeting of the Board of Managers on Thursday, the 20th, which Miss. Osborne will attend, and will then find out more definitely in regard to Harriet's needs. She was told of the ten dollars which you had so kindly sent for her use, and desired Miss. Osborne to keep it for the present.

Sincerely yours,
Secr'y.[42]

This note includes details on Tubman's financial condition and sets forth a plan to gain more information on her long-term care and finances. Unfortunately, Harriet Tubman died before the scheduled meeting took place.

Among the letters and papers recently returned to the Home is an unsigned draft of what appears to have been Rev. Charles A. Smith's response to Sanborn. It politely addresses most of the issues raised by Sanborn and in the process provides some important details on the state of the Home in March 1913. This draft letter is missing sections. It consists of two parts written on identical paper but folded separately and differently. Each represents only part of a page. Nonetheless, the details it presents are important. Given the rapidity of events, including Tubman's illness and then her death on March 10, it is

42. Secretary of Thomas Osborne, Auburn, New York, to Franklin B. Sanborn, Concord, Massachusetts, Mar. 11, 1913, carbon copy, Osborne Family Papers.

not known if a final draft was ever sent to Sanborn. It is dated only a few days before Tubman died, so it is possible that it was never mailed.

First part of letter:

> The printed article was a reprint from an appeal written up by a gentleman from [page break here] and is as Harriet told him. Although his ~~mind~~ memory is not as good as in past years. The book you speak of—we have no knowledge of its where about but a later one published in 1891, printed by J. J. Little and Co., New York is extant, entitled: Harriet Tubman Moses of her people also by Mrs. Bradford if you have not that book and would like one I would gladly send you a copy. The home is managed by a committee appointed by the AME Zion Connection who took it upon Harriet's request after she became too feeble to [illegible word] have succeeded in reducing the debt to $800.00 which is under mortgage _____ [line then word erased] is what Harriet is anxious to raise. The original cost was about _____ [blank line]. There are at present six inmates, three from Elmira and three from Auburn who pay $3.83 per week. [page break here]

Second portion of letter:

> That really leaves very little for her needs. Miss H. out and gives some funds for Harriet when she visits her but no stated amount. A friend or relative of Mrs. Osborne allows her fifty dollars per year. The pension from the Government is $60 per quarter. The rent of her house brings her a small sum only as it needs repairs. She has not been able to do for herself as she has been an inmate of the home for over two years, but in consideration for what she has done is charged no board, the connection [AME Zion] pays that. But aside from that her nurse is to be paid and also. The nurse's board, her Dr.'s Bills and her laundry clothing and the many little necessities that constantly arise.[43]

The letter continues, but the remainder is lost. It indicates that Rev. Smith was concerned about Sanborn's response and was eager to address each issue squarely to demonstrate that Harriet Tubman stood behind the request but

43. Unknown letter writer to unknown recipient (probably Rev. C. A. Smith, Harriet Tubman Home, to Franklin Sanborn, Concord, Massachusetts), c. Mar. 5–13, 1913, Harriet Tubman Home Collection. The name "AME Zion Connection" refers to the broader AME Zion Church body and its connection to the laity. Its use in this letter suggests that Tubman's upkeep in the Home was paid by donations from the church membership.

that the Home was a legitimate facility. There was good reason to believe that it was important to gain Sanborn's goodwill because he had helped Tubman in the past. The note does not say who authored the article Sanborn disliked so much, and it is possible that it was simply a document on file that was sent to him along with the request, and Smith did not know its author. The response shows that Smith was very familiar with Tubman's finances, including the money she was receiving from her government pensions as well as regular support from members of the Osborne family, such as "Miss. H.," who is likely Helen Storrow, Eliza Wright Osborne's daughter, well known for her philanthropy in Boston.

Regardless of its specific author and its incomplete state, this draft of a letter from the Home is filled with important details about Harriet and the Tubman Home in early 1913. It says that rent to Tubman for her house brought only a small sum of money and that most if not all of that amount was used for repairs. The AME Zion Church charged her no board, which was paid by the AME Zion Connection. It also indicates that Tubman's financial needs had to be met, which included a salary and room and board for a nurse as well as laundry and living necessities that "constantly arise."

The final part of this exchange was written on March 24, 1913, when Thomas Osborne wrote to Franklin Sanborn to tell him that Harriet Tubman had died. He also tells Sanborn that the $10 that Sanborn had sent for Tubman's care before her death "will be used in accordance with Harriet's request, toward paying her nurse."[44]

Right up to the time of her death, Tubman continued to receive small-scale financial donations from friends and admirers. On February 19, 1913, Thomas Osborne wrote to Emily Howland about Tubman: "The last time I saw her, tho' in bed she was bright and talkative very clear in mind. Told me what she wanted to do with her gold pieces, which were given to her by Mrs. Osborne and her children, in case she didn't live very long." He thanks Emily Howland for a check and tells her that Tubman's pension is spent paying for a nurse, but "it isn't quite enough": "I think, the annuity that she receives in the fall she will not let me use for that purpose, she wants to keep that on hand for her own personal use, she gave the last that she had to pay for a cow for the Harriet Tubman home a nice fine cow she is too, gives lots of milk they told me. . . . I shall try to see Harriet Tubman next week."[45]

44. Thomas Osborne, Auburn, New York, to Franklin B. Sanborn, Concord, Massachusetts, Mar. 24, 1913, carbon copy, Osborne Family Papers.

45. Thomas Osborne to Emily Howland, Feb. 19, 1913, Osborne Family Papers.

March 10, 1913: The Death of Harriet Tubman

Harriet Tubman Davis died of pneumonia on March 10, 1913. Before she died, a group gathered at her bedside for religious services led by Rev. E. U. A. Brooks and Rev. Charles A. Smith. Those in attendance included Frances R. Smith, who had served as Tubman's nurse and as the Home's matron, Eliza E. Peterson of the Women's Christian Temperance Union of Texas, and Charles and Clearance Stewart (two of Tubman's grandnephews) (*Auburn Daily Advertiser*, Mar. 13, 1913). Newspaper accounts report that Tubman's last words were "I go away to prepare a place for you, that where I am you also may be." She was buried on March 13, 1913. On the morning of the funeral, several hundred people met at the Home. After a service at the Home, she was taken to Thompson AME Zion Church on Parker Street for a viewing and another service.[46] The respect paid to Tubman by the AME Zion Church leadership and its parishioners at the church service illustrates her bonds with the church (D. Armstrong and A. Armstrong 2020; Krieger 2018). After the services at the church, she was carried across the street to her final burial place at Fort Hill Cemetery in Auburn.[47] In her casket were placed the silver medal sent to her by Queen Victoria and a crucifix. The casket was draped with an American flag ("Goodbye: Death of Aunt Harriet," *Auburn Daily Advertiser*, Mar. 11, 1913). The graveside service included many church and community leaders as well as friends who reflected on Tubman's many accomplishments ("Harriet Tubman Is Dead," *Auburn Daily Advertiser*, Mar. 11, 1913). In addition, her burial was afforded military recognition out of respect to her service during the Civil War. The service was closed by the Relief Corps of the Charles H. Stewart Post of the Grand Army of the Republic (*Auburn Citizen*, Mar. 14, 1913). On March 14, the day after her burial, the *Auburn Citizen* published a long tribute to Harriet Tubman written by Mrs. Mary Talbert.

46. Photographs show Tubman's casket in the church and the procession from the Thompson AME Zion to her burial plot across the street at Fort Hill Cemetery (Krieger 2018). The church is now part of the Harriet Tubman National Park (referred to by the US National Park Service as HART). The building and grounds are currently being restored. Much of the cement work in front of the church has changed since 1913; however, granite stones that mark the east side of a bridged culvert remain. These stones mark the edge of the property and what at the time was a dirt road upon which wooden planks were placed to provide a pathway for Tubman's burial procession.

47. In the fall of 2019, I conducted excavations in the front yard of the church and rediscovered a stone curb feature that shows up in photographs of the front of the church during the era of the funeral.

When Tubman died, tributes flowed in, and several fund-raising campaigns were initiated in support of an appropriate commemorative service, a tombstone, a bronze plaque, and her legacy at the Home for the Aged. A year later, on June 12, 1914, a formal ceremony was held in Tubman's honor. This gathering was organized around a visit and speech by Booker T. Washington and was held at Auburn's Auditorium Theater. It included the unveiling of a bronze plaque, which was later placed on an exterior wall at the Cayuga County Courthouse.

IN MEMORY OF
HARRIET TUBMAN
BORN A SLAVE IN MARYLAND ABOUT 1821.
DIED IN AUBURN, NEW YORK, MARCH 10, 1913.

CALLED THE "MOSES" OF HER PEOPLE
DURING THE CIVIL WAR, WITH RARE
COURAGE, SHE LED OVER THREE HUNDRED
NEGROES UP FROM SLAVERY TO FREEDOM,
AND RENDERED INVALUABLE SERVICE
AS NURSE AND SPY.

WITH IMPLICIT TRUST IN GOD,
SHE BRAVED EVERY DANGER AND
OVERCAME EVERY OBSTACLE: WITHAL
SHE POSSESSED EXTRAORDINARY
FORESIGHT AND JUDGEMENT SO
THAT SHE TRUTHFULLY SAID

"ON MY UNDERGROUND RAILROAD
I NEBBER RUN MY TRAIN OFF DE TRACK
AND I NEBBER LOST A PASSENDER."

Fund-raising efforts continued, and through the efforts of Mary Talbert and the Empire State Federation of Colored Women's Clubs a stone monument was erected on Harriet Tubman's grave on June 13, 1915.

With the opening of the Home in 1908, it appears that women under Tubman's care moved to the new facility, and men, including her brother William, remained in her brick house. Although Tubman's ownership of her house and farm was clearly recognized, those in her house continued to be considered part of the Home. However, the Home more formally switched from the inclusion of both females and males to housing women only after Tubman's illness in 1911 and her movement from her house to the hospital and then to John Brown Hall. These changes were followed by the removal of William Henry Stewart Sr. and James E. Smith to the Cayuga County Almshouse in Sennett. The change to a woman-only institution is more apparent after 1913, when Tubman's personal residence and farm were sold to settle her estate and thus were no longer available for use by the Home.

The settlement of her estate included some debts as well as stipulations in her will to distribute the proceeds from her worldly goods to three relatives and friends: Mary Gaston (her niece), Katy Stewart (her grandniece), and Frances R. Smith, her health-care provider and matron at the Home for the Aged during the final years of Tubman's life.[48] Her farm, including her brick farmhouse, was sold to the Norris family in 1913; however, the twenty-five-acre farm continued to operate as the Home for the Aged under ownership and management of the Tubman Home Board of Directors and the AME Zion Church.

Archaeological Reconnaissance at John Brown Hall

John Brown Hall served as the residential dormitory and infirmary for the Home for the Aged when it opened in 1908 (figures 1.9–1.11).[49] It was initially built to house brickyard workers in the 1860s and was rented out for the

48. Harriet Tubman, Last Will and Testament, 1912, copy in the Harriet Tubman Home Collection. Louis K. R. Laird, a white man who served as executor of the estate, sold the property to a white neighbor, William Norris, but William Freeman, at the time caretaker and sometimes listed as superintendent of the Harriet Tubman Home, claimed that Laird had refused his offer to buy the property, even after Freeman had even upped his initial offer of $1,400 to $1,500. For his part, Laird claimed that no neighbor had offered anywhere near as much as was paid by William Norris and that he had acted in accordance with his responsibility to the heirs to obtain the best price for the land. Much of the funds received went to cover debt, and so when the remainder was divided by three, there was little net gain for each of the three heirs. The result was a general feeling of dissatisfaction as well as long-standing resentment that a property so important to a key African American figure was sold and separated from the family and the AME Zion Church. Hence, when the land was offered for sale to the AME Zion Church in 1990, the church jumped at the opportunity to buy the property and include it as part of Harriet Tubman Home, Inc.

49. This effort was assisted by hundreds of volunteers who participated in weekend dig days in 1998 and 1999. Clearing of debris within the basement of the house was assisted by teams of inmates from the Butler Correctional Facility, Victor, New York. The brick and stone were removed from the basement and stacked in an area to the west of the house. These materials might be used in future reconstruction or restoration of the building.

first decade after Tubman acquired the twenty-five-acre farm.[50] When sufficient funds were raised, this structure was refurbished to create the dormitory
and infirmary for the Home. It was the operational and housing center of the
Home from 1908 through Tubman's death in 1913. After her death, new
funds were generated to refurbish the wood-frame building at the front of the
property (the Legacy House). By mid-1915, the primary dormitory had been
moved to that site, and the John Brown Hall structure was rented out to raise
money to support the Home.[51]

The ruins of John Brown Hall (Locus 3) were rediscovered in the woods in
1994.[52] In 1997, my proposal for research was approved by the Harriet Tubman Home Board of Directors, and, along with my graduate student Bonnie
Ryan, I began doing background research on the property (Ryan 2000; Ryan
and Armstrong 2000). Our goal was to demonstrate the potential for archaeological recovery at John Brown Hall with a broader objective of expanding
archaeological research to the entire site to assist with restoration.

The John Brown Hall site was completely overgrown by trees, brush, wild
rose bushes, and blackberry brambles. The first step in assessing the structure
involved clearing the vegetation and mapping. As we did this, we laid out a
five-meter site grid and began to test the site for middens and features.[53] We
began digging shovel test pits in and around the ruins in 1998 and expanded
to excavation units in 1999.[54]

Brickyards in the area had begun operation in the 1850s, but there is no
specific record for the construction of the building that came to be called
"John Brown Hall." John W. Farmer and his wife, Polly, purchased the
twenty-five-acre farm on which the building stands from William Seward in

50. An historical overview of archaeological studies of institutional life can be found in
Beisaw and Gibb 2009, which addresses a range of topics from charitable schools for girls and
cloistered communes to places of forced incarceration, such as asylums and prisons.

51. John Brown Hall was still in use as the Home's dormitory on March 27, 1915, when
Mrs. Winifred Johnson died there.

52. The rediscovery of John Brown Hall is discussed in chapter 1.

53. The site datum was established 7.2 meters west of a power pole located about 25
meters north of the ruins of John Brown Hall. The datum point, an axis, and a baseline were
surveyed by Gordon DeAngelo, a well-recognized amateur archaeologist and a professional
surveyor who then worked for the New York State Department of Transportation.

54. Excavations were organized as part of Syracuse University's summer field schools
and a series of public dig days in October 1998 and 1999. The October public dig days were
supported by a Vision Fund grant and ear year involved more than three hundred volunteers
of all ages, including buses full of students from the Syracuse City School District.

1864.[55] John Farmer may have leased the land to Clark Pierce for his brick-yard.[56] In 2002, Alice Norris gave us a picture from the 1940s showing the Norris children skating on a pond behind the barn at the front of Tubman's personal farm. In the background, one can see the south side of John Brown Hall (figure 9.2).[57]

Most of the daily activities at John Brown Hall took place in the ground or basement floor, which was divided into seven rooms. This level had large windows with limestone lintels and sills, indicating that the basement had substantial sources of light. The sleeping area was upstairs, and privy-style bathrooms were attached to the ground floor and sill stones at the southeast corner of the structure.[58] The presence of a full basement and its use as a primary activity area, including a kitchen and a living area with two fire-places, is consistent with nineteenth-century houses along South Street, such as Tubman's own personal residence and the William Seward house. Both the Seward house and Tubman's residence had kitchens in the basement in the nineteenth century. The Sewards moved their kitchen to the first floor soon after the Civil War, and Tubman moved hers to the first floor between 1904 and 1905.

Recovery of Structural Information

Pictures of John Brown Hall taken between 1908 and 1911 show and excavations confirm a substantial brick structure built on a stone foundation with a full basement divided into seven rooms and a first floor divided into two bedrooms and a central parlor (figures 1.7, 1.9–1.11). The building was initially constructed from local brick to serve as a dormitory for workers in the brick-yards that stretched out along the creek that runs south to north through

---

55. The land was inherited by Seward's wife, Frances Miller Seward, and her sister, Lazette Miller Worden, from Judge Elijah Miller (Cayuga County Deeds Book 106, 1864, p. 51, Cayuga County Clerk's Office).

56. Pierce's business was short-lived and was dropped from the *Auburn City Directory* after 1875.

57. Mrs. Alice Norris did not think we would be interested in a group of family photographs because they were of her family rather than of Tubman and her era. Fortunately, Beth Crawford and I convinced her of their value. In fact, they provided important information on both buildings used to house inmates at the Harriet Tubman Home in John Brown Hall and the wood-frame building at the front of the property.

58. This feature has not been tested.

the property.[59] The majority of artifacts we found there were construction debris—bricks, mortar, and plaster, which were weighed (not counted)—as well as other construction debris, such as nails, coal, metal, and roofing material. These data came from twenty-two units excavated within the foundation. The building had two chimneys and glazed windows with stone lintels. The main entrance was on the north side, with three doors on the south side of the ground, or basement, level.

The data recovered provided information on structural details relating primarily to the ground floor. The kitchen (room one) is an interior room at the northwest corner of the main western block of the building (figures 9.3–9.4). This room had a six-over-six window on its northern wall, defined by a stone sill that was still in place. A fireplace and chimney were located in the southwest corner of the room and probably once had an attached stove, fragments of which were recovered through excavation. The kitchen was accessible through a doorway marked by a stone sill to room four to the south. The floors of the kitchen and of rooms two and three were approximately thirty centimeters higher than the floors of rooms four and five. The stone walls on the west and north sides of the building were lined with plaster painted shades of pink, green, and blue.

Room two is an interior room located between rooms one and three on the north side of the building. A limestone sill indicates the presence of a large window, as shown in early twentieth-century photographs (figure 1.10). Stone foundation walls had unpainted plaster, and an interior wall was indicated by a single course of brick. This brick footing may have held a wood framing because framing nails were recovered from this area. Room three is similar to room two, except that it has a cement floor. The blue-painted plaster on the wall of this room is in the best condition of any area of the structure. Some pink paint survives on the plaster on the northern wall. This room also has a doorway leading to room six and the eastern half of the building (figure 9.5).

59. Several brickyards bracketed the property, and bricks were made at a brickyard on this farm (A. Armstrong and D. Armstrong 2012). One of the brickyards was operated from 1872 through 1875 by Clark Pierce (*Auburn City Directory* [Boyd's] 1873, 1874, 1875, Cayuga County Historian's Office). Details on brick production are included in the discussion of the brick kiln on the property in chapter 11. A report in the *Auburn Morning News* on October 4, 1873, describes Harriet Tubman's husband, Nelson Davis, as a person who "is at work at Pierces' brickyard, near the South street toll gate." This article also focuses on Tubman being robbed in a complex "gold" swindle.

Room four is on the southwest corner of the building. The west wall of this room is made of stone, but the wall has a brick lining. The floor of this room was not in as good shape as the floor of any of the other rooms, but the amount of brick in the area suggests that it once had been made of brick. There is no definitive evidence for this room having a window, but it may well have had one on its south side. The foundation of the south wall was constructed out of two rows of brick. The wall fell outside the structure and remained articulated on the ground, covering a predestruction-period surface (i.e., before the hall was demolished by the City of Auburn) (figure 9.6).

Room five, the main living or gathering room, is in the southwest corner of the ground floor. This room had two exterior doorways and the base of a chimney. The amount of burned brick suggests that the room had a fireplace. It had a pine-plank floor aligned on a north–south axis. Based on surviving wood fragments, it appears that the planks were of uneven widths ranging from ten to eighteen centimeters. Stone sills were found in excavation units on the south and east walls of this room. These sills rested on foundation stones that projected twelve centimeters into the interior of the room. These wooden floors were apparently elevated about twenty to thirty centimeters above the ground so that the surface elevation of this room was even with the brick-and-mortar flooring of the other rooms of the western part of the building. It is likely that the basement was connected to the upper living floor by an interior staircase, but no evidence of a footing for a staircase was found on the ground floor.

The eastern section of the building was divided into two rooms (rooms six and seven). Room six was like room five in that it had both exterior and interior doors leading outside the structure and to other parts of the building. It had a wooden-plank floor built in a manner like the floor found in room five. Room seven did not share a doorway with any of the other rooms in the house, and we found evidence of wood-plank flooring there, too, much like that in rooms five and six. Based on the structural features, it is probable that room seven was used for storage of foods and supplies.[60] There may also have been an attached bathroom at the southeast corner of the building; however, exploration of this area was prevented by the presence of a large tree.

60. Only about half of the ground floor of John Brown Hall was excavated. Although we have been able to reconstruct the general outline of the rooms, additional excavation, particularly in rooms two, five, six, and seven, will provide further details on how the various specific activity areas of the building functioned. In particular, we are interested to know about the possible use of room seven as a storage area.

Because the second floor was destroyed, we have little definitive information on its layout except for information gleaned from photographs. However, as described in accounts of the opening of the Home (given earlier in this chapter), we do have details on the contents of furnishings in two rooms and a central hall upstairs.

Arrangement and Furnishing of John Brown Hall

Furniture found in the building include chrome-plated drawer pulls from dressers or cabinets and metal hardware from a wooden bed frame. A clock spring indicates the presence of a clock. Bake-a-light electric plug parts suggest electricity even though there is no evidence of electric wiring at the site. A reporter's account of the refurbished Home in 1908 provides significant details of the décor. The reporter began on the living floor and described a "light and warm" central corridor landing "east from the large sitting room off from which are the sleeping rooms." This room was furnished with "Brussels carpet," "exquisite lace curtains," "upholstered furniture," and "many small articles" by Mrs. Cregor of Geneva, New York, and Mrs. Lee. This room was flanked by two dormitory rooms. In the basement were the dining rooms, a "spacious kitchen," and a furnace purchased by the lady managers (*Auburn Semi-Weekly Journal*, May 18, 1908).

Artifacts from John Brown Hall

The primary function of this structure during the Tubman era was a dormitory for elderly African Americans, so it was not surprising to find large numbers of pharmaceutical bottles and health-care-related items, including bedpans, in the yard (figure 9.7). Two metal pillboxes, including one that is heart-shaped (figure 1.15), are of note. We do not know to whom this pillbox belonged, but its shape is provocative and perhaps emblematic of the character of those who lived at the site, not the least of whom was Harriet Tubman. It still contained pills. In addition to the pillboxes, the large number of pharmaceutical bottles support the use of John Brown Hall as an infirmary for the Home. Several glass jars held medicinal ointments such as Frank's Petroleum Jelly and Vick's Vapo-Rub (figure 9.7). The second most common group of bottles and bottle glass fragments found ($n = 126$) included those used to hold pharmaceuticals, such as patent medicines. The majority of the bottle glass present was from jars and storage bottles, including canning jars to put up food, containers to store condiments, and milk bottles ($n = 219$). Census records indicated that Tubman almost always owned a milk cow, and as late as 1913, the year she died, she used the proceeds of donations to her to buy a cow for the Home.[61] The presence of milk bottles indicates that in addition to the milk produced on the farm, the Home purchased and its residents consumed milk from local dairies. At the time, a dairy was in operation across South Street. Other small finds include a toothbrush and a metal toothpaste tube, both of which attest to personal hygiene. Window glass ($n = 475$) made up 44 percent of the glass present, a number that is not surprising given the many windows shown in photographs of the building. Bottle glass ($n = 405$) and glassware ($n = 133$) were also common, and items associated with lights and lighting were present ($n = 14$).

Consistent with other places on the Tubman properties and with Tubman's and the AME Zion Church's views on temperance, there was a paucity of bottles reflecting alcohol consumption from deposits dating to the Tubman era.[62] The virtual absence of beer and wine bottles and of liquor bottles confirms the specific historical context of this site and its association with individuals who were supporters of the temperance movement. Other sites from this period, even during Prohibition, generally are loaded with an abundance of beer and alcohol-related vessels (Orser 1988).

Most of the ceramics present were recovered from a refuse deposit located to the east of the structure ($n = 227$). The majority were tableware fragments, including from plates and bowls. The next most common form was from storage vessels, consistent with the property's combined farm and group-home functions. Numerous tea and coffee service items were found. Most prominently, these items included fragments of cups and saucers from a "Lace' pattern of teal-blue transfer-printed wares made by L. (Lazorus) Straus and Sons, a significant group of wares that I have already discussed in terms of complex gender roles expressed at the site (figure 2.1). Matching pieces from this set were also found at Tubman's residence, specifically in trash deposits in the basement of the structure defined as Locus 4 (a wood-frame structure near South Street that burned) as well as along the road leading to John Brown Hall (Locus 5) and in the woods adjacent to the brick kiln (Locus 6). Only

61. Thomas Osborne to Emily Howland, Feb. 19, 1913, Osborne Family Papers.

62. Any bottles of types used for alcohol that we found were almost always found on the surface of the site and probably reflect consumption of alcohol by those who made use of the site after it was formally abandoned. We found ten beer bottle fragments and one wine bottle fragment. The wine bottle fragment clearly dates to the period following the demolition of the structure and has a foil seal.

small quantities of service platters were present, which was rather surprising given that each meal would have involved the many residents of the Home. We recovered evidence of one chamber pot and one bedpan from deposits in the surrounding yard of the hall.

Nine white-clay tobacco pipe fragments were found at John Brown Hall, the majority of them just outside the southeast door at the structure. One had a gray-bodied bowl with a red-glaze ribbed design; another was a white pipe stem etched with the name of its maker, "Peter Dorni."[63] It is possible that these pipes correlate with the use of the house as a brickmakers' dormitory that preceded its use as a dormitory for the Home. However, this type of pipe continued to be in use into the late nineteenth century and may have been favored by the elderly residents of the Home. The relative scarcity of tobacco pipes and other tobacco-related paraphernalia at the John Brown Hall site no doubt relates to its turn-of-the-twentieth-century context (Gordon DeAngelo, personal communication to the author, Apr. 15, 2000; Walker 1970, 19).

The buttons we found (n = 41) included almost equal numbers of shell (n = 12) and porcelain (n = 11) buttons, along with some metal buttons. The majority of the buttons were found at the south doorway. The variety of button types suggest a range of clothing styles. Other items associated with clothing include several garter clips probably used by the women of the home to hold up hose or stockings (figure 9.8A). Other clothing fasteners included a cuff link with an inlayed shell front (figure 9.8B). The site yielded a number of hook-and-eye fasteners and safety pins as well as two buckles, all of which would have been useful in maintaining the appearance of one's clothing and should be considered the personal effects of those who resided at the property.

As at other ruins on the property, toy parts were found at John Brown Hall, including eight porcelain-doll fragments and most of a porcelain dog (figure 9.9).[64] The dog may have been part of a craft industry in which details on undecorated porcelain items were painted with gold paint and then heated. Several bottles of gold paint used in this type of craft production were found at Tubman's house and barn (Locus 1) and at the wood-frame house (Locus 2).

63. The marking "Peter Dorni" found on the decorated pipe stem refers to a popular brand of pipe produced everywhere in the United States as well as Europe. The date range of the Dorni pipes has been listed as between 1850 and 1880 (Brewer 1989, 158; Gordon DeAngelo, personal communication to the author, Apr. 15, 2000), The ribbed pipe is similar to the Point Pleasant reed-stem varieties by James Murphy dating to between 1894 and 1891 (Murphy 1976, 12).

64. See the discussion of gold painting of porcelain as a craft industry in chapter 10.

Other toys at John Brown Hall include parts of a lightweight baby carriage that was probably used to hold dolls. These items may have been used by visitors to the site, including youthful relatives of the residents or children of the home's administrators. Although the designated intent of the Home was to provide for the aged, visitors were not restricted by age. It is also possible that these items represent the personal keepsakes of elderly residents.

Coins present include a well-worn 1858 flying eagle cent and a 1916-S Lincoln cent in excellent condition. The coins were found in the area of the porch and steps at the hall's front entrance (north side of the building). The presence of coins in doorway areas is common as people reached into their pockets to find keys or clear their hands of change while entering or leaving the building. The dates of the coins are consistent with the historical information on the site. The well-worn 1858 coin could have been lost any time during the use of the building, and the 1916-S attests to the coin's continued use in the late 1910s and early 1920s, when John Brown Hall was rented to an elderly couple.

Personal items include a pressed penny token, probably made at a local carnival, with the names "Wayne" and "Auburn" pressed within the form of an eagle (figure 9.8C). Personal jewelry includes a gold-plated ring with five empty settings (figure 9.8D) and an earring clasp. An ornamental five-by-seven-inch gold-plated, cast-iron picture frame (figure 9.10) probably once contained someone's photograph and was either held in place by brass screws or displayed on a bedroom dresser.

Evidence of literacy includes the presence of two pencil erasers, one with part of a pencil lead still attached. Some of the people associated with the Home and its management were literate. Also, even though Tubman was not literate in the formal sense of being able to write, this would not have preempted her from making use of writing implements like those found at the site.

9.1. "Votes for Women" postcard and note, Anne F. Miller to Harriet Tubman, July 1, 1911. Images courtesy of Harriet Tubman Home, Inc., Auburn, NY.

9.2. Norris family photograph from the 1940s showing children ice skating in the yard behind what was formerly Harriet Tubman's barn. This is the only known image of the south side of John Brown Hall. Photograph courtesy of Harriet Tubman Home, Inc., and Special Collections Research Center, Syracuse Univ., Syracuse, NY.

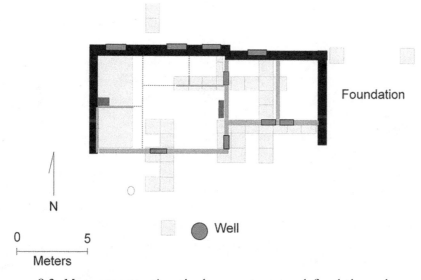

9.3. Map reconstructing the basement rooms defined through excavations at John Brown Hall. Map by D. Armstrong.

John Brown Hall, Harriet Tubman Home

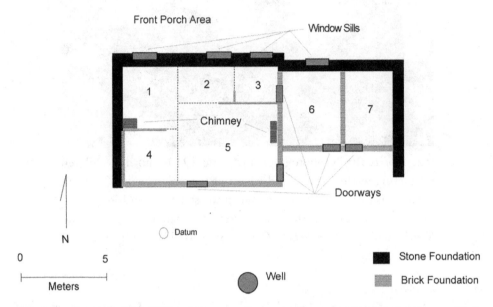

9.4. Map showing the location of excavation units in and around John Brown Hall. Map by D. Armstrong.

9.5. Excavation in the basement of John Brown Hall showing cement floor, interior brick wall, interior doorway, and plaster on exterior wall. Photograph by D. Armstrong.

9.6. Brick-wall fall from the south side of John Brown Hall; the bricks were pushed over from the north side and remained articulated, covering the ground surface in the 1940s. Photograph by D. Armstrong.

9.7. Whitall Tatum patent-medicine bottle (*left*) and Vick's Vapo-
Rub bottle (*right*) excavated at John Brown Hall. Photograph by
D. Armstrong.

9.8. (A) Garter, clothing fastener. (B) Cuff link with shell inlay and gold plating. (C) Flattened penny with "Wayne" and "Auburn" pressed on surface. (D) Gold-plated ring with five empty facets. Photograph by D. Armstrong.

9.9. Porcelain doll head (*left*) and dog with gold paint (*right*). Artifacts recovered from John Brown Hall. Photograph by D. Armstrong.

9.10. Gold-plated, cast-iron picture frame, John Brown Hall. Photograph by D. Armstrong.

10

Legacy House

The Wood-Frame House at the Harriet Tubman Home

In sunshine she was willow, and in storm she was oak. Through summer's heat, through autumn's blast, winter's frost and springtime's whistling rain, she was ever found at the post of duty. She gave the best of her life, the best she possessed, for the benefit of others. Hers was an inspiring service, with high and exalted ends. From the lowest plane of ignorance and superstition, she rose to a commanding altitude, to be admired by queens, to stand before kings and to be honored of mankind.

> —James Edward Mason, Secretary, Livingston College, Salisbury, NC, speaking of Harriet Tubman, *Auburn Advertiser-Journal*, Saturday, June 6, 1914

A Complex History: The Harriet Tubman Home Moves Forward in Tubman's Honor

Often referred to singularly as "the Harriet Tubman Home," the white wood-frame "Legacy House" (Locus 2) at the front of the twenty-five-acre property played a significant role for the Home when it was opened and an even more integral role after Tubman's death (figure 10.1). The history of this building is complex and varied. In the years following Harriet Tubman's acquisition of the second farm to facilitate her dream of a home for the aged, this house was rented out and served as a source of income in support of her effort.[1] It con-

---

1. Among the renters were the Sincerbeaux family, a white family whose head of household, like many other whites and Blacks in the neighborhood, worked for a time for the Osborne Manufacturing Company. The son went on to become a prominent local doctor whose patients included the elderly women of the Home for the Friendless on Grant Street in Auburn. For a short time between 1907 and 1908, the wood-frame house on South Street had been vacant, probably in anticipation of being refurbished to create an industrial school for girls. However, after the Home for the Aged was opened in John Brown Hall, plans for the school were dropped.

tinued to be rented after Tubman's transfer of the property to the AME Zion Church in 1903 and the opening of the Home in John Brown Hall in 1908. At that time, the plan was for this house to be the site of Tubman's industrial school for girls, but this school was never opened. From 1908 through the end of Tubman's life and for a short period afterward, the Home's dormitory was in John Brown Hall. Proceeds from the entire farm supported the Home. Funds were raised from crops grown in its fields, hogs were raised for both food and sale, and buildings were rented out.

By the year of Tubman's death, 1913, the wood-frame house was no longer rented, and fund-raising efforts were used to refurbish this house in early 1915. Later that year, the Home's dormitory was moved from John Brown Hall to this house. Refurbishing included painting the red house a lighter tan or brown color. Though smaller than John Brown Hall, the house had a wraparound porch where inmates could sit, and it was far more accessible to the elderly than John Brown Hall, which required climbing an exterior staircase to access the sleeping areas. From 1915 until the closing of the Home in the late 1920s, the wood-frame house served as the dormitory for Tubman's Home for the Aged (figure 1.12). Having swapped roles, this house was now the dormitory, and John Brown Hall was rented out to a family, with the rent used to support the Home.

Though this house was used as a dormitory for the Home only after Tubman's death, it came to be considered "the Home" due to its more recent use as the dormitory. Located at the front of the Tubman property, where activities were clearly visible from South Street, it was not only the place where the inmates lived through the late 1920s but also the place where fund-raising events, including picnics and ice cream socials, were organized by the women of the AME Zion Church.[2] Moreover, in time it became the solitary standing building that survived on the property owned by the church. Hence, it came to be remembered as "the Home."

By the early 1940s, both the wood-frame house (Locus 2) and John Brown Hall (Locus 3) were abandoned and in disrepair (figure 10.2). Even as the AME Zion Church sought funds to restore both buildings, the decline continued through the 1940s, and after a series of small fires John Brown Hall was ordered to be torn down by the City of Auburn. From that point forward, the wood-frame house became the focus of an effort to restore the

2. See additional detailed discussion of community outreach and gifting associated with the Harriet Tubman Home in chapters 9 and 12.

Home and Tubman's legacy, beginning with a successful fund-raising effort and a reconstruction of the house from the ground up in the late 1940s and early 1950s.[3] Hence, even though it was only one of several structures, including Tubman's personal residence and John Brown Hall, that had served as a living space and refuge for African Americans in need, for decades it was the symbolic and spiritual link between Tubman's dream and new generations of supporters—hence my reference to it as the "Legacy House."

The Home continued to pursue Tubman's mission after her death. Following the successful model of fund-raising used when Tubman had become ill in 1911, the trustees arranged for newspaper solicitations of support when she died. Newspapers were used to spread the word of the need of financial support to continue the work of her Home as a legacy to her life's work. One example of this is an announcement, "Funds Are Much Needed," in the *Auburn Citizen* on October 23, 1914.

> To Carry on the laudable Work of the Tubman Home. We now have six inmates whose ages range from 60 to 113 years. Life in the Home has passed in its usual even tenor, unmarked by any event of special Interest. The committee of management has exercised its usual vigilance and each month has been able to report satisfactory results. During the past year three of the inmates have been very sick. But thanks to Almighty God they have been spared to again mingle their voices with those of others at the home. One of our inmates has celebrated her 113th birthday which was made very pleasant for all through the kindness of Mr. William Freeman and wife who are members of the Board of Managers and to whom the managers feel very thankful.

3. In 1947, the Home Missionary Department granted Secretary Rev. Herbert Bell Shaw $2,500 for restoration of the Tubman Home, and $1,300 more were raised in a contest for social service led by Miss Lillian L. Browder (William Walls, note on the AME Zion Church sesquicentennial celebration, n.d. [c. 1951], Bishop William Walls Papers, AME Zion Church, Special Collections Research Center, Syracuse Univ., Syracuse, NY). The balance of $30,100, the cost of re-erecting and furnishing the Home, was raised by the conference under the leadership of Bishop Walls with the support of churches throughout AME Zion's several conferences (Walls, note on the AME Zion Church sesquicentennial celebration, n.d. [c. 1951]). Walls indicated that the house was finished in 1949 but awaited the action of the AME Zion Church General Conference for a plan to operate it. When Bishop Walls wrote this note, he was awaiting a final plan of action with the hope that they could expand use of the Home property for "an Annual meeting place for the Youth Conference and a Rest-in-Station for needy farm migrants." He felt that this would honor the practice begun by Harriet Tubman of making this property "an institution for the service of all people" (Walls, note on the AME Zion Church sesquicentennial celebration, n.d. [c. 1951]).

The holidays have been appropriately observed and have brought a ray of sunshine to the entire household. The craving for., religious services is a part of the life of these aged people, and whatever contributes to this is hailed with pleasure and thanks. We welcome at all times anyone who may assist in this particular way. We do not want to weary our friends with a repetition of our urgent needs. But in the face of the recognized financial stringency that has prevailed and is still prevailing and with the increased cost of living, we cannot but feel very deeply a degree of concern, lest our expenses in the future may continue to exceed our sources of income.

We are greatly in need of funds as our only source of income is from the board of these old ladies and the contributions of our friend with the aid of the AME Zion Church, Western New York Conference, which holds the property in trust.

The following amounts have been received and expended during the year, commencing July 7, 1913 and ending June 12, 1914:

Forward cash July 7.	$5.68
Received from Board of Inmates . . .	$93.56
Received from Board of Mrs. Dale, two week	$6.00
Received from rent of farm	$103.75
Received from rally held at Zion Church	$113.20
Received from friends and members of Board Donations	$66.90
Received from AME Zion church agent	$32.00
Received from sale of pigs	$9.00
Received from sale of calf	$12.00
Received from sale of apples	$9.00
Received from sale of milk	$7.30
Received from sale of badges	$7.10
Received from sale of ice cream and by donation	$21.58
Received by picnic held July 25, 1913	$32.06
Cash received	$1,174.43
Expenses	
For groceries	$211.22
For meat	$142.46
For matron	$154.75
For doctor and medicine	$16.95
For labor	$124.70
For house furnishing	$145.24

For phone and telegrams	$39.55
For coal and fuel	$31.00
For tablet for Aunt Harriet	$10.00
For fruit trees and shrubs	$10.00
For lumber	$6.00
For postage and stationary [*sic*]	$6.60
For taxes on one house	$1.85
For traveling expenses	$99.70
For miscellaneous	$127.94
Total expenses	$1,141.92
Cash Bal. on hand	$32.61

Mrs. H. T. Johnson, Corresponding Secretary.

This straightforward request for funds with its detailed accounting of expenses was no doubt designed to address concerns about how funds donated to the Home were being expended.[4]

Bolstered by a wave of donations and hoping to solicit greater support, the Home put forward a plan for remodeling and expanding the Home in April 1915. The Board of Lady Managers put out an appeal for support for repairs and remodeling of the buildings. The appeal provides detail on the Home during this era: at "present there are but five inmates at the Home, but the plans for enlargement of the place, if carried through, will make it possible to accommodate a far larger number of aged colored women" (*Auburn Citizen*, Apr. 17, 1915).[5]

The appeal indicates that the buildings at the Home needed paint. It also suggests moving several small structures adjacent to the main building. The idea was that one large building could be operated at less cost than

4. Such concerns had been explicitly stated in correspondence, such as the letter received by both Rev. Smith, chaplain of the Harriet Tubman Home, and Thomas Osborne from Franklin Sanborn in the weeks before Tubman's death (see chapter 9). See Franklin B. Sanborn, Concord, Massachusetts, to Rev. C. A. Smith, Chaplain of the Harriet Tubman Home, Auburn, New York, Feb. 3, 1913, Harriet Tubman Home Collection, Harriet Tubman Home, Inc., Auburn, NY; Franklin B. Sanborn, Concord, Massachusetts, to Honorable Thomas Osborne, Auburn, New York, Feb. 3, 1913, along with a copy of the letter Sanborn sent to Rev. C. A. Smith, Osborne Family Papers, Special Collections Research Center, Syracuse Univ., Syracuse, NY.

5. In 1915, Rev. E. U. A. Brooks was the superintendent in charge of the Home. Formerly in Auburn, Brooks was attached to a church in Saratoga in 1915.

several structures.[6] The wording of this appeal implies that the primary dormitory was in the process of being switched from John Brown Hall to the wood-frame house at the front of the property. It also notes that at present the wood-frame structure did not have a cellar and that the digging of a cellar would be provided for in the total projected cost of improvements, which was pegged at $1,200 more than the funds currently available.[7] As part of this effort, a shed kitchen was moved or constructed and attached to the building. It is possible that the tollhouse building was moved and positioned on the east side of the house from its former position on the west side of South Street. Archaeological evidence of this two-room wood-frame building was found during excavations after a garage built in the 1950s was removed.[8]

Mrs. Winifred Johnson, who had been in residence at the home since 1912, died in 1915. Her obituary reports her age at the time of death as 113. She was born into slavery in Winchester, Virginia, made her way to Elmira, New York, in 1863, and lived there for more than fifty years. She was "well acquainted with Harriet Tubman, being a firm friend of one who did so much to bring slaves to the north" (*Auburn Citizen*, Mar. 27, 1915).[9] On November 17, 1917, Elizabeth Shephard died at the Home. Her obituary indicates that she had been a resident at the home for nine years, and until her death she had been in good health. She was survived by her children

6. This same argument had been used earlier when the wood-frame structure was being targeted for use as the dormitory of an industrial school for girls.

7. Records related to the restoration of the white wood-frame house between 1949 and 1953 indicate that the cellar had not yet been dug and that it was finally dug along with the installation of a heating unit as part of that later reconstruction effort. The walls of the cellar are made of a variety of cement cinder block that was not yet available in 1915.

8. These excavations indicated that this was a wood-frame structure built on top of a foundation wall made of unmortared "waster" brick from local brickyards (see chapter 11). It is possible that these buildings were moved from other sites on the property or that what was once the tollhouse on the west side of South Street (about two hundred meters north of the Tubman properties) could have been moved to the house. The tollhouse was no longer in use and is frequently mentioned as a structure that could or should be moved next to the wood-frame house to increase the house's capacity.

9. Mrs. Johnson had no living relatives. She had come to know Rev. E. A. U. Brooks when he was a pastor in Elmira, and he arranged for her to come to live at the Harriet Tubman Home. Mrs. Johnson was taken to Elmira for burial. The *Poughkeepsie Daily Eagle* (Mar. 29, 1915) also reported on her death and indicated that "the officers of the Home believe the record of her longevity is accurate."

and was taken home for burial in Elmira (*Auburn Citizen*, Nov. 26 and 17, 1917).[10] Newspaper accounts and records in city directories provide otherwise difficult-to-reconstruct information on those who were cared for by the Home (appendix A). These records and obituaries indicate that several Home inmates had escaped slavery in the South and had made the journey north to freedom. Most had not lived in the Auburn area but rather were attracted there by Tubman's offer of help for those in need. Most, like these two from Elmira, were recommended to the Home by a network of AME Zion clergy from throughout the region.

Efforts to gain support for the Home took place on both local and national levels. In 1917, Rev. I. K. Fonvielle, pastor of the Auburn AME Zion Church, went to Chicago on behalf of the board of trustees. He attended an AME Zion convention, at which he urged improvements to the Home, including the installation of a plumbing system (*Auburn Citizen*, Aug. 9, 1917). Locally, on Thanksgiving Day in 1917, the children and teachers of the Genesee Street School contributed food to the Home for the holiday. The school provided the Home with "vegetables, canned goods, jellies, olives, and canned fruit. In addition, Rev. E. W. Clark's church [Thompson AME Zion Church] donated a bushel of potatoes and the Needlework Guild gave the women of the home three night dresses and sixteen pairs of stockings, and one pair of towels" (*Auburn Citizen*, Dec. 5, 1917). That December a call went out to the people of Auburn to support a "Real-Old Fashioned Yuletide Setting" for the holidays. This account describes an effort to provide a dinner of "chickens, roasts, fruit, candy, and delicacies" at the tables of local charities, including the Harriet Tubman Home, the Old Ladies Home, the Cayuga County Almshouse, and the prison (*Auburn Citizen*, Dec. 24, 1917).[11] The New York State Board of Charities also organized celebrations, including dinners and entertainment to mark the beginning of the New Year at the Harriet Tubman Home, the Home for the Friendless on Grant Avenue, the County Home, and Sunnycrest Sanitarium (*Auburn Citizen*, Jan. 2, 1918).[12]

October 1918 saw the accomplishment of the final payments on the Home's mortgage. This was announced along with a ceremony to burn the retired mortgage. Also on people's minds was the involvement of the United States in World War I. They gathered at the AME Zion Church, discussed

10. Newspaper accounts reporting the deaths of these elderly Black women provide otherwise difficult to reconstruct information on those who came to the Home for support.

11. The "Old Ladies Home" referred to was the Home for the Friendless in Auburn.

12. See discussion of the array of care facilities for the elderly in Auburn in chapter 8.

issues related to the war, and "honored negro soldiers in the war" (*Auburn Citizen*, Oct. 3, 1918).[13]

In 1923, the Home held a picnic to celebrate Labor Day. The event, defined as the annual picnic to benefit the Home, was organized by the Board of Lady Managers and included a luncheon, a dinner, a baseball game, running events, croquet, and quoits.[14] The main program began at 4:00 with a lecture by Rev. Bishop James E. Mason, financial secretary of Livingston College and chairman of the Tubman Home Board of Directors (*Auburn Citizen*, Aug. 29, 1923). Rev. E. U. A. Brooks was once again the pastor of the Auburn AME Zion Church and was the assistant superintendent of the Home, and Rev. C. S. Witted, DD, was the superintendent. A couple, Mr. and Mrs. George Johnson, served as matron and manager of the farm.

That same year, 1923, William Perry and his wife came to live in John Brown Hall. They rented the house rather than being formal inmates of the Home. Williams was a "colored veteran of the Civil War, who was born and reared in slavery" and emancipated during the war (*Auburn Citizen*, June 28, 1925). Williams and his wife paid the rent from his Civil War veteran's benefits. Over the next few years, William Perry became well known to the editors of the local press for his stories of escaping from slavery and coming aboard Commodore [Matthew] Perry's ship to serve as cook. Reporters recounted his stories, so we not only know who lived in the house but have some colorful details of his life. During his years in Auburn, "his eyesight [was] almost gone and his palsied legs and waning strength made travel uncertain and unsure"; however, each year he would make his way from the Tubman Home at the edge of the city and up the stairs of the newspaper building. Once a year the reporters and editors were sure "to hear the feeble tap of Perry's cane as he groped his way up the stairs for an annual visit to the newspapermen." He would tell the story of his escape and "would dwell on his war experiences and lament the neglect of the government in regards to his pension" (*Auburn Citizen*, June 28, 1925). On occasion Perry would overestimate his strength and not be able to return home, causing him to seek lodging at the city hall in order to recover enough strength to go home the following day. On June 28, 1925, William Perry passed away, and following services he was buried in Fort Hill Cemetery in Auburn with military honors (*Auburn Citizen*, June 28, 1925).

13. It is possible, given the number of deaths among the elderly at the Home in 1917, that this age group was hit by a first wave of the flu pandemic of 1918–19.

14. Quoits is a game that is like horseshoes. Round loops of rope called "quoits" are thrown a distance of eighteen feet in an effort to encircle a spike or stake and score points.

In contrast to William Perry, during the Home's later years there is more information about the end of the life of each of the inmates and renters than details about the lives they lived. On February 27, 1923, Jane Decker, a seventy-six-year-old resident of the Harriet Tubman Home, passed away. Her services were overseen by Rev. E. U. A. Brooks, who also accompanied her remains for burial in Binghamton, her former city of residence (*Auburn Citizen*, Feb. 28, 1923).

During the Christmas season in 1924, each of the city schools of Auburn selected a charity to which it would contribute and interact with as part of the school's Christmas celebration. The Parent–Teacher Association at the Seward School chose to support the Home. Its Christmas plans included sending "goodies" to the Home (*Auburn Citizen*, Dec. 18, 1924). During this period (1924–25), Mrs. Sarah Penn is listed as the matron of the Home (appendix D).[15]

In the late 1920s, with the Home in disuse, the Western New York Federation of Women's Clubs of New York State asked to take it over so that it could be used as a home for girls in memory of Harriet Tubman. By 1828, the last resident of the Home had passed on, and the Home was effectively closed. On July 16 the Home and the Empire State Federation of Colored Women's Clubs announced plans for the transfer of the property to the Women's Clubs.[16] The transfer was initially confirmed by the Bishop's Council in Hartford, Connecticut. Meanwhile, at its convention in Buffalo, the Women's Clubs voted to take over and finance the Tubman Home and operate it under their own auspices. This proclamation shows a continuity of objective concerning care for the elderly but also a new direction with respect to the school. Instead of rescuing girls from the "Jim Crow" South, it proposed providing training for "problem girls" (*Auburn Citizen*, July 16, 1928). One report projected that the Home would be open to up to "11 women and an equal number of girls and indicated that the funds had been raised through a subscription at the summer meeting of the federation" (*Poughkeepsie Daily Eagle*, July 26, 1929). Even though the project was apparently fully subscribed and funded by the Women's Clubs, the transfer of the property never took place. In fact, the Women's Clubs' plans were rejected by the AME Zion Church,

15. Sarah Penn is listed in the *Auburn City Directory* of 1924 and 1925 as living on Danforth Street (Cayuga County Historian's Office, Auburn, NY).

16. By the late 1920s, successful models of homes for African American girls and women were in operation, including the Phillis Wheatley Home for Girls on Rhodes Avenue in Chicago (Agbe-Davies 2011).

which wished to retain control of what had become an abandoned property. Interestingly, after being rebuffed, the Women's Clubs redirected their funds to the construction of a monument to Frederick Douglass in Rochester, New York. The Home would not reopen as a care facility for the elderly, nor was it ever opened as a school.

Closing and Rebirth

Reviewing the history of the Home, Bishop William Walls says few words about its closing other than that it was finally forced to shut down and that by 1944 "everything was in decay" and had been so in ever-increasing dimensions since the late 1920s (1974, 440, 444).[17] The *Auburn City Directory* for 1933 indicates the Home was vacant.[18] In October 1934, the buildings of the Home were still empty when the AME Zion Conference proposed to create a summer home dedicated to Black youths. However, no doubt the church was cash strapped in the depths of the Depression, so this plan went no further than discussion at the conference (*Auburn Citizen Advisor*, Oct. 12, 1934).[19] In 1939, at a time when the buildings on the property were in a state of severe neglect, another call was made to convert the property into a retreat for youth (*Auburn Evening Recorder*, Nov. 11, 1939). However, once again no action was taken.

In the meantime, the condition of both the wood-frame house and John Brown Hall continued to decline. Neither building was in condition to be rented out, and the site was left uninhabited. Because it was no longer used

17. In his discussion of the final period of the Home's operation and its closure, Walls appears to mistake the white wood-frame house at the front of the Harriet Tubman Home property for "her old residence" (1974, 444). One cannot be certain regarding the reasoning behind this statement because earlier in the text he describes how "for years Harriet had looked from the porch of her residence [the brick house on the farm in Fleming] over a 25 acre expanse of adjoining terrain, dreaming of what a fine community farm it would make" (441). This clearly shows that Walls knew that Tubman's residence was the brick house, not the white wood-frame house. It does appear as if Walls purposely shifts his interpretation of Tubman's "old residence" in redefining the importance of the wood-frame house that he had been involved in restoring.

18. *Auburn City Directory*, 1933, Cayuga County Historian's Office. The wood-frame house is listed as 1 Danforth Avenue. In 1933, a Mrs. Reginald Cadelia Carter is listed as in residence at 18½ Parker Street (the AME Zion Church parsonage).

19. In 1936, the *Auburn City Directory* (Cayuga County Historian's Office) lists George W. Robinson in association with the Harriet Tubman property, but there is no specific information regarding his role as either a superintendent or resident of the property.

to care for the elderly, little was recorded about John Brown Hall except for brief reports to the Western Conference of the AME Zion Church and a *Syracuse Post-Standard* newspaper article in early 1939 that both describes it and includes a photo of it as abandoned and in considerable disrepair:

> Scraggly shoots of grass have grown around it, roving bands of youths with a hidden pride of marksmanship have stoned the windows, and part of the porch railing has been ripped away. This describes the state of the modest home of the late Harriet Tubman, the famed heroine of the "underground railroad" of civil war days, which is situated in a field off South street road, almost on the border line of the city limits, for several years the house has been unused although it was the owner's last wish that it might become a haven for deserving old people of her race. It just stands in the field, weeds and tall grass almost hiding it from view from the road, not even a marker to denote its presence. Decaying rapidly, it will take but a few years before it will be a mere shamble. She will occupy a place in history long after her home has gone into a twisted heap of brick and rotted wood.[20]

John Brown Hall continued to be plagued by vandalism by "wood-burning filchers" and a succession of small fires, while the wood-frame building at the front of the property was gradually stripped of its porch and clapboard siding and interior so that one could see clear through the building (figure 10.2).[21]

The AME Zion Church tried to organize plans to reopen the Home as part of the church's sesquicentennial observations. This effort included a Miss AME Zion contest, which helped to raise $1,300 for the project, but the effort fell short of its goal, and the church became silent in relation to the property until 1942, when due to lack of use and in the absence of having filed necessary not-for profit tax papers the property was made subject to a tax auction.[22] The threat of losing this important property for unpaid taxes was

20. *Syracuse Post-Standard*, Mar. 16, 1939, Walls Papers.

21. Walls notes that Rev. E. U. A. Brooks reported that the impressive stone foundation of John Brown Hall had been vandalized and parts of it had been carted away (Walls, note on the AME Zion Church sesquicentennial celebration, n.d. [c. 1951]). The state of the wood-frame house was reported in a pamphlet titled *Harriet Tubman* written by Bishop W. Walls as part of fund-raising efforts to restore the building (Walls 1949, 15). Also, Mrs. Alice Norris described to me how during the Depression and war years her family would often strip wood from this building to heat their home during long cold winters (Alice Norris, personal communication to the author, May 25, 2002).

22. In 1942, Christopher McLeod is listed in association with the Harriet Tubman Home at 182 South Street, but no one was in residence on the property. In 1943, the *Auburn*

followed closely by the arrival on the scene of Bishop William Walls in 1944. Walls worked with the City of Auburn to negotiate a tax deal and to establish a new not-for-profit charter that protected the property from taxes and provided a governance structure that once again allowed for contributions toward a new effort to make the property viable. The plan was to restore both John Brown Hall and the white wood-frame house. The first effort, beginning in 1947, focused on John Brown Hall, but before sufficient funds could be raised, the building was damaged by a series of fires started by children playing in the vacant building.

There are accounts of other fires, too, including a brush fire and another fire in the hall, so the City of Auburn deemed the hall beyond restoration and a nuisance to the community and so slated it for demolition.[23] With the possibilities for restoration and reconstruction now limited to the white wood-frame house, all attention was focused on rebuilding this structure, which by this time was barely standing, having lost much of its porch as well as its siding. This also appears to have been when this building began to be billed as "*the* Harriet Tubman Home" rather than being referred to as only one of the buildings on the Home's property.

Bishop William Walls (1974) documented details related to the wood-frame house's reconstruction. He recorded the cost of constructed at $23,000, plus an additional $7,000 for equipment. Except for $2,500 from the Home Missions Department of the Church, Bishop Walls raised all funds. He points out that Mrs. Daisy Caldwell Tucker introduced a resolution at the 1948 AME Zion General Conference that the Home be deeded to the AME Zion Connection, but until 1952 expenses for the Home continued to be paid by the Second Episcopal District, which raised funds and began construction of the house. In 1953, the AME Zion Church held a celebration to mark the completion of the rebuilding of the wood-frame house, calling it "A Pilgrimage to the Harriet Tubman Home" (figure 10.3). Two years later more landscaping and a cinder block garage were added, and the Home commemorated

---

City Directory (Cayuga County Historian's Office) changed the address for the listing and referred to the property as "180–182 South Street." No one is listed as being in residence. In 1945, the *Auburn City Directory* once again lists Christopher McLeod in association with the Home property at 180–182 South Street, but the condition of the Home suggests that no one was in residence. In 1946, the directory defines the property as the "Harriet Tubman Home, 180–182 South Street," and indicates that the property was vacant.

23. Even though John Brown Hall was demolished by the City of Auburn, it was actually located just south of the city line in the Town of Fleming.

the project in the Third Annual Pilgrimage to the Harriet Tubman Home (figure 10.4).[24]

Still in plain view but largely overlooked during this period because ownership was out of the control of either the AME Zion Church or family members, Harriet Tubman's own brick residence, barn, and associated farm continued to be owned by the Norris family. Meanwhile, the location of the ruins of John Brown Hall, the building that had been so important to the opening of the Home and Tubman's last place of residence when she was taken in and cared for from 1911 until her death in 1913, was gradually fading from memory as supporters and visitors began to interpret the restored white-frame structure as the Home. In subsequent decades, this house would often be misidentified as both Harriet Tubman's house and the Home for the Aged.

During this time, Rev. James C. Brown was the presiding elder who oversaw the reconstruction, but after its completion Rev. Arthur E. May was appointed presiding elder of the Rochester-Syracuse-Buffalo District of the AME Zion Church and superintendent of the Home. At the completion of the reconstruction, the building was rededicated as a legacy and "national shrine" to Harriet Tubman and was enrolled on the National Register of Historic Places. Bishop Walls recalls that the house was made livable and that a new concrete-block garage and driveway were added in 1953–54 (1974, 444). Rev. May and his wife, Margaret, "gave full measure of devotion in supervising the property for twelve years" and lived in the Home until Margaret died in 1964 (Walls 1974, 444). Rev. Samuel L. Brown was appointed presiding elder and supervisor of the Home from 1965 until 1972, at which point Rev. Guthrie Carter was appointed superintendent, and Bishop H. B. Shaw, DD, became the chairman of the Harriet Tubman Foundation Board (Walls 1974, 444).[25]

The property had been operated from AME Zion Connection funds since 1952, and money continued to be saved for an envisioned new "Old People's Home."[26] Bishop Walls arranged for the accumulated saved total of $107,000 to be made available for new projects on the site. The result was the construction

24. *Third Annual Harriet Tubman Home Pilgrimage*, pamphlet, Oct. 14, 1955, Stewart Family Collection, papers collected by Judith Bryant, Auburn, NY.
25. Rev. Guthrie Carter was the second of three AME Zion ministers named Carter who have served the Home. Rev. George C. Carter was a longtime superintendent of the Home in the era of its founding and operation, and Rev. Paul Carter and his wife, Christine, have been the managers of the property from the early 1990s to the present.
26. During this period, the Home fell under the jurisdiction of the First Episcopal District of the AME Zion Church (Walls 1974, 444).

of two buildings, an administrative center (which has also served to house the library and for a time a small museum) and a multipurpose community building that over the years has housed social functions, dinners, and pilgrimages. Although plans move forward for a new interpretive center for Harriet Tubman National Historical Park, this multipurpose building continues to serve as a small museum and is the starting point of interpretive tours of the property.

Archaeological Study of the Wood-Frame "Legacy" House

In our initial survey of the property, the wood-frame structure was defined as Locus 2. We plotted the location of the existing building and conducted walking surveys of the yard from the driveway into the property and then into the woods on the north side of the property. We also examined early photographs and records related to the rebuilding of the structure between 1949 and 1952 as well as more recent photographs of it. Prior to a fundraising effort in 1914 and early 1915, this house had been painted red; when it was refurbished as the dormitory for the Home, it was painted a light tan or brown, with a darker trim (figure 1.12). However, when the house was reconstructed, it was painted white. Restoration of the house was completed in 1953 (figure 10.3). To facilitate modern use of the house, a double garage was constructed out of cinder block and placed on the east side of the house in 1955, after the house was reconstructed (figure 10.4). Photographs indicate that during the period of its use as the dormitory for the Home from 1915 to 1928, the wood-frame house had been flanked on its east side by a low, one-story building and shed (figure 1.12).

This house had been rented out until about the time of Tubman's death in 1913. However, from 1903 until 1908 the house was discussed as the location of a planned industrial school for girls. These plans often made mention of the fact that the building had no basement and was too small for its intended purpose, so it was suggested that either the tollhouse be moved from across the street and attached to the building or other small buildings from elsewhere on the farm be moved. When plans were made to remove the "noncontributing" 1950s-era cinder block garage, we turned our attention to the wood-frame house and its yard.

Our initial archaeological efforts focused on John Brown Hall, Tubman's farm, and a brick kiln site, but in 2009 and 2010 we turned our attention to the wood-frame house and began a series of archaeological tests. As part of the effort to remove non-Tubman-era structures from the site, the cinder block garage that had been added to the house in 1955 was removed, and we monitored this project. Based on photographs from the 1910s through the 1930s, I knew that a Tubman-era structure had abutted the house in the area where the cinder block garage was later built. This building was no longer standing by the 1940s and thus had not been part of the rebuilding plan in 1949. Working with the demolition team, I directed the backhoe operator to simply pull up the cement foundation rather than dig it out, thus preserving any underlying cultural deposits. Given the era in which the garage was built, I had expected a gravel base and at least twelve centimeters of cement. However, as the operator started pulling up the cement, we found that it was only two to five centimeters in thickness and that it was built on a soil substrate rather than on gravel. Significant credit must be given to the care taken by the demolition team as they peeled the 1950s-era cement flooring away with no damage to underlying features. Once it was removed, we used shovels to skim the debris off the surface and began to encounter rows of brick indicative of an earlier brick foundation.

Over the next two years, we conducted excavations at the site that exposed the entire foundation and identified a two-room structure that had probably served as a kitchen for the house and dormitory (figures 10.5–10.6). Excavation of the foundation demonstrated that this structure was tied directly into the foundation of the house at two points and had a doorway into the house. The foundation brick outlined a two-room structure. The bricks used to construct this foundation were unusual in that all were irregularly shaped waster brick made at a local South Street brickyard, and no mortar was used between the brick (figure 10.5). Hence, the foundation was rather loosely constructed, two bricks wide and up to four courses deep, and the top level of brick was offset to support a wooden sill and floorboards. The waster bricks had been misfired in the shape of irregular loaves rather than square-sided brick. Neutron Activation Analysis of brick samples from the foundation indicate a chemical composition that matches closely with samples from the brick kiln on the property (Locus 6), from Tubman's brick house (Locus 1), and from the Ross-Sullivan brickyard two hundred meters south of the Tubman property. It is likely that the misshapen bricks used to construct this foundation were available at little or no cost from the local South Street brickyards (A. Armstrong 2011; A. Armstrong and D. Armstrong 2012).

Large fieldstones were used at key points to augment the foundation. These large stones were present at the junction between the frame house and the abutting foundation, at the junction of the two rooms, and at the northeast corner of the building. It is probable that these stones helped to support the building that was set atop the loose courses of bricks that made up the rest of the foundation. It is unlikely that this type of foundation could have supported a heavy structure, but the neat lines of brick suggest that it served its purpose during the life of the building (circa 1915–30).

We continued excavation to the east of this brick foundation and recovered evidence of burned wood that we initially thought might have been an additional woodshed without a foundation. However, in consideration of the fact that this feature included an abundance of burned wood, including flooring, clapboard, roofing materials, and nails, we concluded that it was a result of the burning of the small one-story structure that had sat atop the adjacent foundation. It is probable that this structure was pulled away from the house and then burned in such a way as to protect the old dormitory building. It is also possible that the kitchen caught fire, perhaps in an accident related to a heater, stove, or even a canning stove, one of which is visible at the southeast corner of the structure in one of the photographs of the building, and that the one-story structure was pulled away from the rest of the house in order to preserve it. Either way, the kitchen area was removed and purposely burned, and so the older farmhouse/dormitory was retained without damage from fire.[27]

As excavation of the ruins of the kitchen area were completed, we began a series of shovel tests and excavations of the yard behind the house. Our objective was to try to identify the location of structures and activity areas in the yard. Unfortunately, when the house was reconstructed, the backyard was dug up, and a grid pattern of septic lines was dug across the yard, which destroyed the stratigraphic contexts of virtually everything located immediately north of the house. Hence, we did not find evidence of any fencing, even though a fence is present in one of the photographs. However, some well-preserved contexts were defined for the area north of the foundation ruins and along lines of shovel tests to the west and north of the house and near the edge of the woods. Testing north of the northwest corner of the house identified some stones and brick that probably supported a small shed. Testing within this feature did not recover any evidence of a privy. We did not carry out deep testing of the areas where artifacts were recovered about thirty meters north of the house (at the edge of the woods). It is possible there was a privy in this area.

---

27. There are no accounts of fires at this house during this period, so I think it is more likely that the kitchen building was pulled away from the house and burned in place just east of where it had stood on top of the loose brick foundation.

With respect to the wood-frame house, the early 1950s-era reconstruction was a near total rebuilding of the house. This project included the construction of a basement, a project that had been in the proposed list of improvements in 1915 but was not done at that time. Hence, the foundation of the wood-frame house is a 1950s-era cinder block construction, and most of the detailed treatments in the house reflect materials available for construction at that time. Fortunately, however, the construction of the garage did not involve digging out the foundation of the two-room structure attached to the house during the period in which the house served as the dormitory for the Home from the mid-1910s to the late 1920s.

Artifacts from the Kitchen and Yard

The materials present in the ruins of the two-room structure suggest its use as a kitchen and storage room and perhaps as lodging for a cook. They consist of a range of domestic wares dating to the first three decades of the twentieth century. Even though this was a twentieth-century house, the kitchen area apparently did not have electricity. Several metal fragments from at least two oil lamps and several glass lampshades indicate that they were the primary means of lighting (figure 10.7).

Ceramics found consist primarily of plain, undecorated ironstone wares, some with decaled and transfer-printed decorative patterns. In terms of cost, nearly all represent relatively inexpensive table and service wares. We also found some brown and gray stoneware storage crocks. There were no distinguishable sets of tableware dishes present at several of the other loci. Most of the ceramics date to the early twentieth century. We pieced together the ceramic sherds to reconstruct a bone-china plate with overglaze, gilded with a scene of a girl cutting a piece of pie for a boy and lettering saying, "For a Good Girl" (figure 10.8). The plate dates to the early twentieth century.

One of the interesting sets of artifacts recovered from this site was a gold-painted porcelain dog and a bottle of gold paint (figures 10.9). The two items reflect a popular cottage industry revolving around the painting of porcelain that dates from the late nineteenth century through the 1920s. People would buy plain porcelain figures and plates and apply gold paint to decorate them. The gold paint was a deep red when applied to the pottery. This overglaze paint was then heated in an oven at a far lower temperature than required to fire the porcelain, and it would turn gold from the residual gold suspended in it. The finished products were resold for a profit. Two other bottles of gold paint were found on the Tubman properties, one in the midden near the porch at Harriet Tubman's house (Locus 1) and one in deposits under the barn on her farm.[28]

Glass artifacts from the kitchen area included fragments from many canning jars. This type of food-storage device is expected given the presence of a canning stove at the side of the house by the kitchen. Carrying on a practice that Tubman established when she acquired her initial farm in 1859, the Home continued to have a vegetable garden and produced many of the fresh foods eaten at the Home. It also had fruit trees and certainly used the canning stove to preserve the produce of the farm to assist the residents through the long months of winter and early spring. Moreover, numerous newspaper accounts describe the continual gifting of foods, including canned goods, to the Home. This practice was particularly popular during the period from Thanksgiving through Christmas, and at times large groups, such as the families of the Seward School in Auburn, would work collectively to collect fresh and canned goods for the elderly at the Home. The variety in the types of canning jars present at this site as well as at John Brown Hall (Locus 3) and Harriet Tubman's house (Locus 1) indicate that this gift giving was a long-term practice that added significantly to the inmates' diet at the Home.

The abundance of tableware and glassware, including plates, storage vessels, and cooking utensils, as well as of personal items connected to clothing and craft production attest to the range of domestic uses associated with the artifacts from the ruins of this kitchen. The site yielded numerous porcelain, bone, and metal buttons for clothing. Two of these buttons are particularly interesting. The first is a metal button with a gold six-pointed star (figure 10.10A). This button was one of four buttons with six-pointed stars recovered from the site, but the only one with gold on it. The presence of star buttons to adorn clothing at two house sites at the Tubman Home projects symbolism that may have many meanings, but, given the context of this site and its occupants, the star probably correlates at least in part to the North Star and its meaning as a symbol of freedom.

Another button is an ivory-colored bone button with a simple loop for fastening on the reverse and a triangle pattern on the front (figure 10.10B). Triangles are a basic design, and this button may simply reflect an idiosyncratic choice by one of the occupants of the household. However, in the context of a

---

28. Interestingly, this form of craft production has become popular again for both personal art and for resale, and supplies to assist the craft are sold at most hobby and yardage stores.

10.1. Legacy House (Locus 2), white wood-frame house during excavations in 2009 (after removal of mid-1950s-era garage). Photograph by D. Armstrong.

Home operated by the AME Zion Church, it could be tied to the church's use of the triangle as a primary symbol to indicate the Holy Trinity: Father, Son, and Holy Spirit. A range of possible meanings for artifacts like these are discussed more fully with respect to Tubman's spirituality in chapter 12.[29] Finally, a glass stopper from a perfume bottle (figure 10.11) allows us to reflect not on the themes of age or deep spiritual meaning but on the softer side of a woman's choice of fragrance and reminds us to consider the array of scents, colors, and sounds that were an active part of the lives of those who occupied the site.

29. In chapter 12, I discuss the significance of another artifact found in the kitchen area, a Liberty Bell medallion produced for the centennial of the Declaration of Independence (figure 12.1).

10.2. Wood-frame house showing siding stripped away, late 1940s. Photograph courtesy of Harriet Tubman Home, Inc., Auburn, NY.

10.3. Legacy House restored, 1953, Harriet Tubman Home. Photograph courtesy of Harriet Tubman Home, Inc., Auburn, NY.

10.4. Legacy House restored after the addition of a cinder block garage at east side of house in 1955. Photograph courtesy of Harriet Tubman Home, Inc., Auburn, NY.

10.5. Excavated two-room kitchen shed structure at Legacy House (Locus 2). Its roof was probably pulled away from the house and burned in the yard on the east side of the structure (black ash visible at top of picture). Photograph by D. Armstrong.

10.6. Excavated two-room kitchen shed area at Legacy House (Locus 2). Photograph by D. Armstrong.

10.7. Lamp parts found on the east side of the white wood-frame house (Locus 2). Photograph by D. Armstrong.

10.8. "For a Good Girl" plate. Photograph by D. Armstrong.

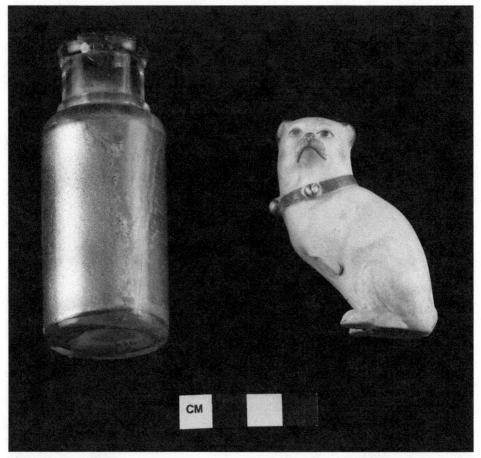

10.9. Bottle of gold paint and porcelain dog. Photograph by D. Armstrong.

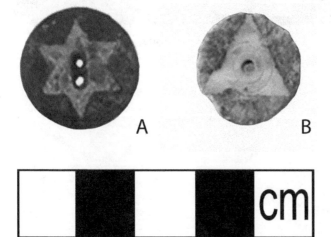

A   B

10.10. (A) Six-pointed star button made of brass with gold-plated star. (B) White metal button with a shell inlay triangle. Photograph by D. Armstrong.

10.11. Glass perfume stopper. Photograph by D. Armstrong.

11

A Brick Kiln and Brick Production
in the Auburn Community

Of all the whole creation in the East or in the West,
The glorious Yankee nation is the greatest and the best,
Come along! Come along! Don't be alarmed,
Uncle Sam is rich enough to give you all a farm.
            —verse of a song sung by Harriet Tubman
                to African American Union soldiers
                in South Carolina, in Sarah Bradford,
                Harriet: The Moses of Her People (1886)[1]

Brickmaking on the Property

The brick kiln (Locus 6) found on the twenty-five-acre Home property is an important element of the site that would not be known without archaeological investigation. This part of the site represents a very different set of archaeological contexts from the personal residence and Home-based domestic contexts associated with Tubman's farmhouse and the dormitories at John Brown Hall (Locus 3) and the wood-frame house (Locus 2). However, the study of the brick kiln and brickmaking at and near the site on South Street provides important linkages to the overall social context and articulation of the cultural landscape represented at the property.

As soon as we started doing background research for the study of John Brown Hall, we realized that brickmaking was an important part of the cultural landscape of the area in and around the Tubman properties. Maps of the area showed brickworks to the north and south of the property and

1. Colonel Montgomery encouraged Tubman to sing this song during her service to the Union army in South Carolina, as recorded in Bradford 1886, 53.

along the creek that crosscuts the Tubman properties on a meandering north–south line. We determined that John Brown Hall was initially constructed to serve as a dormitory for brick workers in the late 1850s or early 1860s, that brickmaking was taking place on the property, and that many of those who lived in Tubman's household, including her husband, Nelson Davis, were engaged in brickmaking in the South Street brickyards.

In surveying the property in 2002, we defined a distinct rectangular-shaped rise in the grass northwest of the museum building when we surveyed the field (Locus 6) (D. Armstrong 2003c). We felt that the distinctive rise was probably either the foundation of a barn, as one was shown to have been in the vicinity on a 1904 map of Auburn (figure 1.14), or a site associated with brickmaking. The possible association with brickmaking was reinforced by a pedestrian survey when we found large "borrow pits" where brickmakers had dug to extract clay to make bricks in the nineteenth century. These pits were found along the creek bank in the woods on the north side of the property, north of where the 1980s-era multipurpose and museum building is located. The importance of learning more about bricks and brickmaking in the area was made clear during our first week of excavations in the yard of Tubman's brick residence (Locus 1). We found evidence that the brick house on the property was built on the site after a house fire on February 10, 1880. In fact, there was an abundance of information pointing to the importance of bricks and brickmaking to Tubman and the local African American community that became more and more compelling when we considered similarities in the bricks in John Brown Hall, in Tubman's farmhouse, and even in many houses in Auburn. Moreover, at the time of the survey, this area (Locus 6) was being projected as the site of a proposed new structure (Beardsley Design Associates 2002). Thus, we needed to determine the nature of any cultural deposits or structures hidden in the ground in order to develop a plan for their protection or mitigation. For this reason, I took immediate action to contract for remote sensing to quickly test the area for unseen underground features and structures.

Remote Sensing and the Definition of a Brick Kiln Feature

As we initiated excavations outside Tubman's residence (Locus 1), we also brought in a team of remote-sensing experts with R. Christopher Goodwin & Associates to run magnetometer and resistivity surveys on two areas. One area included a target that traversed the open field on the north side of

Tubman's farmhouse and behind her barn.[2] For the second area, we focused on generating a subsurface profile to provide a basis to quickly evaluate the presence of possible features in what we would define as Locus 6 (R. Christopher Goodwin 2002). Surface-trend maps from magnetometer and resistivity surveys in the area of Locus 6 showed a very discrete anomaly centered in the area of a distinct mound in the grassy yard area to the northwest of the Home's 1980s-era building that houses a museum on the property. Based on the archaeological evidence, the area was immediately removed from consideration for use in site development and placed on a priority list for future subsurface archaeological explorations; however, it was not tested further until 2005 (A. Armstrong 2011; A. Armstrong and D. Armstrong 2012; D. Armstrong 2003c).

Excavation and Analysis of Brick Production
on the Tubman Property

In 2005, shovel test pits (STPs) were excavated at five-meter intervals throughout the area (figure 11.1). Guided by the data from remote sensing, the first STP was placed at the center of the hypothetical feature and came down directly on a brick feature. This test picked up the edge of the base of the bottom layer of bricks that had been fired in the kiln and ash marking the base of one of the fireboxes that had fired the brick. As we dug STPs, we quickly delineated the parameters of a brick kiln with several fireboxes. Within the area of the kiln itself, units were excavated to an average depth of twenty centimeters to expose the pattern of the underlying feature. Each row of brick in the base of the kiln was oriented on a north–south axis, with each row separated by three to five centimeters. In areas with a larger space between brick, evidence of wood ash was found. Beyond the area of the kiln, we found large quantities of both brick and coal but no associated features. These units were dug to an average depth of fifty centimeters, at which point we reached sterile soil but not clay. Probe coring was done at the case of each unit to extend the depth to nearly eighty centimeters. We found that clay began to appear at a depth of between seventy and eighty centimeters. The

---

2. This study area confirmed the location of a foundation in the field north of Tubman's house that we defined as Locus 4 as well as a probable density of iron objects in the field immediately behind her barn.

distribution of brick, coal, and charcoal showed a dense pattern of accumulation of broken brick along with wood ash. Many of the brick fragments were blackened and multicolored and had melted and twisted shapes (A. Armstrong and D. Armstrong 2012).

In 2006, the area of the brick kiln, defined by STPs, was excavated entirely to the level of the base of the brick kiln (figures 11.2–11.3). Even though the site was very close to the surface, a substantial portion of the base of this kiln had survived. The intact feature includes evidence of fireboxes (dark-ash and charcoal layers) bracketed by linear groupings of brick. Each row of brick has a space of three to five centimeters between it and the next row. Four rows of brick made up the wall bracketing the side of each firebox. Each firebox was forty to fifty centimeters wide. The surviving elements of the brick kiln suggest that there were originally two sets of fireboxes separated by a brick-paved area, but only the southern half of the kiln survived intact.

The kiln was created when stacks of dried brick were built up around a series of fireboxes, with the brick aligned to enclose the top of each box but with space for air to pass through. Once the kiln was constructed, fuel was placed in the base of each firebox, and the kiln was lit. The fires of the kiln cured and hardened the brick. After firing, the kiln was disassembled, and the bricks removed from it were sold. Bricks from this site are very similar to many incorporated into houses and industrial buildings in Auburn and surrounding communities and may have been used in the construction of Tubman's house (Locus 1) and the foundation to the kitchen attached to the wood-frame house (Locus 2). The site shows evidence of a single use and single firing of the kiln, with the bottom course of brick simply left in place after the firing. The specific location of this site is not reported in any accounts of the property; however, the general area is well documented for brick production and brick kilns (Anderson 1996a). The boundary of the kiln was defined through excavations to expose the pattern of brick and ash areas left in the base of the kiln's fireboxes and brick stacks, and it was confirmed by the extension of a grid of STPs well beyond the boundary of the kiln.

Given the importance of brickmaking to the site, we began to study the history of brickmaking in the region as well as the composition of the clays used. The clay found at the Tubman site derives from glacially ground shale bedrock and redeposition of alluvium in streambeds. This process produced excellent brickmaking clays in the Finger Lakes region of Central New York. The mining of clays was a seasonal task that revolved around the digging of clay in the fall and the flooding of clay pits in the spring (Anderson 1996a;

Dobson [1850] 1971, 2; Dobson and Tomlinson 1882; Storke 1879). This research helped to explain numerous features associated with procuring clay on the Tubman properties and on neighboring properties along the creek on the east side of South Street.

Karl Gurcke (1987) describes three basic types of molded-brick technology used in the brickyards of the United States: soft-mud brick (20–30 percent water), stiff-mud brick (12–15 percent water), and dry-pressed brick (up to 10 percent water). While earlier techniques for brick production involved pressing prepared clay into brick-shaped wooden molds, by the mid- to late nineteenth century mechanized brickmaking machines were in use. The bricks found at the Tubman Home site correspond with soft-mud and stiff-mud bricks, which were either formed in molds or pressed in machines. By at least the first decade of the twentieth century, a press mold was in use at the Saunders brickyard in the area (figure 11.4). Among the brick workers in figure 11.4 is Tubman's great-nephew Charles Edward Stewart.[3] The photograph shows that most of brick workers were African Americans and that whites and Blacks worked side by side. This photo also provides details on the industrial equipment in use to produce bricks as well as the type of pallets and specialized carts used at the South Street brickyards near the turn of the twentieth century.

At the Tubman property, the kiln type used is defined as a "scove" or "field kiln," made up of the green (unfired) bricks.[4] Following the North American tradition of brickmaking, I use the terms *clamp kiln, scove kiln,* and *field kiln* interchangeably in this discussion. The scove kiln is built of green bricks, fired, and then disassembled when the firing process is complete. Gurcke (1987) describes a typical field kiln made in sections of about thirty-five thousand bricks, stacked thirty-five to forty courses high. The kiln at the Tubman site is made up of a series of fireboxes bracketed by stacked brick, with the brick above the firebox gradually offset to the center and ultimately forming an arch that closes together at a height of just less than a meter from the surface. The course at the top of the arch is called the "tie course." Courses of brick are then added with either one-finger spacing or three-finger spacing, or two to three centimeters width, between bricks at the base of the stacks, as found at the Tubman site (A. Armstrong and D. Armstrong 2012).

3. Charles Edward Stewart was William Henry Stewart Jr.'s son and Judith Bryant's great-uncle (Judith Bryant, personal communication to the author, Aug. 19, 2017).

4. The terms *clamp* and *kiln* are generally used interchangeably in North America; however, in England a clamp is considered a specialized type of kiln.

Material Analysis of the Brick Kiln
at the Harriet Tubman Home

The brick kiln site yields information on both the details of brickmaking and activities associated with the practice. This was an industrial rather than a domestic site, and by far the most common artifacts were the bricks themselves and the fuel used to stoke the kiln. The bricks found at the Tubman home were 2-by-4-by-8 inches (or approximately 5-by-10-by-20 centimeters). The National Brickmakers Association adopted 2-by-4-by-8 inches in 1887, and the National Traders and Builder's Association adopted 2¼-by-4-by-8¼ in 1889 (Vogel 2009). The Tubman bricks are consistent with the standards of the National Brickmakers Association. However, as noted earlier, a significant number of the bricks present on the site are waster bricks of irregular, exploded shapes, like loaves of bread that have risen, rather than the standard flat-sided bricks.

In 1881–82, Tubman and her family rebuilt her house with bricks that appeared similar to those used in buildings that were known to have been made with brick from the South Street brickyard. Because of this, we wanted to determine if the bricks used in constructing this and other structures on the property were from the excavated brick clamp on the Tubman properties (Locus 6). To test this, Alan Armstrong carried out a study of brick from across the site and used Neutron Activation Analysis to test element composition. The samples were sent to the University of Missouri Research Reactor (MURR) Archaeometric Laboratory.[5]

We tested samples of brick from the kiln site (Locus 6) and from buildings on the two Tubman properties (including Tubman's brick residence, Locus 1; John Brown Hall, Locus 3; and the foundation of the shed next to the wood-frame Legacy House, Locus 2). Our sample also included samples of brick from the former "Ross-Sullivan" and later Saunders brickyard located on the property south of the Tubman properties. The Neutron Activation Analysis study found all the samples from the South Street brickyard district to contain similar element compositions. Thus, we were not able to tie specific kilns or batches of brick to specific buildings, but we could determine that all the brick used in construction at the site were from the local South Street brickyards.

5. This study was supported by National Science Foundation Grant no. 802757, and testing was conducted under the supervision of Dr. Michael Glascock at MURR. Details of findings and the related data are included in other reports, such as one produced by the MURR laboratory (A. Armstrong 2011; Salberg, Ferguson, and Glascock 2010).

The brick and clay samples were defined as part of a local "Auburn Compositional Group" made up of samples that show a strong compositional correlation. Samples clustered within the Auburn Compositional Group. The clay in these bricks may have come from any production source in the South Street area. This is consistent with a uniform deposit of glacial clays that included crushed silica from local shale bedrock.[6]

Only two "branded" bricks identifying the brick manufacturer were found on the Tubman properties. Both were from disturbed or post-1913 contexts at Tubman's residence (Locus 1). One, found near the surface under the north porch of Tubman's residence, was impressed with the name "ROSS," and the other, found in a disturbed area at the west end of the brick walkway leading form Tubman's house to South Street, had the initials "WW." Their composition fell well outside the pattern established for the Auburn Compositional Grouping (A. Armstrong 2011; Salberg, Ferguson, and Glascock 2010). It is possible that the ROSS brick was made in the Ross-Sullivan brickyard on South Street (south of the Tubman property) using a different clay recipe, hence the distinct difference in element composition for this brick.[7]

Social History of Brickmaking:
Brickmaking as Craft Production

The study reveals details of an almost forgotten industry that was important to the area in the late nineteenth and early twentieth centuries. Brickmaking was a source of employment for African Americans living in the Auburn area.

6. A sample included from an off-site location but deriving from a source on the Seneca River was also placed within the Auburn Compositional Group, suggesting a general homogeneity of clays within at least five kilometers of the site (A. Armstrong and D. Armstrong 2012).

7. The other clay-based objects analyzed using Neutron Activation Analysis were a group of clay marbles found on the surface of the walkway in front of Tubman's residence. These marbles showed variation in composition, but all fell well outside of the compositional grouping found for local South Street brick. The range in composition may be a result of an idiosyncratic collection of clay that was rolled into clay balls for marbles that did not have to conform with production standards necessary for uniformity in bricks used in construction. It is also possible that the clay marbles were acquired from outside the South Street area. They may have been marbles placed in soda bottles, which were broken off-site and the marbles found and brought home by children who played with them in Tubman's yard. A key problem with this idea is that examples of marbles in soda bottles indicate that they tended to be made of glass. Glass probably would have survived better under the pressurized and unstable environment of a soda bottle. It is felt that these clay marbles were made in a variety of places, whether used as stoppers in soda bottles or not. In any case, they were clearly used as toys by children.

The industry was important in providing materials used in the construction of houses, businesses, and roads. Although much smaller in scale than the brick-making industry along the Hudson River and in Buffalo, local and regional clays were of sufficient quality to facilitate the production of a wide array of products.

Not only was there a brick kiln on the site, but Harriet Tubman's house was made from brick produced by this or a neighboring kiln, and both the bricks and the house were made by African Americans, including family members and Black brickmakers The archaeological studies of the property produced an abundance of information on bricks as an important local indus-try that reflected a small craft-production scale. Significantly, although the archaeological record was clear, this local industry and its importance to the local community had been omitted in historical research or lost in the records. Finding the brick kiln site boosted our interest in learning about the broader role of brickmaking in the community. We found that this site was part of a small-scale, cottage brickmaking industry that produced common building brick for local houses, industries, and municipal buildings as well as agricul-tural tiles used to drain fields and expand productive agricultural acreage. In contrast to well-documented centers of brick production along the Hudson and in Buffalo (G. Hutton 2003; La Chiusa 2004, n.d.; Vogel 2009), the South Street brickyards were part of what was essentially a cottage industry involving no more than a few employees at seasonal brickworks and kiln sites. The large-scale brick industry on the Hudson grew dramatically at the end of the nineteenth century. The result of the dramatic shift to large-scale indus-trial production of extruded brick was the creation of cheap and uniformly sized brick at a price that simply could not be matched by the local brick industry (Crary 1971; G. Hutton 2003). By the end of the first decade of the twentieth century, this local industry ceased operations.[8]

The data suggest that the brick kiln (Locus 6) on the Home was con-structed and fired during John Farmer's ownership of the property, before Tubman bought it. However, we researched the use of brick on the property, the role of local brickmaking and of African Americans in local brickmaking became apparent. Local brick was used in the construction of Tubman's house

8. Alan Armstrong (2011) provides details of the broader role of brickmaking in New York State and the growth of large-scale brickmaking along the Hudson River Valley and near Buffalo, New York (see also A. Armstrong and D. Armstrong 2012; Gurcke 1987). He also reviews findings from a number of brick kiln sites excavated across the United States (A. Armstrong 2011; A. Armstrong and D. Armstrong 2012).

and in the foundation of the kitchen at the wood-frame house, and the industry created the structure that Tubman and the Home converted into a dormitory for inmates, John Brown Hall. Moreover, brickmaking provided an important source of employment and income for many within Tubman's household, including her husband, Nelson Davis, and her nephew William Stewart Jr.

Brickmaking was considered a minor industry and apparently did not merit the detailed descriptions one finds for larger industrial corporations that emerged in this area (Snow 1908; Storke 1879). The only records of brickmaking on South Street derive from maps, census data, advertising, and listings in the cities "Blue" books of business and businessmen.[9] African Americans living at or near Tubman's property make up the majority of laborers engaged in the South Street brickyards. The *Auburn City Directory* for 1868 lists several "colored" laborers employed in the brickmaking industry on South Street "near the Toll Gate": for example, Jacob Jasper (brickmaker, who resided for a time in Tubman's house and later owned property near Tubman), Frank Brown (brickmaker/laborer), Eli Rossum (brickmaker/laborer), Charles Harper (brickmaker), and William Copes (brickmaker).[10] All of them are described as boarders on South Street near the tollgate. In addition, Tubman's brother John Stewart is listed as living in the area and working as a teamster.[11] The *Auburn City Directory* for 1869 lists William Copes (colored, laborer) and John "Stuat" (Stewart) as working in the South Street brickyards and living on South Street.[12]

The earliest evidence of brickmaking in relation to Tubman's seven-acre farm is found in correspondence between Tubman supporter Martha Coffin Wright of Auburn and her daughter Ellen Wright Garrison of Boston.[13] The

---

9. The most complete record for brickmaking in Auburn relates to the competing Kelsey-Harvey brickyards located along the same creek but on the opposite, northwest, side of town on the city line (Anderson 1996a, 1996b, 1996c) or about five kilometers northwest of the South Street brickyard district.

10. *Auburn City Directory*, 1868, Cayuga County Historian's Office, Auburn, NY.

11. *Auburn City Directory*, 1868, Cayuga County Historian's Office.

12. *Auburn City Directory*, 1869, Cayuga County Historian's Office.

13. Martha Coffin Wright and her family were longtime supporters of Tubman. Wright's daughter Ellen married William Lloyd Garrison Jr., the son of the renowned abolitionist. Letters written by Wright show that she was keeping track of activities on the Tubman property (Livingston 2004). Wright as well as her sister, Lucretia Coffin Mott of Philadelphia, and Elizabeth Cady Stanton of Seneca Falls organized the first women's rights convention in Seneca Falls. Tubman stayed with the Garrisons and several other prominent Boston families during several visits to Boston before and after the beginning of the Civil War.

letter, written October 20, 1869, focuses on Tubman's financial condition, the use of a $50 gift to Tubman from a Mrs. Birney, and problems on Tubman's farm. Wright states that Tubman's "garden had failed, by the wet season and the masons turning water on it."[14] The clay pits used to make brick were dug in low-lying areas and were flooded with water; then clay was dug from these ponds to produce bricks. Apparently, in 1869 the flooding extended beyond the intended pits and inundated Tubman's fields. It is probable that the clay pits on the Tubman property were along the creek that meanders south to north across the property about 250 meters east of South Street. There may also have been additional pits at the back or east end of the property.[15]

Harriet Tubman's husband, Nelson Davis, was a brickmaker, as he listed in the New York State census of 1875.[16] These records do not specifically say that Davis was operating a brickyard, as they do for a series of white brickyard owners, but the fact that Davis was listed as a brickmaker suggests that he was recognized as more than just a laborer in the brickyards. This interpretation is supported by Harriet Tubman's testimony to Congress in 1894 as part of her claim for a widow's pension based on her marriage to Nelson Davis. In this affidavit, Tubman reported that Davis was a brickmaker.[17] Jean Humez indicates that Davis and Tubman "were carrying on the business together" and suggests that Harkless Bowley, a brickmaker and resident at Tubman's house, worked in Davis's brickyard (2003, 86). It is quite possible that clay was dug to make brick during the period Tubman owned the property and that she would have been compensated for this use of her property. The brickyard on the twenty-five-acre farm that became the Home dates to the period prior to Tubman's ownership, but brickmaking continued to be an economic activity at sites north and south of her properties on South Street until about the time of her death.

An advertisement for "Ross and Rice brick and tile manufacturer" in the *Auburn City Directory* for 1875–76 was typical of written descriptions of

14. Martha Coffin Wright to Ellen Wright Garrison, Oct. 20, 1869, Garrison Family Papers, Sophia Smith Collection, Smith College Library, Northampton, MA, at http://asteria.fivecolleges.edu/findaids/sophiasmith/mnsss175_bioghist.html, cited in Humez 2003, 309.

15. However, this area was disturbed when the entire width of the property was dug out to acquire soil to build up the grounds for the Seward School, located just north of the Tubman properties on Metcalf Street, when the school was constructed in the 1960s (A. Armstrong and D. Armstrong 2012).

16. New York State census, 1875, including an agricultural census, Auburn and Fleming, Cayuga County, NY, Cayuga County Records Office, Auburn, NY.

17. Harriet Tubman, affidavit testimony in pension claim, Nov. 10, 1894, State of New York, County of Cayuga, Cayuga County Records Office, cited in Humez 2003, 93, 404.

South Street brickyards. It provides a detailed list of brick types and prices per thousand for brick and tile made at the local brickworks, including two-inch flat brick for $10 per thousand.[18] By 1884, the brickyard had been sold to S. J. Saunders. An advertisement for Saunders brickyard in the *Auburn City Directory* for that year describes the types of brick being made in the area as "hard and light hard brick" and notes that a supply of these bricks is "constantly at hand" and that "all kinds and styles made to order" (figure 11.5).[19]

The Auburn population was 21,891 in 1880; 25,859 in 1890; 30,345 in 1900; and 34,668 in 1910 (Anderson 1996b). In this period, several industries were expanding in the area, including manufacturing plants that produced farm implements, rope, and shoes. Records of the Kelsey-Harvey brick company, located across town from the Tubman properties, show that 1,231,700 bricks were made and 1,225,750 were sold in 1893 (Anderson 1996b). The peak year for production was 1903, with 2 million bricks made and 1,872,180 sold (Anderson 1996b). A note in the Kelsey-Harvey corporate records shows that the Saunders brickyard on South Street produced more brick than the Harvey yard in 1899—hence, more than 2 million bricks (Anderson 1996b).

After 1900, South Street brickmaking appears to be limited to the properties south of Tubman's farms, with Nicholas Saunders operating the former Ross brickyard.[20] Robert Anderson (1996b) reports prices of between $5 and $6.50 per thousand bricks just after the turn of the twentieth century. This is about half the price per thousand advertised by the Ross brickyard twenty-five years earlier.[21] By 1910, the brickyards on South Street had closed, and the Kelsey-Harvey yard ceased full-scale operations in 1911. The brickmaking industry on South Street and in the broader Auburn area had succumbed to the combination of stagnation in the Auburn economy and competition from the rapidly expanding large-scale industrial mechanization of brickyards in the Hudson Valley and Buffalo, which intensified their scale of production by shifting to permanent "tunnel" kilns and mechanized movement of bricks within the site (G. Hutton 2003; see also US Army Corps of Engineers 2006 and Vogel 2009). The local Auburn industry simply could not compete with the larger businesses.

18. *Auburn City Directory*, 1875–76, Cayuga County Historian's Office.

19. *Auburn City Directory*, 1884, Cayuga County Historian's Office.

20. Map of Auburn, 1904, and map of Fleming, 1904, Cayuga County Historian's Office; *Auburn City Directory*, 1905, Cayuga County Historian's Office.

21. *Auburn City Directory*, 1875, Cayuga County Historian's Office.

In addition to the inability to compete in the industry, the decline of the Auburn brickyards can be tied to a decline in growth and building in the City of Auburn. After increasing by nearly 70 percent between 1880 and 1910, the net gain in population for Auburn was only two thousand (about 5 percent) for the next forty years. The demise of this industry ended a source of employment and income that had been open to African Americans, so they may have gone to other places where there was employment.

11.1. Brick kiln as seen at base of first shovel test at Locus 6. Photograph by D. Armstrong.

11.2. Brick kiln. Sets of rows of brick alternating with ash base of firing furnaces (Locus 6). Photograph by D. Armstrong.

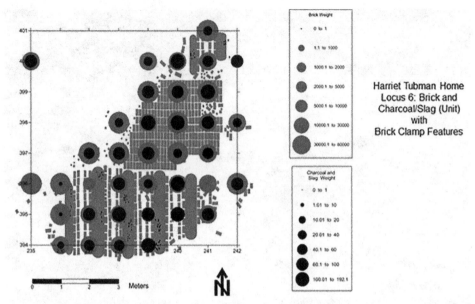

11.3. Map of brick kiln excavations showing layout of brick clamp walls and fire-boxes as well as the distribution of brick fragments, charcoal, and lag (Locus 6). Map from A. Armstrong 2011; A. Armstrong and D. Armstrong 2012.

11.4. Brickmakers and extruding machine, Saunders brickyard, South Street, Fleming, New York, approximately two hundred meters south of the Tubman properties, n.d. Charles Edward Stewart is on the far right of the middle row of brick workers. He was William Henry Stewart Jr.'s son and Judith Bryant's great-uncle (Judith Bryant, personal communication to the author, Aug. 19, 2017). Photograph courtesy of the Harriet Tubman Home, Inc., Auburn, NY.

S. J. SAUNDERS,

(Successor to Sylvester Ross,)

Brick Manufacturer.

☞ **Hard and Light Hard Brick constantly on hand. All Kinds and Styles made to order.**

South Street Brick Yards, South Street, near Toll Gate.

11.5. Advertisement for S. J. Saunders Brick Manufacturing, South Street, *Auburn City Directory*, 1884, Cayuga County Historian's Office, Auburn, NY.

PART FOUR

Integrating Tubman's Social Activism

The Past Inspires the Future

12

Keep on Going

Spirituality, Belief, Suffrage, and Fulfillment

Mine eyes have seen the glory of the coming of the Lord;
He is trampling out the vintage where the grapes of wrath are stored;
He hath loosed the fateful lightning of His terrible swift sword:
His truth is marching on
(Chorus)
Glory, glory, hallelujah!
Glory, glory, hallelujah!
Glory, glory, hallelujah!
His truth is marching on.

> —Julia W. Howe, "Battle Hymn of the
> Republic" (1861)[1]

The Battle for Freedom: Archaeology
of a Liberator and Liberty

In a real sense, the abolition movement was in a battle for freedom, and Harriet Tubman was a spearhead of the cause before and after formal emancipation was achieved. She stayed with Julia Howe and her husband, Dr. Samuel Gridley Howe, during her visits to Boston before and in the early years of the Civil War. Howe's "Battle Hymn of the Republic," written at the start of the war, captured the era's philosophical mood and spiritual sentiment

---

1. Julia W. Howe wrote the lyrics for "Battle Hymn of the Republic" in 1861, and the hymn was published in the *Atlantic Monthly* in February 1862. Howe was an active abolitionist who interacted with and supported Tubman during the latter's visits to Boston in the late 1850s and early 1860s. She was married to Dr. Samuel Gridley Howe, a wealthy backer of John Brown who supported and "conspired" with Brown leading up to the Harpers Ferry rebellion (Renehan 1997, 4). The words of "Battle Hymn of the Republic" were set to a slowed version of the then popular tune "John Brown's Body," which was being sung at a Union encampment that Howe was visiting.

for physical action to correct a wrong. At Auburn's centennial celebration of Abraham Lincoln's birth in 1909, nearly fifty years after the resolution of the slavery issue, Tubman was "greeted with enthusiasm as she came on stage decked from head to foot in miniature American flags and joined in the singing of 'The Battle Hymn of the Republic.'"[2] From her prominent position on the stage, Tubman was not shy in expressing her feelings and the spiritual bonds that linked her religious beliefs, those who had assisted the cause, and (what she saw as) the triumphant unity of her country. To Tubman, the words of the hymn retained their intense meaning nearly fifty years after the initial battle for freedom had been won. Though sometimes critiqued for its gender bias, the hymn retains its strength of message and its statement of convictions in relationship to human justice in today's world. Its metaphorical message was carried forward in *The Grapes of Wrath* (1939), John Steinbeck's literary (and later cinematic) exposé on the plight of the poor and homeless during the Depression of the 1930s (Steinbeck 1939). Moreover, it was used in the civil rights movement of the 1960s, most notably being incorporated into many speeches by the civil rights leader Martin Luther King Jr. It still resonates with meaning and has become an anthem sung at yearly pilgrimages to the Home.

In his speech at Canandaigua, New York (west of Auburn in Central New York), on August 3, 1857, Frederick Douglass captured the essence of the coming war and the ongoing battle for freedom in his assertion that "if there is no struggle, there is no progress" (Douglass 1857), and by the late 1850s the shift from philosophical and moral battle to physical battle was quickly approaching. Tubman, long a quiet mover of people to freedom, likewise became more visibly active within the abolitionist community, raising funds for the refugee community of St. Catharines, Ontario, and traveling to Boston to engage with the philosophical and financial leaders of the cause. In 1859, she acquired her house and farm on South Street from William and Frances Seward in an action that asserted her family's freedom within a setting of strong support and that suggests she was directly confronting the issue of living freely as an African American on American soil. At the same time, she was engaged in communications with more radical leaders, such as John Brown, who was already planning a campaign for liberation. Within months

2. The celebration was held in Osborne Hall and featured a speech in which General William H. Seward (son of Secretary William Seward) reminisced about Lincoln. The event was reported in a story on Tubman titled "To Harriet Tubman" in the *Auburn Citizen*, May 3, 1909. These details are provided to contextualize Tubman's intimate involvement with Howe, Brown, and the song that she sang with such emotion at the Lincoln celebration in 1909.

of Tubman shifting her home base to New York, John Brown and his follow-ers would initiate armed rebellion at the Harpers Ferry Armory in Virginia on October 16, 1859. Though Tubman did not participate at Harpers Ferry, Brown had turned to her for support and to assist in recruiting for his cam-paign. They met several times, and he referred to her as "General Tubman" (Sanborn 1863). She felt a spiritual bond with Brown and throughout her life was steadfast in her support for his actions and praised him as a martyr to the cause of freedom, a cause that for her had both civil and spiritual conno-tations. Throughout her life, Tubman would sing the "Battle Hymn of the Republic" with unbounded spiritual vehemence and forceful enthusiasm.

Tubman as Seer: Religion and Spirituality

Harriet Tubman was a person of strong personal beliefs, both inside and out-side of the formal confines of the church. During her life, she was associ-ated with several churches. In her work to establish her Home for the Aged, she was most closely associated with the Thompson AME Zion Church of Auburn and more generally with the whole of the AME Zion Church and its leadership. It is not known if Tubman had been formally baptized prior to 1897, but in March 1897 she declared her desire to be baptized by immersion at the Bethany Baptist Church in Syracuse during its Sunday evening service on March 28. In a public announcement of this event in the *Syracuse Daily Journal* on March 26, the story of her life, her contributions as a conductor and agent for the Underground Railroad, and her roles with the Union army was recounted along with fact that she was known as the "Moses of Her Peo-ple." This and other renewed tellings of her story show the strong influence of the second edition of Sarah Bradford's biography of Tubman (1886), which declared her to be a Black Moses.

Historical accounts are replete with stories of Harriet Tubman's seem-ingly supernatural ability to elude pursuers in her dangerous flights of con-veyance as part of the Underground Railroad. Her "seerlike" abilities were heralded by supporters and integrated into stories of her legendary deeds. She was known as a woman of strong beliefs who would talk directly to God. She used the verbal metaphor of verse and song to convey information to intended parties on her travels and to obscure the meaning of that infor-mation to those wishing her harm. In freedom, she continued to project strong beliefs and to trust in the goodwill of God in providing the means to achieve her mission to assist others. Having met Tubman before the Civil War, Franklin B. Sanborn wrote of the mystique of her success as a conductor and described how she always managed to elude her pursers when escorting people to freedom. He explained her remarkable ability as due to "her quick wit" and what she felt were "warnings from heaven." He asserted that "she is the most shrewd and practical person in the world, yet she is a firm believer in omens, dreams, and warnings" (Sanborn 1863; see also Sernett 2007, 134). During Sanborn's interviews with Tubman prior to his writing about her in 1863, she claimed that she had a vision of Brown before she met him: "She laid great stress on a dream which she had just before she met Captain Brown in Canada" (Sanborn 1863). Tubman described a reoccurring dream in which she thought she was

> "in a wilderness sort of place, all full of rocks and bushes," when she saw a serpent raise its head among the rocks, and as it did so, it became the head of an old man with a long white beard, gazing at her "wistful like, jes as ef he war gwine to speak to me," and then two other heads rose up beside him, younger than he,—and as she stood looking at them, and wondering what they could want with her, a crowd of men rushed in and struck down the younger heads, and then the head of the old man, still looking at her so "wistful." This dream she had again and again, and could not interpret it; but, when she met Captain Brown, shortly after, behold, he was the very same image of the head she had seen. But she could not make out what her dream signified. (Sanborn 1863; see also Bradford 1869, 82–83)

When Tubman met John Brown in St. Catharines, she immediately recognized him as the man in her dreams and felt that he was ordained to carry out his mission on behalf of freedom. Brown was unlike any white man she had met before, and their mutual admiration and respect both elevated Brown's stature among the fugitive community and likewise raised Tubman's own stature in white antislavery circles (Larson 2004, 158).

An account of Tubman's opening a home for the aged in her house in the *Syracuse Sunday Evening Herald* on April 17, 1896, included rich details about her spirituality, such as a series of dreams and visions she had experienced, some of them premonitions of floods in China and the fatal torrents that would sweep away Johnstown, Pennsylvania, on May 31, 1889. It also tells of the recurrent dream of the snakes and her connection of the snakes to John Brown and two of his sons. The author of the article notes the scant rewards that Tubman had received for her service, only an $8 a month widow's benefit and no pension, and projects Tubman's positive reception at the "great white gates": "A loving voice will say 'Friend come up higher.' And if then the happy, wondering Harriet should ask why such a welcome should await a poor, ignorant, black slave, she will doubtless hear the answer: 'Inasmuch as ye did it unto one of the least of these, my brethren, ye did it unto me.'"

In his biography of Tubman, Milton Sernett addresses the issue of the ways in which biographers have addressed her beliefs and spirituality. He presents the juxtaposition of how Sarah Bradford "dressed her subject in the garments of Christian righteousness" and the way in which modern biographers "present her in the role of a secular saint—a social activist who should inspire the present generation to seek the greater good" (2007, 308).

For Tubman, living in freedom with her family in Auburn, New York, was equivalent to finding the promised land (Larson 2004). She achieved this goal by following her beliefs and what she felt was God's guidance. The spiritual and transformative aspects of her deliverance from enslavement are easy to follow, even if they are wound up in the confusion expressed by chroniclers who were sympathetic to her actions but not fully cognizant of the context of her underlying beliefs. The spiritual basis of her life in Auburn and the new causes that she took up after the war were perhaps no less strong. It was easy for her to communicate the spiritual guidance in achieving and maintaining her goals of living freely and sharing her resources with her family and others. However, it was more difficult for the broader network of her supporters to understand the rationale behind her communal use of her property or her dream of opening a home for the aged and infirm (Bradford 1886, 7, 78–79).

Akinwumi Ogundiran and Paula Saunders argue that "ritual has been at the core of Black Atlantic studies" since the early twentieth century (2014b, 2–3).[3] W. E. B. Du Bois begins *The Souls of Black Folk* with a chapter titled "Of Our Spiritual Strivings," in which he describes how he and African Americans in general had been "shut out from their [white America] world" by a "vast veil," the existence of which, once realized, he had no desire to "tear down" or "creep through" ([1903] 1994, 2). He addresses the deep structures of belief, the constructions of separation expressed through the metaphor of a "veil," and the resulting dual roles that each African American lives as both an "American and a Negro." He explains that African Americans have "two souls, two thoughts, two unreconciled strivings; two warring ideals in one dark body, whose dogged strength alone keeps it from being torn asunder" (2).[4] In the broadest sense, spirituality and ritual are universal to human experience.

---

3. The phrase "Black Atlantic" derives from Robert Ferris Thompson's (1984) approach to studying people of African descent on both sides of the Atlantic.

4. Megan Springate (2014) discusses a similar framework of "double consciousness" for an African American archaeological household context in northern New Jersey.

Archaeologists have explored an array of sites where African Americans have lived and worked and have looked closely at ritual and religion associated with their African roots and their lived experiences in the Americas.[5] Along these lines, Ogundiran and Saunders explore the role of ritual as the "conceptual and empirical starting point for investigating ritual practice in the Africa world" and examine how "seemingly ordinary objects become ritualized, assume essence, and become coparticipants in the construction and transformation of reality" (2014b, 2–3). The approach focuses on ways in which ritual is used to create and negotiate "values, ideas, beliefs, spirituality, and socio-political/ideological interests" (3). As such, this approach challenges us to carefully consider alternative uses and meanings of the material world and to infuse a "level of ancestral awareness and spiritual practice" in our assessment of the spatial and material world that is being assessed (LaRoche 2014a, 314).

Those who wrote of Tubman during her lifetime pointed to her strong sense of spiritual motivation and guidance, but how might this sense be translated in our interpretation of the material record recovered from her house, farms, and Home for the Aged in Auburn and Fleming, New York? How might we better know her spiritual side? A simple answer is the mere fact of these sites' existence as a vindication of Tubman's beliefs and of those moved by her deeds. In a multitude of ways, the landscape and the material record recovered from these sites project aspects of her life and elements of her beliefs. Tubman and many in her household had beat the odds and survived the trek to freedom. In her many clandestine trips shepherding enslaved African Americans to freedom, Tubman relied on and gave credit to her spiritual intuition and help from others. In Auburn, the qualities expressed in her actions, character, and beliefs continued to cause others to see and support her vision. Her spiritual strengths served as a basis by which she acquired her initial farm and gained support for its maintenance even though she had no financial means. Moreover, her belief in the importance of the calling to create a Home for the Aged ultimately attracted the support that she needed to bridge the shortfall of resources and to ensure that the Home was finally opened. The fulfillment of this dream was made possible by the actions of the people of the AME Zion Church, who stepped forward, took over the property, organized fund-raising, and opened the Home. Hence, in no small way the sites represent an embodiment of Tubman's spiritual dream, a sacred

5. Among others, see Fennel 2007; Ferguson 1992; LaRoche 2014a; Leone and Fry 1999; Leone, Knauf, and Tang 2014; Ogundiran and Saunders 2014a.

ground. They defy the probability that a poor, uneducated, enslaved woman as well as her family, friends, and associates would find such a sanctuary for life lived freely on their own terms.

Franklin Sanborn wrote that Tubman believed that she had the "spiritual gift of protective foresight." She felt that she had inherited this spiritual gift from her father, who "could always predict the weather" and who "foretold the Mexican war" (Sanborn 1863; see also Bradford 1869, 80, and 1886, 115).[6] Given her incredible record in successfully conveying people to freedom, few doubted her spiritual beliefs, and it was common during this era for people to openly declare their spirituality. This was particularly the case in the "Burned-Over District" of Central New York (Sernett 2002 2007). Some suggest that her spiritual powers became more acute after she was hit on the head as a slave in 1848. When Sarah Bradford interviewed her for a biography that would eventually be published in 1869, Tubman told Bradford that she always knew when danger was near; "she does not know how, exactly, but 'pears like my heart go flutter, flutter'" (Bradford 1869, 79–80, and 1886, 115; see also Sernett 2007, 5). In freedom, she continued to trust in God's assistance.

Jean Humez asserts, however, that Tubman's view of her relationship to God was very different from how Bradford understood it. To Bradford, God was a remote but kind savior to the good and a stern judge of evildoers.[7] In contrast, Tubman's spiritualism projected a direct and unmitigated means to express her ideas, which Humez describes as "an informal, God-guided ministry, which had both activist and spiritual components" (1993, 162). Yet even with this gap in understanding, Bradford wrote of Tubman: "She seemed ever to feel the Divine Presence near, and she talked with God 'as a man talketh with his friend.' Hers was not the religion of a morning and evening prayer at stated times, but when she felt a need, she simply told God of it, and trusted Him to set the matter right" (1886, 23). Humez notes that neither Sanborn in 1863 nor Bradford in 1869 made any explicit reference to Tubman attending church. However, during her fifty years in Auburn, Tubman interacted with many church organizations. Her parents attended church each week, and she married Nelson Davis in the First Presbyterian Church in Auburn. Her husband, at least two of her brothers, and many relatives were members of the

6. My point in listing several sources is to illustrate how prominent a role her spirituality played in her perception of her powers and in how her actions were interpreted.

7. Bradford was a Presbyterian associated with the integrated First Presbyterian Church in Auburn. Her father was also the president of the Auburn Seminary, which later merged with the Union Theological Seminary in New York City.

Thompson AME Zion Church,[8] and she is reported to have been instrumental in the construction of that church. She worked in philanthropic activities such as clothing drives with the Methodist Episcopal Church in Auburn, and, as noted earlier, she was baptized at the Bethany Baptist Church in Syracuse. Moreover, she is documented to have enjoyed singing hymns of praise in numerous houses of worship. From the mid-1890s until the end of her life, she engaged with and came to rely on the AME Zion Church. However, even though she ultimately turned over responsibility for her dream for a home for the aged to the AME Zion Church in 1903, she was not a formal member of that church.[9]

Humez explains Tubman's spirituality in terms of a transformation story interwoven with her story of liberation. She points out how Bradford found it difficult to tell this story in acceptable Christian terms, tripping on issues such as Tubman's prayer for her master's death (1993, 174). Hence, we have a "partial, mediated, spiritual autobiography, whose meaning is contested by two women who, though politically allied and sharing a respect for spiritual item[,] [sic] have clearly different understandings of God and of the relationships of human and divine in history" (174). Tubman's is a "story of heroism and religiosity, but one that does not clearly separate the human and the divine, nor minimize the passions, actions, pleasures, and pains of the embodied women in order to create the spiritual heroine" (174).

Milton Sernett discusses how Tubman's life in Auburn projects her as a "homespun heroine" whose identity had taken on "remarkable seer-like powers" that had been "honed since her youthful years and used during her raids on a hostile South but now, as she grew older, folded into the notion of her as the model Christian—pious, saint-like, and self-sacrificing" (2007, 5). The archaeological record also offers specific examples of how the material realm of her lifeway or lifestyle manifested her spirituality and beliefs, from the communal way in which she shared her worldly goods to her adherence to a temperate lifestyle and to the abundant evidence of goodwill extended to her in the form of gifts of charity to her cause.

The material evidence of Harriet Tubman's belief system and spiritualism is everywhere in the landscape and history of the property. In fact, it is reflected in her very presence in New York and vested in the family with

8. Moreover, Tubman's husband, Nelson Davis, was a longtime member and officer of the local chapter of the Colored Masonic Society.

9. Harriet Tubman is not listed in any of several registries of membership of the Thompson AME Zion Church.

whom she lived in Auburn. We see it in the retention of the lands on which her Home for the Aged was located and the reacquisition of her farmsteads by the AME Zion Church and supporters of the Home. Her good deeds are commemorated on her tombstone at Fort Hill Cemetery in Auburn and on a bronze plaque displayed in her honor in a position of importance on the front wall of the Cayuga County Courthouse. Moreover, I experienced the by-product of those beliefs carried forward in my first encounter with Rev. Paul Carter on the Tubman property in 1994 and continually in the context and syntax of discussions regarding the importance of the sites' interpretation. In fact, I embed the evidence of her spiritualism in the titles of papers relating to the archaeology of the site, where I use such phrases as "Uncovering Inspiration" (D. Armstrong and Hill 2009) and "Excavating Inspiration" (D. Armstrong 2011). There can be no doubt about the strength of her beliefs as well as her facility to express those beliefs in action through her many trips to secure the freedom of others, her work as a nurse, the openness of her home to those in need, and her efforts to establish a home for aging African Americans on her property.

Artifacts as Reflections of Beliefs and Actions

Material remains may be interpreted in a variety of ways to illuminate issues related to agency, economy, social connections, ethnicity, gender, and age. Given Tubman's spirituality and the role of the AME Zion Church as owner and caretaker of the Tubman properties, in this project we sought to define ways in which the artifacts we found project symbolic reflections of beliefs and practices.[10] Studies by Mark Leone (2008) and others have shed light on African Americans' religious and spiritual practice. During excavation, we specifically selected areas in proximity to doorways, windows, corners, and staircases, but no specific areas were found to contain discrete, purposely placed, or hidden spiritual caches. Certainly, many objects reflect Tubman's spirituality, beliefs, goals, and actions, but these objects were dispersed everywhere within her household, at the Home for the Aged, across the landscape, and in her public interactions.[11]

10. This effort was spurred on by the work of Mark Leone (2008) in Tubman's home state of Maryland, which has identified a range of artifacts that are thought to reflect African American beliefs, rituals, and religious practice.

11. The materials selected and communally used by Tubman reflect her beliefs, ideals, and values—some of them directly but most of them indirectly and reflexively. Women's rights

Through archaeology, we found thousands of artifacts and personal items from the Tubman household. We even found caches of goods related to the clearing out of her house (Locus 1) after the fire of 1880, but we found nothing to suggest a set or subset of artifacts cached away as a shrine. This house site was inhabited by Tubman and dozens of other African Americans over a period of more than fifty years; they rebuilt the house after the fire and over time reshaped and reconfigured almost every space on the property. What shows up in the archaeological record reflects a combination of acting upon one's belief and caring for others, traits that best fit the individual who was the head of the household—Harriet Tubman. The absence of alcohol bottles (except those associated with medicinal use and some beer bottles in the builder's trench, probably left there by the men who rebuilt her house) reflects a combination of religious beliefs and women's rights advocacy. Abstinence is consistent with Tubman's overall belief system, including the doctrine of the AME Zion Church and temperance associated with the suffrage movement of the nineteenth and early twentieth centuries. Evidence of the communal nature of Tubman's spirituality was found materially in the array of canning jars recovered and in the historical accounts of foods, materials, and supplies donated to Tubman and her Home.

The 1852 Bank of Quebec penny found in deposits just outside her front door projects ties to Canada (figure 4.1). Was it lost between the cracks of the porches floorboards or purposely placed there? Probably the former, given its location under the porch. The combination of a set of teacups and matching saucers and a brass calling-card nameplate projects complex ritual-laden behaviors of social interaction among women (figures 2.1–2.3). The nameplate was used to send cards making and accepting invitations to social events. Pieces of the tea set were distributed across three structures and a total of five deposits on the property. The "Lace" pattern tea wares date to the era of the opening of John Brown Hall and probably represent a gift of a tea set of substantial size (figure 2.1).

Teas were social gatherings often organized around specific causes. We have records of a tea honoring Tubman at which a new edition of Bradford's biography of Tubman was sold in support of Tubman 1888 (*Auburn Bulletin*, Apr. 6, 1888), a tea in her house linked to the founding of her Home in 1896, and a tea held on New Year's Day 1903 at the home of Tubman's benefactor

---

are reflected by her ownership of property. Communality is reflected in her sharing of her house and her efforts to open a home for those in need.

Eliza Wright Osborne.[12] When Susan B. Anthony returned home from the tea in 1903, she commemorated the meeting with a note in her copy of Bradford's *Harriet Tubman, the Moses of Her People*.[13]

Four metal buttons depict six-pointed stars (figures 1.4 and 10.10A). The three found in the deposits at Tubman's residence are like buttons recovered from the W. E. B. Du Bois (Burghardt family) house site in Great Barrington, Massachusetts, projecting a possible AME Zion or at least an African American connection. A fourth six-pointed star with gold plating was recovered at the white wood-frame house on the twenty-five-acre property that was purchased for the Home for the Aged in 1896—the house that became the primary residence for the Home after Tubman's death in 1913. A wide range of associative meanings may be projected for the selection of these six-pointed star buttons, including a backdrop of possible African contexts. They were also a Judeo-Christian symbol and adopted by African American churches, including the AME Zion Church. More directly, the star was adopted as a symbol of freedom that had meaning to Tubman, her family, and associates, Black and white, in relation to following the North Star to freedom. This connection with the North Star does not negate other complex meanings and interpretations, but it is likely that in the context of the Tubman properties the selection of these particular buttons correlates with the quest for freedom.[14]

We see Tubman's spiritualism materially in the way she lived, in her sharing of her house, and in the opening the Home for those in need. It is expressed in an array of artifacts indicating a life lived on her terms following her ideals and in the faith she expressed in turning one of her farmsteads over to the AME Zion Church for use as the Home.[15] The designation of her farm, house, and Home as a National Historic Landmark in 1975 and a National

---

12. Whereas the teas organized within Tubman's home and reported in the press were organized without restrictions on gender because they were focused on gaining support for the Home, the teas within the affluent white community of women's rights activists included only women.

13. Susan B. Anthony's copy of the 1901 edition of Bradford's biography of Tubman was donated as part of the Susan B. Anthony Collection to the Library of Congress, Washington, DC, where it is housed in the Rare Book and Special Collections Division.

14. See chapter 13 for a description of new meaning applied to these buttons in relation to their inclusion in the artwork of the Harriet Tubman $20 bill.

15. Her spiritualism is also reflected in her community's response to her in the celebratory commemoration of her life and the outpouring of support to construct her tombstone at Fort Hill Cemetery in Auburn and in the bronze plaque that honors her on the front wall of the Cayuga County Courthouse.

Historical Park in 2017 identifies these properties as protected, sacred spaces for future generations to visit, learn from, and reflect on.

Tubman was known to let the spirit take hold and guide her in her actions. As Bradford noted, "When she felt the need, she simply told God of it, and trusted Him to set the matter right" (1886, 23), and she was vocal in singing out praise for her Lord and for those who assisted her in her goals—from abolition to women's rights to the care for the elderly. Moreover, she was known for telling others about her direct messages from God and her frequent chats with the Lord (Bradford 1886, 29, 60).

She believed that God had given her the power to deliver people to freedom through visions that came to her in dreams and spells of unconsciousness. She related dreams of "lying over fields, towns and mountains 'like a bird'" and of how ladies "all drest in white ober dere, reach out to Tubman and pull her across to safety" (Sanborn 1863). In his account, Sanborn added that later, when she in fact came north, she "remembered those very places, as those she had seen in her dreams, and many ladies who befriended her were those she had been helped by in her visions" (Sanborn 1863; see also Sernett 2007, 134).

Suffrage and Freedom: Tubman as a Women's Rights and Social Welfare Activist

In framing a context for the examination of Harriet Tubman's life in Auburn (chapter 2), I outlined the importance of multivalent roles played by perceptions of gender and her role as an activist for women's rights and suffrage. Now that we have reviewed the historical, material, and spatial record of her life in her house and her efforts for her Home, it is important to reflect on to the initial questions posed in this book: What role did gender and race play for Tubman? And how was Tubman involved in the era's women's movement? The treads of history and the material record of archaeology provide a means to sew together details of how she was perceived as a woman as well as of her role in the women's rights movements of her era. Because of her strong role as a leader and her risky role as a conductor of people to freedom, John Brown referred to her as "General Tubman" and used the pronoun *he* in describing her (Larson 2004, 158). In 1863, Franklin Sanborn quoted Brown as saying about Tubman, "He is the most of a man that I ever met with" (Sanborn 1863). This characterization of Tubman blurred gender conventions of the time and related to Brown's perception of her as a doer who was willing to act on her convictions in a manner that stood out from both women and most men he knew.

While pursuing her efforts on behalf of African Americans and striving to open her Home for the Aged, Harriet Tubman retained old ties and developed new, strong ties with the proponents of women's rights and suffrage. She was considered and felt herself to be a supporter and activist for this cause (Sernett 2007, 5). Tubman was not only a woman but also an African American, a head of household, and an American icon. Her multiple roles as a symbol of free, independent, self-sustaining women as well as role model and heroine open a series of questions with respect to the corresponding multimodality of the archaeological record.

Tubman's gender has become a highly negotiable commodity in contemporary feminist politics, but the "symbolic use of her as a woman who battled against the restrictions placed on women in her day is complicated by the factor of race" (Sernett 2007, 150). There is consistent agreement that Tubman was a symbol as a strong woman and was presented as such at many women's rights and suffrage conferences and public forums, but there is less agreement on her role as an activist, and over the years there has even been some tension regarding that role and the belief among some more recent Black feminists that she may have been misappropriated by white feminists both in the nineteenth century and now (Sernett 2007, 150). Certainly, there is an abundance of evidence of Tubman being present at and even speaking at suffrage meetings, but there is less clarity about the message she was presenting to these audiences.

At the New York State Women Suffrage Association meeting in Rochester, New York, on November 18, 1896, Susan B. Anthony came to the stage leading Harriet Tubman by the hand. A reporter in the audience reported: "Miss Anthony introduced her as Mrs. Harriet Tubman, a faithful worker for the emancipation of her race, who had reason to revere President Lincoln"; "the old woman stood before the assemblage in her cheap black gown and coat, and big black straw bonnet without adornment, her hand held in Miss Anthony's, she impressed one with the venerable dignity of her appearance." Tubman "bowed modestly as Miss Anthony presented her, and when she commenced to speak, her voice[,] low and tremulous at first, rose gradually as she warmed to her subject, till it was plainly heard throughout the hall" (*Rochester Democrat and Chronicle*, Nov. 18, 1896). She was there, and she was a symbol of both freedom and women's rights, but her speech was directed more to her escape and activities as a conductor on the Underground Railroad and perhaps at gaining support and funding for the new farmstead and plans for her

Home for the Aged. It would not be surprising to find that Tubman mixed these messages, but certainly the audience responded most favorably to her based on her known role as a freedom fighter. The reporter commented: "The old woman, who can neither read nor write, has still a mission, which is the moral advancement of her race. She makes her home in Auburn, but depends on the kindness of friends to assist her, by a dollar now and then, or a bed, or a meal, as she travels from place to place" (*Rochester Democrat and Chronicle*, Nov. 18, 1896). Quite possibly missed by Anthony and the reporter was the primary reason for Tubman making the trip: to gain financial support to pay for the farm that she had just purchased and the Home she dreamed of opening on it. The reporter stereotyped Tubman as a poor woman dependent on handouts from friends rather than as a woman who had owned her own property for nearly forty years by that point.

Anne Fitzhugh Miller, the feminist granddaughter of Gerrit Smith, visited Tubman in 1911 on behalf of the Geneva Political Equality Club and later related elements of this visit to an African American student who was involved in raising funds for the Home building fund (Conrad 1943, 200; Sernett 2007). Miller indicated that she had told Tubman that she had seen Tubman at a suffrage convention in Rochester and that Tubman had responded: "Yes, I belonged to Miss Susan B. Anthony's association." In describing this account, James Clarke concluded, "Aunt Harriet proved by this answer that she is a good suffragette and an independent, self-assertive woman" (1911, 118).

Tubman was part of the women's suffrage movements, was present at gatherings and in the parlors of many involved in the movement, and interacted with key leaders. Moreover, she was considered a symbol of the movement by its early leaders. Tubman was someone who sought liberty, took it for herself, and assisted others to attain it. At the National Association of Colored Women's first convention in Washington, DC, in 1896, Tubman was the oldest and perhaps most honored delegate. When she was presented to the gathering, "the audience rose as one person and greeted her with the waving of handkerchiefs and the clapping of hands" (Sernett 2007, 162). So although some may see Tubman's active role in white female activist suffrage groups as debatable, others see her firmly established as a leader—of both Blacks and whites. Shortly after Tubman's death, Mary Talbert, president of the Empire State Federation of Colored Women's Clubs, proclaimed, "The last star in that wonderful galaxy of noble pioneer Negro womanhood has fallen" (quoted in *Auburn Citizen*, Mar. 11, 1913).

Harriet Tubman's farms were busy with a wide range of activities. The sights, sounds, and smells there included those associated with raising pigs and chickens, milking cows, harvesting grains, and making bricks.[16] It is easy to picture Tubman tending her pigs, consulting with family and friends on her porch, and traversing South Street to sell the produce from her garden or gather food waste for her pigs (*Syracuse Sunday Herald*, Apr. 19, 1896). Some of the activities that Tubman engaged in no doubt fit within gender-based expectations (Spencer-Wood 2004, 235; Walls 1974). However, others do not. In fact, it is probable that the historic links between Tubman and brick-making on her properties have been muted by the fact that the brick industry was a male-dominated profession. Who would think to look for Tubman in that arena? It is such limiting assumptions that impact the breadth of our understanding of her life today and prevent us from seeing her in a brickyard setting or surrounded by African American families and friends who worked in the brickmaking industry (Sørensen 2000, 7).

The objective is to examine Tubman's life in terms of the permutations of expressed behaviors associated with gender, gender roles, and gender actions. The expressions and impacts of gender are dependent in part on the social constructs engaged in by the society of which the individual is a part. The important point is to assess and evaluate gender as a variable within these specific contexts of social interaction (Sørensen 2000, 7). Thus, one can expect that gender roles displayed in mid-nineteenth-century Central New York may very well reflect aspects of the variances advocated within sectors of society during a period of social change and within a context of strong advocacy for social reform. Harriet Tubman thus breaks most if not all of the stereotypes for women and women of color in this era if viewed from the broader context of the nation as a whole or of mid- to late nineteenth-century women in general. However, within the social fabric of Auburn, New York, this variance was definitively within the social construct of a significant and vociferous segment of the population, including both men and women. That social construct revolved around advocacy for social reforms (abolition, temperance, women's rights, health care, distributed property ownership, and voting rights), all of which were advocated both individually and collectively within the community.

As opposed to the restricting notion of separate spheres often discussed in feminist archaeology as a means of defining women's space and to finding only gendered spaces in the archaeological record, the contexts of Harriet

16. See the US censuses for 1870–1920, Auburn and Fleming, Cayuga County Records Office, Auburn, NY.

Tubman's properties allow us to look more broadly on the intersection of gender, race, ethnicity, and identity (Spencer-Wood 2009; Walls 1974). The archaeological and historical record indicates that Tubman drank tea in her parlor and was a welcome guest in the parlors of others, in particular those engaged in social reforms and the ongoing women's rights movement of the nineteenth and early twentieth century. She was a champion of such efforts and an invitee to gatherings to discuss such issues in the heartland of the nineteenth-century women's rights movement from Rochester (Susan B. Anthony) to Seneca Falls (the Henry and Elizabeth Cady Stanton household) and east to Peterborough (the Gerrit and Ann Smith household).[17]

Within the Tubman contexts, gender is a significant part of the processes of social constructs, interaction, and reproduction but must be viewed within the broader social fabric of social interaction in which it is a significant element that has bearing on our interpretations (Sørensen 2000, 7). In other words, gender is important but not the only or perhaps even the most important lens through which to view Tubman's life and her social interactions as expressed in the historical and archaeological record. We find ceramics used to serve tea and coffee within the Tubman household, but we really have no basis to establish a limitation on who within the household used them or if such gatherings had gendered parameters, such as the casual exclusion of men. We know that she was invited into upper-middle-class and upper-class households for formal teas and conversations, so we can project more specific gender relations into those specific interactions, but teas of this type did not take place at her own residence or in her Home for the Aged. Further, we have found a relatively uniform set of tea and coffee wares in middens located throughout the site, from her residence to John Brown Hall, as well as scatters associated with trash deposits on the site. These artifacts project a more broadly defined adoption of tea service for all of those within her household and in the care of the Home for the Aged. There is also no indication of her discrimination between men and women in the Home, and those of each gender probably

---

17. Ann Smith was Elizabeth Stanton's cousin. Ann and Gerrit's daughter Elizabeth Smith Miller started the practice of wearing pantaloons and knee-length skirts that became known as "bloomers." These clothes were part of the broader movement of social reform that women in the region were engaged in. Bloomers were not only a rebellion against the limitations placed upon women in the restrictive clothing of the day but also a symbol of change in the role of women. Though Tubman was within the social circles of these reformers, there is no indication that she took up this type of clothing as part of her reform efforts.

had access to such service wares and the social exchanges involved in the times in which individuals and groups sat down to enjoy tea or coffee.

Harriet Tubman was a nineteenth-century activist who was, among other things, a feminist. In keeping with her active engagement in many forms of action aimed at social and economic equality, including emancipation and women's rights, she lived her life advocating for women the same rights she wanted for men. She was a person of action who would come to the podium to state her case and to advocate her beliefs, but for the most part her beliefs were demonstrated by the actions she took, and it would be others who would commemorate these actions in terms of their meaning for her selected causes. Unlike the wealth of information we have about Jermain Loguen, an AME Zion bishop in Syracuse who espoused his beliefs from the pulpit and in both public and published forums, including an autobiography, or about Frederick Douglass, who was a great orator, motivator, publisher, and author, putting to pen both his beliefs and his autobiography, our knowledge of Tubman is more constrained. It has moved forward to us in fits and gaps over time, reflected upon in biographical form first by Sarah Bradford (1867, 1886) in the nineteenth century, then by Earl Conrad (1943) in the mid–twentieth century, and now more completely in synthetic histories by Kate Larson (2004) and Milton Sernett (2007) and by studies of the physical and material record of her life recovered from her properties (D. Armstrong 2011, 2015; Ryan and Armstrong 2000).

Although in other US regions African American women may not have been welcome among those engaged in the women's reform movement, this was not the case in Central New York, at least during Tubman's lifetime (Amott and Matthaei 1999, 152–53). She was considered part of the women's movement there and an example of the transformative properties of freedom and equality.[18] She was a guest in the homes of whites for both formal and informal gatherings. Although the records of the Seward house generally place her in the kitchen or places where cleaning was being done and up and down South Street to sell produce and gather garbage to feed her pigs, she appears to have developed relationships that ensured markets for her produce and stock. These regular encounters allowed her to inform her supporters of

18. Theresa Amott and Julie Matthaei report that such openness to African American women was not always the case among women's rights activists (1999, 52–53), and even famous Black leaders such as Sojourner Truth were not invited to the women's rights convention held in Akron, Ohio, in 1851 (L. Davis 1989, 52–53; Stone and McKee 1998, 97).

the status of current affairs in her house and the Home and to solicit offerings and gifts based on those needs. On numerous occasions, she was the noted guest at parlor meetings of middle- and upper-middle-class women engaged in women's rights and other reform activities. In the archaeological record, we find the direct evidence of these social engagements in the brass plate used to print Tubman's name on the cards she used to respond to social calls. We have not found the resulting calling cards in the records of these households, but this is not surprising because they would have been viewed as informal responses that could be discarded with other such written materials.

In discussing gender, Michelle Rosaldo emphasizes the distinction between public and private spheres of life and finds women to be subordinated because they are more frequently associated with the domestic sphere of housework and childcare. She argues that "this sphere is universally less valued than the public world dominated by men—the world of politics, leadership, and extra-domestic economic life" (1974, 10). Critiques of this work on distinct spheres include the fact that such relationships are not universal because in some societies women do play prominent public roles; moreover, other scholars insist that the domestic world of women is not so strongly devalued in all societies; still others point out that not all societies have a sharp division between public and private spheres (Lamphere 1993).

Linda Stone and Nancy McKee note that one of the problems related to the women's rights movement for women of color was that it was organized to address the needs of the white upper-middle and upper classes and tended to frame arguments that served to demean the value of housework, subsistence, and sustenance—all of which were rudimentary bases of survival for most African American women and, really, for the clear majority of women. Hence, one of the problems of the movement was and would continue to be the embedding of class structures into the articulation of arguments for and against the maintenance of gender roles. Many women's rights reformers expressed contempt for the forms of housework that were in fact the areas of opportunity and employment for women of color outside of their own homes. Or, put another way, who would assume these roles when the affluent women liberated themselves from housework? No doubt, that gap would be filled by women of color and others, often new immigrants, in need of employment. Thus, in many settings, reform involving women was elitist and not inclusive of all women. It is the realization of this elitism that led Tubman and the AME Zion Church to contemplate the creation of a training school for African American girls to learn the skills of household service that could ensure them gainful employment in late nineteenth- and early twentieth-century Central

New York. This mode of training was consistent with Booker T. Washington's mode of education of African Americans but today would be viewed as limiting and demeaning. As we have seen, Booker T. Washington was influential in Tubman's life and in the AME Zion Church, which he attended and which he used to organize the Tuskegee Institute. The Home ultimately concentrated on the care of elderly African Americans, but considerable time and energy were also expended to open an industrial school for girls.

There can be little doubt of Tubman's rightful inclusion in the nineteenth-century women's rights movement and of her regular interaction with many of its leaders. Early women's rights activists had been involved in the abolition movement and had been a key element in Tubman's establishment of residence in Fleming and Auburn. Throughout her life, Tubman had connections with these women. However, when Earl Conrad sought input from leaders of women's rights activities as background for his book on Tubman, he found that within a short time of her death the new generation of women's rights leaders had lost sight of her contributions to the cause or were divided on the level of her involvement and contribution. With the passage of time between Tubman's death in 1913 and his research in 1939, her perceived significance to the suffrage movement had shifted (Sernett 2007, 154).

A Material Legacy: Artifacts Projecting the Theme of Freedom and Liberty

Freedom and liberty were of paramount importance to Harriet Tubman and are part of her legacy to us. The fact that Tubman owned, maintained, and expanded her property is a spatial manifestation of her ideal of life lived free. The whole of the thirty-two-acre property vividly projects a space where freedom was lived. However, the importance of the political ideals of freedom are also projected in the small things lost and forgotten in the archaeological record. Here, I focus on two tokens that were the personal possessions of Tubman or of any one of the many people living on her property: an 1876 Liberty Bell medal and an 1861 Union token.

The Liberty Bell medal was produced in 1876 as part of the US centennial celebration (figure 12.1). The medal depicts the Liberty Bell and includes the words "Memory of the Constitution." This item was acquired and worn by Harriet Tubman or another member of her household and then lost in the yard along with many other personal items damaged by the house fire of 1880. It was a memento of the centennial, but the symbol of the Liberty Bell also had meaning to the principals of liberty and the abolition movement. The actual Liberty Bell, located in the town where Tubman first experienced free-dom, Philadelphia, was commissioned by the Pennsylvania Assembly in 1751 to commemorate William Penn's dedication to religious and social freedoms. It was inscribed with the words:

PROCLAIM LIBERTY THROUGHOUT
ALL THE LAND UNTO ALL THE
INHABITANTS THEREOF LEV. XXV.V X.

BY ORDER OF THE ASSEMBLY
OF THE PROVINCE OF PENNSYLVANIA
FOR THE STATE HOUSE IN PHILADA.

PASS AND STOW, PHILADA, MDCCLIII

In place at the Assembly Hall at the time of the signing of the Declaration of Independence, the bell was no doubt rung to publicly announce the signing of this declaration of liberty (Paige and Kimball 1986). Initially known as the "State House Bell," the bell achieved its iconic status and link to liberty when abolitionists adopted it as a symbol for the emancipation movement. An image of the bell was first used as the frontispiece to an 1837 edition of the periodi-cal *Liberty* published by the New York Anti-Slavery Society. In 1856, William Lloyd Garrison's antislavery publication the *Liberator* reprinted a Boston aboli-tionist pamphlet containing a poem about the bell entitled "The Liberty Bell" (Paige and Kimball 1986). It is from this abolitionist pamphlet that the bell took its new name, the "Liberty Bell." The abolitionists' call for emancipation drew upon the well-established principal of liberty associated with the bell.

Reinvigorated as a symbol of liberty in the post–Civil War era, the bell took on enhanced meaning during the American centennial celebration in 1876, when the Liberty Bell medal was made. The Liberty Bell and the ring-ing of bells have remained symbolic representations of freedom and liberty, adopted by the women's suffrage movement in the early twentieth century and incorporated repeatedly in Martin Luther King Jr.'s "I Have a Dream" speech (1963).

The second distinctive artifact that chronicles the fight for freedom is a Union token dating to 1861, the beginning of the Civil War (figure 12.2).[19]

19. See also Kenneth Brown's (2011) discussion of holed coins at sites associated with African Americans.

This well-worn coin was probably worn on a chain, as indicated by the hole in it. On one side is a Union shield, on the other crossed cannons of the American Revolution "76" and the Civil War "61." From the perspective of self-emancipated persons such as Tubman, the Union cause was synonymous with the abolition cause. Ultimately, the Union's victory delivered freedom and the ability of Tubman and her family to live as they wished on her property in New York for nearly fifty years. In 1861, when the token was made, the conclusion of the war and the outcome of abolition were unresolved. But evidence of wear indicates that the Union token was worn for a considerable period of time and thus had ongoing meaning in the battle for freedom. The key point here is the importance of land ownership. It provided Tubman with the means of securing her liberty in a new landscape of freedom. Land ownership was tied to legal systems defining citizenship, and the ownership of a productive farm provided her with the means of production necessary to maintain herself and her family in freedom. Ownership of land and the fruits that it yielded allowed persons of color to move away from slavery and be economically productive.

Harriet Tubman's house and farm as well as the farm she acquired to expand her Home for the Aged represent a landscape of expressed freedom. Archaeological excavations have demonstrated the value of the archaeological resources at the Home and will be of significance to public interpretation of the sites. The wide range of artifacts recovered from the sites provide details of her life and her legacy of caring for others. This chapter has described a range of artifacts and focused on two that highlight the symbolic importance of liberty and freedom to Tubman and those living at the site. The Liberty Bell medal and the Union token were acquired and worn as personal adornments and as statements of the profound importance of the cause of liberty to those who had boldly freed themselves from the shackles of slavery.

Harriet Tubman is well known for her heroic acts in liberating African Americans from slavery and fighting for emancipation. She has been described as "America's Joan of Arc" and "the Moses of her people." Archaeology is contributing significantly to a new and in-depth understanding of Harriet Tubman's life and legacies and filling in heretofore missing details of her history, including her role as a property owner, her continued concern for and advocacy of those in need, and her long-term commitment to causes of social reform. This complex examination of her life simply had not occurred prior to archaeological study. Archaeology has forced us to reexamine the historical interpretation of this well-known figure and has provided a material basis to understand the complex of sites and structures from the past as well as the corresponding social interactions involving Harriet Tubman and the communities with which she interacted. Our findings have interpretive value as they demonstrate the material record of a person who cared for others. I find the record of Harriet Tubman's life inspiring and hope that its spatial and material interpretation will inspire new generations of people to care for others.

For the Liberty Bell medallion and the Union token, as for many such symbols, direct confirmation and correlation between the attribute and associated belief systems, spiritual connotations, or inspiration are difficult to pin down but nonetheless important to consider (LaRoche 2014a, 300). Coins can project more than simply the value impressed on them by their manufactures. In the case of the trade token, the manufacturer imbued the coin with meaning by the imprinted script that heralds the Union cause and celebrates the fundamental principles of liberty. One need not be able to read the words to understand the meaning of the Union shield as a symbol of the cause of the preservation of the union or the implied meaning of the expansion of liberties through the battles engaged in at the time of the token's manufacture in 1861.

Holed coins have been found in association with many African American sites, and several archaeologists have linked them with special caches and bundles of artifacts that have special ritual and spiritual significance (Brown 2011; Leone 2005; Leone and Fry 1999; Leone, Knauf, and Tang 2014, 212).[20] The holed Union token and the Liberty Bell medallion recovered from domestic contexts at the Tubman Home property project specific meanings related to abolition and freedom that continued to be commemorated by Tubman and her associates for many years after the war. Though we do not know exactly who wore them, both were recovered from post-1880 contexts, and both show wear suggestive of regular use and personal display of ideology and belief.

20. However, holed coins are found in a wide range of contexts and probably project different meanings and intents depending on those contexts. For other archaeological examples of ritual use of coins by African Americans, see LaRoche 2014a, 301, 311.

12.1. Liberty Bell medal (1876) from the Harriet Tubman Home site. Photograph by D. Armstrong.

12.2. Union token from 1861, holed for wearing, found at Harriet Tubman's brick residence (Locus 1). Photograph by D. Armstrong.

13

Epilogue
The Legacy of Inspiration—Serving Others

I had reasoned dis out in my mind; there was one of two things I had a
right to, liberty, or death; if I could not have one, I would have de oder;
for no man should take me alive; I should fight for my liberty as long as
my strength lasted, and when de time came for me to go, de Lord would
let dem take me.

> —attributed to Harriet Tubman in Sarah Bradford,
> *Harriet: The Moses of Her People* (1886)

From Decay to Reconnaissance and Restoration

Just as Tubman struggled to care for others and to open her Home, it was a
difficult struggle to maintain the Home and retain it intact for future generations. Through the very lean years of the Great Depression in the 1930s, the
property was retained and protected by the AME Zion Church. During the
1930s and 1940s, the physical structures, often unoccupied and subject to
the region's severe weather, began a rapid process of decay. Still, in the 1930s
advocates who understood aspects of the importance of Tubman and her
works obtained formal recognition of the property and sponsored the forging
of a New York State Historic Site marker on South Street in front of the property. The marker remained in place as a reminder of Tubman's works of more
than nearly eighty years. Ironically and unfortunately, this marker projects
both respect and a detached misunderstanding of Harriet Tubman and the
complexity of her efforts on behalf of others at the site. It does acknowledge
her role in relation to the Underground Railroad but states only that she
"frequented this site after the Civil War." This vague statement projects the
distanced and fragmented knowledge of her life and omits both her direct
presence and ownership of the properties and her long-term humanitarian
efforts at the site. For many years during the 1930s and 1940s, the sign sat
against a backdrop of abandonment and decay.

Photographs from the mid-1940s show that John Brown Hall (Locus 3) was abandoned, and photographs from 1947 show a stripped-down-wood frame house (Locus 2) barely standing. Its wrap-around porch is gone, and nearly all its clapboard siding stripped away for firewood (figures 1.13, 10.2).[1] However, as indicated by the New York State Historic Site marker, even as the site declined, it continued to be recognized for its significant association with Harriet Tubman. The marker served as a sentry to remind passersby of the importance of Tubman's deeds and her place on the landscape.

The first wave of efforts to protect the site took place from the mid-1940s through the early 1950s. These efforts were led by the AME Zion Church and owe much to the efforts of Bishop William Walls (US National Park Service 2001, 19; Walls 1974). This was a difficult era for historic preservation in the United States. It was a time when the country was focusing on new construction and when there was little protection of historic properties, particularly on private lands. The initial fund-raising campaign for restoration funds targeted John Brown Hall and included former First Lady Eleanor Roosevelt as the honorary chairwoman of the campaign.

Unfortunately, this initial effort failed as people continued to make use of the abandoned structure and fires did structural damage to the building. Ultimately, after a fire on February 1, 1949, the City of Auburn bulldozed the condemned building (*Syracuse Post-Standard*, Feb. 1, 1949). The loss of John Brown Hall solidified resolve, though, and Bishop Walls spearheaded an AME Zion Church fund-raising campaign aimed at restoring the wood-frame structure at the front of the property. Fortunately, this effort was successful and provided the funds for a ground-up rebuilding of this structure. At a ceremony celebrating the completion of the rebuilding project on April 30, 1953, the wood-frame house was rededicated as a "historic site," although it is unclear if this was a local designation, a reconfirmation of the state designation already indicated in the signage on South Street, or placement on the National Register following guidelines of the Historic Sites Act of 1935 (US National Park Service 2001, 16).

In time, confusion emerged regarding the context of the site and its structures. Beginning in the 1950s, the restored wood-frame house, now painted white, which had been part of the Home for the Aged but was not used to

---

1. Alice Norris informed me that during the Depression members of their family would on occasion gather wood that had fallen from the white wood-frame house to burn in their furnace to heat the Norris house (formerly Harriet Tubman's brick house) (Alice Norris, personal communication to the author, May 22, 2002).

house the elderly until after Tubman's death, became the focus of attention and often was represented as both Tubman's residence and *the* Home for the Aged.[2] At the time, Tubman's seven-acre farm and her house were owned by the Norris family, who had purchased them from her estate in 1913, and so were not available for interpretation. As noted, John Brown Hall had been knocked down by the City of Auburn just as restoration efforts got under way in the early 1950s. Thus, the only remaining Tubman-era structure on the twenty-five-acre property was the wood-frame house that from soon after Tubman's death until the late 1920s served as the dormitory for the Home. The restoration campaign had initially tried to generate funds for both structures, but after John Brown Hall was demolished, attention was focused on the frame house at the front of the property. This house had been so badly stripped that its porch was gone, and one could see through the house. Between 1949 and 1953, the house was rebuilt, and for the next several decades the history of Tubman's house and home were publicly fused in the interpretation of the Home.

When the United States began to reawaken to the importance of Harriet Tubman in the 1960s, the Home was featured in a *Life* magazine photographic essay published on November 22, 1967. At the time, *Life* was a leading photographic journal depicting American life. The article brought national attention to the AME Zion Church's effort to preserve Tubman's legacy. The fact that the wood-frame house was the only standing structure under the control of the AME Zion Church led to a singular emphasis on this structure as *the* Harriet Tubman Home.

This *Life* article illustrates a new thirst for knowledge about Tubman, but it also shows how little was known or remembered about her life or her properties. It ignores Tubman's farm and even the broader context of the Home for the Aged property and instead centers attention on the restored white wooden house that was the only remaining structure accessible as a physical symbol of her life. Meanwhile, the ruins of John Brown Hall, which was in fact the heart of the Home for the Aged when it formally opened in 1908, was lost from memory. Her personal farm and home for fifty years, which was within view of the adjacent property, was obscured by the veil of history and the social, historical, and spiritual separation of fact and fiction, reality and imagination, and would not return to the scope of focus and interpretation in the context of Tubman's life for another half century.

2. An historical overview of archaeological studies of institutional life can be found in Beisaw and Gibb 2009, which addresses a range of topics, from charitable schools for girls and cloistered communes to places of forced incarceration such as asylums and prisons.

From the 1960s through the 1980s, much of the AME Zion Church's efforts went toward making the property an active part of the life of the church and its communities (local, regional, and national). During this period, two new buildings were constructed on the property. The first, located near the wood-frame building, was designed to house offices for a resident manager as well as a library and small museum. The second was a multipurpose building with community hall, kitchen, restrooms, and porches, aimed at encouraging active use of the property for social gatherings, pageants, and ultimately pilgrimages aimed at honoring Tubman and raising funds.[3]

When the seven-acre farm that had been Tubman's property and residence came up for sale in 1990, the AME Zion Church raised the funds and purchased it for $118,000 on June 11.[4] This act set in motion a chain of events working toward restoration, including the appointment of Rev. Paul Carter as site manager in 1990, and began a legacy of public interpretation of the entire site that is still unfolding.

In 1994, when I first visited the site and conducted my first informal survey, efforts were under way to begin the process of gaining the funds necessary for a complex series of restorations. Those directly involved in the project clearly understood the importance of Tubman's brick farmhouse, barn, and farm on her original seven acres. This brick farmhouse was where Tubman began her Home for the Aged. Yet the story of the wood-frame house as "the Home" had become so ingrained by this point that even the importance of John Brown Hall, which had opened in 1908 as the first formal dormitory of the Home, remained obscured. Even as plans went forward for restoration of Tubman's brick house, the interpretation of the site tended to focus on the wood-frame house, probably mostly because of the energy that had already been put into its restoration and because it was open and available to a public that was beginning to awaken to the property's importance. Meanwhile, behind the scenes at Tubman Home board meetings and in City of Auburn offices, plans were made to seek funds and develop studies that aimed to project a broader historical understanding of the properties and their many structures and activity areas. At the same time, a group of scholars began in-depth

3. These actions are indicative of the retention of the values of family, church, and community seen in Tubman's and the local African American community's social interactions in Fleming and Auburn and are described more broadly by Cheryl LaRoche (2014b) for free Black settlements across America in the nineteenth century.

4. This purchase is recorded in Cayuga County Deeds Book 809, June 11, 1990, Cayuga County Clerk's Office, Auburn, NY.

examinations of Tubman's life in Auburn and elsewhere (D. Armstrong 2011; D. Armstrong, Wurst, and Kellar 2000; Larson 2004; Ryan 2000; Ryan and Armstrong 2000; Sernett 2007). Based on these studies, including historical, architectural, and archaeological investigations, formal recognition of the significance of the site was gained, and funds for its restoration were generated from both public and private sources.

New laws beginning in the 1960s brought new legal mechanisms aimed at historic-site protection, preservation, and restoration. These laws confirmed and bolstered the stewardship legacy of the AME Zion Church and provided mechanisms for funding. The potential for funding provided in this set of historic-preservation laws led the nonprofit Harriet Tubman Home, Inc., to begin the process of evaluating ways to best preserve the property and Tubman's legacy. Working in cooperation with the City of Auburn and its director of capital projects and grants, Michael Long, the Tubman Home sought formal historic-site designation and funding for restoration. The first step toward reinforcing the historic significance of the wood-frame building was in gaining a grant from the Preservation League of New York State to prepare nomination of this building for National Historic Landmark status (US National Park Service 2001, 17). In 1998, the Home was listed on the National Register of Historic Places as part of a multisite Harriet Tubman theme designation. In 2000, the lands, structures, and ruins of the Home, including both Tubman's original farm and the twenty-five-acre farm that she acquired in 1896, were designated a multisite National Historic Landmark, which also encompassed Tubman's gravesite in Fort Hill Cemetery in Auburn and the Thompson AME Zion Church on Parker Street in Auburn (US National Park Service 2001). These designations initially focused on recognizing the historical importance of standing historic buildings and providing a basis for access to an array of historic-preservation resources. However, they also established the significance of the site as part of the landmark and defined the period of historical significance as 1859–1913, the period of Tubman's presence on the property. This recognition of the importance of the site coincided with a series of national, state, and local efforts to advance the historic significance of Tubman herself as well as of social themes of historical importance in the nineteenth century, including the Underground Railroad and efforts toward the legal recognition of women's rights. The formal designation of significance and the reawakened social consciousness regarding the importance of Tubman's actions and life set in motion broader evaluation of past uses of the property, including archaeological surveys to assess areas where buildings once stood and where activities associated with Harriet Tubman's life took place (A. Armstrong and D. Armstrong 2012; D. Armstrong 2003b,c, 2011, 2015; Armstrong and Hill 2009; Armstrong, Wurst, and Kellar 2000; Ryan 2000; Ryan and Armstrong 2000).

Archaeological studies at the Home were and are in cadence with the emerging preservation and interpretation efforts.[5] The objective has been to do more than just excavate and restore historic sites and report on our findings. It has been to honor Tubman and her legacy and to utilize these sites to engage, inspire, and assist the public in gaining an understanding of her life. Mark Leone has described sites such as the Tubman Home as "teaching landscapes" that can provide a context in which to examine complex interactions (2010, 219). In an approach that can be defined as interpretive historical archaeology (Beaudry 1996), the type of investigation conducted on the Tubman properties similarly seeks to "connect the artifacts to the people" (Ferguson 1992, xliv). Analysts can employ such an approach to illuminate the "close relationships between people and things in the past" (Beaudry 1996, 496). The study takes on the task of bringing forgotten elements of Tubman's life to public light through reconnaissance, interpretation, and public engagement. Paradoxically, although Tubman herself was a storyteller, those of us involved in the study were challenged by omissions in the scope and breadth of accounts of her life and so set out to recover all details pertaining to her, the property, and the cultural landscape.

The act of recovery of data on the site has allowed for the generation of a more exact representation of life on Tubman's farmstead and within the setting of the Home for the Aged, which she established after acquiring the adjacent farm. The emphasis is on usable detail so that future interpretation can project "accurate research findings in an interesting and compelling manner" (Aplin 2002, 22).

The rediscovery of the site of John Brown Hall in 1994 and the recovery of artifacts at this site as part of excavations in 1998–99 show the value of archaeology to yield significant information on the use of this facility as the primary dormitory for the Home during Tubman's lifetime. Once the value of archaeological studies to the site was demonstrated, we became involved in all phases

---

5. The data presented in this volume derive from fieldwork completed in 2016. In fact, archaeological studies continue to expand our base of knowledge of these properties, with an emphasis on targeted excavations linked to restoration efforts. Additional work has been done at Harriet Tubman's brick house, and excavations will soon begin at the Thompson AME Zion Church and associated parsonage, which are part of the Harriet Tubman National Historical Park.

of the restoration of the property. Over the years, as restoration initiatives were begun at the Tubman farm—including barn restoration; garage demolition; water-, sewer-, and electric-line installation; demolition of basement floors and heating systems; and reconstruction of porches and sheds associated with the property—we assessed each context prior to demolition and reconstruction to maximize data recovery and information feedback. We worked under porches, beneath the raised barn prior the resetting of its foundation, under a demolished garage, in the basement kitchen of the brick house, in and around a wooden cistern and a stone-lined well, as well as in an area where there had been a chicken coop. In the process, we gathered a wide breadth of information about the house, its use, and the material record of Tubman, her family, and associates. We also pursued a series of other research questions related to the cultural landscape associated with the Tubman property. Our initial survey in 2002 defined an anomaly in an area that was being considered for construction of a new building. We carried out remote sensing (magnetometer and resistivity) and found very distinct indicators of an anomaly, which we then tested. The result was the recovery of the base of a brick kiln. This finding led to detailed analysis of brickmaking at the site and in the vicinity that had involved numerous members of the Tubman household and substantial numbers of African American laborers. Moreover, the kiln may well have been the source of the brick used in the construction of Tubman's own brick residence (A. Armstrong 2011; A. Armstrong and D. Armstrong 2012).

The Creation of the Harriet Tubman National Historical Park

This study has used archaeological and historical research to examine and illuminate Tubman's lesser-known but nonetheless significant continued role as a social activist after the Civil War based in her home in Auburn, New York. Archaeological and historical studies provided a body of evidence related to the significance of the property, and the artifacts recovered were integrated into the effort to expand the scope and quality of interpretation of the site. As this research proceeded, the AME Zion Church through its not-for-profit Harriet Tubman Home, Inc., sought funds for restoration and to expand public interpretation. Bishop George Walker, the Home's immediate past chairman, organized meetings with leading scholars, National Park Service director Robert Stanton, and Special Assistant Vincent deForest to begin discussions about ways in which the resources of the National Park Service could be drawn in to support the preservation and interpretation efforts while still allowing Harriet Tubman Home, Inc., to retain control of the property. Initial ideas included a multisite park situated in New York and Maryland as well as an international component in St. Catharines, Ontario. Ultimately, two National Parks were created, one celebrating Tubman's early life in her birth state of Maryland, and the second comprising a series of properties associated with her life in Fleming and Auburn, New York. The formal creation of the Harriet Tubman National Historical Park was a difficult task because the legislation went forward in Congress during an era of financial restraint. On July 10, 2014, a bill authorizing the park was passed by the US Senate; however, this bill never made it to the floor of the House of Representatives.[6] Finally, at the end of the 2014 legislative session, Harriet Tubman National Historical Park was included in the National Defense Authorization Act of 2015 and received necessary bipartisan support, leading to congressional authorization for its creation. The new park was to include the thirty-two-acre Home property, the Thompson AME Zion Church on Parker Street, and the parsonage next-door to the church. Unfortunately, the authorizing legislation included narrowly defined definitions for the boundary of the property, and all the property was owned by the church. To create the park, the National Park Service had to secure ownership of at least a piece of land within the park. Under the leadership of Karen Hill, executive director of Harriet Tubman Home, Inc., an agreement was made to transfer title to the parsonage on Parker Street as a legal foothold for the park. Finally, after two years of negotiations and planning, Sally Jewell, the US secretary of interior, formally signed documents establishing the Harriet Tubman National Historical Park on January 10, 2017 (figure 13.1). At the signing, Secretary Jewell discussed Tubman and the importance of the park: "She lived her principles: her strong faith in God, her love of family, belief in the dignity of all humans and a vision for a better life for all people in this country, so what better place to tell her story than within America's storyteller and that is the National Park Service."[7] Present at the signing ceremony were a bipartisan group of congressional supporters, including the US legislators for New York, Senators Charles Schumer and Kirsten Gillibrand and Congressman John Katko. The delegation in Washington included Tubman descendant Judith Bryant, representatives of the AME Zion Church, and scholars engaged in the study of Harriet Tubman

---

6. S.247, 113th Cong., 2nd sess., July 10, 2014.

7. The events at the signing, including Jewell's speech, are covered on the Team Ebony website, Jan. 10, 2017, at http://www.ebony.com/news-now/harriet-tubman-national-historical -park#ixzz4X5Vc9k4L.

and the Tubman properties. After the signing, some of those present were invited to the US Bureau of Engraving to examine the draft of a painting of Tubman that will be used as the basis for engraving the image of Tubman that will appear on a new $20 bill that has been approved by the Department of the Treasury and authorized by Congress. In anticipation of the new $20 bill, a banner of Harriet Tubman was flying outside of the Bureau of Engraving. As discussed earlier, this bill will incorporate images of artifacts recovered from excavations of archaeological deposits on Tubman's properties.

The new Harriet Tubman National Historical Park in Fleming and Auburn is operated jointly by the National Park Service and Harriet Tubman Home, Inc., which retains ownership of the Tubman Home properties. Moving forward, park interpretation and management of grounds will be organized by the National Park Service. The first tangible benefit of this cooperative effort involves the National Park Service working to graft cuttings from old apple trees adjacent to the ruins of John Brown Hall to preserve the last of these old trees. When we first started work at the site of John Brown Hall in 1999, we noted the presence of a group of apple trees from the Tubman-era orchard (figure 1.10); however, all but two of these trees had died by 2014. In 2015 and 2016, Michael Long and I cut grafting specimens from the last-surviving tree located next to the ruins of John Brown Hall.[8] We are hopeful that the grafts will generate new generations of the variety of trees that provided apples for Tubman and the other elderly persons who lived in the Home.

Inspiration Uncovered

Archaeology is playing an important role in the reconstruction of the Tubman site and a reawakening of the legacy of Harriet Tubman, an individual who did not have access to a formal education and who did not write about her own life. The site is complex, with many components, all of which were virtually undocumented prior to our investigations. The subtitle of this chapter, "The Legacy of Inspiration," relates to the important role that contemporary archaeology has in bringing to life to Tubman's activities through the full and expanded interpretation of archaeological sites associated with her life. We are fortunate that the land and sites associated with her life and continued legacy of social activism have survived, albeit in ruins and modified forms. We can now engage

---

8. These specimens were sent to the US National Park Service's Olmsted botanical facility. We do not yet have results from this effort.

in the process of reconstructing and presenting her stories to the public. The venue facilitates discussion of a wide range of social issues pertaining to American history, African Americans, networks of social interaction, women, the aged, and the combination of elements that constitute personal freedom.

Harriet Tubman is well known for her heroic acts of resistance in liberating African Americans from slavery and fighting for emancipation. She has been described as "America's Joan of Arc" and "the Moses of her people." In the recent movie *Harriet* (Kasi Lemmons, 2019), her heroic actions as a conductor before the Civil War have been vividly portrayed in Cynthia Erivo's powerful Academy Award–nominated performance as Harriet, bringing new meaning to her efforts to millions of viewers worldwide. Yet the full story of her life is still little known, and her continued, lifelong commitment to social causes and reform has not found its way into the pages of history—*until now*. Archaeology has contributed significantly to this renewed interest and depth of knowledge regarding Harriet Tubman's life and legacy. Most studies of her have focused on her efforts to liberate herself and others as an Underground Railroad conductor who escorted African Americans out of the bondage.[9] These acts and her efforts as a soldier, nurse, and spy are retold in countless stories and historical accounts and have elevated Tubman to iconic status in American history, but they do tend to lose track of her after emancipation. Certainly, one cannot and should not underestimate her early accomplishments prior to and during the Civil War; however, given her fame and contributions as well as the length of her life, it is surprising how little was known of her later years and her continued efforts for social justice, women's rights, and care for the elderly.

Tubman's residence and the Home for the Aged represent an interesting nexus projecting the strength of an individual's actions in combination with complex networks of social interaction. Harriet Tubman's house and seven-acre farm represent a property owned by this key African American woman since 1859. The property was acquired on favorable terms from US senator William Seward (later Abraham Lincoln's secretary of state) and his wife, Frances Seward, at a time when Tubman was considered a slave and a fugitive under federal law (the Fugitive Slave Act of 1850). Land ownership was—and is—an important way of ensuring one's own and one's family's autonomy and

---

9. Accounts of the number persons Tubman escorted to freedom give from sixty to four hundred, with scholarly examination documenting a minimum number in the range of sixty to seventy-five (Larson 2004).

future. Tubman's acquisition of a house and farm provided her with the means to care for her family and others. Tubman, the true social activist, used the site not just to secure her own well-being but also to house and care for her extended family—her parents, brothers, sisters, nieces, and nephews. Many came to her and then established their own homes—hence ensuring their own futures. And other African Americans, in particular displaced elderly persons, came to Tubman's house as a place of refuge, and ultimately this house would become a focal point of Tubman's expanded effort to provide care to those seeking shelter and support.

The artifacts from Tubman's house include a wide array of materials, many of which would not have found their way into a definitive midden deposit without the trauma of a fire in which nearly everything in the original household was destroyed at once. In contrast, the middens associated with the dormitory at John Brown Hall appear to have been built up over time, and the deepest accumulations filled a depression created during the construction of the building. The deposits at John Brown Hall are consistent with the use of the property for the care of the elderly. Canning jars, which were found in relatively high frequency, reflect the practice of putting up farm produce such as fruits and vegetables. The diversity of the types of jars found at Tubman's house, John Brown Hall, and the kitchen area of the wood-frame house also reflect a pattern of gifting of canned foods to the Home, which is well documented in newspaper accounts from the period of Tubman's life as well as after it, up to the Home's closure in the late 1920s. The mix of sizes and manufactures of glass is thus consistent with historical accounts of these properties.

The extremely low volume of alcohol-related bottles, unusual for a site of this period, probably reflected the temperance philosophy followed by Harriet Tubman and the AME Zion Church. Few bottles associated with alcohol were found at any of the sites. This absence of alcohol bottles is in sharp contrast with their frequency in almost any other household data generated from domestic archaeological sites from this era. Alcohol appears to have been limited to medicinal use in the Tubman household and probably was present in medicine bottles, such as the several bottles of headache medicine found at the site and identified as "Dr. Marshall's—SNUFF," as well as in other unbranded pharmaceutical bottles.

Most of the ceramics found at the John Brown Hall site were tableware such as plates and tea wares, with fewer mid- to large-size bowls or other hollowware. The emphasis on tea ware reflects the general popularity of teas as a focal point for social interaction, particularly among women during this era. Tea ware differed from most of the other ceramics at the site in the fact that most of it was decorated, and at least fifteen teacups and saucers of the same "L. Straus and Sons—Lace" pattern of tea ware were found at five different locations on the property, including Tubman's house, John Brown Hall, the basement of a house that burned in 1902, and two isolated middens (figure 2.1).[10] The large amount of ceramic stoneware storage vessels corresponds with their glass storage jar counterparts and attests to the harvesting and preservation of homegrown foods by the Home's residents.

Materials from Tubman's house indicate a wide range of uses and the wide age range of those present. Although many artifacts correspond with a generally older population, the presence of children is indicated by toys, including doll parts and pieces of miniature porcelain tea sets. A group of marbles along a brick walkway that was uncovered on the west (street side) of Tubman's house suggests that this area was used by children, and a newspaper illustration of the Home from 1896 shows Harriet with a small child in this same location (figure 6.3). At the dormitory and infirmary at John Brown Hall, small objects, such as metal pillboxes, including a heart-shaped one (figure 1.15), were found, along with a wide variety of pharmaceutical bottles (including Bromo-Seltzer bottles and Vick's Vapo-Rub). The archaeological record of medicine bottles, toothpaste tubes, a toothbrush, and a metal bedpan demonstrate that health and hygiene were an important part of the daily life of those who resided at the Home.

In contrast to the initial National Historic Landmark nomination, which focused almost solely on standing structures, our surveys and excavations have pursued documentation of the site using a holistic approach aimed at examining the entire cultural landscape and the material record. This approach views the properties as composite farmsteads made up of many interrelated features, structures, and midden deposits across the site. The site yielded the excellent preservation of previously unknown and rediscovered structures and material finds. The archaeological record for the site provides information on how Tubman and those she cared for lived on and used the property, including the discovery of a previously unknown brick kiln and clay borrow pits (Locus 6); the rediscovery of important buildings such as John Brown Hall (Locus 3), which was of critical importance as the primary dormitory of the Home; and

---

10. However, tea wares were not found at the white wood-frame house (Locus 2). This house was rented out to others until just before Tubman died and was not refurbished for use as a dormitory for the Home for the Aged until after her death. Hence, the Lace-pattern tea wares appear to be a marker of activities across the two Tubman properties during her life but were not a part of the post-Tubman-era restoration and outfitting of the properties.

the recovery via remote sensing of the foundation and basement to a structure (Locus 4) that probably burned in a house fire in 1902. We have explored many of these contexts, but others, such as the structure at Locus 4, remain undisturbed but protected for future research. Perhaps most exciting from an archaeological standpoint was the realization that so much archaeological data associated with Tubman's house, barn, yard, and associated features survived at these sites, each artifact and feature yielding both significant new information on the trajectory, events, and interaction of Tubman's life on the property as well as the discrete information connected to that unique artifact and artifact grouping.

Evan as this book is being prepared for publication, research at the site is ongoing, and restoration aimed at public interpretation is under way. In late 2019, excavations took place in the front yard of Tubman's brick house prior to the digging of a new gas line. It yielded additional ash deposits as well as burned household items from the 1880 fire. Also, restoration of the Thompson AME Zion Church and parsonage is under way, and excavations were conducted in the front yard and curbside prior to the construction of new walkways, yielding deposits of construction-era brick and window glass as well as the rediscovery of street-side curbstones over which Harriet Tubman's funeral procession passed on the way to her final resting place in Fort Hill Cemetery in Auburn (D. Armstrong and A. Armstrong 2020).

Reflecting on Tubman in the Setting of Her House and Her Home

This interpretive study of Harriet Tubman in Central New York has drawn upon the material record and cultural landscape of her properties as well as on an array of historical accounts, census data, and information on those with whom she interacted in her house, at her Home, within her community, and on a broader national scale. It is a story of the inspirational life of Harriet Tubman and the final fifty years of her life lived in freedom and dignity. Her continuous dedication to individual freedom and collective social justice was played out in the way she lived her life and can still be seen in the material and spatial context of the artifacts of her life and in the historical evidence of her deeds over more than fifty years in residence in Fleming and Auburn, New York.[11] This approach to life is repeatedly and explicitly expressed in the

---

11. As this book goes to press, new generations have recently been shocked into action to address many of the same problems that Tubman confronted regarding human rights and

archaeological record of how she lived and how she interacted with others as well as in contemporaneous accounts of her unbounded generosity. The collective record clearly projects her undaunted faith, her spiritual intellect, and her dedication to life lived in freedom and liberty by all, most specifically by those whose freedoms were and are challenged, including her fellow African Americans, women of the presuffrage era in which she lived, and, more generally, the poor, the aged, the sick, and the infirm, for whom this era offered very little support and protection.

You have now read an account of Harriet Tubman's life in Auburn and Fleming, New York, from 1859 to 1913 as well as the ongoing sagas associated with her Home and its ultimate recognition as a significant National Historic Landmark and National Historic Park. I ask you to reflect on Tubman's life and imagine the setting of Harriet Tubman's farm and the adjacent Home for the Aged in 1908, the year John Brown Hall opened. Imagine walking up her driveway and meeting Harriet Tubman in her later years. She is standing by the porch of her brick farmhouse, hands full of produce or the tools of her latest task. The farm is full of life. There are the smells of cooking and the background sounds of hogs and chickens in the yard. She has one eye on the children in her care, who are busying themselves playing marbles on the front walk, while she engages an elderly woman in her charge. Tubman greets you and asks you to join her on the steps of her porch, where she welcomes you and asks you to look out across the adjacent farm to the back of the property at a brick building that she calls John Brown Hall, which has just been refurbished by the women and men of the AME Zion Church in fulfillment of her dream for a home and care facility for aging African Americans. As you sit with her, or, perhaps more likely, as you try to keep up with her movement around her farm, she regales you with stories of her abolitionist past, her views on women's rights, and her goals for her home for the elderly. She might even recount one of her spiritual dreams or break into poetic song. Perhaps she hands you an apple from her farm, but if there is an immediate need within the household, she is not shy in soliciting support from you, your church, or your school. When you depart, perhaps with a photograph of Tubman in hand, you have much to think about. Are you inspired by the breadth of her experiences, the importance of her work, and the depth of her spirit? Or do you wonder why she is compelled to share her worldly goods and care for

---

social inequality and to demand that society take action to ensure that society as a whole recognize that Black Lives Matter.

13.1. Secretary of Interior Sally Jewell signing document formally establishing the Harriet Tubman National Historical Park on January 10, 2017. Photograph by D. Armstrong.

those in need? As you walk away, can you hear Tubman break into a song of jubilation as she and her household get back to the work at hand?

Harriet Tubman's life serves as an inspiration, and the Harriet Tubman Home that she established remains hallowed land, consecrated by the actions of a free woman reinforced by her community as she supported those around her. Archaeological remains recovered from the property, including buildings, foundations, and small broken pieces of this and that allow us to reconstruct the actions and details of Tubman's daily life. The study of the ruins on Tubman's farms allows us to piece together the texture and context of a landscape that is worth reconstructing and saving, so that we remember and reinforce the values Tubman continues to represent. It is hoped that these details of a life lived in freedom, passion, exuberance, and concern for others provide inspiration and challenge you to emulate Tubman—to find worthy causes and take actions aimed at achieving social justice, furthering causes of freedom, and improving the lives of those around you.

APPENDIXES
REFERENCES
INDEX

People and Activities
at the Harriet Tubman Home

The data in the appendix tables were compiled from *Auburn City Directory*, 1896–1939, Cayuga County Historian's Office, Auburn, New York; US and New York State censuses, 1900–1930, Auburn and Fleming, Cayuga County, New York, Cayuga County Historian's Office; "Conference and Thompson Memorial, Parker Street AME Zion Church Register, Auburn, 1892–1938," Harriet Tubman Home Collection, Harriet Tubman Home, Inc., Auburn, New York; and newspaper accounts.

APPENDIX A

Residents at the Harriet Tubman Home, 1896–1925

Owner / Relative / Assisted Resident* / Boarder	1896	1897	1898	1899	1900	1901	1902	1903	1904	1905	1906	1907	1908	1909	1910	1911	1912	1913	1914	1915	1916	1917	1918	1919	1920	1921	1922	1923	1924	1925	Information	Race/ Color **	Age at Death
Harriet Tubman (owner, assisted resident)					87					90						97															Died 10 March 1913 John Brown Hall	B	91
William Stewart (brother)					70					70					90																1911 removed to County Almshouse, Sennett. Died 1912	B	82
Kate [Kay] Stewart [Northrup] (relative)					6					16																					1905 away at school	B	
Mary Wright [Knight] (boarder)					74					80																					1900 and 1905 censuses	B	
Max Shaw (relative]					8																										child in home	B	
Caroline Blane (boarder/assisted resident)										90																					1905 census only	B	
Robert J. Newberg (boarder/assisted resident)										28																					on census only, day laborer	B	
Anna Newberg (boarder/assisted resident)										30																					on census only, servant	B	
woman - name unknown (boarder/assisted resident)																															caused disturbance, removed by police (*Auburn Citizen* 1906)	B	
Ursula Johnson (assisted resident)																															resident at Tubman Home (*Auburn Citizen* 1909)	B	
Margarette Printey (Tubman's nurse)															70																Tubman's nurse (1910 census defines her as a servant)	W	
James Smith (boarder/assisted resident)															63																1911 removed to County Almshouse, Sennett. Died 1912	B	65
James Whitman (boarder/inmate)															85																1910 census only	B	
Mrs. Rebecca Leiss [Cross] (widowed)															70																	B	
Mrs. Maria Jones, widow of James R. Jones (assisted resident)															74																Died 1 August 1917, 1 Danforth	M	81
Mrs. Susan Van Schaick (assisted resident)																															Refused to stay at Tubman Home. Sent to Oxford	B	
Elizabeth Shepherd (assisted resident)																															Died 16 November. 1917, Elmira (*Auburn Citizen* 17 Nov. 1917)	B	
John L. Jackson (assisted resident)																															Moved to John Brown Hall, died 2 March 1913 at John Brown Hall	B	
Mrs. Winifred Johnson (assisted resident)																															Died 27 March 1915, John Brown Hall, Elmira (*Auburn Citizen*)	B	113
Jane Cornell (assisted resident)																															Died 18 July 1819, 1 Danforth	B	73
Mrs. Christina Van Slack, widow of William (assisted resident)																										78					Died 25 April 1924, 1 Danforth	B	82
Mrs. Isabel Berry, widow of Robert R., (assisted resident)																										91					Died 3 December 1921, 1 Danforth	B	90
Anna Graham (assisted resident)																															Died 28 July, 1921, 1 Danforth	B	82

* Referred to at the time as inmates   ** B: Black; M: Mixed; NAT: Native American; W: white

Tubman Residence (Locus 1)   John Brown Hall (Locus 3)   Legacy House (white wood frame house, Locus 2)

Year of death   90 Age recorded in census

(continued on following page)

417

Owner / Relative / Assisted Resident* / Boarder	1896	1897	1898	1899	1900	1901	1902	1903	1904	1905	1906	1907	1908	1909	1910	1911	1912	1913	1914	1915	1916	1917	1918	1919	1920	1921	1922	1923	1924	1925	Information	Race/ Color **	Age at Death
Mrs. Harriet Jefferson (assisted resident)																									78						Moved to Moravia 1921	B	79
Mrs. Nettie Tylor, widow of John (assisted resident)																									75						Died 16 May 1923, 1 Danforth	B	75
Heather Mountpleasant (assisted resident)																									70						Not listed in 1921	NAT	
Jane Decker (assisted resident)																															Died 27 February 1923, 1 Danforth, Binghamton (*Auburn Citizen*)	B	76

* Referred to at the time as inmates   ** B: Black; M: Mixed; NAT: Native American; W: white

Tubman Residence (Locus 1)   John Brown Hall (Locus 3)   Legacy House (white wood frame house, Locus 2)

Year of death   90 Age recorded in census

APPENDIX B

Superintendents or Supervisors of the Harriet Tubman Home, 1896–1930

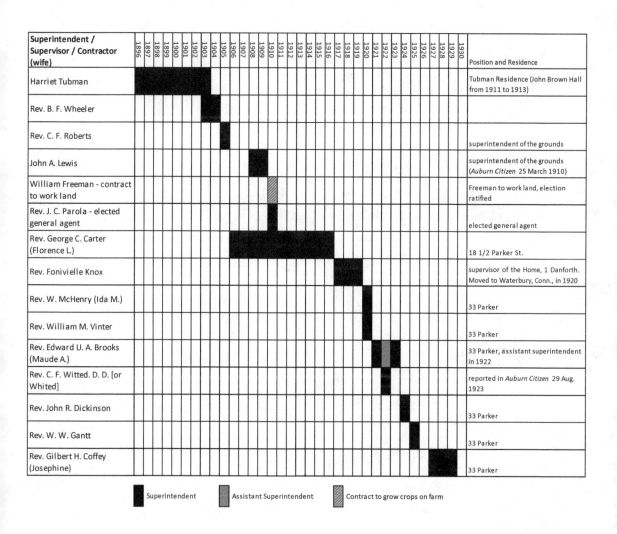

Superintendent / Supervisor / Contractor (wife)	1896–1930	Position and Residence
Harriet Tubman		Tubman Residence (John Brown Hall from 1911 to 1913)
Rev. B. F. Wheeler		
Rev. C. F. Roberts		superintendent of the grounds
John A. Lewis		superintendent of the grounds (*Auburn Citizen* 25 March 1910)
William Freeman - contract to work land		Freeman to work land, election ratified
Rev. J. C. Parola - elected general agent		elected general agent
Rev. George C. Carter (Florence L.)		18 1/2 Parker St.
Rev. Fonivielle Knox		supervisor of the Home, 1 Danforth. Moved to Waterbury, Conn., in 1920
Rev. W. McHenry (Ida M.)		33 Parker
Rev. William M. Vinter		33 Parker
Rev. Edward U. A. Brooks (Maude A.)		33 Parker, assistant superintendent in 1922
Rev. C. F. Witted. D. D. [or Whited]		reported in *Auburn Citizen* 29 Aug. 1923
Rev. John R. Dickinson		33 Parker
Rev. W. W. Gantt		33 Parker
Rev. Gilbert H. Coffey (Josephine)		33 Parker

Legend: ■ Superintendent   ■ Assistant Superintendent   ▨ Contract to grow crops on farm

Harriet Tubman Home Board of Directors 1896–1925

Board of Trustees	1896	1897	1898	1899	1900	1901	1902	1903	1904	1905	1906	1907	1908	1909	1910	1911	1912	1913	1914	1915	1916	1917	1918	1919	1920	1921	1922	1923	1924	1925	Position, Residence
Bishop Alexander Waters	█																														New Jersey
Rev. James E. Mason	█							█			█			█	█			█	█	█								█			1896 and 1923 chairman, Rochester, NY
Rev. G. C. Carter	█									█	█																				Wilkes-Barre, PA, 1907 vice chair and agent
Rev. B. F. Wheeler	█							█																							1903 superintendent, Ithaca and Auburn, NY
Rev. E. U. A. Brooks	█													█	█	█	█	█													Lived in Auburn, Elmira, and Saratoga, NY
Judge George Underwood	█							▓																							attorney for Home, Auburn, NY
Rev. W. A. Ely	█																														1896 president, Syracuse, NY
Rev. M. H. Ross	█																														first vice president, Elmira, NY
Rev. S. L. Carruthers	█																														2nd vice president, Rochester, NY
Rev. J. H. Anderson	█																														3rd vice president, Elmira, NY
Cyrenus Wheeler Jr.	█																														treasurer, former mayor of Auburn, NY
Dr. Brainard	█																														
Dr. Ivy	█																														
Dr. Beecher	█																														
Dr. Hopkins	█																														
John H. Osborne					█			▓			█	█																			treasurer, Auburn, NY
Bishop James Walker Hood								█																							
Bishop Alexander Walters								█	█	█	█	█																			president of general committee
Bishop George Wylie								█																							
Bishop J. B. Small								█																							
Hon. J. C. Dancy								█																							
Rev. Dr. Martin R. Franklin								█																							
J. S. Caldwell								█																							
C. A. Small								█																							
Prof. Robert W. Taylor								█																							
R. J. Frazier								█																							
Board of Bishops								█	█																						nine-member board
Hon. Thomas M. Osborne								▓																							
Mr. Meeker [Meaker]								▓																							used as a reference for fundraising
Dr. Stewart								█																							
Rev. C. A. Smith											█	█																			1907 secretary, local board
James Dale											█	█			█	█															1907 president, 1910 treasurer
William Freeman											█	█						█													1907 vice chairman
Thomas Freeman											█																				
J. Lewis											█	█																			

█ : Board Members   ▓ : Proposed Board Members (not seated)

(continued on following page)

Matrons and Spouses at the Harriet Tubman Home, 1908–27

Matron (and spouses)	1908	1909	1910	1911	1912	1913	1914	1915	1916	1917	1918	1919	1920	1921	1922	1923	1924	1925	1926	1927	Details	Race / Color
Asa Lewis (and John Lewis, husband)	▨																					Black
Doreas Griger (and Shaburn Griger, husband)		▨	▨																		moved to Geneva in 1910; Shaburn served as the Home's carpenter	Mixed
Frances Brown				▨									■	■								Black
Frances Smith					▨																	Black
Agnes E. Mickens						▨																Black
Mary Freeman							■	■													moved to Chicago, Illinois	Black
Elizabeth Dale (widow of James G. Dale)									■	■											died 3 November 1918, 1 Danforth, also treasurer of Board of Lady Managers	Black
Jesse Cooper and George Cooper, husband)											■										laborer at Home but was removed from his position	Black
Emma Johnson (and George Johnson, husband)														■	■							Black
Sarah Penn																■						Black
Annie Jackson (and housekeeper)																	■	■	■		left at the end of 1925 or in early 1926	Black

▨ : John Brown Hall, Locus 3   ■ : Legacy House, white-wood frame house, Locus 2

Renters on Harriet Tubman Home Properties, 1900–1937

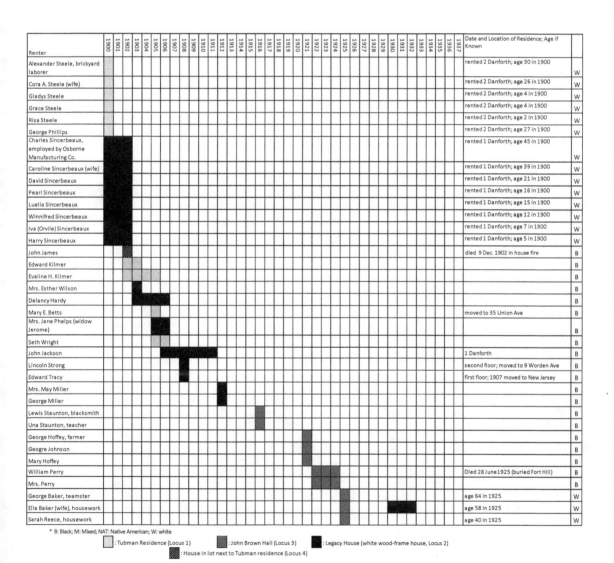

Renter	Date and Location of Residence; Age if Known	*
Alexander Steele, brickyard laborer	rented 2 Danforth; age 30 in 1900	W
Cora A. Steele (wife)	rented 2 Danforth; age 26 in 1900	W
Gladys Steele	rented 2 Danforth; age 4 in 1900	W
Grace Steele	rented 2 Danforth; age 4 in 1900	W
Risa Steele	rented 2 Danforth; age 2 in 1900	W
George Phillips	rented 2 Danforth; age 27 in 1900	W
Charles Sincerbeaux, employed by Osborne Manufacturing Co.	rented 1 Danforth; age 45 in 1900	W
Caroline Sincerbeaux (wife)	rented 1 Danforth; age 39 in 1900	W
David Sincerbeaux	rented 1 Danforth; age 21 in 1900	W
Pearl Sincerbeaux	rented 1 Danforth; age 16 in 1900	W
Luella Sincerbeaux	rented 1 Danforth; age 15 in 1900	W
Winnifred Sincerbeaux	rented 1 Danforth; age 12 in 1900	W
Iva (Orvile) Sincerbeaux	rented 1 Danforth; age 7 in 1900	W
Harry Sincerbeaux	rented 1 Danforth; age 5 in 1900	W
John James	died 9 Dec. 1902 in house fire	B
Edward Kilmer		B
Evaline H. Kilmer		B
Mrs. Esther Wilson		B
Delancy Hardy		B
Mary E. Betts	moved to 35 Union Ave	B
Mrs. Jane Phelps (widow Jerome)		B
Seth Wright		B
John Jackson	1 Danforth	B
Lincoln Strong	second floor; moved to 9 Worden Ave	B
Edward Tracy	first floor; 1907 moved to New Jersey	B
Mrs. May Miller		B
George Miller		B
Lewis Staunton, blacksmith		B
Una Staunton, teacher		B
George Hoffey, farmer		B
Geogre Johnson		B
Mary Hoffey		B
William Perry	Died 28 June 1925 (buried Fort Hill)	B
Mrs. Perry		B
George Baker, teamster	age 64 in 1925	W
Ella Baker (wife), housework	age 58 in 1925	W
Sarah Reece, housework	age 40 in 1925	W

* B: Black; M: Mixed; NAT: Native American; W: white

▢ : Tubman Residence (Locus 1)   ▩ : John Brown Hall (Locus 3)   ■ : Legacy House (white wood-frame house, Locus 2)
▨ : House in lot next to Tubman residence (Locus 4)

(continued on following page)

425

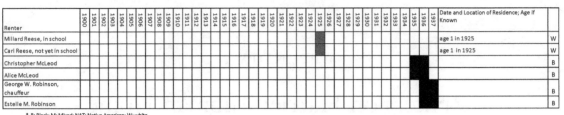

Renter	1900	1901	1902	1903	1904	1905	1906	1907	1908	1909	1910	1911	1912	1913	1914	1915	1916	1917	1918	1919	1920	1921	1922	1923	1924	1925	1926	1927	1928	1929	1930	1931	1932	1933	1934	1935	1936	1937	Date and Location of Residence; Age if Known	
Millard Reese, in school																										■													age 1 in 1925	W
Carl Reese, not yet in school																										■													age 1 in 1925	W
Christopher McLeod																																				■				B
Alice McLeod																																					■			B
George W. Robinson, chauffeur																																					■			B
Estelle M. Robinson																																					■			B

* B: Black; M: Mixed; NAT: Native American; W: white

▢ : Tubman Residence (Locus 1)   ▨ : John Brown Hall (Locus 3)   ■ : Legacy House (white wood-frame house, Locus 2)

▨ : House in lot next to Tubman residence (Locus 4)

APPENDIX F

Pastors of Thompson AME Zion Church on Parker Street, Auburn, New York, 1896–1930

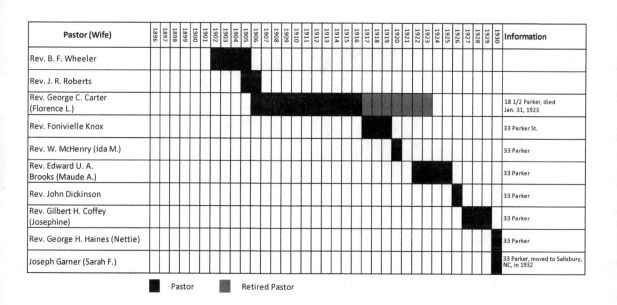

Pastor (Wife)	1896	1897	1898	1899	1900	1901	1902	1903	1904	1905	1906	1907	1908	1909	1910	1911	1912	1913	1914	1915	1916	1917	1918	1919	1920	1921	1922	1923	1924	1925	1926	1927	1928	1929	1930	Information
Rev. B. F. Wheeler							■	■	■																											
Rev. J. R. Roberts										■																										
Rev. George C. Carter (Florence L.)											■	■	■	■	■	■	■	■	■	■	■	▨	▨	▨	▨	▨	▨									18 1/2 Parker, died Jan. 31, 1923
Rev. Fonivielle Knox																						■														33 Parker St.
Rev. W. McHenry (Ida M.)																										■										33 Parker
Rev. Edward U. A. Brooks (Maude A.)																											■	■								33 Parker
Rev. John Dickinson																														■						33 Parker
Rev. Gilbert H. Coffey (Josephine)																																■				33 Parker
Rev. George H. Haines (Nettie)																																		■		33 Parker
Joseph Garner (Sarah F.)																																			■	33 Parker, moved to Salisbury, NC, in 1932

■ Pastor ▨ Retired Pastor

Board of Lady Managers, Harriet Tubman Home, 1903–28

Board of Lady Managers	1903	1904	1905	1906	1907	1908	1909	1910	1911	1912	1913	1914	1915	1916	1917	1918	1919	1920	1921	1922	1923	1924	1925	1926	1927	1928	Information
Mrs. Henry T. Johnson				■	■	■	■	■				■	■														1910 secretary, "Lady's Auxillary"
Mrs. James Dale			■	■	■	■	■	■	■	■	■	■	■														1910–1915 treasurer
Mrs. Myron A. Baker				■	■	■																					1908 corresponding secretary
Harriet Tubman				■	■																						in absentia
Frances Smith				■	■		■		■			■															1911 president, 1914 matron
Mrs. Thomas Freeman					■	■																					1911 president
Mrs. Mary Ball					■	■																					
Mrs. J. A. Lewis					■	■																					
Mrs. S. Grigor					■																						also matron
Mrs. D. F. Diggs					■																						
Mrs. J. H. Washington					■																						1910 vice president
Mrs. M. H. Ross					■	■						■															1910 corresponding secretary
Mrs. E. U. A. Brooks						■																					
Mrs. C. Goodlow						■																					
Mrs. C. A. Cannon												■															1914 president
Mrs. Elmer Cooper												■															1914 vice president
Mrs. C. S. Mathews												■	■														1914 recording secretary
Mrs. F. A. Ridgeway												■															
Mrs. Sarah Reid												■															
Mrs. Fred Johnson												■															Elmira, NY
Mrs. Ella Belcher												■															Ithaca, NY
Mrs. R. Hawkins												■	■														Geneva, NY
Mrs. L. Stanton												■															
Mrs. Emma Nelson												■															
Mrs. Francis Brown												■															
Mrs. Laura Freedman												■															

References

Archival and Primary Source Material

Boston Public Library.
    Anti-Slavery Collection.
Boston University Library, Special Collections.
    Franklin B. Sanford Collection.
Cayuga County Clerk's Office. Auburn, NY.
    Cayuga County Clerk's Deeds Books.
    Cayuga County Tax Records, 1860–90.
    Town of Fleming Tax Rolls, 1855–1915.
Cayuga County Historian's Office. Auburn, NY.
    Auburn City Directory, City of Auburn, 1860–1930. Published in various years
        by Boyd's, Hamilton and Child's, Fitzgerald's, and Laney.
    Auburn City Maps. 1837, 1859, 1871, 1882, 1904.
    Town of Fleming Maps. 1853, 1859, 1875, 1904.
Cayuga County Historical Society. Auburn, NY.
Cayuga County Museum. Auburn, NY.
Cayuga County Records Office. Auburn, NY.
New York State Census, 1855–57, 1865, 1874–75, 1905. Auburn and Fleming, Ca-
    yuga County, NY.
    United States Census, 1840–1940. Auburn and Fleming, NY.
City of Auburn, Health Department, Bureau of Vital Statistics. Auburn, NY.
Cornell University. Ithaca, NY.
    Emily Howland Papers. Howland Museum, Sherwood, NY.
Du Bois National Historic Site. Great Barrington, MA.
Harriet Tubman Home, Inc., Harriet Tubman Home Collection. Auburn, NY.
"Conference and Thompson Memorial, Parker Street AME Zion Church Register,
    Auburn, 1892–1938."
    Stewart Family Papers.
Harvard University, Houghton Library. Cambridge, MA.
    Siebert, Wilbur. Manuscript materials. 1898.

Library of Congress. Washington, DC.
    Rare Book and Special Collections Division.
        Elizabeth Smith Miller and Anne Fitzhugh Miller Collection.
        Franklin Sanborn Papers.
        Susan B. Anthony Collection.
New York Public Library, Schomburg Center for Research in Black Culture. New York.
    Earl Conrad/Harriet Tubman Collection.
Onondaga Historical Association. Syracuse, NY.
Seward House and Cayuga Community College. Auburn, NY.
    William H. Seward Papers.
Smith College Library. Northampton, MA.
    Sophia Smith Collection.
        Garrison Family Papers.
        Helen Tufts Bailie Papers.
        Wright Family Papers.
Stewart Family Collection. Papers collected by Judith Bryant. Auburn, NY.
Syracuse University, Special Collections Research Center. Syracuse, NY.
    Bishop William Walls Papers. African Methodist Episcopal Zion Church.
    Osborne Family Papers.
    William Gould Diary. 1859. Copy also at Onondaga Historical Association, Syracuse, NY.
University of Massachusetts, Robert S. Cox Special Collections and University Archives. Amherst.
    James Aronson Collection of W. E. B. Du Bois.
University of Michigan, William L. Clements Library. Ann Arbor.
    Rochester Ladies' Anti-Slavery Society Papers.
    Seward Collection.
University of Rochester, Rush Rhees Library. Rochester, NY.
    William Seward Collection.

Newspaper Articles

Copies of the following newspapers are available at the Harriet Tubman Home, Auburn, NY, and in the Archaeology Laboratory, Syracuse Univ., Syracuse, NY. Many are also available online at http://fultonhistory.com.

Auburn Advertiser-Journal   *Auburn Daily Bulletin*
Auburn Bulletin   *Auburn Democrat Argus*
Auburn Citizen   *Auburn Evening Recorder*
Auburn Daily Advertiser   *Auburn Herald*

Auburn Morning News

Auburn News and Bulletin

Auburn Semi-Monthly Journal

Auburn Semi-Weekly

Auburn Weekly Bulletin

Auburn Weekly News and Democrat

Baltimore News American

Brooklyn Daily Eagle

Cayuga Chief (Weedsport, NY)

Cayuga County Independent

Christian Recorder

Evening Auburnian

Liberator

New York Age

New York Daily Tribune

New York Evening Telegram

New York Sun

New York Times

Poughkeepsie Daily Eagle

Rochester Democrat and Chronicle

Syracuse Daily Journal

Syracuse Evening Telegram

Syracuse Herald

Syracuse Post-Standard

Syracuse Sunday Evening Herald

Syracuse Sunday Herald

Union Spring Advertiser

Weekly Auburnian

Secondary Sources

Adams, William H. 1990. "Landscape Archaeology, Landscape History, and the American Farmstead." *Historical Archaeology* 24, no. 4: 92–101.

Agbe-Davies, Anna S. 2010. "Concepts of Community in the Pursuit of an Inclusive Archaeology." *International Journal of Heritage Studies* 16, no. 6: 373–89.

———. 2011. "Reaching for Freedom, Seizing Responsibility: Archaeology at the Phillis Wheatley Home for Girls, Chicago." In *The Materiality of Freedom: Archaeologies of Postemancipation Life*, edited by Jodi A. Barnes, 69–87. Columbia: Univ. of South Carolina Press.

———. 2017. "Where Tradition and Pragmatism Meet: African Diaspora Archaeology at the Crossroads." *Historical Archaeology* 51, no. 1: 9–27.

Amott, Theresa, and Julie Matthaei. 1999. *Race, Gender, and Work: A Multi-cultural Economic History of Women in the United States*. Rev. ed. Boston: South End Press.

Anderson, Robert V. 1996a. "The Kelsey-Harvey Brickyard, Auburn, New York. Part 1." *Crooked Lake Review*, June. At http://www.crookedlakereview.com /articles/67_100/99june1996/99anderson.html.

———. 1996b. "The Kelsey-Harvey Brickyard, Auburn, New York. Part 2." *Crooked Lake Review*, June. At http://www.crookedlakereview.co/articles/67_100/99 june1996/99anderson.html.

———. 1996c. "The Kelsey-Harvey Brickyard, Auburn, New York. Part 3." *Crooked Lake Review*, June. At http://www.crookedlakereview.com/articles/67_100/99 june1996/99anderson.html.

Aplin, Graham. 2002. *Heritage Identification, Conservation, and Management*. Oxford: Oxford Univ. Press.

Armstrong, Alan D. 2011. "Bricks and Brick Making at the Harriet Tubman Home: Archaeology, History, and Neutron Activation Analysis." Capstone Project submitted in partial fulfillment of the requirements of the Renée Crown Univ. Honors Program, Syracuse Univ.

Armstrong, Alan D., and Douglas V. Armstrong. 2012. "Craft Enterprise and the Harriet Tubman Home." *Journal of African American Archaeology and Heritage* 1, no. 1: 41–78.

Armstrong, Douglas V. 1991. "The Afro-Jamaican House-Yard: An Archaeological and Ethnohistorical Perspective." *Florida Journal of Anthropology* 7:51–63.

———. 2003a. *Creole Transformation from Slavery to Freedom: Historical Archaeology of the East End Community, St. John, Virgin Islands.* Gainesville: Univ. Press of Florida.

———. 2003b. "Patterns in the Snow." *Dig* 5, no. 1: 28–30.

———. 2003c. "Preliminary Archaeological Survey and Reconnaissance at the Harriet Tubman Home, Auburn and Fleming, New York." Archaeological Research Center, Anthropology Department, Maxwell School, Syracuse Univ.

———. 2008. "Archaeological Testing in the Area of the Tubman Era Shed behind Harriet Tubman's Brick Residence: The Harriet Tubman Home, Auburn and Fleming, New York." Cultural Resource Assessment Report submitted to the Harriet Tubman Home, Inc. Archaeological Research Center, Anthropology Department, Maxwell School, Syracuse Univ.

———. 2010. "Degrees of Freedom in the Caribbean: Archaeological Explorations of Transitions from Slavery." *Antiquity* 84:146–60.

———. 2011. "Excavating Inspiration: Archaeology of the Harriet Tubman Home." In *The Materiality of Freedom: Archaeologies of Postemancipation Life*, edited by Jodi Barnes, 263–76. Columbia: Univ. of South Carolina Press.

———. 2015. "Harriet Tubman's Farmsteads in Central New York: Archaeological Explorations Relating to an American Icon." In *The Limits of Tyranny: Archaeological Perspectives on the Struggle against New World Slavery*, edited by James Delle, 147–74. Knoxville: Univ. of Tennessee Press.

Armstrong, Douglas V., and Alan. D. Armstrong. 2020. "Thompson AME Zion Church and Parsonage HART 2019 B): Archaeological Investigation." Report on archaeological testing at Harriet Tubman National Park carried out by Syracuse Univ. for the US National Park Service, Northeastern Region, Historical Architecture, Conservation, and Engineering Center. Historic Structures, Research, and Documentation Branch, Lowell, MA.

Armstrong, Douglas V., and Anna Hill. 2009. "Uncovering Inspiration: Current Archaeological Investigations of Harriet Tubman in Central New York." *African Diaspora Archaeology Network Newsletter* 12, no. 2: article 21.

Armstrong, Douglas V., and LouAnn Wurst. 2003. "Clay Faces in an Abolitionist Church: The Wesleyan Methodist Church in Syracuse, New York." *Historical Archaeology* 37, no. 2: 19–37.

Armstrong, Douglas V., LouAnn Wurst, and Elizabeth Kellar. 2000. *Archaeological Sites and Preservation Planning in Central New York*. Pebbles Island, NY: New York State Historic Preservation Office.

Auwaerter, John. 2018. "Cultural Landscape Report, Harriet Tubman National Park." First draft, Sept. Olmsted Center for Landscape Preservation, US National Park Service, Lowell, MA.

Balloting Book and Other Documents Relating to Military Bounty Lands in the State of New York. [1825] 1983. Reprint. Ovid, NY: Morrison.

Barile, Kerri S., and Jamie C. Brandon, eds. 2004. *Household Chores and Household Choices: Theorizing the Domestic Sphere in Historical Archaeology*. Tuscaloosa: Univ. of Alabama Press.

Barnes, Jodi A., ed. 2011. *The Materiality of Freedom: Archaeologies of Postemancipation Life*. Columbia: Univ. of South Carolina Press.

Battle-Baptiste, Whitney. 2011. *Black Feminist Archaeology*. Walnut Creek, CA: Left Cost Press.

Beardsley Design Associates. 2002. *Harriet Tubman Cultural Research and Retreat Center, Auburn, New York*. Brochure designed on behalf of the Harriet Tubman Home. Auburn, NY: Beardsley Design Associates.

Beaudry, Mary C. 1996. "Reinventing Historical Archaeology." In *Historical Archaeology and the Study of Material Culture*, edited by Lou Ann DeCunzo and Bernard L. Herman, 473–97. Winterthur, DE: Henry Francis du Pont Winterthur Museum.

———. 2004. "Doing the Housework: New Approaches to the Archaeology of the Household." In *Household Chores and Household Choices: Theorizing the Domestic Sphere in Historical Archaeology*, edited by Kerri S. Barile and Jamie C. Brandon, 54–62. Tuscaloosa: Univ. of Alabama Press.

Beisaw, April M., and James G. Gibb, eds. 2009. *The Archaeology of Institutional Life*. Tuscaloosa: Univ. of Alabama Press.

Bodner, Connie Cox. 1990. *The Development of 19th Century Agricultural Practices and Their Manifestations in Farmsteads in the Genesee River Valley*. Rochester, NY: Rochester Museum & Science Center.

Bourdieu, Pierre. 1977. "Structures and the Habitus." In *Outline of a Theory of Practice*, translated by R. Nice, 72–95. Cambridge: Cambridge Univ. Press.

Bradford, Sarah H. 1869. *Scenes in the Life of Harriet Tubman*. Auburn, NY: W. J. Moses, Printer.

———. 1886. *Harriet: The Moses of Her People*. New York: George R. Lockwood and Sons.

———. [1886] 1897. *Harriet Tubman: Moses of Her People*. Reprint. New York: Corinth Books.

———. 1901. *Harriet: The Moses of Her People* . New York: J. J. Little.

———. [1886] 1993. *Harriet Tubman: The Moses of Her People*. Reprint. Bedford, MA: Applewood Books.

————. [1886] 2004. *Harriet Tubman: The Moses of Her People*. Reprint. Mineola, NY: Dover.

Brandon, Jamie C., and Kerri S. Barile. 2004. "Introduction: Household Chores; or, the Chore of Defining the Household." In *Household Chores and Household Choices: Theorizing the Domestic Sphere in Historical Archaeology*, edited by Kerri S. Barile and Jamie C. Brandon, 1–12. Tuscaloosa: Univ. of Alabama Press.

Brewer, Floyd I. 1989. "Albert Bradt, Tobacco Planter, and the Smoking-Pipe Story in Early Bethlehem, New York." In *Proceedings of the 1989 Smoking Pipe Conference: Selected Papers*, edited by Charles F. Hayes III, 151–61. Rochester, NY: Research Division, Rochester Museum & Science Center.

Brown, Kenneth L. 2011. "BaKongo Cosmograms, Christian Crosses, or None of the Above: An Archaeology of African American Spiritual Adaptation into the 1920s." In *The Materiality of Freedom: Archaeologies of Postemancipation Life*, edited by Jodi A. Barnes, 209–27. Columbia: Univ. of South Carolina Press.

Brumfiel, Elizabeth. 2000. "On the Archaeology of Choice: Agency Studies as a Research Strategy." In *Agency in Archaeology*, edited by Maria-Anne Dobres and John Robb, 249–57. London: Routledge.

Cheney, Ednah Dow. 1865. "Moses." *Freedman's Record* 1:34–38.

————. 1897. "Concerning Women." *Women's Journal*, Apr. 17.

Clarke, James B. 1911. "An Hour with Harriet Tubman." In *Christophe: A Tragedy in Prose of Imperial Haiti*, edited by William Edgar Easton, 113–22. Los Angeles: Grafton.

Clinton, Catherine. 2004. *Harriet Tubman: The Road to Freedom*. New York: Little Brown.

Collins, Patricia Hill. 2009. *Black Feminist Thought: Knowledge, Consciousness, and the Politics of Empowerment*. New York: Routledge.

Comaroff, John, and Jean Comaroff. 1992. *Ethnography and the Historical Imagination*. Boulder, CO: Westview Press.

Conrad, Earl. 1943. *Harriet Tubman: Negro Soldier and Abolitionist*. Washington, DC: Associated Publishers.

Coyle, Katy, David George, Kari Krause, Susan Barrett Smith, Ralph Draughon Jr., James Eberwine, Jean B. Pelletier, et al. 2000. "Historical Research and Remote Sensing of the Former Location of the Braziel Baptist Church and Cemetery Complex (Site 16IV49), Iberville Parish, Louisiana." Report prepared by R. Christopher Goodwin & Associates, Inc., for the US Army Corps of Engineers, New Orleans District.

Crary, John W. 1971. "Selections from Sixty Years of a Brick Maker: A Practical Treatise, 1890." In *Accounts of Brickmaking in America Published between 1850 and 1900*, edited by Joseph Foster, 44–56. New York: Claremont Press.

Crawford, Beth. [2002] 2017. "Timeline/Chronology: Compilation of Primary Materials, Including Auburn Directories and Tax Records, and Secondary Source

Material." Unpublished report prepared for Crawford & Stearns, Architects and Preservation Planners, Syracuse, NY.

Crawford & Stearns, Architects and Preservation Planners. 2002. "Tubman South Street Properties." Unpublished report, Syracuse, NY.

Dabel, Jane E. 2008. *A Respectable Woman: The Public Roles of African American Women in 19th-Century New York.* New York: New York Univ. Press.

Davies, Carole. 2007. *Left of Karl Marx: The Political Life of Black Communist Claudia Jones.* Durham, NC: Duke Univ. Press.

Davis, Lenwood. 1989. *The Black Aged in the United States: A Selectively Annotated Bibliography.* New York: Greenwood Press.

Dawdy, Shannon. 2006. "The Taphonomy of Disaster and the (Re)Formation of New Orleans." *American Anthropologist* 108, no. 4: 719–30.

———. 2010. *Patina: A Profane Archaeology.* Chicago: Univ. of Chicago Press.

Debs, Eugene V. [1914] 1916. "The Coppock Brothers: Heroes of Harper's Ferry." Originally published in *Appeal to Reason*, May 23, 1914. Reprinted in *Labor and Freedom* 1916:39–51. Online at Marxists' Internet Archive, http://www.marxists .org/archive/debs/works/1914/1914-coppock.htm.

De León, Jason. 2015. *The Land of Open Graves: Living and Dying on the Migrant Trail.* Oakland: Univ. of California Press.

Delle, James A., and Kristen R. Fellows. 2012. "A Plantation Transplanted: Archaeological Investigations of a Piedmont-Style Slave Quarter at Rose Hill, Geneva, New York." *Northeast Historical Archaeology* 41, no. 1: 50–74.

Delle, James, Stephen A. Mrozowski, and Robert Paynter, eds. 2000. *Lines That Divide: Historical Archaeologies of Race, Class, and Gender.* Knoxville: Univ. of Tennessee Press.

Dobres, Marcia-Anne, and John Robb. 2000. "Agency in Archaeology: Paradigm or Platitude?" In *Agency in Archaeology*, edited by Maria-Anne Dobres and John Robb, 1–16. London: Routledge.

Dobson, Edward. [1850] 1971. *A Rudimentary Treatise on the Manufacture of Bricks and Tiles.* Facsimile of the 1850 edition published in *Journal of Ceramic History* 5, edited by Francis Celoria. Stafford, PA: George Street Press.

Dobson, Edward, and Charles Tomlinson. 1882. *A Rudimentary Treatise on the Manufacture of Bricks and Tiles.* 7th ed. London: Crosby Lockwood.

Dodson, Howard, and Sylviane A. Diouf, eds. 2004. *In Motion: The African-American Migration Experience.* Schomburg Center for Research in Black Culture. Washington, DC: National Geographic.

Douglass, Frederick. 1852. "What to the Slave Is the Fourth of July?" Speech presented to the Rochester Ladies' Anti-Slavery Society. *The Thistle* 12, no. 2. Online at the MIT Alterative News Collective, http://www.mit.edu/~thistle/v12 /2/douglass.html.

———. 1857. "West India Emancipation." Speech at event commemorating the twenty-third anniversary of emancipation in the West Indies, Aug. 3, Canan-

daigua, NY. Online at Blackpast, https://www.blackpast.org/african-american
-history/1857-frederick-douglass-if-there-no-struggle-there-no-progress/.

———. [1855] 1994. *My Bondage and My Freedom.* In *Douglass: Autobiographies,* edited by Henry Louis Gates Jr., 104–451. New York: Library Classics of America.

Drew, Benjamin. 1856. *The Refugee or the Narratives of Fugitive Slaves in Canada
Related by Themselves with an Account of the History and Condition of the Colored
Population of Upper Canada.* Boston: Jewett.

Du Bois, W. E. B. (William Edward Burghardt). 1903. *The Soul of Black Folks.* Chicago: McClurg.

———. 1913. "David Livingston and Harriet Tubman." *The Crisis* 6, no. 1 (May):
18.

———. [1903] 1994. *The Soul of Black Folks.* New York: Dover.

———. [1909] 2001. *John Brown, 1800–1859.* New York: Random House.

Easton, Edgar William. 1911. "James B. Clarke, Class '12 Cornell University."
In *Christophe: A Tragedy in Prose of Imperial Haiti,* edited by William Edgar
Easton, 106–7. Los Angeles: Grafton.

Eboh, Simeon Onyewueke. 2005. *Inalienability of Land and Citizenship in the African Context: Unity and Diversity in the Age of Globalization.* Frankfort, Germany: Iko Verlag fur Intervulturell.

"Edwin Coppock Memorial at Hope Cemetery, Salem." N.d. At https://testfamily
genealogy.net/History/JohnBrown/EdwinCoppock/Memorial.html. Accessed
Mar. 14, 2022.

Elliot, Rex R., and Stephan C. Gould. 1988. *Hawaiian Bottles of Long Ago.* Hono-
lulu: Hawaiian Services.

Fennel, Christopher. 2007. *Crossroads and Cosmologies: Diasporas and Ethnogenesis
in the New World.* Gainesville: Univ. of Florida Press.

———. 2011. "Examining Structural Racism in the Jim Crow Era of Illinois." In
The Materiality of Freedom: Archaeologies of Postemancipation Life, edited by
Jodi A. Barnes, 173–89. Columbia: Univ. of South Carolina Press.

Ferguson, Leland. 1992. *Uncommon Ground: Archaeology and Early African America, 1650–1800.* Washington, DC: Smithsonian Institution Press.

Franklin, Maria. 1997. "'Power to the People': Sociopolitics and the Archaeology of
Black Americans." *Historical Archaeology* 31, no. 3: 36–50.

———. 2001. "A Black Feminist Inspired Archaeology." *Journal of Social Archaeology* 1, no. 1: 108–25.

Franklin, Maria, and Larry McKee. 2004. "African Diaspora Archaeologies: Present
Insights and Expanding Discourses." *Historical Archaeology* 38, no. 1: 1–9.

Friedberger, Mark. 1988. *Farm Families and Change in Twentieth-Century America.*
Lexington: Univ. Press of Kentucky.

Galbraith, C. B. 1921. "Edwin Coppik." *Ohio Archaeological and Historical Publications* 30:397–449.

Glascock, Michael D. 2010. "An Overview of Neutron Activation Analysis." Univ. of Missouri Research Reactor. At https://www.researchgate.net/publication /228643668_An_overview_of_neutron_activation_analysis.

Green, Rebekah. 1998. "History of Harriet Tubman's Brick House." Cornell University, Ithaca, NY. Paper on file at the Harriet Tubman Home Archives, Auburn, NY.

Groover, Mark D. 2008. *The Archaeology of North American Farmsteads.* Gainesville: Univ. Press of Florida.

Groover, Mark D., and Tylor J. Wolford. 2013. "The Archaeology of Rural Affluence and Landscapes Change at the Clements Farmstead." *Journal of African Diaspora Archaeology and Heritage* 2, no. 2: 131–50.

Gurcke, Karl. 1987. *Bricks and Brickmaking: A Handbook for Historical Archaeology.* Moscow: Univ. of Idaho Press.

Gwaltney, John Langston. 1980. *"Drylongo," a Self-Portrait of Black America.* New York: Vintage Press.

Hardesty, Donald L., and Barbara J. Little. 2000. *Assessing Site Significance: A Guide for Archaeologists and Historians.* New York: AltaMira Press.

Hart, John P. 2000. Preface to *Nineteenth- and Early Twentieth-Century Domestic Site Archaeology in New York State*, edited by John P. Hart and Charles L. Fisher, xi–xiii. New York State Museum Bulletin no. 495. Albany: Univ. of the State of New York, New York State Education Department.

Hazzard, Florence Woolsey. 1971. "Emily Howland." In *Notable American Women*, edited by Edward T. James, Janet Wilson James, and Paul S. Boyers, 229–31. Cambridge: Cambridge Univ. Press.

Hendon, Julia A. 2006. "Living and Working at Home: The Social Archaeology of Household Production and Social Relations." In *A Companion to Social Archaeology*, edited by Lynn Meskell and Robert W. Preucel, 255–71. New York: Wiley-Blackwell.

Home for the Friendless, Auburn, New York. 1866. *Report of the Committee on the Organization of a Home for the Friendless in the City of Auburn with Certificate of Incorporation, Constitution, and By-Laws; December 1865.* Auburn, NY: Advertiser-Journal Print.

———. 1889. *Annual Reports of the Home for the Friendless in the City of Auburn.* Auburn, NY: Advertiser-Journal Print.

———. 1899. *Annual Reports of the Home for the Friendless in the City of Auburn.* Auburn, NY: Advertiser-Journal Print.

———. 1904. *Annual Reports of the Home for the Friendless in the City of Auburn.* Auburn, NY: Advertiser-Journal Print.

———. 1908. *Annual Reports of the Home for the Friendless in the City of Auburn.* Auburn, NY: Advertiser-Journal Print.

———. 1911. *Annual Reports of the Home for the Friendless in the City of Auburn.* Auburn, NY: Advertiser-Journal Print.

————. 1912–13. *Annual Reports of the Home for the Friendless in the City of Auburn, for the Years Ending September 30, 1912, and September 30, 1913.* Auburn, NY: Advertiser-Journal Print.

————. 1915. *Annual Reports of the Home for the Friendless in the City of Auburn.* Auburn, NY: Advertiser-Journal Print.

Howe, Julia W. 1862. "Battle Hymn of the Republic (Words Written by Julia W. Howe in 1861)." *Atlantic Monthly,* Feb.

Huey, Paul R. 2000. "Research Problems and Issues for the Archaeology of Nineteenth-Century Farmstead Sites in New York State." In *Nineteenth- and Early Twentieth-Century Domestic Site Archaeology in New York State,* edited by John P. Hart and Charles L. Fisher, 29–35. New York State Museum Bulletin no. 495. Albany: Univ. of the State of New York, New York State Education Department.

Humez, Jean M. 1993. "In Search of Harriet Tubman's Spiritual Autobiography." *National Women's Studies Association Journal* 5, no. 2: 162–82.

————. 2003. *Harriet Tubman: The Life and the Life Stories.* Madison: Univ. of Wisconsin Press.

Hutton, George V. 2003. *The Great Hudson River Brick Industry: Commemorating Three and a Half Centuries of Brickmaking.* New York: Purple Mountain Press.

Johnson, Matthew. 2010. *Archaeology Theory: An Introduction.* 2nd ed. Chichester, UK: Wiley-Blackwell.

Jones, Joyce Stokes, and Michele Jones Galvin. 2013. *Beyond the Underground: Aunt Harriet, Moses of Her People.* Syracuse, NY: Sankofa Media.

King, Martin Luther, Jr. 1963. "I Have a Dream." Public speech presented at the Lincoln Memorial, Washington, DC, Aug. 28. At https://www.npr.org/2010/01/18/122701268/i-have-a-dream-speech-in-its-entirety.

Klaw, Spencer, 1993. *Without Sin: The Life and Death of the Oneida Community.* New York: Penguin.

Klein, Herbert S. 1999. *The Atlantic Slave Trade.* Cambridge: Cambridge Univ. Press.

Krieger, Rebekah. 2018. "Historic Structure Report Part 1: Thompson African Methodist Episcopal Zion Church." Northeastern Region, Historical Architecture, Conservation, and Engineering Center, Historic Structures, Research, and Documentation Branch, US National Park Service, Lowell, MA.

La Chiusa, Chuck. 2004. "Partial Listing of Buffalo Brickyards and Brands." At http://phwebhosting.com/a/DCRNRY/mat/brick.

————. N.d. "Aurora, New York, Brickyards." History of Buffalo. At http://www.buffaloah.com/a/DCTNRY/mat/brk/aurora/aur.html. Accessed Mar. 11, 2010.

Lamphere, Louise. 1993. "The Domestic Sphere of Women and the Public World of Men: The Strengths and Limitations of an Anthropological Dichotomy." In *Gender in Cross-Cultural Perspective,* 7th ed., edited by Caroline B. Brettell and Carolyn F. Sargent, 97–108. Abingdon, UK: Routledge.

LaRoche, Cheryl J. 2014a. "'As Above, so Below': Ritual and Commemoration in African American Archaeological Contexts in the Northern United States." In

Materialities of Ritual in the Black Atlantic, edited by Akinwumi Ogundiran and Paula Saunders, 296–316. Bloomington: Indiana Univ. Press.

———. 2014b. *Free Black Communities and the Underground Railroad*. Urbana: Univ. of Illinois Press.

Larson, Kate Clifford. 2004. *Bound for the Promised Land: Harriet Tubman, Portrait of an American Hero*. New York: Ballantine Books.

Leone, Mark P. 2005. *The Archaeology of Liberty in an American Capital: Excavations in Annapolis*. Berkeley: Univ. of California Press.

———. 2008. "Overview of Three Reviews of The Archaeology of Liberty in an American Capital: Excavations in Annapolis." *Cambridge Archaeological Journal* 18, no. 1: 102–5.

———. 2010. *Critical Archaeology*. Walnut Creek, CA: Left Coast Press.

Leone, Mark P., and Gladys-Marie Fry. 1999. "Conjuring in the Big House Kitchen: An Interpretation of African American Belief Systems Based on the Uses of Archaeology and Folklore Sources." *Journal of American Folklore* 112, no. 445: 372–403.

Leone, Mark P., Jocelyn E. Knauf, and Amanda Tang. 2014. "Ritual Bundle in Colonial Annapolis." In *Materialities of Ritual in the Black Atlantic*, edited by Akinwumi Ogundiran and Paula Saunders, 296–316. Bloomington: Indiana Univ. Press.

Lincoln, Abraham. 1863. "Gettysburg Address." Nov. 19, Gettysburg, PA. At http://www.abrahamlincolnonline.org/lincoln/speeches/gettysburg.htm.

Little, Barbara J. 2002. *Public Benefits of Archaeology*. Gainesville: Univ. Press of Florida.

———. 2004. "Is the Medium the Message? The Art of Interpreting Archaeology in US National Parks." In *Marketing Heritage: Archaeology and the Consumption of the Past*, edited by Rowan Yorke and Uzi Baram, 269–94. New York: AltaMira Press.

Livingston, James D., and Sherry H. Penney. 2004. *A Very Dangerous Woman: Martha Wright and Women's Rights*. Amherst: Univ. of Massachusetts Press.

Locke, John. [1690] 2012. *The Second Treatise on Civil Government*. At http://oregonstate.edu/instruct/phl302/texts/locke/locke2/2nd-contents.html.

Loguen, Rev. J. W. [1859] 2016. *The Rev. J. W. Loguen, as a Slave and as a Freeman, a Narrative of Real Life*. Edited by Jennifer A. Williamson. Syracuse, NY: Syracuse Univ. Press.

Lowthert, William, IV, Scott Meachem, Nate Patch, Brian Clevan, Jean B. Pelletier, and Katherine Grandine. 1999. "Management Summary for Remote Sensing Investigations at Chapel Park, Frederick, Maryland." Technical summary prepared by R. Christopher Goodwin & Associates, Inc., for the City of Frederick, MD.

———. 2002. "Archival, Architectural, Geophysical Remote Sensing Investigations at the Montevue Property, Frederick, Maryland." Report prepared by R. Christopher Goodwin & Associates, Inc., for the Frederick County Division of Public Works, Frederick, MD.

Marx, Karl, and Frederick Engels. [1888] 2004. *Manifesto of the Communist Party, with a Preface to the 1888 London Edition by Frederick Engels.* Translated by Samuel Moor in cooperation with Frederick Engels. Edited by Andy Blunden. Marxists Internet Archive. At https://www.marxists.org/archive/marx/works/1848/communist-manifesto/.

Matthews, Christopher N. 2019. "Refuge and Support: An Introduction." *Journal of African Diaspora Archaeology and Heritage* 8, nos. 1–2: 1–7.

McGowan, James, and William G. Kashatus. 2011. *Harriet Tubman: A Biography.* Santa Barbara, CA: Greenwood.

McManus, Edgar J. 1966. *A History of Negro Slavery in New York.* Syracuse, NY: Syracuse Univ. Press.

Messineo, Daniel. 2017. "Harriet Tubman's Name Discovered in Old Cayuga Centers' Ledger." *CNY Central,* Mar. 16. At https://cnycentral.com/news/local/harriet-tubmans-name-discovered-in-old-cayuga-centers-ledger.

Miller, Anne Fitzhugh. 1912. "Harriet Tubman: Interesting People." *American Magazine,* Aug., 420–23.

Mrozowski, Stephen A., Grace H. Zeising, and Mary C. Beaudry. 1996. *Living on the Boott: Historical Archaeology at the Boott Cotton Mills, Lowell, Massachusetts.* Amherst: Univ. of Massachusetts Press.

Muller, Nancy Ladd. 1994. "The House of the Black Burghardts: An Investigation of Race, Gender, and Class at the W. E. B. Du Bois Boyhood Homesite." In *Those of Little Note: Gender, Race, and Class in Historical Archaeology,* edited by Elizabeth M. Scott, 81–94. Tucson: Univ. of Arizona Press.

Mullins, Paul R. 1999. *Race and Affluence: An Archaeology of African American Consumer Choice.* New York: Kluwer Academic/Plenum.

———. 2008. "Excavating America's Metaphor: Race, Diaspora, and Vindication Archaeologies." *Historical Archaeology* 42, no. 2: 104–22.

Murphy, James L. 1976. "Reed Stem Tobacco Pipes from Mount Pleasant, Clermont County, Ohio." *Northeast Historical Archaeology* 5, no. 1: 12–27.

Myers, Mildred D. 1998. *Miss Emily: Emily Howland, Teacher of Freed Slaves, Suffragist, and Friend of Susan B. Anthony and Harriet Tubman.* Charlotte Harbor, FL: Tabby House.

National Association of Colored Women's Clubs. 1902. *Official Minutes of the National Federation of Afro-American Women.* Washington, DC: National Association of Colored Women's Clubs.

New York State Board of Charities. 1899. *Annual Report of the State Board of Charities for the Year 1898.* 2 vols. Albany, NY: Wynkoop Hollenbeck Crawford Co. State Printers.

———. 1904. *Thirty-Second Annual Report of the State Charities Aid Association of the State Board of Charities of the State of New York, No. 88 Charities Aid Association.* New York: L. B. Lyon.

————. 1910. *Annual Report of the State Charities for the Year 1909: State Board of Charities of the State of New York*. New York: L. B. Lyon.

————. 1913. *Annual Report of the State Board of Charities for the Year 1912*. Albany, NY: L. B. Lyon.

————. 1914. *Annual Report of the State Board of Charities for the Year 1913*. Albany, NY: L. B. Lyon.

————. 1915. *Annual Report of the State Board of Charities for the Year 1914*. Albany, NY: L. B. Lyon.

————. 1917. *Annual Report of the State Board of Charities for the Year 1916*. Albany, NY: L. B. Lyon.

————. 1918. *Annual Report of the State Board of Charities for the Year 1917*. Albany, NY: L. B. Lyon.

————. 1919. *Annual Report of the State Board of Charities for the Year 1918*. Albany, NY: L. B. Lyon.

————. 1922. *Fifty-Fifth Annual Report of the State Board of Charities for the Year 1921*. Albany, NY: L. B. Lyon.

Ogundiran, Akinwumi, and Paula Saunders, eds. 2014a. *Materialities of Ritual in the Black Atlantic*. Bloomington: Indiana Univ. Press.

————. 2014b. "On the Materiality of Black Atlantic Rituals." In *Materialities of Ritual in the Black Atlantic*, edited by Akinwumi Ogundiran and Paula Saunders, 1–27. Bloomington: Indiana Univ. Press.

Oneida Limited. 2022. "History of Oneida Limited." At http://www.oneida.com.

Oneida Community. 2022. "Our History: History of the Oneida Community." At http://oneidacommunity.org/our history.

Orser, Charles, ed. 1988. *The Material Basis of the Postbellum Plantation: Historical Archaeology on the South Carolina Piedmont*. Athens: Univ. of Georgia Press.

Paige, John C., and David A. Kimball. 1986. "The Liberty Bell: A Special History Study." Unpublished study for the US National Park Service, Denver, on file at Independence National Historical Park, Philadelphia.

Paine, Thomas. [1774] 2003. *Common Sense, the Rights of Man*. New York: Signet Classics.

Painter, Nell Irwin. 1997. *Sojourner Truth: A Life, a Symbol*. New York: Norton.

Paynter, Robert. 1982. *Models of Spatial Inequality: Settlement Patterns in Historical Archaeology*. New York: Academic Press.

Pena, Elizabeth S. 2000. "Prospects for the Archaeology of Nineteenth-Century Farmsteads in New York State." In *Nineteenth- and Early Twentieth-Century Domestic Site Archaeology in New York State*, edited by John P. Hart and Charles L. Fisher, 37–43. New York State Museum Bulletin no. 495. Albany: Univ. of the State of New York, New York State Education Department.

Rafferty, Sean M. 2000. "A Farmhouse View: The Porter Site." In *Nineteenth- and Early Twentieth-Century Domestic Site Archaeology in New York State*, edited by

John P. Hart and Charles L. Fisher, 125–47. New York State Museum Bulletin no. 495. Albany: Univ. of the State of New York, New York State Education Department.

R. Christopher Goodwin & Associates. 2002. *Geophysical Studies at the Harriet Tubman Home*. Prepared for Douglas Armstrong and the Harriet Tubman Home. Frederick, MD: R. Christopher Goodwin & Associates.

Reed, Cleota, and Stan Skoczen. 1997. *Syracuse China*. Syracuse, NY: Syracuse Univ. Press.

Renehan, Edward J., Jr. 1997. *The Secret Six: The True Tale of the Men Who Conspired with John Brown*. Columbia: Univ. of South Carolina Press.

Riello, Giorgio. 2013. *Cotton: The Fabric That Made the Modern World*. Cambridge: Cambridge Univ. Press.

Robinson, John Bell. [1863] 2003. *Pictures of Slavery and Anti-slavery*. Philadelphia: 1320 North Thirteenth Street.

Rosaldo, Michelle Zimbalist. 1974. "Woman, Culture, and Society: A Theoretical Overview." In *Women, Culture, and Society*, edited by Michelle Zimbalist Rosaldo and Louise Lamphere, 17–42. Palo Alto, CA: Stanford Univ. Press.

Ryan, Bonnie Crarey. 2000. "Harriet Tubman Home for the Aged Project: Glass Analysis." Master's thesis, Syracuse Univ.

Ryan, Bonnie Crarey, and Douglas Armstrong. 2000. *Archaeology of John Brown Hall, Harriet Tubman Home, Auburn, New York*. Archaeological Research Center Report, vol. 13. Syracuse, NY: Syracuse Univ.

Salberg, Daniel J., Jeffery R. Ferguson, and Michael D. Glascock. 2010. "Neutron Activation Analysis of Bricks and Brickmaking at the Harriet Tubman Home, Auburn, New York." Draft paper prepared by Archaeometry Laboratory, Research Reactor, Univ. of Missouri, Nov. 11.

Sanborn, Franklin. 1863. "Harriet Tubman." *Commonwealth* (Boston), July 17.

———. 1869. "Announcement of Fund Raising Meeting for Harriet Tubman." *Commonwealth* (Boston), Jan. 5.

———. 1872. "John Brown in Massachusetts." *Atlantic Monthly* 29, no. 174: 420–33.

———. 1885. *The Life and Letters of John Brown: Liberator of Kansas, Martyr of Virginia*. Boston: Roberts Brothers.

Scott, E. J. 1919. "Letters of Negro Migrants of 1916–1918." *Journal of Negro History* 4, no. 3: 290–340.

Scott, Janine Nicole. 2018. "Place and Mobility in Shaping the Freedman's Community of Antioch Colony, Texas, 1870–1954." *Journal of African Diaspora Archaeology and Heritage* 7, no. 1: 1–16.

Sernett, Milton C. 2002. *North Star Country: Upstate New York and the Crusade for African American Freedom*. Syracuse, NY: Syracuse Univ. Press.

———. 2007. *Harriet Tubman: Myth, Memory, and History*. Durham, NC: Duke Univ. Press.

Sesma, Elena. 2016. "Creating Mindful Heritage Narratives: Black Women in Slavery and Freedom." *Journal of African Diaspora Archaeology and Heritage* 5, no. 1: 38–61.

Shackel, Paul. 2000. *Archaeology and Created Memory: A Public History in a National Park*. Contributions to Global Historical Archaeology. New York: Kluwer Academic/Plenum.

Shaw, Anna Howard. 1915. *The Story of a Pioneer*. Ithaca, NY: Cornell Univ. Press.

Singleton, Theresa A. 1999. "An Introduction." In *"I, Too, Am America": Archaeological Studies of African American Life*, edited by Theresa Singleton, 1–15. Charlottesville: Univ. of Virginia Press.

Smith, Adam. [1776] 1909. *An Inquiry into the Nature and Causes of the Wealth of Nations*. Harvard Classics, vol. 10. Cambridge, MA: P. F. Collier and Son.

Snow, Benjamin. 1908. *History of Cayuga County*. Auburn, NY: Cayuga County Historical Society.

Sørensen, Marie Louise Stig. 2000. *Gender Archaeology*. Cambridge: Blackwell, Polity Press.

Spencer-Wood, Suzanne. 2004. "What Difference Does Feminist Theory Make in Researching Households? A Commentary." In *Household Chores and Household Choices: Theorizing the Domestic Sphere in Historical Archaeology*, edited by Kerri Barile and Jamie C. Brandon, 235–53. Tuscaloosa: Univ. of Alabama Press.

———. 2009. "Feminist Theory and the Historical Archaeology of Institutions." In *The Archaeology of Institutional Life*, edited by April M. Beisaw and James G. Gibb, 33–48. Tuscaloosa: Univ. of Alabama Press.

Springate, Megan E. 2014. "Double Consciousness and the Intersections of Beliefs in an African American Home in Northern New Jersey." *Historical Archaeology* 48, no. 3: 125–43.

Steinbeck, John. 1939. *The Grapes of Wrath*. New York: Viking.

Still, William. [1871] 1970. *The Underground Railroad*. Chicago: Johnson.

Stone, Linda, and Nancy P. McKee. 1998. *Gender and Culture in America*. Saddle River, NJ: Prentice Hall.

Storke, Elliot G., assisted by Jason H. Smith. 1879. *History of Cayuga County, New York, 1789–1879, with Illustrations and Biographical Sketches of Some of Its Prominent Men and Pioneers*. Syracuse, NY: D. Mason.

Stottman, M. Jay. 2010. "Introduction: Archaeologists as Activists." In *Archaeologists as Activists: Can Archaeologists Change the World?*, edited by M. Jay Stottman, 1–11. Tuscaloosa: Univ. of Alabama Press.

Taylor, Robert W. 1901. *Harriet Tubman: The Heroine in Ebony*. Boston: George E. Ellis.

Thompson, Robert Ferris. 1984. *Flash of the Spirit: African & Afro-American Art & Philosophy*. New York: Random House.

Truth, Sojourner. [1850] 2017. *The Narrative of Sojourner Truth a Northern Slave*. Dictated by Sojourner Truth. Edited by Olive Gilbert. Boston: Yerrinton.

Tucker, Sheila Saft. 1973. *The Township of Fleming, Cayuga County, New York*. Auburn, NY: Brunner the Printer.

US Army Corp of Engineers. 2006. "The Historic Harmony Brick Works." Pittsburgh District. At http://www.lrp.usace.army.mil/lmon/harmony_brick_works.htm.

US Bureau of the Census, Department of Commerce. 1910. *Benevolent Institutions 1910*. Washington, DC: US Government Printing Office.

US Congress. 1899. *Report 1619: An Act Creating an Increase of Pensions for Harriet Tubman Davis*. 55th Cong., 3rd sess., Feb. 28. Washington, DC: US Government Printing Office.

US Department of Agriculture. 2014. "The American Farm." Chap. 3 of *Agricultural Fact Book*. Washington, DC: US Department of Agriculture. At http://www.usda.gov/factbook/chapter3.pdf.

US House of Representatives. 1888. *Harriet Tubman Davis, Widow to Nelson Charles, Alias Nelson Davis; Pension Claim*. House Report no. 55A-D1. Reports Accompanying Claim of Harriet Tubman. Washington, DC: US Government Printing Office.

US National Park Service. 2001. *National Historic Landmark Nomination: Harriet Tubman Home*. Philadelphia: US National Park Service, Northeastern Region.

———. 2008. *Harriet Tubman Special Resource Study: Environmental Assessment*. Boston: US National Park Service, Northeastern Region.

———. 2017. "Harriet Tubman National Historical Site: National Historic Park, Maryland." At https://www.nps.gov/hatu/index.htm.

———. N.d. "Harriet Tubman National Historical Park, Auburn and Fleming, New York." At https://www.nps.gov/hart/index.htm.

Vogel, Michael N. 2009. *Up against the Wall: An Archaeological Field Guide to Bricks in Western New York*. Buffalo, NY: Buffalo Lighthouse Association and the American Lighthouse Coordinating Committee. At http://www.buffaloah.com/a/DCTNRY/mat/brk/vogel/index.html.

Walker, I. C. 1970. "Nineteenth-Century Clay Tobacco Pipes in Canada." *Ontario Archaeology* 16:19–35.

Wall, Diana DiZerega. 2004. *The Archaeology of Gender: Separating the Spheres in Urban America*. New York: Plenum Press.

Walls, Bishop William J. C. 1949. *Harriet Tubman*. Pamphlet produced for the Harriet Tubman Home. Auburn, NY: Harriet Tubman Home.

———. 1974. *The African Methodist Episcopal Zion Church: Reality of the Black Church*. Charlotte, NC: AME Zion Publishing House.

Weik, Terrance. 2004. "Archaeology of the African Diaspora in Latin America." *Historical Archaeology* 38, no. 1: 32–49.

———. 2019. "Engendering Labor, African Enslavement, and Human–Horse Relations in Chickasaw Territory." *Journal of African Diaspora Archaeology and Heritage* 8, nos. 1–2: 110–30.

Wellman, Judith. 2005. "Uncovering the Freedom Trail in Auburn and Cayuga County, New York: Cultural Resources Survey of Sites Relating to the Underground Railroad, Abolitionism, and African American Life in Auburn and Cayuga County, New York." Study sponsored by City of Auburn Historic Resources Review Board and Cayuga County Historian's Office, Auburn, NY. At http://www.co.cayuga.ny.us/history/ugrr/report/toc.html.

Wells, Lester Grosvernor. 1953. "The Skaneateles Communal Experiment 1843–1846." Paper of the Onondaga Historical Association, February 13, Syracuse, New York.

Wilkie, Laurie. 2003. *The Archaeology of Mothering: An African-American Midwife's Tale*. New York: Routledge.

Wurst, LouAnn, Douglas V. Armstrong, and Elizabeth Kellar. 2000. "Between Fact and Fantasy: Assessing Our Knowledge of Domestic Sites." In *Nineteenth- and Early Twentieth-Century Domestic Site Archaeology in New York State*, edited by John P. Hart and Charles L. Fisher, 17–28. New York State Museum Bulletin no. 495. Albany: Univ. of the State of New York, New York State Education Department.

Yamin, Rebecca, and Karen Bescherer Metheny, eds. 1996. *Landscape Archaeology: Reading and Interpreting the American Historical Landscape*. Knoxville: Univ. of Tennessee Press.

Index

Photos, figures, and tables are indicated by *italicized* page numbers.

Douglas V. Armstrong (PhD, UCLA, 1983) is professor and chair of the Anthropology Department in the Maxwell School at Syracuse University, where he holds a Laura J. and L. Douglas Meredith Professorship and Maxwell Professor of Teaching Excellence. He has been engaged in archaeological and historical research in the Caribbean since the late 1970s. In the Caribbean, he is currently working on archaeological projects in Dominica and Barbados, focusing on cultural transformations and ethnogenesis related to the African Diaspora, household and community archaeology under conditions of enslavement, as well as movements to freedom. He has also been involved in New York State archaeology since joining the Syracuse University faculty in 1986. For more than two decades, his archaeological and historical research at the Harriet Tubman Home and related topics is linked to social movements, abolition, and women's rights.